HOW INFORMATION TECHNOLOGY IS CONQUERING THE WORLD

Workplace, Private Life, and Society

Kai A. Olsen

THE SCARECROW PRESS, INC.
Lanham • Toronto • Plymouth, UK
2013

Published by Scarecrow Press, Inc.
A wholly owned subsidiary of The Rowman & Littlefield Publishing Group, Inc.
4501 Forbes Boulevard, Suite 200, Lanham, Maryland 20706
www.rowman.com

10 Thornbury Road, Plymouth PL6 7PP, United Kingdom

British Library Cataloguing in Publication Information Available

Library of Congress Cataloging-in-Publication Data

Olsen, Kai A.
  How information technology is conquering the world : workplace, private life, and society / Kai A. Olsen.
      p. cm.
  "This book is an extended and updated version of Formalizing Internet, Web and eBusiness Applications for the Real World, Scarecrow Press (2005)."
  Includes bibliographical references and index.
  ISBN 978-0-8108-8720-6 (pbk. : alk. paper) -- ISBN 978-0-8108-8721-3 (ebook) 1. Internet. 2. Internet—Social aspects. 3. Information technology. 4. Information technology—Social aspects. 5. World Wide Web. 6. Electronic commerce. I. Title.
  TK5105.875.I57O484 2013
  303.48'33—dc23
                                    2012029339

♾™ The paper used in this publication meets the minimum requirements of American National Standard for Information Sciences—Permanence of Paper for Printed Library Materials, ANSI/NISO Z39.48-1992. Printed in the United States of America.

To the Internet and the Web for
making this book possible

Contents

Preface

The **future** is in the technical possibilities filtered through the real world constraints.

An abundance of books covers Information Technology (IT), the Internet and the Web. Most predict that these technologies will have a profound impact on everything from business to entertainment. They tell you to jump on the train now to avoid being left in the technological backwoods. This book is somewhat different. We try to view IT without the "hype." Focusing on the interface between the technologies and the real world, we shall see not only where these technologies have their advantages, but also where their limitations become apparent. That is, the future is in the technical possibilities filtered through the real world constraints.

This perspective allows us to focus on the difficulties of introducing a new technology to the real world. The book has the practical goal of giving readers a basic understanding of IT so that they can use the technologies to their full advantage. While we cannot give a formula for evaluating IT applications, we introduce a way of thinking that is helpful for finding the areas where the probability of success is greatest. This will give readers an understanding of where we are today, and where we will be tomorrow.

This book is an extended and updated version of *Formalizing Internet, Web and eBusiness Applications for the Real World*, Scarecrow Press (2005). However, with three hundred new pages, a change of title was appropriate. This new version covers most aspects of information technology, including new parts such as usability (Part 3), system development (Part 4), and cloud computing (Part 8). The last part, on the digital world (Part 9) is also new. In addition, there are many new chapters and subchapters.

This book has nine parts. Part 1 builds a foundation for understanding computer applications. We draw the distinction between formalized and unformalized processes and then discuss how the formalization level of data and processes determines the functionality of applications. This background is needed to evaluate the potential of new technologies. Part 2 presents the constraints, from technical to cultural—the "filters" that determine which applications that are to succeed or not. In Part 3, we discuss usability. This topic becomes more and more important as IT is reaching new user groups. Part 4 is somewhat more technical. Here we present system development, programming,

B2C (business-to-consumer) has a human being at one (final) end of the communication line.

B2B (business-to-business) describes services performed by computers without involving human beings.

software engineering and applications, development for both small and medium-sized companies, and Apps.

Part 5 introduces the basic Internet and Web standards, and gives a discussion of their potential. Part 6 provides an overview of the formalization of e-business applications within the B2C (business-to-consumer) category—what we really should have defined as computer-to-person applications (that is, where a human being is at one end of the communication line, whether a private citizen or a company employee). We shall present numerous examples and analyze these using the basic ideas introduced in the first part of the book. In Part 7, we look at B2B (business-to-business) applications, or what we more precisely may specify as computer-to-computer applications. Here we introduce the standards that are needed to transmit data with a high level of formalization (for example, to transmit an invoice between two computers). Part 8 discusses cloud computing, the idea of centralized storage of data, and centralized implementation of applications. We also explore applications that make use of large data repositories, for example, natural language applications. Finally, Part 9 sums up and takes a look into the future.

Notes are offered at the end of each chapter; however, where there are clear and distinct keywords, notes are not offered because the reader may conveniently perform a search on the Web.

This book will be useful for students taking an introductory course in computing, for social science students who want to know more about IT, for managers and designers of Web projects, and for those who are interested in seeing how the new technology will affect their lives or their jobs. No background in computing science is required, but experience in using PCs and the Internet will be an advantage.

Ways to Use This Book for Teaching

As a text for introductory courses, this book will give students a broad selection of topics, from IT in general and to the Internet and Web technologies in particular. For all of the topics presented, students should be given the opportunity to form their own arguments and opinions.

The book contains a great many topics, and an instructor may not be able to cover all of them in a single semester. It is recommended to allocate readings based on the backgrounds of students and their disciplines. Part 1 may be a good starting point for all types of students. The remainder of the book may be used selectively, with instructors choosing to emphasize different parts and chapters depending on the prerequisites of their students and their disciplines.

Students with a good background in IT can skim through Part 5, but some of the chapters (Chapter 34, Searching; or Chapter 36, Web presence), may be suitable for case studies. Students without an IT background will need most of this part to get a basic understanding of Web technologies but may choose to skip the more technically-oriented chapters (Chapter 39, Dynamic Web pages; and Chapter 40, Embedded scripts).

Part 6 gives an overview over all B2C applications. An instructor may choose to cover the whole or to give exercises and tasks in which students selectively read these chapters to get background material. However, take care that students learn the difference between services that are entirely symbolic and those that also have a physical part.

In Part 7, B2B technology, less technically oriented students can skim through Chapter 52, XML, concentrating on the other chapters of this section.

Accompanying **Web page**:

www.himolde.no/ ~olsen/IT

Note that there is an accompanying Web page to this book:

www.himolde.no/~olsen/IT

The Web page includes a set of exercises, some with answers, as well as additional material, cases, and examples.

Acknowledgments

This book is about IT, especially the Internet and the Web, and is dedicated to these technologies. I could have said that this book could never have been written without the aid and support given by the Internet and the Web, but that seems ludicrous. Instead, I shall express my deepest appreciation for the contribution of all the content providers on the Web, both within the public domain and subscription services that make it possible to get updated news and information at any place in the world, at any time. Google's search engine, its Scholar site with scientific papers, Wikipedia, as well as all the scientific bibliographical Websites have been very useful. With email, I can maintain an important global network of colleagues and students in many countries, independent of difficulties posed by time zones and distances.

In working on this book, I have had invaluable help from colleagues, students, consultants, and friends all over the world. My deepest appreciation goes to Alessio Malizia, Andrea Belluci, Jo Berre, Hans Fredrik Nordhaug, Mike B. Spring, and Jim Williams. Andreas Berre has been of great help in offering advice and in reviewing Part 4. In addition, Martin Dillon and Sally Craley at Scarecrow have offered valuable comments and suggestions. Special thanks go to James Morrison (JamesEdits) who has edited all the 600+ pages. Laura Payne has patiently proofread the final version.

Several of the chapters in this book are based on scientific papers that I have published in *IEEE Computer*, *IEEE Potentials*, *Communications of the ACM* and other journals, some written with Alessio Malizia, Jim Williams, Andrea Belluci, Erling Fagerlie, and Bård Indredavik. A reference to these papers is given in each chapter.

Trademark Notice

The following are trademarks or registered trademarks of their respective companies:

ActiveX, Microsoft, Outlook, Internet Explorer, Visual Basic, Microsoft Access, and Windows are trademarks of Microsoft Corporation; iPod, iPhone, iPad, Apple MacIntosh are trademarks of Apple Computer, Inc.; Facebook is a trademark of Facebook, Inc.; Netscape is a trademark of Netscape Communications; Java is a trademark of Sun Microsystems, Inc.; AltaVista is a trademark of Digital Equipment Corporation; Yahoo! and Flickr are trademarks of Yahoo!, Inc.; Google and Android are trademarks of Google Corporation; eBay is a trademark of eBay, Inc.; Maple is a trademark of Maplesoft; Mathlab is a trademark of Mathworks, Inc.; Twitter is a trademark of Twitter, Inc.; iStockPhoto is a trademark of Getty Images, Inc.; Lotus Notes is a trademark of IBM; Firefox is a trademark of the Mozilla Foundation, Instagram is a trademark of Instagram, Inc; Netflix is a trademark of Netflix, Inc; Huawei is a trademark of Huawei Technologies Co., Ltd.

Introduction

Closed tasks can be formalized and handled by a computer. **Open** tasks cannot be described in a formalized manner; these must be handled by humans. Most services will consist of both open and closed parts.

If an application is *formalized* (that is, with well-defined procedures and data), then and only then can it be handled by a computer. Only formalized or closed applications can be described as a computer program, the part that is needed to turn a general computer into an "application machine," whether it is a word processor, a banking system, or the system for an online store. A computer cannot process tasks that are *unformalized*, open tasks. The advantage of describing an application as a program is, of course, that the tasks and processes can be automated. When tax regulations and tax data, for example, are described as a program, this one program can calculate taxes for all citizens, running repeatedly with a different data set each time.

We find few of these formalized, fully automated programs on our personal machines and the Web. Here the tasks are solved through *interaction* with the user, that is, the user activates the next process by clicking a command button or providing input from the keyboard. This human-computer interaction allows us to use the computer to support processes that have both open and closed parts. Word processing is a typical example. The computer handles the formatting part while the human being takes care of the writing. If the process of writing a document is categorized as occurring on three different levels, lexical (characters, words), syntactic (grammar), and semantic (meaning), we see that the computer takes care of the lexical part, while the human is in charge of the semantics, the meaning of what is written. However, we may get some computer support on the syntactic level through grammar checking programs. Social networks provide a similar example. The computer takes care of users—their "friends," messages and photos—but all the semantic parts (the understanding) are left to the humans.

For the past fifty years, we have seen that many fully "formalized" jobs have disappeared, while others have changed profoundly. We still have accountants, but a computer does the practical part of keeping the books. Telephone companies still have operators, but computers now handle most of their services. Air traffic controllers rely on computers to do their work, but may soon be replaced by machines. Similarly, in cockpits the role of the pilots can be more supervisory than actually flying the plane. In the manufacturing industry, robots and other

Intermediates may no longer be needed when we find terminals in every home and office.

computer-controlled machinery have been replacing workers for forty years, increasing the effectiveness of the remaining workers.

If one or more of the tasks that you perform can be described by a well-defined procedure, a computer probably can do the job. Some formalized jobs have, up to now, been protected from a computer takeover by limited data access. But today, with the Internet, we do not need intermediaries. With improved software, and better user interfaces, the "terminals" are moved to the consumer's PC or mobile phone. The Internet has removed the data access barrier, and is in many ways —as we shall see in this book—revolutionizing the end user markets for banking and other formalized applications.

Automation has a huge impact in our modern societies. Over the centuries, workers have moved from agriculture to industry, and then have been laid off as industry automates. New jobs have appeared in the service sector, in banks, travel agencies, administration, and many other areas. But, many of the jobs in these sectors also can be automated or made so simple that intermediates are no longer needed.

IT supports **automation**. While this was a process mainly in manufacturing, we now see automation in all areas.

While the *unformalized jobs* are better protected from a computer takeover, IT will change the way these jobs are performed. In the medical fields, for example, general practitioners perform tasks that are still unformalized. That is, even if doctors follow procedures while treating patients, these tasks are not so well defined that they can be described as computer programs. In most cases human beings are needed to diagnose and treat patients, but the computer is an important tool for many supporting tasks, for example, for storing, retrieving, presenting, and editing medical records. The Internet and Web will have a profound influence here as well, and are already used for transferring medical records, accessing medical literature, sending prescriptions to pharmacies, and so forth. Some doctors give patients limited access to records online and allow appointments to be scheduled over the Internet. Test results may be communicated to patients by email. Doctors may even be able to perform a checkup for follow-up patients via the Internet, where the patient has a video camera and other special equipment in his home.

As we shall see, the perspective of formalization is invaluable when evaluating computer systems to see where the new technology can be applied successfully, to weed out the overly optimistic applications, and to know where the going is straightforward and where we will meet difficulties. We can use this perspective on a macro scale to predict the future of the Internet, Web, Web services, e-business applications, or a new standard, such as XML. We also can use it on a micro level to identify which functions in a new system that will be most difficult to implement.

In a world where technological development proceeds at a record-breaking pace, it is easy to overlook the fact that the technology needed for many applications may be many years away. We do not have the large, high resolution and lightweight display needed to eliminate paper entirely; neither do we have the everlasting battery needed for true mobile computing. In addition, *cultural and social constraints* may act as boundaries to how far we can go in applying new technology. While the video telephone (a phone that conveys both picture and sound) can be offered at a reasonable price using existing technology, consumers do not seem to want such a product for general calls. There are exceptions, of course. Many grandparents are happy to talk to their grandchildren using Skype or a mobile phone video connection.

As we see, new technologies come with promises of new and interesting applications. However, these theoretical possibilities must be filtered through a set of real-life constraints before highly successful applications emerge. This is our setting.

Symbolic is a key word in this book. Symbols are the building blocks of the virtual world that we have developed. Are you a symbolic worker, that is, do you use a major part of your work time entering, editing, disseminating, and storing symbols? For most of us, the answer is yes. Our business may be education, administration, economy, science, production; we may work with text, pictures, music, money, drawings, or any other type of data, but all of these are symbolic by nature. These symbols may be represented as bits, sequences of zeros and ones (binary digits) in a computer. Letters may be translated to binary form using a code lookup table; pictures can be represented as a collection of pixels (picture elements), each giving the color and brightness values of a certain point in the picture. Music may be represented as grooves on an LP record, but can just as easily be coded as a digital value. Money can be represented as bills and coins, but also may exist as numbers in a virtual form. An insurance policy may be printed on paper with all the correct signatures, but may just as well reside in a computer system, verified by digital signatures.

New applications must be **filtered** through a set of real-life constraints.

Symbols, as distinguished from physical objects, can be represented as bits, stored in a computer and transmitted over the Internet.

Atoms, physical items that have weight, cannot be handled directly by computer systems and can only be transmitted or distributed using traditional channels.

Thus, a new technology that offers the opportunity to transmit data inexpensively from anywhere to everywhere will affect the way we do business. The electronic bits representing the balance of a bank account are as real as the paper bills. The institutions that work with *symbols*, such as banks and insurance companies, are as real as any farm or manufacturing plant. While Internet technologies can support physically oriented businesses, they often can handle the whole job when the raw materials are bits and bytes, as we see with Internet banks and the distribution of music. Then, if the tasks are fully formalized, they also can be automated.

Are you selling groceries, clothes, or working as a mechanic? Clearly, a part of your job is to work with *non-symbolic items, items that have weight* (sometime defined as atoms, in contrast to bits). We cannot transport apples or clothes via the Internet; neither can we use this technology to repair a car (although some manufacturers have Internet-based systems for diagnosis of engine malfunction). While the Internet cannot handle the main part of these jobs, it offers opportunities to change the way we are performing the symbolic or the administrative part. The Internet offers a new channel to consumers that may be used by a technology-optimistic grocer to let customers order their groceries directly from home, or, for a more mundane application such as marketing. The mechanic may use the Internet to get part numbers or repair procedures or he may allow customers to book appointments for inspections, oil changes, and so forth, directly via the Internet.

The Internet will change the way we regard *ownership* of data. A battle lines have emerged over laws to protect copyright. Some want to implement the spirit of the net and make everything accessible, or, where ownership is necessary to protect the income of musicians, authors, and others, they are open to models that will combine protection with open access. Others want more restricted laws to avoid piracy. But we may take this discussion to other areas as well. When medical records were on paper, the only practical solution was to store these where they were used, in doctors' offices and in hospitals. Computerized records and the Internet have opened the way for other solutions. Perhaps the patients should take control of these records and let doctors access the record using the Web. Then all a patient's doctors would have access to the same data, and all the data would be stored in one patient record. If someone is hospitalized during a vacation in Italy, the hospital there

Copyright laws protect musicians, authors, and companies. But strict laws may conflict with the open idea of the Internet.

could both retrieve the records and enter information on the new case.

The basic technology behind the Internet may be complicated, but it is offered to us in such a way that it can be used by *everybody* and can be afforded by almost everybody (at least in the industrial countries). School kids are on social networks, use text messages, chat and send tweets (messages on the social network service Twitter) for communication. Even the owner of a small garage may see the benefits of setting up a system that allows customers to make appointments directly. Thus the Internet can "replace" the office staff that a small business could never afford.

The Web is a *democratic* technology, clearly a medium for the people, which is one of its strengths. Many of the applications presented in this book require a large part of the population to have access to the Internet to get the full benefit of the technology. In contrast to newspapers, radio, and TV, the Web can be used for both input and output. That is, one can take an active and creative role, along with the more passive consumer role on the Web. When everybody is an information provider the Web becomes *anarchistic.* Data is available on everything, written by professionals or amateurs, governments as well as crackpots, superficial or in-depth, left or right, right or wrong.

Democratic, the Web enables users to be both information consumers and producers.

IT also has an impact as a social, communication technology. Many use their spare time to chat with friends through messaging systems or on a social network. Virtual communication has become the norm, in some cases replacing face-to-face communication, or in addition to previous forms of communication. Of course, this is nothing new. We have had telegrams and the telephone for one hundred and fifty years, but IT has much larger bandwidth. It offers many too many connections, multimedia and comes with a low cost. It is also an answer to a more dynamic life, even when we may live far from our friends. That is, instead of going over to the neighbor's for a chat it is often more convenient to meet her on the computer.

We shall explore all these issues in the following parts.

PART 1
Fundamentals

This part begins with a description of the virtual world, a world built by humans through history, but which has accelerated since the advent of computers (Chapter 1). In Chapter 2, we describe the basic technology. We shall see that any task has to be described completely and unambiguously before the computer can do the job (Chapter 3). This will be followed by a set of cases (Chapter 4). Formalization may occur at different levels, which is covered in Chapters 5 and 6.

Chapter 7 presents the types of data that can be represented in symbolic form (as bit codes in a computer). The symbolic parts of our society are replacing physical parts as the most important, and the computer thrives on this development.

Finally, in Chapter 8, we shall discuss the cost-benefit of formalization.

1 Welcome to the Virtual World

Some unknown artist, perhaps a shaman or a hunter, painted animals and hunting scenes on a cave wall thirty thousand years ago. At that time, there was only one world, a world where objects and processes were physical. However, these drawings were of a different kind. Sure, they were made with charcoal on a rock wall, but this was only a representation. The magic of the symbols also would have been retained for other depictions. Since then, creating this virtual world has been an ongoing project for humans. This world of symbols has become an integral part of our lives, and one that the modern computer also has conquered.

To apply computers, we need a formalized and virtual world.

If we could take a laptop with us back in history, we would find few applications for it in prehistoric times. Perhaps the artist could use a paint program to draw sketches, but other than that a computer would have no place in this world (or, perhaps they would have enjoyed an episode of *The Flintstones*?). Seven thousand years ago the Assyrians of Mesopotamia could have applied the laptop to accounting, and text processing would have been a possible task two thousand years later. The logistics officers of the Roman Empire, with the task of supplying large armies during a campaign, would clearly have found applications for a laptop, as would later librarians, bookkeepers, astronomers, and navigators.

With Gutenberg's printing press in 1450, the virtual world represented by books reached new parts of the population. The virtual world gained momentum in the middle of the nineteenth century when a few creative engineers managed to formalize processes such as weaving and spinning. By defining these processes as a set of fixed mechanical movements it was possible to create a machine that did the job. Then, the competence needed was in the machine.

The Industrial Revolution boosted the virtual world.

Although the Industrial Revolution took place in a physical world, it also boosted the virtual world. Until now just a few scientists, priest, bureaucrats, teachers, and traders worked with symbols. Suddenly there was a need to hire vast numbers of clerks, accountants, engineers, and architects. Their tools were pencil and paper, and later on typewriters, drawing boards and mechanical calculators. The "many" part of the Industrial Revolution—many products, many orders, many customers, and many employees—also forced a formalization of administrative processes. With rigid procedures, one could ensure that vast numbers could be handled correctly, independently of the person who handled the order. Expansion became just a matter of hiring.

The virtual world expanded in other areas as well. Where entertainment had been storytelling, a fiddler, concerts, circus, and theater, there was now mass production of books, records, and movies. While the representations were still in the physical—on paper, vinyl, and celluloid—the information, represented by symbols, was part of the virtual world, just as for the cave paintings.

It was into this world that the computer was introduced. The very first computers were used for studying airplane design (Z3, Berlin, 1941), cracking codes (Colossus, Benchley Park, 1943), and running computations for the hydrogen bomb and artillery tables (ENIAC, Philadelphia, 1946). They soon reached applications outside the military area, for example, in banking and insurance. Through the last forty years, we have seen how VLSI (Very Large Scale Integration) technology has advanced to the point where it can offer cheap, high capacity, reliable, flexible, adaptive, and lightweight computers that are embedded in everything from PCs, laptops, and smartphones to washing machines.

Standards are as important as the hardware.

Standards, not least TCP/IP (to transmit packets of information), HTML (to describe the layout of Web pages), and HTTP (to transmit Web pages), have made it possible to interconnect devices, offering a set of applications from email to Web, from Internet banking to booking, from eBusiness to social networks. Previous physical representations could now be replaced by a generic, digital, computer-based platform. Freed from the physical formats, better service was possible at a lower cost.

Symbolic products can be delivered in digital format at low cost.

Music is an excellent example. The move from analog (vinyl) to digital (CD) retained the business model of selling music in stores. However, the next step, from CD to a virtual file had greater impact. Where a record store can offer only a thousand to five thousand CDs, streaming services can provide music lovers nearly everything—for a fraction of the costs. New albums or tracks can be presented to the whole world at the same time. Movies, and to some extent also books, will follow. We see the consequences already. Music and bookstores are closing down as customers move to the more convenient Web-based services.

Many areas were **formalized** before the advent of the first computer.

When the first computers arrived, the table was already set for many applications. That is, one could take advantage of the previous developments in the virtual world. In principle, what the very first programmers had to do was to translate instructions from natural language processes into a programming language, adding extras such as logon processes, data descriptions, and user interfaces. Of course, in many cases the system developers would have to increase the formalization level, as instructions designed for human beings often require an additional clarification before the computer can be applied. We see a need for unique IDs such as social security numbers, account numbers, and email and other addresses. If your employer uses a calendar system for meetings, this will only function properly if everyone applies the system to everything. That is, we need to follow the formalized routines to take advantage of functions such as being able to set up a meeting automatically.

On one hand, the computer offers flexibility and adaption to personal needs, and on the other, it favors a more uniform world. These formalization requirements are apparent when the virtual world interfaces with the physical. While robots, such as a computer-controlled forklift can do the job in a modern warehouse, putting a robot inside a private home is not as easy. An automatic vacuum cleaner looks like a godsend, but it is not that simple. It climbs the legs of chairs and stops, enters a shag carpet and stops, and gets tangled in electrical wires and stops. That is, most apartments are not formalized to the level that the robot requires to work properly. However, when furnishing a new apartment today, perhaps it would also be a good idea to accommodate the needs of robots.

Computers—for **flexibility** or **rigidity**?

With mass production and automatic processes, one could envisage a future of limited flexibility, the "any color as long as it is black" attitude of Henry Ford. However, the computer has given consumers the possibility of customization, at least within the realm of variants. We can choose the color of a car, the language for a user interface, or the operating system for a laptop. A word processing system lets us write what we want, and we can present all types of documents on a Web page. In many ways the computer has offered more ways of personalization than we ever had before.

On the other hand the computer's effectiveness for handling large numbers may result in a more uniform business structure. When a thousand department stores, grocers, bookstores or fast food restaurants can be run with the same software packages as if they were one, variation disappears.

Computers can remove formalized jobs.

While the Industrial Revolution created jobs, the computer may take them away. Jobs in industry have always been productive and well paid, better than farm work and most jobs in the service sector. But manufacturing jobs are disappearing as automation offers dramatic increases in productivity. Nearly everything that can be formalized can also be automated. That is, if you can give a clear and unambiguous description of your job, there is a chance that one day it will be performed by a computer. Computers can replace bank employees, toll booth operators, travel agency employees, salesmen, call center employees, even piano players, as in Kurt Vonnegut's famous science-fiction novel, *Player Piano*. Stock market brokers are losing their jobs as robots take over the task of buying and selling stocks. We already have automatic metro trains at many airports and in some cities. The military uses unmanned aerial vehicles, and the day when commercial airplanes are operated without pilots may not be far off. While passengers may feel uncomfortable with no pilot on board, this will not be a problem for freight planes.

Computers in the home remove intermediates.

The large offices with hundreds of clerks, cashiers, customer representatives, engineers, and architects have disappeared. Today the computer handles all the "many" aspects, from doing accounting to performing detailed strength analysis and drawing windows and doors for office buildings. Engineers and architects are still needed, of course, but modern software packages, such as 3D drawing tools, have made their work more effective today than just a few years ago.

With the computer, amateurs are offered tools that were previously only available to professionals. Where the work of a bank or a travel agency employee was leveraged by their access to a terminal, this "terminal" is now in everybody's home. That is, we can perform our own banking or book hotels and flights without the need of an intermediary. In entertainment, amateurs are offered high quality video cameras at a cheap price. A standard laptop may offer professional video and sound editing tools. As important, there are now several sites were amateurs may publish their work, such as YouTube for videos, Flickr for photo sharing, and Google for creating blogs. With this equipment and through these sites, amateurs offer real competition to professionals. The time that the public spends making or viewing video clips on YouTube, in editing or reading blogs is time that had been spent in front of the TV, radio, at the cinema, or reading newspapers.

Thus, we see fewer jobs in these areas, and the Internet is creating its own paradoxes. In his youth, Steven Spielberg played with a simple video camera to capture action scenes—a good starting point for his career as a movie director. Today, he would probably have launched these clips on YouTube, perhaps also reducing the market for commercial movies.

Today's high unemployment rates in many countries have more than one explanation, but creating new permanent jobs is not so easy when the computer is there to remove intermediates and handle everything that can be formalized. Perhaps the only place to create new jobs is in the unformalized areas where the computer cannot compete, such as in education, healthcare, and care for children and the elderly. Even in these areas, the computer can be used as a tool for making the human caretaker more effective, for example, by taking on heavy loads.

Humans are better at performing open (non-formalized) tasks.

Will the computer also change power structures? At one time in history the ownership of land gave power, clearly to squires and other landowners with control over large areas, but also to the farmer who owned his own land. In many countries, only property owners could vote. During the Industrial Revolution, ownership of factories that could generate huge profits became important. While these values of the physical world are still important, they may be surpassed by virtual values, which recent events illustrate. Apple is now competing with Exxon to be the world's most valuable company. The value of Facebook has been comparable to that of General Motors. The value of many other companies, such as Cisco, Nike, and many more, is not in their production facilities, but in design, brand names, and marketing. Today many of the most important enterprises, such as banks, insurance companies, newspapers, TV stations, and software firms, operate in the virtual world only.

Virtual institutions are the most powerful.

The transition into a virtual world is also indicated by our business heroes. At one time the heroes were John D. Rockefeller (oil) and Henry Ford (automobile manufacturing); today they are Bill Gates (software) and Mark Zuckerberg (social networks). The latter have created as much money from virtual goods as the former did for physical ones. But while the value of Facebook is comparable to General Motors, it generates only a fraction of the more than two hundred thousand jobs that are offered by the industrial giant. That is, even with modern manufacturing methods, employees are necessary to manufac-

The **virtual values** are becoming the most interesting.

Disasters are also a part of the virtual world.

Physical representations are changed into digital.

ture, sell, and service physical goods. On the software side, Facebook can service close to a billion users with just a few thousand employees.

The virtual world is a place for creativity, where good ideas and knowledge go far. Initially, the virtual world was open for all, but now the turf wars from the physical world have invaded the virtual—perhaps an indication of its importance, In the virtual world, the battle is not over borders, minerals, oil, and other resources, but over the capability to make money on ideas. When Google offered more than $12 billion for Motorola's mobile phone business, it was not to get their hands on the manufacturing part, but to control Motorola's more than seventeen thousand patents (with an additional 7,500 pending). This will be important ammunition in the legal battles over mobile technologies (especially over their Android operating system) that are currently taking place. Today, it is clearly not sufficient to develop creative applications; one also needs to be able to protect these in the courtroom.

While the physical world has its tornados, floods, earthquakes, and tsunamis, some of the same instability exists in the virtual world, notably in the financial sector. With all data available, we (or at least the authorities and central banks) should be able to foresee and avoid a financial crisis. However, the system has become as complex as nature. The volume of data and the many hidden connections made a financial crisis as unexpected as an earthquake. If stock prices reflect the underlying values, it is difficult to see the causes for their fluctuations. However, some of these fluctuations may be the result of stop-loss systems in which a computer is ordered to sell if the share falls under a threshold, that is, a formalization of an area that perhaps should not be formalized.

Clearly, the computer has increased the advantages of working in the virtual world, with the lure of automation for tasks that are formalized. "Virtualization" can be expected to gain momentum. In the next decade, we can expect that the vision of a paperless society may at last be realized, replacing the physical representations with virtual. This change has already occurred for many types of documents, such as books, tickets, maps, and photos. A next step may be to replace paper bills with digital money. Standards will be an important issue. When applications can use data already stored (for example, in the cloud), we will see greater functionality, new applications, and simpler user interfaces.

Information technology is changing the world.

Welcome to the virtual world—a world created by humans, but where the computer may do much of the work. New technologies have always had a great impact on society. Today, that impact belongs to information technology (IT). If we go back to the nineteenth century, we see that railway technology had a similar market impact. The technology itself was viewed as so promising that there was an abundance of capital, and after a few years, around 1870, hundreds of companies were engaged in laying new tracks. Not all had valid business models, which is similar to what we have seen with computer technology. This did not imply that railways did not have a future; as we know, they nearly monopolized land-based travel for a century, had a deep impact on society, and made some of the pioneers immensely rich.

IT technology is having a similar impact. It will affect us, as employees, managers, business owners, students, professors, venture capitalists, or private citizens. These technologies will be a threat to some, opportunities for others.

2 Information Technology

For many, the computer is a black box, which makes it difficult to see the inherent **limitations**.

The **intelligent computer** is still far off, even if we have seen prototypes of "intelligent" applications for nearly fifty years.

For many people a computer—and the Internet—is a black box. In contrast to bicycles, cars, and excavators it is difficult to understand how computers work and to see the possibilities and the limitations. Augmenting this problem are media portrayals of all the novel applications—intelligent computers, speech recognition, language translation, and so forth—and the ensuing discussion of the idea of computers' replacing human beings for all tasks. Many find proof of the everything-is-possible idea in the revolutionary developments within hardware. We have all heard how a multimillion dollar, room-sized mainframe of the 1960s is exceeded in functionality by a $300 laptop of today. Since the advent of LSI (Large-Scale Integration) technology, followed by VLSI (Very Large-Scale Integration) Moore's law[1] has predicted that integrated circuit complexity would double every eighteen months. In practice this implies that the price of chips decreases by fifty percent in this time span. Today, even an inexpensive PC offers more disk space, memory capacity, and processor speed than most users need.

In spite of the advances of computer hardware many of the visions from the 1960s and 1970s have not come true. We are still far from the intelligent computer. There have been great advances for an important task such as natural language translation, but we are still far from the point where we can replace human translators. In the seventy years of computer history, we have heard from all kinds of professionals that these radical computer applications are just around the corner. It has been prophesied that in ten, twenty, or fifty years, computers will handle most of the tasks that are performed by human beings, from decision making to language translation. Today, prophets have learned from their predecessors' overly optimistic statements (we can test the twenty-five-years prognostics given in 1975) and are confining predictions to the much safer fifty or hundred year perspective.

Regrettably these prophesies are often given uncritical media coverage, even today. The black box nature of the computer seems to be a barrier against skeptical questions that may follow presentation of other futuristic technological visions. A press conference held to introduce an inexpensive people's helicopter is met with skepticism, especially if the prototype only runs on the ground. However, the same

Many IT applications, such as word processing or email, have been here for decades. The revolution is in the **omnipresence** of these and other applications.

journalists may accept natural language speech-to-speech translation without a critical question. Other examples include a video system that is supposed to detect criminals as they enter a ball game, or the mobile phone in which a person can talk in one language and allow the listener to hear another.

Even more mundane applications that use existing technology can be troublesome. About one-third of all failed or abandoned software projects are estimated to cost the United States alone billions of dollars every year.[2] Many of these failures have been large corporate and government systems. Medical systems and systems for handling Social Security have had especially high failure rates.[3] These systems seldom fail due to the computer hardware; the problems are usually in the software. This does not imply that hardware engineers are smarter than their colleagues in software. Instead, it indicates that software developers have the toughest part of the job.

While hardware is mass produced at low cost, **software** developers must bridge the gap between the formalized hardware and the real world applications.

While hardware is mass produced and sold as general machines, the software developer must bridge the gap between this general machine and the actual application. The software engineer has to build a system that conforms to the requirements of the real world. In the simplest case this may be a translation of real world concepts into computer programs and databases. In practice, however, the software engineer will find that the real world data and its tasks are too *open* to be described directly as database structures and computer programs. That is, in the real world we utilize the flexibility of human beings to interpret data, to apply the right procedure, to make low-level decisions based on an overall strategy or a higher goal. For a computer application these data and processes must be *closed*, that is, they must be described in a formalized manner. As we shall see, this formalization process is not an easy task.

We may experience some of the pain that faces software developers when we fill out a structured questionnaire. Give us your views on the president, the economy, a Saturday night show by inserting a number between one (excellent) and five (poor) in the appropriate box. If you are a conservative or a liberal, check here. These forms translate views from an open to a closed world. We may be able to present our opinions on the president in several pages but here we have to compress our point of view into one digit.

Many of the successful computer applications that we have today were available many decades ago. In the 1970s, we had word processors, spreadsheet programs, and database systems. In the sixties, NASA used digital photos, and the first commercial digital camera came on the market as early as 1981.[4] The first versions of Enterprise Resource Planning (ERP) systems, which integrate functions such as manufacturing, distribution, financials, and human resources, emerged in the early seventies.

In many ways I use my PC today for the same functions as in my first job in 1975. The basic word processing functions of dynamic, editable text were available on my 1975 PC (at that time called a microcomputer), but the one-font, limited-capacity, no-graphics version has been replaced by a word-processing system with full layout control, a variety of fonts, graphics, tables, spellchecker, grammar control, and much more. Still, the greatest advantages of using a word processing system could be realized thirty years ago, but at a $20,000 price tag (with inflation, several hundred times the price of a modern PC). In the last thirty years, the computer has become more affordable. The combination of increased power and smaller size has created the potential for widespread use.

Henry Ford produced the first affordable car in 1914.[5] Although a modern car has a large set of new features, improved engine, transmission, and steering, the greatest advantage of having a car—personal transportation—already existed in the twenties. It may be a sacrilege to compare computer technology, the brainchild of our modern society, with the more mundane automobile industry, but there is perhaps a stronger similarity than we want to admit.

In the early days of PCs we had a fairly optimistic view of the possibilities that lay ahead. Moore's law was already in effect. We could develop applications, knowing that the next version of the hardware would have increased capacity. In 1979, three years before IBM entered the PC market, we connected a twenty megabyte (MB) disc to a PC, creating a database machine, a computer with software and disk drives that could execute high-level commands for storing and retrieving medical records. It was a big deal, also physically, as four men were needed to move the disk drive. We used the machine in a system for primary health care, where a number of doctors, each with an NPC (a network, diskless PC), were connected to this common archive for medical records. It did not take much imagination to envision the continuing hardware development. Of course, just as a modern car would have impressed the

Evolution is more common than revolution, even within the computer field.

If we are going to use the word **revolution**, it should be used for:

- The affordability and power of the PC.
- The Internet and the Web.
- Digitalizing data.

Model T Ford owner, we are really impressed by the functionality, small size, and affordability of the modern PC.

However, the ability to connect to every other computer in the world would have been even more impressive. While the Model T Ford owner would marvel at modern highways, we would have been daunted with the Internet and the Web. Yes, there were roads in the twenties and computer networks in the seventies. But, few of us could have envisioned a future with a road to every place, with an Internet connection in every home. In practice, the Internet is like any other transportation network with local roads, hubs, and highways, but from most users' perspective it looks as if every computer is directly connected to every other computer, like the way we envisage the telephone network.

Similarly, the advances in digital cameras would have been difficult to predict. Although the basic principles behind these devices are fairly simple, what astonishes is the development of cameras with millions of reliable and fast sensors, with enormous memory capacity, and at prices even lower than the previous analog devices.

On the basic level everything is stored as **bits**.

On the most basic level the computer can handle only bits, data stored as zeroes and ones. This representation has been chosen because only two different coding levels need to be represented electronically, using one voltage for a one, another for a zero. Simple transistors can be used to store these numbers physically in the machine. A drawback of this coding scheme is that more digits are needed to represent a number, for example, we need four binary digits to represent the number eight (binary 1000), while the largest number that we can store in a byte (eight digits) is 255 (binary 11111111).

In electronics "**many**" often comes cheap.

However, in electronics, it is far easier to represent *many* of something simple than *few* of something more complex. That is, it is far easier to represent binary digits (two voltage levels) than trying to implement digital digits (ten voltage levels), even if the first requires many more digits than the latter. This is especially true for the large-scale integration techniques used today for producing computer processors and memory. In fact, the cost of repetition of a simple electrical circuit, such as a transistor, is so low that the cost of one gigabit (1,000,000,000 bits) is as low as two dollars (in 2012).

2.1   Binary system

All commercial computers use the binary system;[6] that is, data, whether it is numbers, text, photographs, or audio, are stored and processed as binary digits. This is just another number system, but unlike the digital system that has ten symbols (0 to 9), the binary system has just two (0 and 1).

A digital number such as 13 is made up of $1*10^1 +3$, or 10+3, and 123 is made up of $1*10^2 +2*10^1+3$, or 100+20+3. For binary numbers the base is 2 (binary) and not 10 (digital). The digital number 13 is then represented as binary 1101, mathematically $1* 2^3+1*2^2+0*2^1+1$, or 8+4+0+1. A binary system works similar to a digital, except that we need more digits to represent the numbers.

Mathematical operations are simple to implement in the binary system. For example, let us assume that we are to design the electronics for the ADD function, adding two digits. We have just four cases:

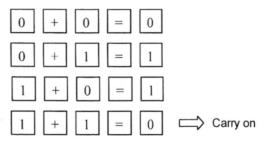

In the last case we have a carryon to the next higher position in the binary number, as indicated by the arrow above. Thus the electronics must also be able to add the carryon (from the previous position) to the results.

Symbol	Value	Symbol	Value	Symbol	Value
,	44	A	65	a	97
-	45	B	66	b	98
.	46	C	67	c	99
/	47	D	68	d	100

Table 2.1 ASCII Table (examples).

While numbers can be stored directly in binary form, other types of symbolic data can be represented using coding schemes, for example, the ASCII table for representing symbols as numbers. Some examples are shown in Table 2.1. As

With **coding**, any type of symbolic information may be represented in a computer (for example, coding letters as numbers).

indicated, an A is coded as the digital number 65, B as 66, and so on. With this simple table we can convert all letters to numbers, and thus they can be represented in the computer. This coding can be performed already by the keyboard. When we type an A, number 65 (digital) is transmitted to the computer. If the A is to be displayed on a computer screen, the opposite conversion will be performed, from numbers to the figure that represents an A on the screen.

2.2   Storage

Once the number system is defined, we need storage space. Typical storage devices today are disks with a magnetic coating in which the zeros and ones are represented by magnetizing the cover. A modern disk may store many terabytes of data. Each byte consists of eight binary digits; a "terabyte" is 10 raised to the power of 12 (1,000,000,000,000) bytes. Although modern disks are reliable, they have mechanical parts: a motor that rotates the disk at high speed, and a head that can move over the surface to read and write data. With solid-state disks (SSD), these moving parts are avoided. SSDs are faster than the magnetic disks, use less power, and are more reliable. As of today, they cannot compare with the storage capacity of magnetic disks, neither with the cost per byte; however, solid-state technology is developing rapidly and is likely to replace the magnetic devices for many applications at some point.

Digital storage devices offer high capacity at low prices.

In addition to the permanent storage, on magnetic or solid-state disk, which retains information even when the device is turned off, a computer has a working memory, typically a dynamic random access memory (DRAM). Here each binary digit is represented by a capacitor, which is either charged or discharged to indicate the values of 0 and 1. Because the capacitors fade, DRAM has to be refreshed periodically. That is, we need power to maintain data. However, DRAM is fast and can be directly accessed, and therefore is used for *working memory*. Programs and data are read into working memory from disks where operations are executed. This explains why we can loose data if there is a power failure in the middle of an operation. Without power, working memory is cleared, and if we did not have time to save it to disk, data will be lost.

Flash memory is a non-volatile type of memory that is used in USB drives, memory cards, or in SSDs and can be erased and reprogrammed electrically. In the future, flash memory may be replaced by phase-change memory chips (PCMs).[7]

2.3   Processing

The central control unit, the processor, works in close contact with the working memory. Most program instructions will reside here, along with the data that the processor is working on. That is, instructions are performed in special registry locations in the processor, really a third type of memory. These registers are in close contact with working memory.

Basic instructions are simple, but can be executed very fast.

Instructions are simple, which adds the advantage of being able to be performed very fast. Instructions may be mathematical operators such as adding and subtracting, or logical operators for performing conditional statements, such as to execute an instruction only if a number is less than zero. More complex operations are then executed by putting together a set of simpler operations.

A modern computer will have several processors. To speed up operations, a PC may have two or more central processors that work in parallel. In addition, there may be several specialized processors or "computers" within the computer, which may be customized for a certain type of operations. A graphics card may be specialized to render 2D or 3D scenes on a display. Other input/output devices may handle storage on disks, and may have special processors to perform these operations. A network interface controller handles all network traffic, sending and receiving data.

2.4   Operating systems

The operating system makes the hardware easier to use.

Hardware alone has severe limitations. With only hardware, we would have to be specialists to use a computer. However, the hardware is only a part of the basics. Most often we need an operating system as well, such as Linux or Windows, which operates on top of the hardware. It takes care of all the "administration" and in this way provides a higher layer for users. Operating systems help us to store programs and data in files and offer a folder structure to organize files and an interface for moving, copying, and deleting files. The operating system handles execution of programs. For example, when the user double clicks on the icon for the text-processing program, the operating system will find the file containing the program, load this into working memory, and start program execution.

Security is another important function for the operating system. It ensures that errors in a program will not affect other running programs and that data is stored securely on disk. To avoid a violation of privacy and the possibility that villains can get access to the computer, it maintains a password system that limits access.

For programmers, the operating system offers a set of shortcuts, premade components to perform standard operations, such as reading from a file, presenting information on the display, performing printing, and so on. Thus the operating system extends the functionality of the hardware both for users and system developers.

Smartphones also come with an operating system.

Until now most mobile phones had their own basic software, but today, modern phones employ a standard operating system such as Android or Windows Mobile. Phones are becoming computers, and there are advantages to have a common system to build on. However, not all computers have a general operating system such as Linux or Windows. More specialized devices such as game consoles come with their own basic software, tuned to the applications. In the future, we may see general application-oriented computers, for example, a Facebook computer that starts directly in this application. If this happens, the operating system will be hidden from the user.

2.5   Programs and applications

The very first programs were written in machine code, replicating the instruction set of the processor:

```
LOAD        230
MULT        300
STO         231
```

In this example, the contents of memory location 230 are loaded into the processor. This value is multiplied with the value in location 300, before the result is stored in location 231. This one-to-one correspondence between the program and the machine is not very suitable for humans, which is why the first programming languages were developed. These special purpose languages offered more convenient instructions to the developers. FORTRAN was one of the first languages. Here a programmer could write statements such as:

```
Total = Items * Price
```

and the FORTRAN compiler would turn this into basic machine instructions, as shown above. FORTRAN is still in use today, but languages such as Java, PHP, and Visual Basic are more common. The idea behind all of these is to offer a more convenient and programmer-oriented language than the basic machine code. However, independent of language and independent of the advanced constructs that are used, the code is eventually turned into low-level machine code—as sequences of zeroes and ones. We return to programming languages in Part 4.

2.6   Devices

Peripheral devices connect the human world to the world of the computer.

The world of the computer, that of binary digits, electronic circuits, memory, and processors, is very different from the world of humans. To connect these two worlds we use a set of devices, such as a keyboard, display, mouse, and printer. The keyboard turns a physical touch into a binary code that is transmitted to the computer. A display or a printer works in the other direction, a binary code from the computer is turned into a symbol. While a touch pad offers an absolute position on the screen, a mouse gives a relative position, that is, a movement of the cursor in either direction.

In the last years, technology advances have offered a set of new devices at low cost, such as cameras, GPS (Global Positioning System), and various types of sensors. With these, we can develop a set of interesting applications, such as navigators, surveillance systems, or more convenient user interfaces.

2.7   Network technology

A computer becomes really powerful when it can be **connected** to other computers.

Computers are connected through data networks. At the lowest level we have physical lines, such as twisted pairs of copper wires (telephone lines), coaxial cables, or optical fiber cables. The advantage of copper wires is that they are often already in place and there is no need to dig ditches as with more modern cables. But modern cables offer much higher bandwidth, which is especially the case for optical fiber cables that can handle a large number of connections simultaneously, multiplexed on the same physical fibers. In addition, there are several wireless technologies, such as NFC (Near Field Communication), WLAN, that have a range of some hundred meters, mobile phone networks, that have a range of a few kilometers, and satellite communication. On all of these systems, data are transferred as bits, even if the coding may vary between the technologies.

Many of us have a PC at home that is connected to the Internet over an old telephone line, a coaxial cable, or perhaps through a fiber cable. With high bandwidth, such as what a fiber cable can provide, applications such as streaming of movies are possible. In practice this will require a bandwidth between 3 and 10 Mbits/sek (Megabits, one million bits). For other applications, such as Web surfing, much lower bandwidths will do the job. Interestingly, considerably high bandwidths can be obtained using twisted pair copper wires using technology called ADSL (Asymmetric digital subscriber line). With a modem at each end, the bits are coded by frequencies that are not used by a voice telephone call. Thus, Internet access is possible with bandwidths up to 3 Mbits/sek, without having to put in new cables.

The twisted pair line or the cables connect each home or business to an exchange, similar to the telephone system. Between exchanges, high capacity networks are needed, which are most often implemented on optical fiber cables. This is the "backbone" net.

On top of these physical networks we find the Internet, an addressing scheme (to give each computer a unique identifier), and a set of protocols to transmit data. We return to these issues in Part 5.

2.8   Conclusion

For many of us, hardware is there to do a job, just as the engine in a car. Most often we can ignore technology, but when we invest in a new device, whether it be a new car or a new computer, we must make some choices. For a car, should we choose a diesel or a gasoline engine, or perhaps a hybrid? How much power do we need? For a computer, we may have to decide how much memory we need for the applications we intend to use, whether it is smart to have more than one central processor, or if we will need a specialized graphics card. But often these choices are simplified by getting the right package, a business computer, a multimedia PC, a game console, for example.

What is important to understand is that all the advanced operations that a modern computer can perform are eventually executed as a set of basic machine instructions, and that all data—independent of type—are stored as sequences of zeros and ones. Take, for example, a spreadsheet with a column of all our income and expenses. Each line has a text and a number. Both are represented as zeros and ones in working memory. In the spreadsheet we expect that the sum at the bottom of the column will be updated at all times, along with the cell that gives total income and the one with total expenses. The spreadsheet program will have the code to perform this. Whenever there is a change in the data, the processor will be asked to go through all the numbers in the column and add these, storing the results in a location in working memory. If we could see the program code for the spreadsheet, we would see this value stored as a variable, a named entity that gives the sum of the column. The programmers who made the spreadsheet did not have to know the actual location in working memory; other systems, such as the operating system, take care of that. We also would see stored variables for the sum of income and expenses. In computing these, a conditional instruction is performed, for example, if the number is positive, add to income, otherwise add to expenses.

This implies that we can use a computer for all applications that, in the end, may be performed as mathematical or logical operations on zeros and ones and for all types of data that may be coded into these digits. The binary sequences are formalized and their interpretation, either as instructions or as data, is exact and unambiguous. Thus, the application must also conform to these requirements—be completely formalized—for it to be performed on a computer. We consider formalization in the next chapter.

Notes

1   Gordon E. Moore, a co-founder of Intel, recognized the trend that became known as Moore's Law, one of the driving principles of the semiconductor industry.

2   Ewusi-Mensah, Kweku. 2003. Software Development Failures, MIT Press.

3   For example, see Jakob Nielsen's Alertbox (http://www.useit.com), April 11, 2005: Medical Usability: How to Kill Patients Through Bad Design.

4   The Sony Mavica, which captured video frames on to a minidisk. True digital cameras, which used image sensors to convert light to digital data came some years later. However, Steven Sasson at Eastman Kodak invented the first digital camera using a charge-coupled image sensor in 1975.

5   For example, see the home page of the Model T Ford Club of America, http://www.mtfca.com.

6   A quantum computer utilizes quantum properties to represent data and perform operations instead of binary digits. These computers are still in their infancy. A few prototypes with very limited capacity have been developed, but the potential is for extremely fast computers, especially suitable for breaking codes.

7   Phase-change materials are capable of storing and releasing energy when they move from a solid to a liquid state. This can be used to permanently store a value in the material, such as a binary 1 when it is in a crystalline state or a 0 when it is in an amorphous state. Today, the technique is used for re-writeable optical storage (e.g., CD-RW and DVD-RW), but promises many advantages over flash memory.

3   Formalization

Formalization,
the process of
giving an exact
and unambiguous
specification of
data, tasks, and
processes.

An understanding of the concept of *formalization* provides the background needed to understand the possibilities and limitations of computer technology. A computer requires that both data and tasks be formalized. For data, an unambiguous representation is needed, for example, numbers represented with binary digits and letters represented with standard code tables (e.g., the ASCII[1] or Unicode[2] character sets). Similarly, tasks must be described by well-defined, unambiguous procedures. These procedures can then be represented in computer programs, for example, in programming languages such as Visual Basic, Java or PHP. Eventually, special systems (compilers or interpreters) will transform these programs into machine instructions, the binary digits that allow functions to be executed on a computer. That is, in the end an application and data will be represented as sequences of zeros and ones, and run on a machine that has an unambiguous interpretation of each digit, which is why the application also must be formalized.

Formalization
has been an
ongoing effort for
hundreds of years.

In many areas, the computer came to a preset table, as both data and routines were already formalized. Banks were among the first institutions to use computers extensively. Why? Perhaps, because they had the capital to buy the expensive mainframes, but that is only part of the answer. The real reason why banks were pioneers in using computers is that the groundwork had already been laid. Banks started their process toward automatic computing several hundred years ago by formalizing processes. A deposit, or a withdrawal, had to be carefully entered in the books under the appropriate account. Customers had to sign withdrawals and got receipts for deposits. Ledgers and cash were balanced at the end of the day. These strict procedures were needed to keep track of a large set of transactions, to safeguard the customers, and to avoid embezzlement. Formalized procedures simplified training and had the advantage that all employees worked in the same way. When the first computers arrived, the software developers could simply rewrite these formalizations in a programming language, transferring data to structured files, or later, to database systems. The advantage was *automation* of procedures, as these could then be executed repeatedly on a computer with new data sets.

In many ways, the introduction of computers resembled what happened during the Industrial Revolution when physical processes, such as spinning and weaving, were given an exact description as a sequence of simple mechanical operations. This "formalization" made it possible to construct machines that automated these processes. The same happens today, but in a symbolic rather than a physical world.

Not all processes in banks are formalized. Credit and loan approval may be based on a careful study of the customer's financial history, and perhaps on what kind of personal impression she makes. However, in order to automate some of these processes, banks are developing formalized procedures for loan approval, for example, for loans below a certain threshold to private citizens. Some customers may exploit possible weak points in such a formal evaluation, but the advantages of introducing a cheap and fast automatic process will often surpass the drawbacks.

When a process is formalized, one often uses the earlier manual processes as a starting point. For the bank loan approval procedure this may imply accessing several electronic records, collecting the customer's financial history with the bank and credit data from other sources, and perhaps also reviewing data from a questionnaire or an interview. Often, however, formalization can take a new approach, independent of manual methods.

The Vikings read environmental indicators to navigate. They used the position of the sun, moon, planets, and stars. The flight direction of a seagull could give important information, as well as the freshness of drifting seaweed, picked up by the waves from a nearby coastline. But modern navigational systems do not have video cameras that try to detect the polar star or seagulls. Instead, they rely on a satellite network, such as the GPS. GPS consists of "formalized stars" in fixed orbits that send coded beacons that make it possible to compute one's position with great accuracy nearly anywhere on the planet by use of small and cheap handheld devices. Cash registers in supermarkets do not use video cameras to identify each item, replicating the human cashier. Instead, the recognition-environment is formalized by giving each item a bar code, a set of vertical bars that can be read by a simple laser scanner. This UPC code (Universal Product Code) uniquely defines any product.

Horses and wagons opened the U.S. continent. To find their way, the pioneers careful evaluated the terrain, avoiding steep cliffs, fast running rivers, marshland, and thick forests. Today, a network of roads simplifies transportation. A freeway offers

When formalizing an application, there may be "**leftovers**," sub-tasks that cannot be formalized.

A first approach to formalization may be to try to **mimic the human being**, that is, to develop programs that work as a human.

expectations of a (relatively) smooth surface, a wide road, divided traffic, entrance and exit ramps, no crossing traffic, and signs indicating necessary directions. These expectations allow us to drive in a relaxed state at high speeds, even at night on roads that we never have driven before. While it is possible to create a car that steers itself on such good roads (several prototypes have been made), it does not seem to be a practical solution. The degree of road formalization is not high enough to defining *driving* as a formalized process. Still, a well-functioning automatic pilot for the car would seem to be an interesting product, since so much of our time is spent (wasted) on driving. In addition, an automatic solution may be more secure. Human drivers may be inattentive, even go to sleep, while a computer will be alert at all times.

To develop such an automatic pilot, engineers can make smart devices that mimic human drivers, or formalize the environment to a higher level, allowing for new ways to solve the driving task. Or, as is often the case, use a combination of the two methods.

The first approach would include video cameras, radar devices, and other gadgets to sense the environment. These data would then have to be entered as input to a program that controls the wheel, gas pedal, and brake. Even with the great advantages in sensory equipment, such a program would not be easy to make. While driving can be very relaxing at times, allowing us to listen to music, look at the countryside, and have a conversation, there are situations when we use all our sensory organs and our brain capacity to make the right decisions. We may unexpectedly see something in the road ahead. Do we have to brake, veer, or can we just go straight ahead? If an automatic pilot has to make these decisions, the tasks must be formalized. The decision program will have to distinguish between a rock (brake or veer), a small snowdrift (go ahead), an empty cardboard box (go ahead?) or a full box (brake or veer). It must be able to interpret the intentions of fellow drivers (Is he really going to turn? Why is she slowing down? Does he want me to pass?).

Humans have a better ability than computer programs to make decisions in these unexpected cases, and we have the context knowledge that is needed to do the right thing. Of course, this does not imply that we always make the right decision. There are unaccountable accidents that occurred because the driver made a reflex action, for example, steering his car out

When formalizing a task one focuses on the result, not on the way the manual processes were performed. This often leads to **radical new ways** of performing the task.

of the way of a cat, saving the cat but ending up with a serious accident.

Clearly, the other alternative—to formalize the road to a higher level—seems to be more promising, such as installing "virtual rails" in the road, cables that gadgets in cars can follow. Timers and sensors can be used to control the distance to nearby cars. Such a system may reduce the driver's workload, but exceptions would still be a problem for a completely automatic system. To achieve automation, we may have to go all the way, as with the automatic trains that run in controlled environments on elevated rails or in tunnels. Doors on the platforms, which do not open before the train arrives, restrict access to rails. Sensors are used to check if all doors are closed before the train leaves, and doors will reopen if they are blocked, perhaps with a prerecorded message that asks passengers to keep away from the doors. In such an environment the actual programming of the automatic pilot will be a simple task. (See the next chapter for a full example.)

If you are a metro train driver, your job may be at risk of a computer takeover. But note that even a metro train needs some additional formalization before we allow the computer to take over. A human driver can at least make an effort to stop if someone has fallen onto the track, but such control would be difficult to achieve with a computer-controlled train. Devices to sense any obstructions could be installed, but an easier and more reliable solution would be to formalize the environment to such an extent that passengers do not have access to the rails, as described above. Formalizing old metro networks is a major task, and a full automation of road traffic may be impossible, even with "virtual rails." However, intermediate systems may be used to improve the driver efficiency. As an example, systems have been proposed in which one driver can control a "train" of virtually connected trucks.

A modern car may also give the driver a warning if the car unexpectedly crosses the midline or is on a collision course with another car. The car can reduce speed automatically if it gets too close to the car ahead, and may even park itself in some situations. However, giving warnings and performing partial functions are much simpler than taking over full control. In the latter case, the system has to handle *all* the situations that may occur. Since a warning is only redundant information, there is no need to handle all cases. False warnings may be an annoyance, but we can handle that.

We formalize our **physical environment** by roads, train tracks, beacons, GPS systems, flight patterns, and so forth. Where formalization goes all the way, a computer may replace human beings, for example, for driving a train or piloting a plane.

The job of an airline pilot is viewed by most as a far more complicated job than driving a bus, but from the view of a computer it is much simpler.

Most of us would view an airline pilot's job as far more complicated than that of a bus driver (and often with better pay), but from the view of a computer, it is much simpler. We already have an environment of satellites and radio beacons used for automatic flight control. With modern navigational systems planes may be controlled by automatic pilots onboard and automatic flight controllers on the ground.

Completely automated systems already handle everything from takeoff to touchdown. These systems will make it possible to pack aircraft closer in the air, reducing congestion and delays. So while a pilot has more data to consider, more instruments to read, more controls to set, less time to make decisions, a lower margin for error, and more catastrophic consequences of an error, the pilot's job is much easier to formalize than that of a bus driver. The decisions that have to be made are to a large extent based on formalized data such as course, altitude, speed, radio signals, engine data, and so forth, and the decisions themselves can be calculated based on these data. The computer works faster than the human pilot and the human flight controller can work with greater accuracy and will be more reliable. On the other hand, the bus driver's job seems much simpler with only a few instruments and controls, but the open nature of the decisions that have to be made make a computer takeover highly improbable. This has, of course, nothing to do with the bus itself, but is a consequence of the environment, determined by the unformalized nature of roads, traffic, and passengers.

Social Security services are not as formalized as bank services.

Although computers have been successful in banks and planes, information systems have been much more difficult to develop in Social Security. The difference is in the formalization level of the institutions. As we have seen, banks have had formalized routines for hundreds of years, but within Social Security, the rules and regulations offer possibilities of interpretation. This ambiguity is not a fault of the regulations, but more a consequence of systems that handle data about people. The need for Social Security comes in all forms, and the regulations need to be flexible. If a computer is to be used to determine support, the rules and regulations have to be formalized to a higher degree, as well as the related data.

Many years ago, Norwegian regulators changed the system for giving social support for housing expenses. Under the new rules, taxable income, rent, and the type of house determined the support level, criteria that enabled the computer to calculate the correct amount for each client. Of course, such a system may give support where it shouldn't (rich ship owners with good tax lawyers) and some clients (perhaps with a dramatically poorer situation today compared to last year when the data was collected) would not get the support they needed. However, the advantage was automation of a manual system that was expensive and time-consuming to administer.

Interestingly, the formalization process for these types of systems often has been carried out as a part of the software development process. In many cases, the results of the formalization, the interpretations chosen for each case, have been described only in the computer programs; the actual background regulations may not have been changed. This is one reason why many organizations still run very old systems and find it difficult to update to more modern hardware and software. The old computer program has become a de facto standard for interpretation of the regulations, not simply an implementation. The ghost is in the machine. Therefore, a reengineering effort will have to extract specifications from the old system.

Similar problems have been encountered within medical information systems. Parts of these applications, for example, the "hotel" part of a hospital or an inventory system, are formalized and are open for a computer takeover. Other parts, such as interpreting test results, are more difficult to handle. While early developers saw medical systems as just another computer application, problems with the level of formalization were apparent. Different doctors used different names for the same diagnosis, medication, and so forth. However, as with Social Security the advantage of using computer systems has promoted efforts to raise the formalization level, for example, by introducing more unique identifiers for diagnosis. Even then, medical systems have proven to be more difficult to implement than other systems.

Enforcing inventory routines in a manufacturing industry is not difficult, but it is not so easy to get doctors and nurses to formalize their responses in an emergency situation in a hospital. The whole hospital environment, treating patients, working toward a diagnosis, selecting a treatment, naturally focuses on the open, unformalized parts—not an easy setting for imposing standardized and strict regulations. One of the most successful implementations of medical information systems has been in a privately owned Japanese hospital.[3] Here the culture may be

> Formalization may change the **nature** of the task, giving somewhat different results from the previous open implementation.

right for establishing rigid rules that are to be followed at all times.

Medical systems need a formalized environment to function, where someone can set the standards and require that these be followed. Other hospitals have given up on the formalization, and have instead chosen to implement image and text-based systems. With document image systems, the old records are stored as images, formalized to the level of pixels, a pixel representing a point in the image. With such systems, doctors get fast access to records, but there is no possibility of using the data for higher-level functions, for example, for statistics or medication control.

Notes

1   ASCII (American Standard Code for Information Interchange) offers a table for digitizing characters as bytes. With ASCII coding, each of the 128 characters in the table is given a seven-bit code.

2   Unicode is a coding standard for text, encompassing more than a hundred thousand characters.

3   http://www.kameda.com

4   Cases of Formalization

A set of cases will clarify the aspects of formalization. Each case is an example of formalization of a real world function so that a computer can perform the function. I shall start with the metro example introduced previously.

4.1   Case 1: Unmanned metro train

Steering a metro train can be a **formalized** task.

For this automated metro project, the most promising starting point is to formalize the environment. For example, to avoid handling situations with people on the tracks, we use a system of sliding doors to make it physically impossible for a passenger to fall into the tracks. With this controlled environment, we can develop a computer system that can take over the functions of the driver. For example, this simple code can take the train out of the station:

```
Close doors (command to all doors)
Repeat
         Read status (from sensors in the doors)
Until status = all closed

Send ready signal to central computer
Wait for go-ahead signal from central computer
Start train (a signal is sent to the engine)
```

The program will close the doors, go in the repeat-until loop[1] (repeating the Read status code) until the "all closed" status for the doors is received, wait until the train is permitted by the central scheduling computer to leave the station, and then start the engine.

The automatic pilot can then accelerate the train until the correct speed is attained, operating the train at that speed until a sensor indicates that the train is approaching the next station. Then the task is to reduce speed gradually and to stop at just the right place in the station (indicated by other sensors). Now the doors can be opened. The train will wait the required time and then repeat the program shown above.

Human driver	Automated system
Able to view ahead and stop if there is anyone on the tracks.	This problem is eliminated by using sliding doors on the platform.
Recognizing signs, for example, for speed reductions.	Replaced by sensors that give signals at appropriate locations.
Stopping the train at the station.	Replaced by sensors that indicate where the train is with regard to the station.
Seeing that all is clear before starting the train (in practice, the driver of long trains will have to rely on the sensors as well).	Using doors that reopen if they are blocked, and systems that indicate when all doors are closed.

Table 4.1 Replacing the human metro driver.

As seen from Table 4.1, the ability of the human driver to see has been replaced by automatic doors and sensors. Thus driving a metro train has become a fully formalized application. Of course, this program is only a superficial sketch. In practice, these systems need fail-safe parts that can handle every contingency.

Today automatic train operation is used in many cities and airports, and will probably become a standard for most modern metro lines.[2]

4.2   Case 2: An alarm function

A program for a digital alarm clock may be as simple as:

```
loop
        read time
        if time = alarm time then
                sound alarm
                stop
        else
                wait a minute
        end if
end loop
```

This program will start by retrieving the current time and check if this is the set alarm time.[3] If so, it will sound the alarm and stop. If not ("else") it will wait a minute. The "end loop" statement will pass control to the "loop" statement, to repeat the program.

Setting an alarm
can be a simple
formalized func-
tion.

Let us assume that the alarm time is set to 8:00, and that the current time is 7:59. Since 7:59 is not equal to 8:00 the "else" part will be executed, that is, the program will wait a minute. Execution is then (by "end loop") transferred to the loop-statement, and the program will retrieve the current time, now 8:00. Since this time is equal to the alarm time, the alarm will be sounded and the program will stop. Clearly, an alarm clock on a mobile phone or any other device will have more options and be more advanced than this, but the principles are the same. In fact, even the simple version above would be useful in many circumstances.

However, all implementations of an alarm clock have to rely on a formalization of the task. Our simple version, as with most other alarms, will sound an alarm on the set time. This is the simple formalized version of the idea of a wake-up or a re-minder. The alarm may sound even if we are already out of bed, or it may persistently remind us of a meeting that we are already attending.

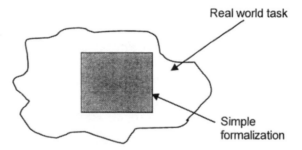

Figure 4.1. Discrepancy between the real world and the formalized version of a task.

The formalization
will not cover all
real-world situa-
tions.

This discrepancy between the real-world idea of an alarm or a reminder and the formalization is shown in Figure 4.1. In some cases the two are fairly equal; in others, there is a discrep-ancy. In this example, the real-world idea is comparable to ask-ing our spouse to wake us at a given time. Then the action will not be performed if we are already awake.

If the discrepancy causes problems, we may try to develop a more advanced formalized description.

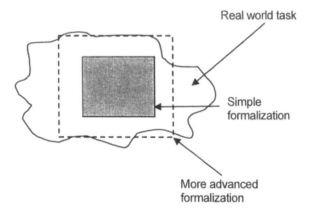

Figure 4.2. A more advanced formalization.

We can add more devices and more advanced options, but there will always be situations that are not covered by our formalized functions.

Figure 4.2 illustrates the idea to allow the formalization to cover more of the real-world interpretation of the task. To do this, we may find that we need more input. For example, by adding a motion detector to the device we may detect that the person is out of bed. If this is the case, the alarm may not sound. The if-statement in the program may then be changed to:

if time = alarm time and no motion then …

That is, the alarm will be activated only if the current time is equal to the alarm time (as before) and if the sensor cannot detect any motion in the room. However, we understand that this will be just another formalization—with drawbacks. Our user may be asleep, but tossing around in bed so often that the motion detector reacts and no alarm is given. Or our user may already be in the shower at the alarm time, and therefore, no motion is detected. Perhaps it is better to sound the alarm anyway. It may be a nuisance in some cases, but we may avoid the more serious situation of oversleeping.

4.3   Case 3: Number of passengers to a car

A ticket collector retrieves a ticket from each passenger, checks its validity, and allows the passenger to embark. This function is quite easy to formalize, and we see implementations everywhere, using bar codes, RFID[4] or magnetic strips to read the ticket, and often opening a gate when the ticket is valid.

However, in some cases, restricting the number of passengers is necessary, for example when boarding a gondola lift or a boat. In such cases, we can add a counter to the gate-keeping function that temporarily stops the reading of tickets when the number has been reached. This solution implements the idea of a passenger as one person, but there may be structures such as families and groups that are ignored. In practice, we cannot allow the kids to enter and then stop the parents when the vehicle is full.

A formalization could be to connect tickets that were bought together, stopping embarking if there is not room for the full family. Yet this procedure will require the family to board at the same time, and make it very difficult to implement if we have more than one gate. In practice, one often needs a human to handle these cases.

4.4   Case 4: Controlling heaters

More advanced formalization will often require **more data**.

As another example, consider temperature regulation in the home, a task that can be described as "keeping my house comfortably heated with as little energy as possible."

When new sensors and cheap digital devices made this possible, many consumers installed such systems. The simplest system reduced temperature at night. For example, one could program the system to turn off heaters at midnight, turning them on in the morning. This simple system may work until Saturday when we have guests and stay up late. Suddenly everyone may get very cold before we realize that the system has turned off all the heating.

A more advanced system may let us program a different shutdown time for the weekends or any other day that we want to stay up late, but it also may require quite a lot of input. Even if the system had a calendar and recognized all holidays and other days that we may want a later shutdown time, the heating may be on for a long time after we are in bed, even on days that we are away. Motion detectors may pose an alternative solution. The system could be programmed to keep the heaters on as long as there is movement in the room, saving us from chilling our guests on Saturday. In addition, the cat may love the system—heating every room as it wanders around.

As we see, the simple task of "keeping my house comfortably heated with as little energy as possible" is not so easy to formalize. To do so in a convenient way, we may need advanced systems and must also spend time providing input to the system, both to describe our needs and the exceptions that may occur. Perhaps it is just as easy to turn the heaters off when we go to bed. At the same time, we could perhaps activate the system that turns the heaters on in the morning.

4.5   Case 5: What is in the freezer?

Formalized tasks are often not working in unformalized environments.

When the first home computers arrived, a useful application was suggested: keeping track of what is in the freezer. Most of us stash things in the freezer, but have problems remembering to take them out. A program that tracked the current contents of the freezer, perhaps with a "best before" date could solve our problem.

To develop this system, we have to formalize the task. Clearly we have to describe what we put into the freezer and what we take out. Each item could be represented by name, weight, and "best before date." This works fine when we store a four-pound steak, a seven-pound salmon, and a pound of blueberries. With these data, the program can show the contents of the freezer at any time, sorted by name, "best before" data, or weight. The program also might remind us when items are approaching their "best before" date.

As long as we remember to enter data on all items, and to notify the system whenever we remove something, this should work fine. However, not all items can be described by weight. Then numbers (quantity) will work better. If we buy four pizzas, the weight of each may be less relevant, so perhaps we should add a number field to the description, an optional value to weight. What if we buy a gallon of ice cream? We fix this by adding a volume attribute, along with the weight and numbers. These solutions may fix the input part, but we now have a problem when we remove two scopes of ice cream from the container. To get an exact value, we have to return to weight, and measure the weight of the remaining ice cream. The new weight can then be entered into the system. Now we know exactly how many pounds we have left, but what is this in gallons?

In addition, we have to find the items in the freezer. We could try to enter the location, for example that the ice cream box is stored to the right, but then we have to take care when we go through the freezer to find items. If the freezer is organized in shelves or compartments, this may be somewhat easier.

However, if the freezer gets full we may have to shift items to get room for everything. This will require that we register new locations for each shifted item.

In practice, such a program will never work. First, it will require an unenforceable data discipline, recording everything, measuring the weight of everything, never forgetting to register a "withdrawal," and finding convenient package descriptions. Second, even if everybody follows the routines, such as never letting the kids take out ice cream without weighting the remainder, the task of typing and measuring will not be worth the effort. Looking into the freezer to see what is there is simpler than trying to run a formalized process.

4.6   Case 6: What is in the company's freezer storage?

This case is similar to the home freezer example, but involves a business environment with huge freezer storage, perhaps with many hundreds of thousands of items and several thousand additions and removals every day. We already failed in the home freezer case, so on the face of it, this new effort seems much more complex. However, as we shall see, this is a much simpler task.

The reason is that the formalization is already in place. Due to the high number of items and the large turnaround every day, the company had to formalize the processes. If not, they would lose track of what they had in storage from the very first day. Because of the shear size, the storage area has been divided into areas and shelves, where each location may be defined by an area and shelf code.

When the formalization is in place, it is often unproblematic to let the computer perform the task.

Packing is standardized. Ice cream may arrive on pallets, with ten crates on each, each of these containing a number of one-gallon boxes of ice cream. The type of ice cream is represented by a code on the packing, presented as a standard product number (such as an EAN code), both with digits and a bar code. By scanning the bar code, it is easy to register input and output. The process only allows for insertion or removal of pallets; one cannot take a crate from a pallet, or a box, and certainly not a scoop of ice cream.

As we see, there is no need to use weight. The bar codes on the pallets are scanned every time a pallet is inserted in the system. Pallets are assigned a location by the system, and a manual or automatic control truck moves the pallet to the correct location. Removing pallets can be performed automatically based on data from incoming orders. The system will know the exact location for each pallet, and can dispatch a forklift to retrieve it.

When developing a program for such a process, we can use the formalization that is already in place, a formalization that was needed to avoid problems inherent in the huge number of items. But huge numbers cause no problems for a modern computer system. In principle, the whole system could run on a laptop, even on a smartphone. As we have seen, "many" is not a problem for a computer.

The IT system may require an additional formalization, for example, requiring that one never try to remove only a part of a pallet. New processes, such as scanning bar codes and using automatic forklift trucks, may also be a part of an IT implementation. But the volume of goods will make implementing automatic or semiautomatic equipment cost effective.

4.7   Discussion

Computer technology requires formalized tasks. In some cases, the formalization is already in place, as in the last case above, handling the freezer storage of a large company. This will often be the case in business, where an environment of "many" (many orders, products, items, etc.) have forced the participants to formalize processes just to be able to handle the large numbers without confusion. When formalization is in place, developing programs is often a straightforward job.

In other cases, we need to formalize the problem as a part of the development project, which can be the really difficult part. In some applications, each part is formalized, but the sheer size of the task and the number of functions and exceptions, make the task too complex to be solved within reasonable time and budgets. I will discuss these cases in Chapter 12.

Notes

1   Loops are important constructs in all computer programs and come in many forms. The repeat-until performs the program sentences in the loop until the condition is true; a while-loop performs the loop as long as the condition is true; and a for-loop lets a variable (for example, a counter) get successive values from a starting value to an ending value (for i=1 to 10). The simple loop-end loop defines an everlasting loop, but will usually have an end-condition inside the loop.

2   For example, Line 14 of the Paris Métro system is fully automatic.

3   The if-statement is one of the most important statements in a program and allows for conditional execution, for example, perform the next sentences only if the condition is true.

4   Radio-frequency identification (RFID), a noncontact system to read tags.

5 Formalization Levels

Data and proc-
esses can be
**formalized on
many levels**. The
formalization level
determines the
functionality of the
formalization.

A formalized application area is a requirement for using the computer, but formalization may occur on different levels, from low to high. In many cases we have a choice of representation, for example, representing images as pixels or using higher-level concepts such as lines, circles, and rectangles. Similarly text can be represented on a low level as strings of characters, or we may try to implement concepts such as words, sentences, and paragraphs.

The following examples will clarify the idea of formalization levels.

5.1   Image representation

**Low-level formal-
ization** offers
flexibility, but does
not often provide
as effective opera-
tions as higher
level formaliza-
tions.

On the lowest level, images are represented as sets of *pixels*, each pixel representing a point in the image. On a display screen, as on a TV or a laptop, each pixel is represented by a red, blue, and green dot. A picture on a 1000 by 1200 screen will consist of 1.2 million pixels (1000*1200). On a good color screen, three bytes (a byte being 8 bits), each capable of representing a number between 0 and 255, are used to set the color and brightness of each pixel. For example, the value 255 indicates maximum value of a color and 0 indicates that this color dot should not light up. If we do the multiplications, we see that we need 3.6 Mb (Megabyte—million bytes) to represent the picture.

The level of formalization determines the functions that can be performed on the data. Note that each level may have advantages and drawbacks. *Paint* programs as well as photo editing programs use a pixel representation,[1] which allows for detailed editing (to control the color and brightness of each pixel). To enhance the user interface, the programs use metaphors such as brushes, spray cans, and geometrical objects, but we can also zoom in and set individual pixels if we want. If we draw a line in the paint program, it will be converted and represented as a sequence of pixels. Thus, any line, straight lines to freehand, can be painted on the image. If we want to change the display, for example, by moving the line, we will have to replace the pixels with background color and try again. In principle, the program does not have an internal representation of a "line," as

High-level for-malizations offer the possibility of performing more advanced opera-tions on each object.

this concept is just a part of the interface, similar to the brushes and spray cans.

In contrast, *drawing* programs implement higher-level for-malization, using a geometrical representation of each object.[2] A line will be represented by its two endpoints, a circle by its origin and radius, a rectangle by the coordinates of the opposite corners, and so on. These are given with attributers for color, thickness, fill options, and so forth. Each object on the display is represented in this form within the program, in an internal data structure. What we see on the display is a generated pic-ture. A rendering algorithm will loop through the picture's data structure and create the pixels that are needed to represent the drawing on the display. The line object, for example, is given as an input parameter to a routine that generates the pixels needed to represent the line. It will start at one endpoint and calculate the x,y-positions along the line one pixel at a time.

With this representation, the user can select an object by clicking on the object or close to the object on the display. The drawing program will compare the click-position to the geo-metrical attributes of each object to identify one of these. If the user hits the delete button, this object will be removed from the data structure, and the display is redrawn without this object. The user can choose to modify objects in many ways, for ex-ample, by moving one of the endpoints of a line, increasing the radius of a circle, or changing the color of a rectangle.

Both the paint and draw representations have their advan-tages and disadvantages, which is the reason why we have both types of programs, the low-level paint and the higher-level draw. But the higher-level representation makes it possible to perform higher-level operations, as moving an object. In prac-tice we may often find a mix of these two types of representa-tions in a commercial program, for example, to add modifiable lines and geometrical objects in a separate layer in a photo-editing program.[3]

5.2   Formalization level of text

Characters are represented by numbers using the ASCII table or any other character-to-number conversion table. On the next level we may represent text as sequences of characters, or what we call strings. A basic string-representation may be sufficient for a simple editor such as Notepad, for storing the text in a file, or for transferring the text via the Internet. However, only basic string operations such as deleting and inserting characters will be available. Higher-level formalizations are needed to handle words, paragraphs, spelling, and grammar.

Level	Formalization	Coding (example)	Functionality (examples)
1	Character	ASCII or similar character-to-number coding.	String editing, inserting and deleting characters.
2	Character sequence, sentence, and paragraph.	Rules to identify words (enclosed by spaces or punctuation) and paragraphs.	Insert and delete a word, avoiding breaking a word at line ends, inserting space between paragraphs.
3	Lexical	Dictionary	Spell checking.
4	Syntactical	Word classification, grammatical rules.	Grammar checker.
5	Semantic	Representing the meaning of words and expressions.	Logical searches, translation, computation.
6	Pragmatic	Representing the "meaning of meaning" or meaning in context.	Full text analysis.

Table 5.1 Formalization of natural language text on different levels.

Table 5.1 presents different formalization levels of natural language text, from a low character to a high pragmatic representation. The higher the level the more functions can be performed automatically. While a simple editor works on the character level, a more advanced word-processing system may work closer to a syntactical level.

As an example, Microsoft Word can provide simple spell and grammar checking in addition to basic editing functions. For spell checking MS Word cannot tell if a word is used and spelled correctly; the function is limited to checking if a word is in the dictionary or not. The function does not replace a human proofreader, but can be of great help in finding and correcting certain kinds of simple typos (those that lead to spellings that are not found in the dictionary). The grammar checker is even more restricted. It can only analyze the simplest of sentences, and its suggestions for improvement may often be wrong or meaningless. The user must know the language in order to accept or reject the suggestions. Still, grammar checking is a very

Most **word processors** work on the lowest formalization levels, leaving the higher level parts to the user.

useful feature, especially when writing in a foreign language when we can easily make the silliest mistakes, some of which the grammar checker will find with ease.

The formalization level of a modern word processor can be determined to be between a lexical and a syntactical level, perhaps getting a score of 3.5 on the scale shown in Table 5.1. For full proofreading features, the system would have to work on a semantic level (that is, the system would then have to represent the meaning of the text). On this level, other functions, such as language translation would be possible.

However, formalization of natural language has proven to be very difficult to achieve. Natural languages are a product of human communication. They are highly dynamic: New words, expressions, and styles of writing are introduced every day. In contrast to programming languages, such as Java, PHP or Visual Basic, natural languages are not designed. Dictionaries and grammar rules are not defined up front, but are mere attempts to keep up with language development in retrospect. (I will return to natural languages in Part 8).

5.3   Tagging

Most **word processors** work on the lowest formalization levels, leaving the higher-level parts to the user.

In some of the first bibliographic retrieval systems, documents were represented as plain text, which has the advantage of simplicity, but does not allow higher-level functions. For example, a search for the author "Addison Wesley" will return books published by "Addison Wesley" or even books in which these words are part of the title. In order to distinguish between title, author, and publisher these concepts must be added to the text, for example, by using tags. This is illustrated in the example below, a record from a bibliographic system using XML[4] markup (a language considered in more detail in Chapter 52).

```
<title>A Doll House</title>
<author>Henrik Ibsen</author>
<publisher>Oxford Press</publisher>
<location>Oxford</location>
<price>£10</price>
<original_title>Et dukkehjem</original_title>
<original_publisher>Gyldendal </original_publisher>
<original_location>Copenhagen</original_location>
<first_published>1879</first_published>
```

This example shows how an abundance of tags can be added to identify all attributes of a data item. Using such a simple scheme, we can limit a search to the author-field, print all titles, find the lowest price, and so forth—but only for documents that follow our scheme and use our vocabulary. Standards such as XML offer a basis for structuring documents, but we have to define vocabularies and identifying fields within the document ourselves, or rely on a standard on top of XML. For example, the above tagging will be most useful if everyone uses it. If some tag the price with <price> and other use <value>, we will have a problem.

Therefore, the major problem is to identify and standardize vocabularies and to have everyone following these standards (I shall return to these issues later in the discussion of XML in Part 4 and the semantic Web in Part 5). Even a markup language, such as in the example above, can only be used in the more "administrative" part of a document—title, author, publication, publisher, date of publication, page numbers, sections, paragraphs, and so on. The textual part of a paper or a book, the content part, must still be an open text, only formalized at a character level.

Note that this is very different from a record-based database system, where every field is uniquely specified. However, markup languages allow us to define something in between, semi-formalized records that can be used for everything from questionnaires to maintenance forms.

5.4   Formalizing data to higher levels

Higher-level formalizations offer improved functionality, but need structured data.

A computer requires tasks to be formalized; however, the formalization level will determine which operations can be performed. For example, a simple editor may represent text as characters. This editor can count the number of characters, but cannot tell how many words are in the document since it has no concept of "word." A more advanced system can have a definition of a word as any sequence of alphabetic letters, with a stop character in front or at the back. Usually we recognize a space, period, comma, colon, and so on as stop characters. By implementing this definition, we have raised the formalization level from a sequence of characters to a sequence of words. With the word definition, we may add a function that avoids breaking a word at the end of the line, for example.

A modern word processing system will raise the formalization level even further. By defining sentence, paragraph, heading, and so on, one can offer more advanced functions. For example, the word processor can avoid having a chapter heading at the very bottom of a page, and can also create and update a table of contents automatically. This function will require that we explicitly define a heading, not simply indicate these by larger font types. By telling the system in what language we are writing, the system can help us to find both typographical and grammatical errors.

Although the computer program cannot tell us if a word is spelled or used correctly, it can tell that a word is not in the dictionary. If we write "var" instead of "car," it can mark the word "var" as unknown. However, if we write the sentence "I have a red far," neither the spelling nor the grammar checker will find the error because "far" is a word in English and the grammar, albeit not the semantics, is correct.

However, even the simple formalization of comparing words to a dictionary and implementing a few basic rules of English grammar, will help us to find many types of errors. There are also methods, as yet not implemented in word processors, that may correct "far" to "car" in the sentence above (a case in Chapter 60).

Formalization of natural language is especially difficult, but the process is not simple even in domains that are more closed. In banking, for example, much effort goes into deciding which data to store on each account, and how this data is to be represented. In such a process, many questions will arise. For example, can a customer have more than one checking account? Can an account be owned by more than one customer? Should state and zip code be stored in one field or two? What about foreign addresses—how shall a name be stored? Most businesses have database administrators who handle this work, but as many of the questions will affect or be affected by business policies, the answers have to be provided on a top-management level.

In fact, a major part of the work involved in making software systems goes into answering these questions. For example, in a system recently developed for a local firm that just celebrated its seventy-fifth anniversary, the concept of a delayed order arose. A formalized description was needed because the system was going to report total delays in each monthly period. "A delay," said the production manager "is calculated as the days between the promised due date and the delivery date. If a delivery was promised Monday, but performed on Wednesday, we have a two-day delay." Reasonable enough, but he was not so sure when the system counted three days between Friday and Monday, or twenty-eight days when the company was not able to deliver on the last day before the

Formalizing data to high levels is a complicated task that is often performed by specialists, by data base administrators.

summer holiday. This case shows that formalizing is a complicated task, and the ambiguousness that has thrived under a
manual system becomes very apparent when a computer system is installed.

Other examples of formalizations are Social Security numbers, other ID numbers, product code identifiers, license numbers, bank routing numbers, and e-mail and Web addresses.
These make it easier for a computer system to identify persons
and objects. Since a clear and unambiguous identification is so
important, we are given these codes to remember. I shall consider some of these cases in the following chapter.

Notes

1   Microsoft Paint, the program that comes as an accessory with Windows is an example.

2   As an example, consider the drawing options in Microsoft Word.

3   For example, Adobe Photoshop.

4   Xtensible Markup Language.

6   Cases of Formalization Level

In this section, a set of cases will illuminate the problems of formalization. In each case, the idea is to raise the formalization level, to ensure more accurate processing, or to allow for more high-level functions.

6.1   Case 1: Personal ID

We need more formalized ways to identify persons than just a name.

At one time, only a forename was used to identify a person. This was unique enough in small communities. But to clarify, one could name the place where the person lived or his or her occupation, such as "Forest," "Hill," "Dale," and "Baker." In archives, we could store persons' birth dates, and then use other attributes such as name and address to distinguish between persons born on the same date. This works in a manual system, but becomes cumbersome in computer systems when we want to combine data automatically on the same person from different sources. To increase the formalization level, to have a really unique identifier, we introduce concepts such as a personal number or a Social Security number. This number follows a person from birth to grave and is unique for the person and is a good example of the need to raise the formalization level to facilitate computer applications.

In many countries, poor people may lack an identification number (ID) altogether. They live in villages where many may share the same name. When they interact with the outside world, they lack a formal ID, which makes it difficult or impossible to get a drivers license, a bank loan, to start a company, and to get any type of state support. To address this problem, India has started a major program to offer IDs to everybody (controlled by the Unique Identification Authority of India). They use biometrics, fingerprints, and iris scan as a basis for offering an ID number. Computer technology is helping to create the basic formalizations it needs to be efficient, in this case creating a unique ID for each citizen.

Although a Social Security number or other IDs are used for formal types of computing (banks, tax authorities, and others), we prefer names in social systems such as Facebook, Twitter, and Google+. Don't they need a unique identifier? Clearly, using a unique ID would facilitate their systems, but since Social Security numbers are considered private and sel-

An **e-mail ad-dress** can be used as a unique identifier; however, a person may have many such addresses and they may change.

dom known by others, these are not practical to use in this setting. Instead social networks allow the user to handle this problem by using names, addresses, schools, and other data in searches for persons. The systems themselves use e-mail addresses as a unique identifier. So when a person is added to a list of friends, the system can use the e-mail address but allow the user to refer to the person by name or alias. The drawback of using e-mail is that a person may have several e-mail addresses, and can thus operate with more than one profile.

Other systems, for example for commerce, may create a special user name for each user. The disadvantage is that the user name will be unique only for the one application. Consequently, we may end up with a large set of user-names. For popular sites, for example Gmail (Google's e-mail service), we may find that someone else has registered with the same name, making it necessary to add random numbers to our name to find something unique. This should be unnecessary. In the <name>@<address> scheme, there should be a possibility of having enough addresses so that <name> can be whatever the user chooses. For all other applications, except e-mail services, the e-mail address may be a better user identifier. However, many of us have several e-mail addresses, for example a work and a private address. This may be an advantage if each address describes a different role. For example, if you use the company e-mail address as an identifier for all applications, you will have a problem the day you change your job. So it is smart to have an e-mail address for each role—employment, personal, volunteer work, and so on.

When parents name their children the idea is that the name should be used through the person's life. While some may change their surnames, few change their forenames. To move toward a more formalized world, perhaps parents should create an e-mail address for the newborn baby based on the forename. This would offer a unique and permanent identifier in the virtual world.

6.2   Case 2: Formalized e-mail

When composing an e-mail message, we start with a blank mail form. The written message is just a block of text, most often formalized on a character level.

> Hi everybody
>
> The meeting tomorrow will take place in room A2 instead of in B3.

Figure 6.1. An e-mail message.

Blank forms have the advantage of full flexibility.

Consider the simple message shown in Figure 6.1. Such messages are easy to write: We start with the standard blank form, enter the e-mail addresses of the recipients (or perhaps a group name identifying a set of recipients), and compose the message, using our own words and style. However, premade forms could raise the formalization level. For example, consider the special mail form for changing information on a meeting, presented in Figure 6.2.

> *Meeting ID*:   Project 12
> *Date and time*: 12.10.13   *New date and time*:
> *Location*:   B3   *New location*: **A2**

Figure 6.2. A form for changing information on a meeting.

With **more formalized solutions,** we can automate many functions.

The advantage of such a form, with clearly identified data attributes such as date and new location, is that this information can be retrieved directly by a calendar system, automatically updating the calendars of each attendee. We can envisage similar forms for all types of messages.

Those who advocate sending forms by e-mail argue that they raise the formalization level, and thus allow for more automation. By using a form, the data will immediately be available for all, both persons and programs. However, the disadvantage is that we need a form for every situation, have to find the right form, and in some cases, may have to enter more information than we really need. In many situations, we may also want to avoid being formal, and the blank page of an e-mail offers many advantages. After all, there is a difference between e-mailing someone to say "what about dinner," and filling out a formal "meeting request" form. Perhaps we should retain simple e-mail formats for human-to-human communication, using more specialized systems when we want to communicate with computer systems.

When using the browser to access an Internet bank or a booking site, we get to a **formalized system**.

There are good alternatives. Web forms will cover many formalized applications better than e-mail, for example, when offering address and credit card data. Some events, as the calendar function, can be handled better by special programs such as Microsoft Outlook or Lotus Notes. If used by all, the program can aid us in finding times for meetings where all can participate. But this will require a high level of data discipline, or formalization. To be beneficial, everybody must use the same program and enter all information on when they are available or not. This may work in some organizations and not in others.

6.3   Case 3: Databases on the Web

Although large parts of the Web are formalized on a low level, using HTML to define the layout of each page, some sites have a much higher formalization level, such as all the specialized systems—Internet banking, booking systems, online stores, bibliographical repositories, and so on. These systems use HTML pages to communicate with customers, but have a much more formal internal data structure. The advantage is that users can apply a standard browser, such as Internet Explorer or Firefox, to access these systems. Customers have no need to install specialized programs.

When we are logged into the Internet bank, or have reached the booking site of an airline, we have left the low formalization level and can operate with higher-level concepts. For example, the banking system will "understand" concepts such as an account, debit or credit, date, amount, receiver, and due date. This allows us to perform all the higher-level operations that are pertinent to banking, such as paying a bill, transferring money between accounts, and activating a credit card. Similarly, in airline booking systems, we may operate with concepts such as airports, flights, one-way, or return trips—all the concepts necessary to perform a booking.

If we had the chance to look into these systems, we would see databases with records for every concept. For example, the airline booking system will have a database record for a flight, identified by a unique flight number, and with attributes for destinations, dates, times, type of airplane, number of seats, and so on. Tickets sold on this flight will be stored in another database record, identified by a unique booking reference number and with various attributes such as flight, passenger name, amount paid, and type of ticket. Seating may be a part of this record, but will often be stored in a separate table. The database system that handles this part will keep track of all records, offer facilities for locating records, combining records, and so forth.

The operations that we perform in these formalized systems are exact and unambiguous. If we want to see a list of all flights out of Pittsburgh International, we expect the system to include all flights. That is, we get an exact answer because the data is formalized to the level of our query.

This is not the case when we search the open Web. A search for "apple" may return pages on both apples and computers. We may make the query more specific by adding the keyword "fruit," but there will still be pages that are left out, for example, a page on apples that does not mention the word fruit, or pages on Apple computers that also use the word "fruit" ("we use Apple computers to distribute fruit to all grocers").

When we are on the Web, we may be operating in an area with low formalization (performing Google searches), or in those with higher levels (specialized databases).

6.4   Discussion

Data can be formalized on several levels. The lower levels, such as characters for text or pixels for images, are simple and offer great flexibility. With a pixel representation, each dot in the image can be changed independently of other dots. On the Web, it is convenient to represent documents as HTML, but HTML is only a "layout" language and is very close to low-level character coding.

The disadvantage of low-level formalizations is that they limit the operations that can be performed. If an image, for example, is built of higher-level blocks, such as circles, rectangles, and lines, operations can be performed directly on these higher-level objects (move the circle, change the width of a line, or delete the rectangle). When text is formalized to higher levels, we can distinguish between different concepts that are represented with the same character sequence, for example between the fruit apple and the computer Apple.

For many systems, a high formalization level is required to be able to return accurate answers and automate functions. For example, to open a bank account, we need to provide some identification, either a personal ID number or an organizational ID. Without these identifiers, the bank would not be able to report to tax authorities or confirm that you have the right to access the account.

However, higher-level formalizations come at a cost. They may reduce flexibility. For example, it is not easy to remove just a pixel from the rendering of a rectangle. If someone tags an Apple PC as <computer> and another uses <laptop>, it may not be easy to perform high-level operations because a search for the laptop Apple may not turn up all occurrences. Similarly, statistics based on these data may be wrong, as the items tagged with <computer> may not be included.

7 Symbolic Data

Over the last ten thousand years, we have created a world where the **symbolic processes** often seem more important than the physical.

In the introduction, I described the development of the virtual world. Over ten thousand years, more and more symbolic tasks have been introduced. "Symbolic" jobs are created when one works with symbols instead of physical objects. Some entire institutions are "symbolic" (banks and insurance companies). Even in companies that produce physical objects (manufacturing plants), the symbolic parts often become more important than the physical. The competitive advantage of car manufacturers, shipyards, computer manufacturers, and others lies more in handling design, logistics, marketing, and finance than in the basic physical processes, such as assembly or welding.

For most employees, the ability to read, write, and organize becomes more important than physical skills. This development from the physical to the symbolic workplace has accelerated over the last fifty years. In modern industrial plants, workers become symbolic operators; instead of handling a tool directly, the worker performs operations through an advanced computer-programmed machine. In an aircraft, more automation and control mechanisms such as automatic pilots are removing the physical aspects of flying. Working with data from manifests, instruments, and guidance systems, the modern pilot is to a large extent a symbolic worker, like most others in Western societies. Not only are more and more jobs symbolic, but also symbolic institutions are becoming the most important, among these banks, insurance companies, and media organizations.

Symbolic objects may have physical **representations**, such as paper bills, coins, tickets, videotapes, and books.

Many of our everyday objects are symbolic. The cost of the paper for a hundred-dollar bill is marginal. However, the paper bill is a *symbol* of a value, and because this symbol is globally recognized, it can be changed into goods or services. The paper bill is just one out of many *representations* for the symbol "value." A book is a physical object. It has weight. So does the DVD. The book and the DVD are representations for the text and the movie, respectively. In some cases we are interested in the representation itself, the first edition of an old book, a book printed on exquisite paper or bound in leather. But in most cases, the content is what interests us (the symbolic weightless book). Characters on paper are just one of many possible representations.

The airline ticket is a document that allows us to board a certain flight on a certain date. This "right to board" is a symbol

The physical representation can easily be replaced by **digital** numbers, for example, money represented as bits in a computer.

that can be represented using other media than paper, for example, a frequent flier or credit card, or perhaps just a code we offer at the gate.

An alternative and convenient form for representing these symbols is as bits, as binary digits in a computer. That is, instead of representing the hundred-dollar value as a paper bill, we store this number in a computer. Here it may represent the balance of a bank account, the amount of a transaction, interest calculated, and so on. We get a compact representation, independent of wear and tear, but most important, we get a representation that is open for automatic handling: storing, calculating, or transmitting. A computer program can automatically calculate interest on this amount, or use it as a basis for computing an account balance. Electronic amounts can be stored efficiently on computer disks, or transmitted at high speed over global networks. The advantages of an electronic representation are so clear that today, only a small fraction of monetary value is represented in its original form, as bills or coins. We get many of the same advantages in using bit representation for other types of data as well, whether they are text, music, video, pictures, tickets, or any other type of symbolic data.

A drawback of using a different internal representation from the external is that we need to convert data from the outside to the inside form, and vice versa. That is, from digital numbers, letters, pictures, and sounds to bits during the input process, and from bits to other symbolic forms during the output process. This mapping is performed through peripherals, which convert binary digits to characters, graphics, or physical operations (or vice versa).

Device	Function
Keyboard	Character input
Mouse	Input of (relative) position
Printer	Character and graphical output
Display	Character and graphical output
Video recorder	Continuous graphical input
Loudspeakers	Sound output
TV	Graphical output (video)
Scanner	Graphical input (pixels)
NMC machine	Physical output (positions, speed of tool)
Robot	Output of physical operations

Table 7.1 Peripheral devices.

Table 7.1 lists some of the most common peripheral devices. Since all of these are bit driven, we get the benefits of both worlds—an internal representation that is easy to represent electronically and various representations suitable for the real world.

7.1   Transmitting symbols

Transmitting the value of a hundred dollars represented by a paper bill may be difficult, but this is no problem with a bit representation. For example, this amount can be withdrawn easily from one account and deposited into another. The data can be sent directly over a communication network, at great speeds, without any costly change in the underlying representation. Compare this to the cumbersome operations needed to do the same task with paper money.

With the Internet, a business letter can be transmitted as an e-mail or as an attachment to an e-mail. On the receiving end, the electronic letter can be forwarded automatically, stored on a disk, made searchable based on contents, and edited if necessary. Compare this to sending the same letter through the mail, which requires translation of the bit representation used within the word processor to paper and a form that requires physical handling of letter and envelope. At the receiving end, the envelope has to be sorted and physically transported to the addressee. All further handling of the letter such as copying or archiving has to be done manually. It may also be necessary to enter data from the letter—date, sender, receiver, title, and more—into information systems.

Some institutions have chosen to avoid manual letter handling by scanning all documents when they are received and storing these as page images (pictures). The documents can then be transmitted, stored, and forwarded in electronic form. The formalization level, however, is that of pixels, and the document data cannot directly be searched or edited. Another disadvantage is that image files tend to get very large, even if packing methods can reduce file sizes. However, with the disk and bandwidth capacity we have today, companies with a modern IT infrastructure can handle images without problems.

The image version of the document can be enhanced by using OCR (Optical Character Recognition) techniques.[1] OCR programs can recognize characters with high accuracy and will translate these from image form to character codes. At best,

*Symbols represented as bits can be **transmitted** over data networks at high speed.*

*Some organizations try to cope with a paper-based world by scanning all incoming mail, storing letters in **image form**.*

OCR (Optical Character Recognition) is used to transform a document from an image representation to a higher-level character representation.

these programs can translate the document back into its original electronic form.

Image scanning and OCR offer businesses the advantages of electronic document handling, without forcing any standard on their customers. For example, the image scanning systems are solely based on the paper format, and can handle documents independently of whether they are produced through handwriting, typewriters, or modern word processing systems. While OCR systems will have problems with handwriting, they can handle any form of typed document as long as the typing quality is reasonable.

Image scanning, OCR, and fax machines, along with other systems that rely on paper, should be considered temporary systems that help us transform from a paper to an electronic world. In the long run, we should expect that the majority of documents that are received by a business will be electronic, sent as e-mails, attachments to e-mails, or as highly structured XML documents. The advantage with the latter is that they can be handled with higher-level functions. These functions can retrieve fields such as item number, quantity, and customer number from purchase orders and can insert these in an order file, available for other functions higher up in the value chain. To get to this "nirvana" of computing, we need standards, from the network level and up to document levels, from the way we send bits on communication networks to the way we structure an order form.

To automate we need standards, from the network level and up to document levels, from the way we send bits on communication networks to the way we structure an order form.

Data communication networks have been available for decades. Businesses have used this technology to transmit data between branch offices and the head office computing center using call-up or fixed telephone lines. But the Internet has introduced standardization, affordability, and availability. Proprietary protocols, as defined by the different computer manufacturers, have been replaced by an open standard—TCP/IP. The IP, Internet Protocol, offers means of accessing every server on a global basis, using a unique IP address. The TCP (Transmission Control Protocol) allows computers to exchange data in a standardized manner.

Standardization has promoted widespread communication, along with physical breakthroughs in technology such as optical fibers, wireless technology, and faster processors that have made data transmission inexpensive. Telecommunication companies have made huge investments in digging ditches and laying down new cables, setting up communication towers all over the world, and launching new communication satellites into space. Smart solutions have been found for the utilization of existing installations. Power companies, for example, use their power lines as a skeleton for a communication network by spinning optical fiber around the lines. With audio modems, digital to audio converters, data traffic can be transmitted over ordinary telephone lines. New technology allows twisted pair copper lines to be used for moderately high bandwidths, offering the possibility of having several telephone "lines" and a fast data "line" all on the old telephone line, without laying a new cable into every office and home.

When Bill, Joe, and Susan get data communication from their homes, this is a revolution, offering possibilities for new ways of symbolic communicating, for new ways of doing business. While TCP/IP defines the underlying standard for transmission, standard formats for messages and contents are as important. For messaging, the global standards are SMTP (Simple Mail Transfer Protocol) and MIME (Multipurpose Internet Mail Extension), and for contents, HTML with the accompanying HTTP standard for transmitting the HTML pages. On the next level, XML seems to be the promising tool.

7.2   New representations change the world

Digital representations change society!

The change from paper to electronic communication is not only a matter of efficiency. As we shall see, it is changing the world. Take digital money. Each year we see a decline in transactions using paper bills and coins, and a similar increase in electronic payments. Toll booths where one stopped to pay are now being replaced by electronic counterparts. These have the advantage for drivers that the transaction, paying to pass, can be performed at full speed. A radio responder in the car is used to identify the account for paying the toll, or a camera may pick out the registration number. In the latter case, the driver may receive a bill later on. Of course, these are only intermediate technologies. In the end, each car will have an electronic registration number in addition to the visual. This will open the way for quite a few new methods to enforce speed limits or to pay for the usage of roads.

When the paper money disappears, so will a lot of crimes. Income will be more difficult to hide from tax authorities. A more formalized system for payments will be possible, with both advantages and disadvantages. (I shall return to these issues toward the end of the book—in Chapter 66.4.)

Digital representations have a great impact also in other areas. When music goes from CDs to streaming, there are direct implications for music stores that are no longer a necessary part of the chain from record companies to consumers. But record companies are also affected. Their model has been to offer contracts to promising new artists, hoping that some of them will succeed. At one time, this was the only way into the business, as the record company had all the resources needed to produce, distribute, and market records. However, today a new artist will have good editing equipment on a laptop, and also channels for distributing the music. Possibilities emerge for making a career without the record company.

Digital representations change the way we do business!

Similarly, publishers are no longer a necessary part of the value chain from the author to the reader. Good typesetting systems are available on a PC. If the book is to be printed, the author can take advantage of standard formats such as PDF. The printers can receive the manuscript, including the book cover, in this format, turn it directly over to their printing software, and produce the number of books that the author wants. The book can be offered to bookstores or put on sale on the Web. In the latter case, the author may sell books from her own site, or get a distribution deal with Amazon[2] or any other established site. If the book is to be offered in electronic format, several sites can be helpful to the author. However, a publisher may still add value to a book, from proofreading to distribution and marketing. Therefore, we may expect to have different models here, as with music.

Web-based newspapers have found a somewhat different model than their paper counterparts. Since it is more difficult to read online, even with modern displays, many Web-based newspapers offer shorter stories, but offer headlines, pictures, animations, and video. In many countries around the world, free Web papers are putting the paper-based newspaper out of business, in some cases the very paper-based newspaper where the Web version gets its stuff. But new technology may change this. In the future we may expect to get larger, color displays with high resolution, not backlit as LCD screens, but displays that use ambient light and have the reading quality of paper. This may offer a new start for newspapers. By skipping physical printing and distribution, high quality papers may be offered for much less than today.

Such a technology may also change the market situation dramatically. Since everything is digital, a national newspaper may offer local versions, with local weather forecasts and local advertisements. With a few freelance journalists in every town, a national paper also can offer local news.

We see that new technology not only comes as a replacement for old technology, but also offers quite new products and applications. While digital cameras have replaced analog, the greatest change is in the availability of cameras. Now all of us have a picture and video camera in our pockets. This has lead to the downfall of many politicians and perhaps regimes (see the Internet and democracy in Chapter 65). Celebrities, too, have to be much more careful. One never knows when a camera is running. Even youths on "drinking holidays" are being more careful, as an unfavorable video on YouTube may have consequences both in the near and the far future. To a certain extent, news sites are relying on ordinary citizens to provide coverage. The banner "Do you know more? Contact us…" is now a standard in many news stories.

For ordinary users, digital cameras are not only much easier to use than the analog, but they also have no limit to the number of pictures that can be taken. The ability to see the picture the very instant that it is taken is also a great aid to the amateur. In addition, pictures can be edited, cropped, or the darker parts made lighter and lighter darker. The amateur is also offered sites to publish his photos and videos, such as Flickr and You-Tube. All of this is driven by digital technology.

Today we may even see the "unseen." Architects can describe buildings using 3D software, and may then insert the building in a street photo, as if it were already built. Builders of cabins and houses can present realistic photos on each model with such a good quality that it is difficult to see the difference between a computer-generated image and a real photo.

One of Norway's largest producers of cabins created a brochure with pictures that I expected to be real photos. However, since they presented different models on the same piece of land, there were only two options: Either they built a model, took a picture, tore it down to build a new model on the same spot, or it was a computer generated image.

At one time, ship building was associated with riveters and welders. While welding is still a necessary part of constructing a modern ship, many of the important phases are now performed in front of a computer. The 2D graphical packages used to design ships have been replaced by 3D systems, which makes it possible to visualize the whole ship before it is built.

New and improved **technology** will push new services and applications.

Today we may see the "unseen." Architects can describe buildings using 3D software, and may then insert the building in a street photo, as if it were already built.

As we shall see in Chapter 40, it is possible to view not only the exterior, but also the interior. Using simulators one can also study how the ship will operate in heavy seas, that is, in the virtual world of virtual ships and virtual waves. Of course, the company buying the ship will not be satisfied with a virtual ship; they want something that can carry passengers, oil, iron ore, or containers. But when the design is complete, the process of building the ship, the welding of the hull and installment of engines and other equipment, can be viewed as a "printing" process.

In practice, it is not that easy. Those building the physical ships will have to make many decisions during this process; however, we are moving towards more and more decisions being made during the design phase. 3D drawing programs, systems similar to the one above for specifying interiors, and simulators are all moving the work towards the virtual phase.

For many types of manufacturing, we are there already, where design and specifications, the virtual process, is the important part, and where the production can be left to the factory with the lowest tender. This requires that the design is complete, that is, that the product is fully specified. Standards are also important here, so that the design company can transmit the design in a form that the manufacturer of the physical product can understand and apply. That is, we are close to the "printing" metaphor.

We have reached this level for book printing. The author can print the book, with text, pictures, and complex layout, as a PDF file, which printers can use directly on their printing presses. The same direct implementation of printing is also available for simple physical objects, for example when we apply a 3D printer device to make prototypes or parts. Based on a CAD model (Computer Aided Design, a full 3D-model of an object), these printers use plastics or metal powder to build layer upon layer of the object.

3D printers have found applications in many areas.

There are limitations as to size and to the material quality. Further, the costs of printing an object can never be compared to the unit costs of mass production, but there are instances where one is enough. It may be prototypes or, very promising, printing "parts" to be inserted in a human body, as a hip replacement. For other types of spare parts, it may be more convenient to store a 3D description of the part than the part itself. When needed, one can perform a "print." The 3D printing process also has the advantage that the interior of a part may get smooth curves, something that is difficult to achieve with traditional methods, such as when machining parts.

7.3 Discussion

The virtual world is becoming more important. Many of our activities, from work to leisure and entertainment, are of this world. Change started with books; then came newspapers, magazines, radio, movies, and TV. Today we play games in virtual worlds, chat with friends on Facebook, or go to a Web site to get the news.

Even some of the traditional processes of the physical world, such as farming or manufacturing, are performed virtually. Today, farmers install computer systems that both feed and milk the cows. In industry, the virtual world is becoming the most important, where the complex decisions are made, where ideas are implemented, and often where the money is. Design is often more important than production. When the design can be performed in a 3D world it becomes possible to make detailed specifications. These virtual products can be shown to users; for example, an architect can present a "picture" of the new house, rendered into its surroundings, long before it is built. Designs can be tested, for example, running virtual ships on virtual seas. For some products, it is also possible to print prototypes in metal or plastic on a 3D printer.

However, even if the virtual world is becoming the most important, we still need the physical world. We cannot eat virtual products, neither can we live in virtual houses.

With complete specifications, the actual manufacturing of the products, the copy phase from a virtual to a physical product, will often be simplified to the degree where it can be left to others, a situation ripe for outsourcing. Alternatively, since the specifications are fully formalized, manufacturing can be automated to a large extent. That is, the specifications can be turned into programs that control the machines that produce the parts. Many companies choose this strategy instead of outsourcing, knowing that it is difficult to outsource production without also outsourcing product knowledge.

Notes

1   For example, see Bunke, H. and Wang, P.S.P. (eds.). Handbook of Character Recognition and Document Image Analysis. World Scientific Pub Co. (May 1997).

2   Amazon has become a long tail retailer (see chapter 46) by also being a distributor for small publishers.

8   Cost-benefit of Formalization

Formalizing may offer great **advantages**, but comes at a price.

To avoid theft, we need to limit access to our property, so that only authorized persons can get into our house. A few may implement this function by hiring a butler or a doorman, but most of us have to rely on locks. A lock offers access to anyone with a key. This is a simple and cheap way of formalizing the concept of access. However, while a doorman can use his intelligence to handle special cases, the lock opens only for those with the right key. There is no way to handle exceptions. We feel foolish when we have locked the keys in the car, and we are worried when the keys are lost since they may get into the hands of the wrong persons.

"Intelligence" in computer systems can break down where the formalizations are too simple.

A refrigerator that orders food automatically via the Internet has been proposed as one possible futuristic net-application.[1] Very convenient—we will never be out of milk or any other item. But we have to remember to tell the fridge that we will be away this weekend; that we no longer can stand chocolate milk; that we are trying to stay away from high-fat cheeses; that we are expecting a lot of guests this weekend; that we have been recommended to eat more vegetables; or that the cheese we bought was an unsuccessful experiment. An alternative solution offering less autonomy to the refrigerator would allow us to use a mobile phone to call the refrigerator on our way to the grocer, and have the refrigerator describe its contents. Still, this idea will need complicated technical implementations. (How much milk is left in the carton? Are the tomatoes still good?) While such a product is possible, the task of administering such a fridge may be extensive, perhaps just the type of work that we wanted to avoid in the first place.

In our homes, and in many smaller institutions, we enjoy the flexibility of open functions. We buy when we like, what we like, and at the last moment we may decide to go to a restaurant instead of eating at home. A "smart refrigerator" that does its own ordering will violate this flexibility. Alternatively, we will have to give it all the data needed so that the system can keep track of our decisions (that is, to "follow" the irregular border of the open function). So when we decide to eat at a restaurant instead of going home, we must call our intelligent fridge. It may even protest, if it already bought the ingredients for tonight's dinner! Some users may get a kick out of having

Formalization and automation often run counter to **flexibility**. In our homes we may prefer flexibility, while a business may prioritize efficiency.

Not all formaliza-
tions for automatic
functions work.

these dialogues with their refrigerators, but most of us would feel very silly.

In computer systems, "intelligence" is used to simplify the user's tasks. For example, Microsoft Word can give us an automatic bulleted list. This is triggered when we write a bullet symbol, such as a minus sign, at the beginning of a line. The word processor assumes that we've started a bulleted list, and will automatically insert this symbol in front of successive lines. This feature is often useful, but I found it irritating the day I tried to make a simple budget using both minus and plus items. MS Word assumed that the minus sign was the start of a bulleted list, and started all successive lines with this symbol.[2]

Similarly, in Norway, many typists encountered the problem of having the preposition "i" (meaning in) automatically changed to a capital "I."[3]

Microsoft Excel's way of saving unnecessary typing can be as irritating and even more dangerous. When typing grades—A, C+, and so on—I suddenly found that all subsequent C grades became C+ grades; that is, whenever I typed a C (after giving the grade C+ to another student), Excel would suggest C+. Since the enter key is used both to leave the field and to confirm this suggestion, all my C students got C+ grades. Of course, this feature, and others, can be turned off, but that requires that the user notice the problem, that he understands that this is a feature and not an error, and that he knows how to turn if off. The program is designed to assume what the user wants to do and to act on it before having the complete picture—just like any other dumb assistant. Now, when I get a new version of any piece of software, the first thing I do is to turn off most of this "intelligence."

This must not be seen as an argument against automation. Automation makes our lives simpler in many cases. Lights that go on when it is dark (controlled by a light sensor) or when someone passes by (infrared sensors), sprinkler systems that water the lawn when necessary, and the automatic choke system on modern car engines that regulates the air/gas mixture are all useful. These systems work because there is a good fit between our needs (the open part) and the formalization (the closed part). Sure, there may be situations where these devices do not perform ideally, such as turning on the lights for a passing cat or sprinkling the lawn before a downpour, but these exceptions come at a minor cost and do not affect the overall goal of the system.

Open functions
are **flexible**, while
closed (formal-
ized) functions
often are more
rigid.

For most applications, the formalized functions will be more rigid than the open, manual functions. Whereas a human being can use her intelligence to handle exceptions, the computer needs to be preprogrammed for each special case, and also will need data to enable it to distinguish between the cases. The costs of formalization lie in the lack of flexibility; the advantages are in the possibility of automating the formalized tasks.

However, large organizations or those that handle many transactions already have accepted many of the formalization costs, as more formal systems were needed just to keep track of all the data and to provide efficient processes. Here, the number of transactions itself is a barrier to flexibility, and the extra formalization needed to use a computer is often negligible. Thus, the lowest formalization cost are often found where the advantages of automation are the greatest, which explains why a computerized inventory and ordering system may function very well at a grocery store, but not at our homes. The grocer will have thousands of different articles, with a large quantity of each on the shelves, and a formalized system for identifying each item, for ordering, taking inventory, and for cash registers is required for efficient handling. The grocer's formalized system is needed independently of the use of computers, and the cost—rigid routines and a loss of flexibility—has already been paid. The grocer cannot make a last-minute decision to close the store and take a walk in the park instead.

Open systems
are more common
in our private lives
than in a business
environment. In
the latter case,
high transaction
volumes often
require closed
systems.

In the end, the possibility of automation is a strong incentive for formalization. But there may be parts that will not be covered. One strategy is just to ignore these parts. Pure Internet banks do this. If you need to deposit cash into your account, they ask you to find another bank. This is no problem, as most customers do not need this option, or may solve the problem by having an additional account in a physical bank. Another strategy is to have other channels for parts that automation cannot cover. For example, our Internet bank will assume that customers perform their own banking using the automated systems, but may offer help over chat or telephone. Similarly, telephone systems that ask you to type 1 for this and 2 for that, usually have an alternative for "other"—inquiries that cannot be clearly categorized.

Notes

1   The first (prototype) products are already on the market.

2   In newer versions, the backspace key will undo the automatic bulleting.

3   This feature is turned off in a Norwegian version of the software.

PART 2
Constraints

Information technology is most often presented through the possibilities, and all new gadgets, applications or businesses are given hyped presentations. For example, when Google has success with its business model, many see the "Google Way" as an answer to all future businesses, just as one talked about the "new digital economy" some years earlier. Even hardcopy books are written to show that the future is in e-books.

As we all know, there are constraints, which become apparent when the new technology meets the real world. These constraints may be fundamental, such as whether we design an intelligent computer (Chapter 9), or technical (Chapter 10 and 11).

Sometimes the constraints are in the details. The example presented in Chapter 12 is from the Telecommunication Act, where the idea was to make way for more competition by splitting up monopolies. New companies were guaranteed access to the infrastructure, as lines and exchanges, also including the software that was needed to set up calls and do the accounting and invoicing. Still, many of the new companies failed. An important reason was that the companies did not master the details.

Cultural constraints may arise in the form of laws governing intellectual property. Old movies are a good example. In practice, offering these online—mostly for historical reasons as few commercial interests remain—should be simple. However, doing so would require a contract with every copyright holder, not only the company owing the copyright, but also with all actors, musicians, and everybody else who participated in creating the product, because an online option was not envisaged when the movies were produced. Chapters 13 and 14 discuss cultural constraints in more detail.

Privacy and security may limit the use of the data we gather and the systems we employ. These issues are discussed in Chapter 15 and a case study on Internet elections is presented in Chapter 16.

9   Computer Intelligence

Is a computer that performs bookkeeping intelligent? Clearly not, but can we call it intelligent when it beats us at chess? Imagine Kasparov,[1] one of the best chess players, looking intensely at the board. We can see that he is thinking hard, analyzing the current situation, and evaluating possible moves. In the end, we see him throw up his hands and leave the table—he has lost to the Deep Blue program from IBM.[2] Or look at the robot-driven cars that go through the Mojave Desert on narrow, winding dirt roads.[3] No humans are aboard. They are in a car behind with a stop button ready to kill the robot car if goes awry, but they have problems keeping up. Driving a car does not demand much intelligence, but still many decisions must be made. Is the robot-driven car another example of the intelligent computer?

From beginning of civilization, human beings have compared their brains to the very latest in technology. In Babylon, five thousand years ago, the brain was said to be like a watering system, with thoughts floating through pipes, spreading out in fountains, and accumulating in chambers. Since then, the brain has been compared to wax tablets, astronomical clocks, and telephone switchboards. We should not be astonished to see that people are comparing the brain to the most advanced technology that we have today—computers.

> From the very beginning of civilization, humans have compared their brains to the very latest in technology.

But what is intelligence? This has been and still is an interesting topic, and you would expect to find a review of this discussion here. But no! I will not discuss intelligence. Instead, I bypass this complex question and look at formalization, that is, the task of describing processes in a clear and unambiguous manner. An example will illustrate this point.

9.1   Is a chess-playing computer intelligent?

Chess is played on an eight-by-eight board, defining a "world" of sixty-four squares. Each side controls eight pawns, two knights, two bishops, two rooks, a queen, and a king. Each player, white or black, starts with all sixteen pieces on the board in a fixed initial position. White has the first move. Every piece can make certain types of moves. For example, pawns can move straight ahead, bishops can run diagonally over the board, rooks in straight lines. Each piece threatens opposite pieces in

Chess is played in a **formalized** world; therefore, the computer can play chess.

It is quite **easy** to make a program that plays chess.

its path. When it is your turn, you can move to capture the opponent's piece, or you can make a move to improve your position in accordance with your own game strategy, such as setting up your next move, or in the one after that. The aim of the game is to checkmate the opponent's king. Checkmate occurs when one of the opposing pieces threatens the king such that it cannot escape to an unthreatened position. In chess, every contingency has been considered; there is a rule for everything, even for specialized situations in which there cannot be a winner (stalemate or draw).

Developing a computer program that plays chess is quite easy. The rules are translated into a programming language such as Visual Basic or Java. The board can be represented as an eight-by-eight matrix, each cell being able to hold one piece. When the game starts, the computer has placed all thirty-two pieces in their initial positions. For each turn an algorithm will consider each piece and make a list of possible moves, depending on the type of piece, its position on the board, and the position of the other pieces. This is the straightforward part of the chess program, a part that could, for example, have been given as an exercise in a programming course.

Strategy is more difficult to program. One possibility is to let the program calculate possible wins and losses, for example, by estimating that a captured pawn is worth a 1, a captured bishop 3, a rook 5, and so on, using similar negative values for losses. By giving a very high value for placing the opponent in a checkmate position, we can ensure that the program will pursue this situation. We can now compute a score for each move, choosing the one with the highest value.

But an opponent can offer the program a piece as bait in order to achieve higher gains in consecutive moves. Thus, we need an algorithm that can see several moves ahead, choosing the move that offers the best overall gains for us, and the poorest opportunities for the opponent. This is called a minimax algorithm.

Our program would probably be a poor player, but with some effort it could beat many human players. To defeat the very best players, we must estimate scores for many moves ahead, which requires excessive computational power. For example, in the middle of the game, we may have about thirty possible moves. For each of these, the opponent will have as many countermoves. Since we cannot know which counter move the opponent will make, we have to evaluate all. Our best

To make a program that **beats** the best human players, we need excessive computational resources, or a **brute force** solution in which we analyze many moves ahead.

move will be the opponent's worst. So just to see two moves ahead we need to evaluate 30*30 = 900 positions. There are 810,000 positions if we look four moves ahead, and 729 million if we want to see six moves ahead. To analyze all game situations, the number rises to 10^{120}, higher than the number of atoms in the universe. The complexity of chess is not in rules, pieces, or moves, but in the sheer number of possibilities.

A human player has no chance of evaluating millions of moves. In practice, a good player will consider only a few, chosen by experience or intuition. But the computer cannot play this way. So we construct special processors, such as Deep Blue, that can evaluate millions of moves in a split second. This enables the computer to look far ahead. While a chess program needs some sense of strategy, a program to play tic-tac-toe or Sudoku needs brute force only, which is the capability to try all possibilities.

Brute force programs are used in industry.

Brute force solutions are also used in industry. For example, a "best-fit" system for a foundry making ship propellers has been developed. Casting is not an exact science; blades are cast somewhat larger than required. After casting, the best-fit program will find the optimum placement of the specified propeller within the cast (see Chapter 26).

In practice, the computer performs bookkeeping similarly to the way it plays chess or Sudoku or performs smart functions in industry—by performing fast and accurate calculations. None of the tasks are any proof of intelligence. They are all formalized applications, performed by exact rules.

9.2　Does driving need intelligence?

Normally we can listen to music and have a conversation when driving because driving takes only a part of our brain capacity. However, in difficult situations—bad weather, traffic lights that are out of order, or entering a highway with heavy traffic—we have to concentrate and we have less capacity for other tasks. Conversation halts until we are out of the complex situation. Clearly, there are situations when driving requires thinking.

DARPA organizes races for **robot cars**.

DARPA, the military research organization, organizes a race for robot cars, both in rural and urban environments. These are not robots that we know them from science-fiction movies, but are ordinary cars and trucks, modified to be computer operated. Mechanisms are implemented to allow the computer to control servomotors that turn the wheel and put pressure on the pedals. The advances from the very first race in 2004 to those in 2005 and 2007 have been astonishing. In the 2004 race in the Mojave Desert, none of the cars managed to complete the course. A year later, five vehicles successfully completed the seven-mile track.

Is intelligence involved? No, this is also a matter of formalization. By using GPS (Global Positioning System) and a long list of waypoints (intermediate positions), the program knows the overall route. GPS is not accurate enough for making detailed decisions, for example, avoiding a rock. For such events, the cars use lasers that scan the road ahead. The program looks for even surfaces, using this as a definition of the roadbed—not as simple as it sounds. A dirt road is difficult to distinguish, and the program has to make many decisions as to which route to follow, combining the GPS and the laser data.

Several tests have been executed for driverless cars on ordinary roads, with good results.[4] Google have a driverless car project, and in a test situation, the Google driverless cars traversed San Francisco streets without problems. It has now been given the very first license for a driverless car.[5]

Will robots some day be our fellow drivers on the roadways? It depends on to what degree we can formalize roads. Today, allowing a computer-driven vehicle into traffic on its own would be impossible in many countries. One example for requiring a human driver is the rule that one must yield to a car coming from the right, but not if the car enters from a parking space or a private road. Today this situation requires complex decisions, but it can be "formalized" by setting up yield-signs. Another problem is that lanes are not clearly marked in many cities. Drivers have to make too many decisions based on judgment. In fact, it would be much easier to let the computer replace an airline pilot than a bus driver. As discussed earlier, an airplane operates in a formalized environment, which is clearly not the case for cars on all city streets today.

Therefore, computers can fully replace human drivers only in the most formalized areas, such as driving forklifts in modern warehouses and metro trains on special lines. Similarly the DARPA vehicles may have an application in special environments, perhaps driving trucks on company roads or for the military.[6] These techniques also will produce safer cars—aiding the human driver. In the future, if roads can be formalized to a higher level and open situations can be closed, perhaps a driverless car may be an option.

> Will robots some day be our fellow drivers on the roadways? It depends on to what degree we can formalize roads.

9.3   Natural language applications

Natural languages are not formalized.

Natural languages, such as English or Italian, are not formalized, and dictionaries and grammar rules are only of limited help. Many of the most prominent authors write sentences that abuse the rules; new words and meanings are introduced all the time. At one time, "grandmother is rocking in the corner" would have implied that she sits in a rocking chair, but today she could just as well be listening to the Stones.

These nuances limit many natural language applications, such as getting precise answers to search queries or translating from one language to another. If you tell the Microsoft Office Assistant that "I do not want any help on printing" it will offer advice on how to print because the parser reads only keywords, not the meaning of the sentence. Similarly the natural language translators found on the Web are of limited use. They may give the overall idea if the original text is simple, but are useless for more complex instances. Applications are successful when there are limited vocabularies and structured sentences, for example translating weather forecasts from English into other languages. (I return to natural language translation in Part 8.)

A human may use intelligence to perform a task, in which the computer can use **calculation**.

We have seen that chess programs needed powerful computers to perform well. Will faster processors give us better translators? The answer is no. Chess is formalized; natural language is not. The main problem is that natural languages rely on context. When we say "see you at lunch," our meaning is quite clear. A computer would have to ask for the time and place. Take the word "right." How should it be translated into Italian: as *destro, giusto, adeguato,* or *correttamente*? A human translator would know the correct answer from the context. A computer could try the same thing, but would then need full world knowledge. Looking at the sentence is clearly not enough; "He took the right path" is still ambiguous. Both "right" and "path" have multiple interpretations. That is, the feasibility of natural language translation is not a question of computer power, but of the possibility of formalizing natural language applications.

9.4   The smart solutions

Early prophets on computer technology told us in the 1960s that there would be intelligent computers in twenty-five years.[7] They have lived to see that their expectations have not come true, not even in fifty years. Today, some have very cleverly dated their forecasts several hundred years into the future. Others have refined their statements to "applications that would be considered intelligent if they were performed by humans." But that is something quite different. While the Vikings needed intelligence and creativity to navigate, we do the job today by simple GPS devices that compute the position with an accuracy of a few meters. No intelligence is involved.

We do not set up video cameras in groceries to distinguish different types of items. Instead, we formalize the environment by marking the packaging with a bar code that can be recognized by a simple laser scanner. Similarly computer systems do not use face recognition to identify customers. Instead, we use plastic cards with magnetic strips or embedded circuits, along with secret PIN numbers, a method that is not foolproof, but simple and workable for most applications.

9.5   Turing test

Alan Turing, one of the fathers of computing, wrote a paper in 1950 in which he introduced this test: You are sitting at a terminal. A computer or a person may be at the other end, and your job is to find out which.[8]

What kind of questions would you pose to distinguish between a human and a computer? We know that the computer can only handle what is formalized, but since humans also can work in this area, albeit slower, we should ask questions within areas that are not formalized. We could try natural language, and ask for the meanings of words or phrases. But why not select an area that is clearly not formalized, such as jokes. Only humans have the context knowledge to get the point, and as we know from experience, one cannot deviate far from the script before the audience misses the point.

Here is a one-liner found on the Internet: "What happened when the computer fell on the floor? It slipped a disk." Can we formalize the difference between an ordinary sentence and a one-liner like this? What if "disk" were replaced with CD or "slipped" replaced with "lost"? A smart program may detect the double meaning, but this is not enough to determine the humor. "It broke its back" also has this double meaning, but is not funny. The program could store a list of all jokes and generate a "ha-ha" sound whenever it found a joke, but this would not handle variations. For example, the one-liner above would work even if we replaced "computer" by "DVD player." Thus, by keeping our questions in the realm of funny, sad, boring, interesting, moving, and so on, we should be quite safe that no computer could give us the human answer.

9.6   Conclusion

This chapter has not discussed intelligence—that was not necessary. Instead, we have looked at formalization. A computer program must be and is a formalization. Basic data and processes must always be given a formalized description. We can use the computer to perform tasks that would have been considered intelligent if they were performed by humans, such as navigation or playing chess, but after the problem is formalized the computer finds solutions by adding numbers. No intelligence is involved.

Notes

1   Garry Kimovich Kasparov, a Russian chess Grandmaster and World Chess Champion.

2   The first six-game match was played in 1996. Here Kasparov won three games, lost one, and drawing two, 4-2 in his favor. In another match the following year, Deep Blue won (3½–2½).

3   See DARPA Grand Challenge.

4   For example, see the VisLab Intercontinental Autonomous Challenge.

5   In Nevada (May, 2012). A Toyota Prius with Google's driverless technology.

6   Mining companies, such as Rio Tinto, already are using driverless trucks.

7   For example, see Simon, H. A. (1965). The Shape of Automation (for Men and Management). New York, NY: Harper and Row.

8   Turing, Alan (October 1950), Computing Machinery and Intelligence, Mind LIX (236): 433–460

10   Constraints on Technology

In the previous chapters, fundamental issues, such as symbolic processes and formalization, were discussed. While these issues set limits for what we can achieve with computers, there are also practical considerations that can set barriers against implementing all the theoretically possible applications for a computer. In this chapter, we consider some of the practical limitations we face when using technology.

10.1   Hardware development, standards, and integration

In the last few decades, **hardware development** has given us more and more powerful computers.

In 1975, my university received one of the first PCs, or microcomputers, as they were called at that time. It had an Intel 8080 processor, 32 KB[1] RAM memory, no hard disk drive, but two eight-inch diskette stations, each with a capacity of 128 KB. The price tag was about $20,000 in 1975! Today, we can get a computer that is a thousand times more powerful at a fraction of the cost.

Perhaps the *cost* factor has been the most important. Our early PC was used for word processing, spreadsheets, and for storing and processing data records, not very different from the use of a modern PC. But while only a few could afford the 1975 version, today a PC is affordable for nearly anyone—at least in the industrial countries.

Increased computer power has been used to improve the **quality** of applications, such as better word processors and higher quality video and music.

The rapid increase in computer *power* and the functionality of peripheral devices has made it possible to increase the quality and functionality of these applications. The 1975 version of word processing was character based, but modern versions offer graphics, a choice of many font types, spelling and grammar checking, and more. We do not need a several gigahertz (GHz) processor for this functionality. The processor capacity offered years ago (for traditional computer applications) could satisfy most users' needs.

However, many new applications need these processor speeds. Today we can play interactive games with amazing graphics. High-speed servers can let us search huge databases in a split second, and offer interesting possibilities for developing and executing complex mathematical models, for example, to improve the accuracy of weather forecasts.

These technological advances can also be seen in the form of *smaller* components, for example, those that can be used to create laptops, tablets, and smartphones. With advances in wireless technology, in principle, we can be connected at all times. Wireless technology is discussed in more detail in Chapter 37.

Although tremendous technological breakthroughs have occurred in certain technology areas, we cannot expect important advances in all areas. Batteries, for example, still have very limited capacity, are often heavy, and are not too good for the environment. Even if the incentive to develop something new and better is enormous, in this and in many other areas, we see only a slow evolution of technology, far from the "Moore's law" development for chip integration. Display technology is another area where developments have come more slowly. The CRT (Cathode Ray Tube) technology, developed in the 1930s, is replaced by LCD (Liquid Crystal Displays), but this technology has other drawbacks. The large resolution, high quality, and inexpensive displays needed for so many applications are still far into the future.

Novel technology often has to compete with established technology and new standards have to compete with the existing ones. While the new TV technology could rely on the NTSC[2] and PAL[3] standards already in place, they are also restricted by the limited resolution of these standards. To really get the benefit of larger TV screens, we need a higher bandwidth signal, as in the digital HDTV (High Definition TV) standard, which offers theater-like TV performance in our homes. But here we face the problem of moving from one standard to the next, a step that requires large investments from all parties involved.

These collective switching costs were accepted when moving from black and white to color TV because the advantages of getting color were clearly a good enough incentive. Color technology also was *compatible* with the previous technology (color signals could be received as black and white on old sets). Viewers could take this step at their leisure, waiting until the old TV set had to be replaced anyway.

The current incentives for the next step, to HDTV, were not as strong. An additional problem is that HDTV not only affects the TV itself, but also the equipment that consumers use along with the TV, such as a cable box, DVD, and video game console. That is, the infrastructure we build to support one technology makes it more difficult to introduce another, noncompatible, technology. However, new and better displays have aided

While we have seen tremendous **technological breakthroughs** in some areas, development moves much more slowly in others. Research and development does not always give us the products that we need.

After making investments in building **infrastructure** for one technology, we need very good arguments to replace all this equipment with another.

the move to HDTV; as one changes from the old-fashioned CRT devices to LCD or plasma displays, it is natural to get HDTV resolution at the same time.

With everything digitized, TV, telephone, data transmission, and so on, an integration of the different media is possible. The first implementations of two-way interactive TV are already here, thereby making it possible for viewers to send responses to programs or advertisements from their remote controls. With interactive TV a user following a broadcast from an marathon, can order the pizza shown in the advertisement just by pressing a button. The backward channel can be established by using the TV cable, an Internet or telephone connection, or by using the mobile phone network. With an Internet TV, Web and traditional TV are merged, making it possible to switch between broadcast TV and streamed services.

Integration, using one technology for many applications, often seems both a simple and flexible solution. In practice, however, different functions may have very different technological requirements.

However, integration of services may cause problems. An example is the integration of telephone and data services, which poses a difference in priorities. Telephone companies work to reduce delays and to keep the line open as long as possible, accepting some loss of information. This is seldom a problem as human beings correct minor missing parts in a conversation automatically. Data network providers tolerate delays, but cannot accept loss of information. Redundancy through fault-tolerant coding may correct a few missing bits, but if more information is lost, data networks are programmed to send the lost packages once more.

Integrating these two different strategies on one network is difficult, but clearly possible with the advantages seen in today's network technology. TV and video signals may be transmitted on the same network, but since these media require much higher bandwidth, there may still be practical and economical reasons for keeping TV on separate networks.

10.2   Software

Software has always been a problem area of computer-based applications. While hardware engineers can give us reliable, fast, and cheap equipment, software is often unreliable, expensive, and time-consuming to build. Software development is a shaky business. As we have seen, hardware development takes place in a formalized manner, defined by the specifications for the new equipment. This is not the case for application software that has to adjust to an eternally changing world. In short, hardware designers can create a computer according to their

A computer program may be flexible and easy to **modify**. However, large programs, especially programs that have been developed and maintained over many years by many different programmers, have a complexity that makes them extremely difficult to change.

own specifications, while the software developers' job is to increase the functionality of the machine so that it can be useful for a real-world application.

On a superficial level a computer program is very flexible. With an editor the program can be changed in minutes; new functions can be added and existing functions modified. In practice, large programs may be more resistant to change than brick buildings. Computer programs may have been developed over a long period of time and may have reached a stage where they are no longer just a representation of an application or a set of specifications. The program *is* the application and the specification. That is, there may not be any manual way of performing the tasks, and the task may not have a complete specification outside the program. The program has made itself invaluable, just like an employee who refuses to document what he does or to teach others the tricks of the trade.

This situation became all too apparent at the new millennium. Companies had to rehire retired Cobol[4] programmers with a competence in yesterday's tools to modify the programs to handle dates into the 2000s. Systems that had an expected lifetime of five to ten years were still in use twenty to thirty years later. The cost of replacing these systems was enormous, and since they can be used yet another day—why not?

While most bugs may have been removed from these legacy systems, we can in no way expect that modern software will be bug free, partly because software is complex, but also that minor errors may have large effects. A house will not fall down if the carpenter did not put in a nail correctly or if the concrete for the foundation did not have the optimal amount of water. But even small errors in a software product may result in a collapse of the whole system. That is, the physical world is *analog*, continuous in a way where everything is fine as long as we are on the right side of the line. A house may have a much stronger foundation than it needs, and the carpenter may put in many more nails than the theoretical minimum, but every line of program code is important in a software system. An error in one of the million lines of a big system may not only have an effect on the actual function, but may also bring the whole system crashing down. In a world of interconnected systems, such an error may also bring other systems down.

The race to get new systems on the market poses another problem: The first versions of a new software product are often released before they are completely tested and may therefore

The first versions of a new software product are often released before they are completely tested and may therefore have serious flaws.

have serious flaws. Smart users acknowledge the problem and avoid installing the very first versions of a software product, at least for systems that are used for important tasks. Within the world of software it is very often a good idea not to be number one. The positions somewhat farther behind in the implementation queue are safer.

Developing software for Web applications is especially hard. On the Web we do not have the same control as in stand-alone or client-server systems in terms of the number of users or the available resources. A portal may break down when it becomes too popular, and the streaming video application may not work if the backbone Internet or the ISP (Internet Service Provider) does not manage the load. Instead of having a set of friendly users, as within a company, we may be faced with in-experienced users, those with very different backgrounds, and even hostile users who try to break the system.

However, in recent years, tools for developing Web applications have advanced. These tools handle at least some of the problems. A few are so easy to use that a full online store can be set up in a couple of days. While this provides efficient solutions, to a large extent, we have to rely on the toolmaker for the quality of the solutions, for example, to ensure that the system does not have any security loopholes.

10.3   Usability constraints

Following technological breakthroughs of size, power, and price, the electronics market is flooded with computer gadgets of all types. Some may be really useful, but the tendency often is to make what is possible, instead of using the technology to support the customer. This technology-centered view is to some extent supported by a market where it is "cool" to have and use the latest of the latest.

These tendencies exist among products that fill traditional roles, too. Digital watches show the time, but also will offer an abundance of easy-to-implement functions, which may interest only a minority of users. Modern telephones come crammed with functions, and often become so complicated to use that most users only master the most basic functions of making and receiving calls. A more productive approach would be to focus on the users and the functionality that they need.

Fewer, generic functions that are easy to use are perhaps better on these devices than an abundance of specific functions hidden within complicated menu structures. My office telephone, for example, looks like and is a small computer. It has an LCD display and a full but primitive keyboard, and offers numerous functions. But 95 percent of our faculty and I never use it for anything other than the most basic functions. While many of the functions offered would be useful, they are hidden within a primitive user interface. It seems that very few are willing to study the manual, even if this could be more efficient in the long run.

Next to my telephone I have this wonderful PC, with its full-size keyboard and two excellent thirty-two-inch displays. That is, a new technology, the PC, comes in *addition* to phones, but as both technologies become commodities, integration may be required. Instead of putting a primitive PC in the telephone, put the telephone into the PC. Then we can use the large display on the PC to make functions visible, to select from the address book by a mouse click, to set up forward and reply functions, and so forth.

The modern smartphone is an implementation of these ideas. Using a touch display, a visual interface, and an Internet connection, these devices may have an abundance of functions, and still be rather user friendly. A disadvantage is the small display and, most often, the on-screen keyboard. Apple has been especially successful. Their user-oriented approach is at full advantage within these constraints.

On the Web, we have the benefit of being able to make functions and data visible, at least where the browser runs on a standard PC with a full display. With scripts,[5] small pieces of code that are embedded in the HTML pages, we can offer error checking and advanced help facilities on the client system. Without scripts, all communication has to go via the servers (the user provides input, the page is sent to the server, and a response page is then returned to the user).

We should expect to see an evolution toward more standardization, to a de facto "look and feel" of systems. The good systems will form "standards" that others will follow.[6] Users will become more knowledgeable and will master more complex interfaces, but they also will learn to require quality, rejecting the worst examples.

A disadvantage for user interface designers on the open Web is that users may come from many cultures, use different languages and terminology, and have different backgrounds, experience, and knowledge. In more closed cases, as within a company, the situation is simpler because more is known about the users, and variation in knowledge can be leveled with training. This is not possible in the open Web (we shall return to usability in Part 3).

10.4   Errors

Do you have a complete, updated backup of all documents and data? What are the risks to your privacy or company security if the laptop data falls into other people's hands?

A laptop can be carried everywhere, and it is quite convenient to be able to take along important documents and databases on a business trip. But a laptop can also be lost, destroyed, or stolen. Do you have a complete, updated backup of all documents and data? What are the risks to your privacy or company security if the laptop data falls into other people's hands? The same considerations apply to smartphones. With large memory capacity and a full operating system, these will soon be able to carry as much information as a PC.

In the long run we do not need criminals to help us to lose information. Even if modern technology is reliable, disks will crash some day, batteries will stop working, and processors and computer memory may become unreliable. Without good backup routines, data may be lost. Or you may find yourself in front of a large gathering with PowerPoint slides that will not come up on the big screen.

Errors in hardware, software, or in use are, alas, an inherent part of using technology.

Errors can occur in networks, in software, as well as in hardware. Errors performed by users can be reduced by good user interfaces, especially by "undo" commands that help us avoid the consequences of unwanted actions. But there are always possibilities for making creative errors.[7] In personal computer systems, the fear is of losing data; in other systems, the consequences may be even more serious. For example, the billion-dollar accident at Pennsylvania's Three Mile Island nuclear power plant in 1979 occurred when the operators were misled by a status light. Although they thought that the light indicated that an important valve was closed, the light indicated only that the "close button" had been pushed.[8] There are numerous other examples in which "human error" is really a fault of the user interface.

In 1996, the European Space Agency lost its $7 billion Adriane rocket forty seconds after takeoff due to a programming error. An automatic guidance system shut itself down after failing to store a 64-bit number into a 16-bit space. The error checking code that is often used to detect such errors and to perform a graceful recovery had been determined unnecessary in this case. There are numerous other examples of similar pro-

Automation
simplifies, but
makes systems
vulnerable. Often,
little can be done
when the automa-
tion breaks down.

gramming errors, many of which have led to huge monetary losses and some that have resulted in loss of life.

Automation is necessary in rockets, but automation is also used in many other cases to improve efficiency, that is, letting the system handle the process without, or with a minimum, of intervention from the user. The first cars had to be started through a process of pumping gas, opening switches, and turning a handle. Today, this is automatic. We turn the ignition key and an electric starter turns the engine. An automatic process has replaced a manual one, simplifying the everyday use of a car. The cost is that we become more dependent on the technology. Today, few car owners have the mechanical knowledge to perform anything but the simplest error checking when the car will not start.

Modern stores rely on point-of-sale (POS) terminals. The cashier's task is limited to scanning the tags. All other functions, such as finding the right price, adding, checking a credit card, performing the payment transaction, withdrawing items from inventory, and printing a sales slip are performed by the POS terminal. If the terminals do not work, the store must close because there is no way that these functions can be handled manually. Many cashiers would even have problems adding up the items as the ability to add numbers is not important in a computerized world.

Fifty years ago, office workers could light a candle during a power failure and continue working. Today, we might just as well go home in such a situation. In the store, the doors will not open without power. To some extent our reliance on technology may be considered dangerous. However, our willingness to allow technology to heavily influence our everyday lives and our organizations may demonstrate our trust that the systems will work correctly, at least most of the time. In life-critical situations redundant systems can reduce the probability of a hardware breakdown, perhaps using as many as three computers so that we will know which machine to ignore when the results differ.

Errors are a part of using technology, and will be reflected in lost time, service costs, and lost efficiency when we are not able to work as planned. In error situations, the capacity of modern technology is a two-edged sword. In Norway, centralized banking transaction systems offer an efficient infrastructure, but a large number of customers were affected for a whole week during the summer of 2001 when the system was down

Centralization of processing offers effective solutions, but may have dramatic consequences in error situations.

following human errors in the installation of new disk units.[9] In 1990, a programming error caused a major service outage on the AT&T telephone network in the United States, an outage that probably affected the most customers since the invention of the telephone. In 2003, a seven-hour blackout occurred across large parts of North America, affecting fifty-five million people. With heavy loads, the power system did not manage to adjust to demand, and many power plants and generating units closed down. Modern technology may make the systems efficient, but the consequences of serious errors are much greater than in the simpler, distributed systems that they replaced.[10]

Errors in Web systems are frequent. For example, few systems check that the back office systems are up and running before presenting the input forms to the user. We often find that only the input part is functional, allowing us to enter all data before we get an error message that tells us that our transaction cannot be stored due to an unavailable database. Most users would never have accepted a similar lack of service in the physical world or on the telephone, but we seem to blame ourselves when companies offer us error-prone Web systems.

10.5   Maintenance

Technology, both hardware and software, needs **maintenance** that may be expensive both in time lost and in direct costs.

While it is easy to focus on functions and be amazed by the specifications available in a new electronic device, technology comes at a price that is much higher than what we pay in the store. Maintenance of a simple home computer can be both expensive and time-consuming. Portable equipment needs recharging or new batteries. Displays, disks, mice, and keyboards do not last forever. Many users are astonished the day the disk drive makes funny noises, and crestfallen when they find that data is no longer accessible, although the question is just *when* this will happen, not *if*. However, modern hardware is very reliable, and basic operating systems work much better than before. Plug and play—the features that help new devices install themselves—are very useful. Thus, changing to a new device, something that could be a major undertaking some years ago, is much simpler today. For example, moving data from an old to new device is often quite simple.[11]

Software also needs to be maintained. Few PCs have everything working as it should. While the installment process of new products and versions has become simpler with modern operating systems, we often experience unwanted results. The new program may not work on our system, it may need a newer

Many technical problems arise from **incompatibility**, between different versions of a system or between systems.

version of the operating system, and if it works, we may find that other programs no longer start. The reason may be that the new program comes with common software components that other applications do not accept. As we use more devices— laptops, tablets, and smartphones —the challenges will increase. However, standards and better software can help.

While operating systems may present a version problem, data may pose a format problem. This is seldom a big issue when we go from one version to the next, as new programs usually have the ability to read and convert older formats. However, for most users, the data stored on eight-inch and five-inch diskettes are no longer accessible. Document formats only from a few years back may be impossible to import to the current version of the system. Just in the last twenty years, a myriad of storage devices have been used, VHS and Beta recorders, zip drives, jaz drives, diskette stations of various sizes, USB keys, CDs, DVDs, videodisks, and many different kinds of solid-state memory. The Beta format of videocassettes has been forgotten; the VHS tape standard (with different formats such as NTSC and PAL) have been replaced by DVDs, which may be replaced by high-definition DVDs (the Blu-ray), and so forth.

While I can go through the photographs taken by my great-grandfather a hundred years ago, probably no one will be able to see my videos or digital pictures in a hundred years, perhaps not even in ten, unless someone takes the time to convert them into the new media before the old disappears. A printout on a typical ink jet printer will be to no avail, as the ink will fade in only a few years' time.[12]

10.6   Scalability

Client-server systems allow us to compute fairly accurately the resources needed for a system to give adequate response times, by taking into account the number of users and the resources they will need from the server. This is very difficult on the Web, where there are an unlimited number of potential users. In peak situations, during ordinary office hours, or for example in the pre-Christmas period for an online store, we may experience service deterioration, when the numbers of requests are higher than servers and networks can handle.[13] Some systems manage this situation by limiting access, at least letting some users get their request through, like having a queue of customers outside the store, while other systems admit

New technology gives us more powerful servers and faster networks. This may give us **faster access**, if the additional resources are not consumed by new and resource-intensive functions.

everyone with the consequence of lowering throughput as most system resources are consumed in handling the queues. A sluggish Web system is often worse than no system, as so many Web processes demand good response times to function. This is the case for browsing, searching, or all processes that have to be performed in many steps, such as booking an airline ticket.

We may hope that new technology can keep abreast of the bandwidth needs. Fiber optic technology will offer increased bandwidth and faster routers (net switching devices), developments in software and hardware support scalability of sites, making it easier to adjust demand and resources.[14] Servers may be geographically distributed, allowing for the workload to be dispersed, and offering systems that are robust despite failure in parts of the network. Rush-hour traffic will come at different hours around the world and may differ from company to company. Some may even have a slack around Christmas time, and free server capacity may be sold or lent to others. Users may learn to do their heavier Web work outside rush hours, and will be able to do their transactions faster and more accurately as user interfaces get better and as they get more experience. (See Part 8 on cloud computing.)

Scalability, offering service to everyone independent of the number of users, is a problem on the Web where the whole world is full of potential users.

The danger is that content providers may offer data in new and more demanding formats, such as high-quality sound and video, thus offsetting any capacity improvements that can be made. At worst, we may end up with a situation similar to the one on many roads, where the demand-capacity equation is balanced by the time we are willing to spend waiting. However, with advances in hardware technology, we may keep abreast of such a situation.

10.7   Display quality

The promised **paperless society** is still far off, but displays are competing with paper in areas where the electronic medium offers other advantages.

The quality of displays is an important factor for the success of many Internet applications. A computer display has inferior contrast and resolution to that of paper. Even in favorable conditions and with a good display, one will find that it is more tiring to read from the screen than from paper. A newspaper lets us see two big pages at a time, and we can spread the pages of a report over a desk, enabling us to see many pages simultaneously. Paper is often lightweight compared to displays, and does not need batteries or a power connection, nor an expensive viewer.

LCD displays have offered us portable viewers, with fairly low weight and reasonable resolution. But we are still far from

Display quality is improving, but still cannot offer the contrast, light weight, and flexibility of paper.

making displays or viewers that can compete with paper in resolution, size, weight, or contrast. The "electronic paper" devices that are used for book reading may have paper-like letter quality, but do not resemble paper in any other way, as they need a display device. However, direct manipulation interfaces enable the user to flip to new pages with a slide movement, making electronic formats as easy to use as flipping through paper.

While we wait for the ideal viewer that manages to combine the advantages of both paper and electronic systems, the choice of medium will be based on cost-benefit functions. Today, documents are created on computers. The flexibility offered by word processing systems overcomes any disadvantage in display quality. The direct and mechanical key-to-paper connection of the typewriter has been replaced by a flexible digital system. The binary digits produced by the keystrokes, a code for each character, can be stored temporarily in computer memory, permanently on disks, and viewed on a screen where the opposite conversion, binary digits to graphical symbols, is performed. The flexibility of displays retains the flexibility of bits in the computer, allowing easy editing and WYSIWYG[15] updates on the screen. Modern word processing systems allow us to go beyond characters, creating multimedia documents that include hypertext links, graphics, images, video, and sound as part of a document.

The Internet makes **electronic distribution** of documents easy.

Until recently the end result from the word processor was often a printout of the document, necessary because dissemination was based on letters and fax. Today, many documents that we produce are not converted to paper form; instead, they are mailed as attachments to email messages or stored on the Web. In the end, they may be printed on paper before they are read. However, dynamic documents can exist in their full version only online. In the paper version, we find no hypertext links, no video, no sound.

Even for more traditional documents the electronic versions have advantages over their paper counterparts. Electronic documents can be edited, forwarded to others, stored on a disk, or subjected to automatic searching. In some cases, however, paper may be an advantage, such as when protecting copyright or a signature.

Computer programmers were always heavy paper users. We used to joke about the prophecies of the "paperless society" among the piles of program printouts in our offices. Even if the

If we can avoid the paper printout and read the document on the **screen**, we can utilize all the dynamic features, such as searching, hypertext, and animation.

final program had to be represented as bits, we used paper and pencil to sketch, to write code, and for proofreading, and we printed a new clean paper copy of the program after every change. Today, programming is performed directly on the computer. The program editors are better; displays are larger and have increased resolution. We also use tools, such as form layout programs and wizards that are only available online. The printouts no longer clutter a programmer's office.

Neither the author's. This book has been written and edited on the screen. Even the final proofreading, previously performed on paper, is now electronic. To get all the details, and in some way compensate for the reducing in display quality, I enlarge the text. A 200-percent enlargement gives a very different view: Suddenly many minor typographical errors are visible. The search function is also helpful when proofreading, and, of course, the ability to correct an error immediately. As display equipment improves, we will see a gradual reduction in the paper usage, first in applications that utilize the other advantages of online devices.

Function	Paper representation	Bit representation
Reading	High quality	Acceptable quality
Presentation	Book, binder, sheets	Computer display, projector
Continuous update	Not easy	Easy
Links	Manual	Automatic (hypertext)
Searching/retrieval	Manual, limited	Automatic, on all attributes
Storing	Manual	Automatic, unlimited storage
Copying	Semiautomatic	Automatic, inexpensive
Dissemination	Mail, bookstores	Over Internet or on digital media
Annotations	Pencil, limited	Typing, extensive
Multimedia	Not available	Yes
Simulations	Not available	Yes
Conversion	Not available	Yes
Equipment needed	None	Computer, display, power
Competence	Basic reading skills	In practice, only reading skills

Table 10.1 Advantages of paper versus bit representation.

Table 10.1 shows the advantages and disadvantages of paper and bit representation. Since the electronic medium has both pros and cons, we should expect that the effects are different for different types of documents. Today, programming and typing are performed on the computer. Manuals are often disseminated and presented in a bit-format as all the bit-advantages favor online manuals. Online we can exploit multimedia presentation forms, easy updates, searching, hypertext links, dynamic examples, and so on. For software manuals, the disadvantage of using a computer is converted to an advantage. The user is already on the computer when help is needed—no additional equipment is required. For other manuals, the unlimited storage capacity, the possibilities of simple updates, and excellent online search possibilities often make electronic dissemination the only choice.

10.8   Cost-benefit

Since technology comes at a cost, we need **clear advantages** before going for a technical solution. These advantages are often found within a critical mass of data, computation or frequency of use.

Technology comes at a price that includes the initial cost of buying the equipment and training as well as recurring costs for maintenance, upgrades, and error handling. These costs vary with the complexity and the robustness of the technology, but as all computer users have experienced, nothing ever works smoothly. To compensate for these costs we need a real advantage in using the technology. For computer systems, the efficiency of automation and the improvement in quality are the important advantages, which are clearly linked to the frequency of use. All of us experience a beginner's problems when using a program or navigating a Web site. For a one-time user, booking airline tickets online may be a tedious process, while a frequent user will give the right commands immediately, having stored all profile data in the system, keeping abreast with updates and changes, and so forth.

For most applications, we have a *critical mass* of usage before the cost-benefit equation balances. Most of us prefer a word processing system to pen and paper, a spreadsheet system to using a calculator (for complex calculations), and perhaps e-mail to letters. Within business environments, the data volumes are so huge that these critical masses can be obtained for most functions, and for some functions, there are really no alternatives since only a computer can handle the huge transaction loads.

It is a challenge to keep the cost side to a minimum.

For private use, the advantages of an application may not be as strong, and it can be a challenge to keep the cost side to a minimum. We need robust hardware that runs with a minimum of maintenance. We need operating systems that simplify installation of new software and that protect inexperienced users against making errors. We need systems that can reinstall themselves when errors occur. We need automatic backup systems so that we do not lose all documents, software, photos, and so on, the day when the disk drive will not work. Most important, infrequent users need intuitive user interfaces.

In many areas a new application may fulfill a need. Business rapidly embraced word processing systems, spreadsheets, copiers, mobile phones, and fax machines, even these advancements demanded new equipment and in some cases, also extensive training. However, in other cases the advantage of the new technology may not be so apparent.

Finding killer applications is not easy, but sometimes an application just emerges out of nothing. The SMS (Short Message Service), the ability to send short text messages between mobile phones, has become enormously popular and provides an important revenue base for mobile phone companies. This was a killer application that found itself, as nobody thought that customers would be willing to type these messages on numeric keypads.

SMS (Short Message Service) or text messages, was an application that found itself. It uses existing and simple technology, but still creates important revenue for many telecommunication firms.

To identify a killer application for the promised broadband services, we need to find something more sophisticated, probably something oriented toward multimedia. The telecom companies are trying to teach the customers to send picture messages as an enhancement of the simple text messages. With the resolution that is used today these pictures can be sent without broadband. The problem is that we now run into areas where few users have any expertise. How do we apply pictures in a useful way in everyday communication? To introduce the technology, we will have to teach users how they can apply the new media (companies have to create a *need*). This is time-consuming, expensive, and very risky. Further, the companies that create this new market have no guarantee that they are the ones that will reap the greatest benefits.

In some cases, the new technology offers functionality that customers have not yet experienced.

Since the first computers, the Colossus[16] and the Eniac,[17] enormous breakthroughs in technology have occurred, giving rise to computers that are extremely powerful, fast, reliable, and so small that they can be portable. Advances in network technology, routers, and optical fibers make it possible to connect these computers in global networks. Still, in the quest for *killer applications*, we have a tendency to look toward futuristic technology, such as high bandwidth wireless networks or even further into the future, quantum computers—significantly more powerful than what we have today.

Waiting for the **next generation** of technology to get a killer application seems to be a bad excuse: What we have today was yesterday's next generation.

However, the PC you can get from your local computer store for $500 is already significantly more powerful than the million-dollar computers from the 1950s. That is, the technology for the killer applications should already be here. However, when the applications meet the real world, technology is only a small part of the success equation.

Notes

1   KB, kilobyte, 1,000 bytes, where a byte is eight binary digits, sufficient to hold an ASCII character.

2   National Television System Committee (NTSC), a television standard first developed in the early 1950s, which is used in the United States, Canada, Japan, and in many South American countries.

3   Phase Alternation by Line (PAL), adopted in 1967 and used mainly in Europe.

4   COBOL, formerly the most common programming language, has been replaced by more modern, often object-oriented, languages.

5   Scripts are discussed in detail in Chapter 40.

6   Amazon (www.amazon.com) has, for example, excellent Web pages.

7   Using Microsoft Word, I inadvertently gave the "close" command instead of "print," and subsequently answered "no" to the "Do you want to save the changes you made to X" question (I did not want to save, I wanted to print), losing the last updates to my document.

8   President's Commission. 1979. Report of the President's Commission on the Accident at Three Mile Island. New York: Pergamon Press.

9   Since then, the system has been down several times, but at most for a day or two.

10 On the other hand, modern technology allows us to keep numerous copies of data at different locations, all updated to the last second. A disaster at one location may affect performance, but may not result in loss of data.

11 For example, many smartphones can transfer data from previous models, also for models made by other manufacturers.

12 Use of special photo paper will prolong the lifetime of printouts.

13 In this infancy of online shopping, an overloaded Web system may even be considered an advantage as it restricts the number of orders that can be received.

14 CNN clearly had a good plan for handling a crisis. On September 11, 2001, after the World Trade Center terrorist attack, the network managed to service all requests by removing all graphics from their sites, using all available servers to provide simple text-based news.

15 What You See Is What You Get (WYSIWYG).

16 A machine made by the Government Code and Cipher School, Bletchley Park, Bletchley, England during World War II, perhaps the world's first computer.

17 Developed by University of Pennsylvania, Philadelphia, under a secret project for the U.S. Army's Ballistics Research, often recognized as the world's first computer.

11 Case Studies: Technical Constraints

This chapter examines a set of applications that are affected by technical constraints—electronic newspapers, e-books, and scientific journals, as well as the distribution of software, music, and video. All of these applications seem well suited for the Web, as they are both formalized and symbolic, but as we shall see, various constraints may delay the introduction of some of these applications.

11.1 Electronic newspapers

If the purpose of a newspaper is to provide the reader with the latest **news;** the Web offers the ideal distribution media.

General information can be sold in the form of newspapers, journals, books, pay-per-view TV, encyclopedias, and more. With the advent of the Web, another channel for sale of information has been opened. The advantages of this new channel for providing general information are:

- 24/7/365 service
- Continuous updates
- Customized information—the customer can choose what he or she wants to see
- Fast and inexpensive dissemination
- Multimedia formats, text, pictures, audio, animation, and video
- Background information from archives
- Unlimited storage

Today's electronic newspapers try to exploit all of these technological advantages. They use all the multimedia capabilities, offer hypertext links between related articles, and offer search tools for retrieval. They give continuous coverage of news events, with many "editions" a day and use video cameras and weather stations to give an update on local conditions. The interactive capabilities are exploited in full, accepting input from readers in the forms of reviews, scorings, comments, and online discussion groups.

However, despite utilization of the technology, creating a revenue base for electronic newspapers is difficult. Many online newspapers depend on a paper-based version from which to get news and articles. If the latter gets into financial

Once the online newspaper is as easy to **read** as the paper version, the latter will disappear.

trouble, it is difficult to maintain a quality Web version on its own.

Some of the traditional newspapers have been able to keep readers even with online competition. That is, some readers are willing to pay for higher quality. One reason may be that the online papers, even if free, are not viewed as real newspapers. Perhaps the new medium has created a new market in between TV and the traditional newspapers. The online newspaper's advantage over broadcast TV is that readers can select what they want to see, and their advantage over traditional newspapers is more updated information. Their disadvantage is that they require more input from the users than the other media. When accessing an online paper from a PC, the hands are on keyboard and mouse. With TV, we only have to choose the channel, and with traditional newspapers "administrative" overhead is restricted to scanning and turning pages. The traditional newspaper can be read everywhere; it does not require an expensive and heavy viewer, batteries, or a power outlet.

How important is the online advantage of offering **updated** information at any time?

The disadvantage of not being updated to the last minute is to a large extent solved by the paper-based newspaper's "symbiosis" with TV. With TV, we do not require newspapers to bring us the latest update. Instead, newspapers can provide in-depth and more developed information. The traditional newspaper may not offer the possibility of online chat channels, but it is a cost effective way of getting information. So, instead of a takeover, in many countries, electronic newspapers exist alongside paper versions. In others, such as in the United States, online sources have put many traditional newspapers out of business.

The electronic versions are mostly offered as an add-on source, perhaps to generate interest for the paper version or to try to get revenue through advertisements. The electronic version also has the advantage of generating data on which articles the readers actually access, by counting "clicks," by surveying search terms and, of course, by studying readers' response in the form of reviews or email. Newspapers that have only an online version, struggle to survive regardless of whether they use subscriptions or advertisements as a basis for their revenue.

However, the balance between electronic and paper versions may change. Radically new display techniques, combined with high bandwidth connections and wireless technology, may alter this balance of pros and cons. If a newspaper can be automatically downloaded over high bandwidth Internet connec-

The newspaper as we know it will still **prevail**, even if it becomes online. That is, online technology will be a part of the evolution that started with Gutenberg's printing press.

tions to one or more cordless viewers with large displays and readability similar to print, all papers will become "online." Most of the functionality of the paper version will be retained, and the electronic advantages will come as a bonus.

With this technology, paper-based and electronic newspapers will merge. For the traditional newspapers, the change will just be another technology breakthrough, following offset printing, electronic communication of text and photos, word processing, and editing systems. Clearly, the shift will have a large impact on the printing and distributing processes, but the effect on journalists and editors may be less.

However, an online paper has a somewhat different style from the traditional "deadline-based" papers. Not only will online media be able to run the same story from different viewpoints during the day, with continuous updates, but they also can give the reader the option of getting in-depth information, provided by links to background data, historical information, or to other articles. But again, care must be taken to provide these services in a way that does not require a higher activation level from the user than she is willing to accept. The role of the newspaper is to provide a general overview in the form of well-prepared articles that require limited energy or activation from the user. In special cases, we may be willing to spend more time in retrieving information, but that may exceed the role of newspapers.

Therefore, technology breakthroughs may not be a threat to traditional newspapers, but only to their printers and distributors. However, literary skills may change in an online society, where information is more likely to be presented as headlines, pictures, and videos. We may find fewer and fewer *readers*, people who are willing to spend time and energy on long articles. Online media may increase the trend that we already see in some on-paper versions, toward giving information in ways that require less effort on the part of the "reader." (I return to newspapers as an example in Chapter 44 and in Part 9).

11.2   Electronic publishing—eBooks

The help system that comes with software products today is always online. Here one can exploit context-dependent help, offering the user information relevant to the problem at hand. A search system is invaluable in finding information in these formalized settings, and hypertext is used to link related articles. The most advanced systems offer automatic demos, anima-

Today, reading from a **display**, is a disadvantage, and therefore, electronic versions must offer clear advantages in other areas.

tions, and dynamic examples. The help system can be updated with every new version of the software, or offered in an always up-to-date version on the Web. Since we are already online when using the software, the disadvantages of an online system are removed. The online help system is now easier to access than any paper counterpart.

This online functionality also will be important for many other forms of manuals, especially when the manuals are so large that they are difficult to access in printed form. So, the online version may be preferred even if one needs a viewer, a PC, or a customized device to access the manual.

For other types of publications, the dynamic advantages may not be so clear. For example, a novel is read from start to end and the degree of formalization is low. The reader does not usually jump back and forth in the text. We do not really need a dynamic link from page 215 to page 18 to find out if James was the cook or the butler. If such a link were needed, it would be simpler for the author to add the job title when he reintroduced James on page 215. That is, the author's responsibility is to organize the text so that it can be read sequentially. Similarly, updates and electronic searches are not usually needed in a novel.

Some of the online **advantages** are directly connected to the formalization level of the publication, the more formalized the greater the advantage of indexing, search, and hypertext systems.

The advantage for a novel in e-book form may be the low cost of disseminating and the large electronic storage capacity. But this must be balanced against the disadvantage of having to use a special viewer, a laptop, or a mobile phone to read the book. Take the viewer out in the sun and the text disappears; it is not recommended to take it to the beach and it is a catastrophe if it is lost. The advantage with the paper version of a book is that it comes with its own high-quality, low-priced "viewer" that can be adjusted to the type of book: paperback, art book, or an atlas.

Modern viewers, especially those that are based on electronic paper[1] are changing this situation. With reasonable reading quality and a battery life of weeks, many see the advantages of an electronic device, especially for disseminating and storing. Some of the money saved for paper, printing, and freight are returned to readers as discounts.

With the high costs of storing paper books, only the most popular books may find a place in the bookstores and in publishing houses' storage rooms. In electronic format, books need not go "out-of-print," and with the low storage costs, it may be profitable to keep all books that have a minimum of interest in the system. In the long run, with heavy competition from e-books, fewer bookstores may survive, and a higher market share for e-books may force all books toward electronic versions.

Textbooks and scientific journals fall between manuals and novels. Today, most of these are still disseminated on paper. However, better viewers may change the situation, enabling the very last update of journal papers and textbooks to be downloaded to the viewer via the Internet, complete with footnotes and references in hypertext format. The author can include further readings, and search tools can be used to find what we are looking for. There will be no need to keep errata, as errors can be corrected at once, and new updated editions can be created as needed.

Formalization	Examples
Organization	Parts, chapters, headers, exercises
References	Author, title, publisher, URL
Terminology	Formalization, symbol
Equipment	Computers, displays, printers
IT applications	Web, e-mail, Word processing
Directions	B2C, B2B, P2P
Concepts	e-music, e-book
Standards	ASCII, HTML, XML

Table 11.1 Formalized terms in this book.

Table 11.1 shows a list of some of the formal terms discussed in this book, terms that can be used for organizing and searching an electronic version. In a more traditional textbook, we would find more of these formal terms and definitions, which could support an electronic version to a greater degree. If we go all the way to handbooks, we are close to the manuals described above, and at this stage the advantages of having an electronic version become very apparent.

Disseminating books in electronic form also opens the way for new business models. Instead of buying expensive textbooks from publishers, states that need textbooks for their schools can organize textbook development themselves, such as using the "competition model" often found in other creative activities like architecture and art. The winners can then be paid to develop their textbook concept in full, and the books can be

An **e-textbook** opens the way for new business models.

The **e-textbook** of the future will be so dynamic that the distinction between a book and a piece of software will disappear.

put on the Web available for all students for free. While this model also could be used with paper-based books, the simplicity and savings of disseminating via the Web will be a powerful incitement.

With an "evolving" book metaphor, the writer may incorporate comments and make modifications suggested by readers or reviewers. Thus, if you download the book tomorrow, you may get a different version than you would get today. This will change our concept of editions and make referencing somewhat more difficult (the part referenced may no longer exist), but may give us better books.

The next generation of textbooks can be *dynamic* far beyond hypertext. A book on physics can include virtual experiments in which students perform simulations within the textbook, such as driving cars around narrow curves, letting objects slide down ramps, or swing on strings. In college mathematics, the textbook will have an interface to mathematical program packages that can simplify, execute, or visualize formulas. Teaching material, such as slides, comments, and references given by the lecturer, can be connected to "hooks" provided in the book. Similarly, students can add their own comments and examples. In this way, a dynamic book may be customized to the particular educational institution, lecturer, and student.

Most of the technology for these things is available today, and it will just be a matter of time before the standards and the equipment needed are more readily available. Then, the question will not be if we *want* to read a textbook on the screen or on paper, but we will *have* to use the online version in order to take full advantage of the dynamics. As we have seen earlier, writing has already moved online, and it is just a matter of time before reading will follow, at least for some type of books.

Transferring scientific journals, textbooks, and other documents from paper to electronic media will have a great impact on publishers, bookstores, and libraries. The tasks of printing, handling, storing, and transporting the physical copy will disappear. As with software, the cost of making an additional copy will be close to zero. Thus pricing schemes of dynamic books will most probably follow those of software—individuals or an educational institution will pay a license for the right to download books. In all respects, it may be better to view a dynamic book as a piece of software. As with software, the cost of creating an application will be high. In addition to the more traditional services, such as editorial tasks, graphical design, and marketing, dynamic books will need expertise in creating animations, video, and sound clips. Thus, it will be a major effort to produce and maintain a dynamic book. However, as with software, the high cost of development can be spread over a large number of users.

Document type	Easy update	Hypertext	Search tools	Dynamics
Manuals	High	Very high	Very high	High
Textbooks	Medium	High	Medium	Low-High
Other books	Low	Low	Low	Low
Scientific journals	High	High	High	Medium
Other journals	Low	Low	Low	Low
Newspapers	Medium	Medium	Medium	Low

Table 11.2 Advantages of electronic representation, degree of importance.

Until the day that we can make viewers as large, flexible, and with as good a quality as paper, we will need additional arguments to find the electronic document representation most useful. Table 11.2 shows how important the added online functionality will be for different types of documents. For example, the online functionality of easy updating, hypertext and extensive search tools will be more important for a textbook than for a novel. So, while we find the electronic form convenient for manuals, even with the limited quality displays we have today, an electronic version may be useful for textbooks in the near future, but we may find it advantageous to read a novel in paper form for many years to come. For all document types, the possibility of accessing the document electronically will be important.

11.3   Video on demand

Today, we can buy or rent movies in DVD representation. The large rental market, also pay-TV, shows that the customer accepts a pay-per-view model, and that the lack of a symbolic value of ownership will not be a barrier for online video. However, we do not always have the infrastructure in place for downloading and playing high-quality videos interactively as such a service demands high bandwidth networks from the source to the consumer.[2] Currently, the only viable solution (if we want quality video and a high level of functionality), is to

Video on demand is a formalized and symbolic service. It is here already for some users, but needs new technological breakthroughs either in compressing or in network technology to be available to all in full quality.

lay optical fiber or cable into each home, clearly a very expensive enterprise. Thus, while it is easy to say that video on demand may be an important Web application, with very much of the same advantages as downloading music, it will take time to get the infrastructure in place or to develop new technology that bypasses the need for high capacity networks.

With such technology in place, we may get a larger "underground" market for movies than we have for music. The industry will try to protect copyright by putting movies on formats with built-in encryption (that is, they will try to bind the business models of today with the technology of tomorrow). The problem is, of course, that there are numerous intelligent and often well-educated hackers who will see view breaking these formats as a challenge. The best model for countering such a situation will be to offer inexpensive subscription models. (These matters are discussed in more detail in Chapter 14.)

11.4   What can we learn?

When discussing new technology, it is easy to focus on the possibilities, trusting the scientists and engineers to filter out the weaknesses and limitations. But history tells us that enormous breakthroughs may be achieved in some areas, while the development may be very slow in others. Also, prophecies often are too optimistic in the short-term view, and yet perhaps too pessimistic in the long-term.

The future lies in the **boundary** between possibilities and constraints.

Although the constraints of formalism are fundamental, technological constraints can be removed by long-term scientific and engineering efforts. Sometimes development may take a great leap forward, surprising everyone. The development of VLSI techniques and the microcomputer suddenly offered much smaller and much cheaper equipment, removing many of the barriers that limited computer usage. HTTP and HTML offered a similar leap forward, enabling us to use the emerging Internet for many new services. Less spectacular, but as important, are the surprisingly high bandwidths available today on the ordinary twisted pair telephone line. The boxes installed on either end of the existing cable enables us to use the infrastructure for telephone, built over many years, for totally new applications. Perhaps the next surprise will be a print-quality display, or an everlasting battery.

Notes

1 Amazon has had success with its Kindle, an e-book reader based on electronic ink, which has reasonable reading quality and can be used for weeks without recharging. Books are downloaded over a Wi-Fi phone connection.

2 The more patient Web users download movies as a background task over today's "broadband" connections, but this operation may take many hours, even days to complete. These movies, often pirated copies, are usually viewed on a PC.

12   The Devil Is in the Details

We often look at ideas and overall concepts, but ignore the details. This natural and top-down approach is often the only way to master the complexity of large systems. However, the details may be important. A fancy new mobile phone that drops conversations because of a bad antenna is perhaps not what users want. That is, for a product or a policy to succeed it must master all details.

In this chapter, the Telecommunication Act is used as an example. The idea for the law was good—split up monopolies, let new companies enter by guaranteeing access to the existing technical infrastructure, and get competition, better services, new services, and lower prices.[1]

12.1   Deregulation

The idea behind the **Telecommunication Act** was to open the market for competition.

The Telecommunication Act of 1996 opened competition in the local exchange telecommunication market in the United States. This act was followed by detailed orders that forced the incumbents to open both their physical and logical infrastructure for the competition, so that these could access existing copper wire, exchanges, databases, and software systems. However, telecommunication is a very complex business, and this unbundling is not easy to accomplish.

Since the 1970s, deregulation efforts have occurred in many sectors of the US economy as well as in many other countries. Government organizations that were established during the "New Deal" period to safeguard public interests have been weakened to let the marketplace work more freely. Interestingly enough, both liberals and conservatives have supported these efforts. The agenda of the liberals has been to reduce corporate interest over the regulatory agencies, while the conservative's agenda has been to get the "government off the backs of industry." The basic idea has been to increase competition, to get better service, and to lower prices.

Airlines, trucking, railways, intercity busing, and telecommunication have been some of the targets for deregulation. To a large extent, these activities have led to increased competition and lower prices. Airlines are a primary example. In many areas the new bargain airlines, such as AirTran in the United States and RyanAir in Europe, are determining the way the air travel business is conducted. They are forcing incumbent airlines to lower prices, but also to change the level of service. While air travel was previously viewed as a luxury product, characterized by excellent service, food and drinks "on the house," and hotel accommodation if one failed to reach a connection, the air travel business is now down to basics—transportation only.

In the telecommunication sector, an abundance of new firms have emerged since 1996, both to provide new services such as data networks and wireless, but also to compete with established wire line telephone services. While deregulation opened the telecommunication sector for competition in these areas, many of the novel services were made possible by the advent of new technologies: wireless services, broadband on a twisted pair cable, optical fiber, digital switchboards, the Internet and the Web standards. In many cases, the new entrants were the first to apply these technologies.

While deregulation can offer many success stories, some of the disadvantages of giving free market control over important infrastructure are apparent. Britain is now, after a set of serious accidents, considering more governmental control over their railways, and in both the United States and in Europe there have been severe blackouts because of an inadequate power system. Long-term investments and preemptive maintenance, it seems, are not the primary focus for private enterprises that have stockholders with a short-term view of their capital investments.

12.2   Deregulation in the telecommunication sector

Billing and Operations and Support Systems (OSS) is a problem area.

The Telecommunication Act of 1996 opened up competition for local voice and data services. The incumbents, the Regional Bell Operating Companies, were forced to lease infrastructure to the new entrants, called Competitive Local Exchange Carriers (CLEC). Many CLECs managed to get their business and their networks up and running in a remarkably short time. However, as Martin F. McDermott states in his book *CLEC*,[2] problems occurred primarily in other areas, one of which was billing and Operations and Support Systems (OSS).

"An incumbent Local Exchange Carrier (LEC) shall provide nondiscriminatory access...on an unbundled basis to any requesting telecommunication carrier for the provisioning of a telecommunications service..."

"...Operations Support Systems functions consist of pre-ordering, ordering, provisioning, maintenance and repair, and billing functions supported by an incumbent LEC's databases and information."

"An incumbent LEC must provide electronic access... Providing access to OSS functions...is a critical requirement ..."

Table 12.1 FCC Orders.

The Telecommunication Act opened access to both networks and software systems.

The Federal Communications Commission (FCC) recognized the fact that access to the physical infrastructure was not enough to attain real competition. In their first order,[3] an interpretation of the Telecommunication Act, they determined that the OSS systems and the data within the incumbent's networks constituted a "network element." Thus, the CLECs were to be granted access to these parts as well. The idea was to let CLECs have the possibility of operating "at parity" with the incumbent Local Exchange Carriers. As seen from the FCC orders in Table 12.1, the CLECs also were granted electronic access to these systems.

Thus, by 1996, both a political ruling and orders that laid a foundation for competition in local exchange telecommunication were in place, giving a go-ahead signal for many new companies. In 2000, there were more than 700 newcomers. Some of these were sales companies only (they owned no infrastructure), using the existing infrastructure to sell telecommunication services offering different market plans and often lower prices. Others used new types of equipment and technologies, for example, to provide both data and phone services on the standard local loop, that is, DSLs (Digital Subscriber Line).

Many of the new telecommunication companies failed.

Even if many of these companies were established in the euphoric "dot-com" years, we would expect them to have reasonable market and business plans in place. Yet, more than 90 percent of these companies failed. Thus, the US Congress did not get the highly competitive market it wanted, and huge amounts of money were spent on this, often futile, race. While investments in new companies and new technologies are always a risky business, the huge losses in telecommunications have reduced the amount of venture capital available today and has made investors very reluctant to enter into new projects in the telecommunications sector.

12.3   What went wrong?

Telecommunication is an extremely complex business.

We shall try to present one critically important part of the answer to what went wrong, based on the experience of running a competitive local exchange carrier.[4] Although the FCC orders were reasonable enough, the implementation of these orders were not simple and straightforward. Telecommunication is an extremely complex business, based on a technology that was invented 150 years ago. Much of the infrastructure has been laid down over a very long period of time at a very large expense. The telecommunications industry has been in the process of converting from an analog-based technology to a digital-based technology, and where we found exchanges (Central Offices) full of electrical switches and relays, we now find computers and complex software.

Telecommunication also is research driven. Equipment that was in the research laboratory just a few years ago is now used by large parts of the population. New developments within wireless systems, satellite communication, and electronic devices are offering great challenges for the future. In addition, there are reasons to believe that it may be more difficult to get adequate revenue out of basic communication services alone. For example, today lucrative voice-oriented telecommunication (the traditional telephone service) is under threat from new entrants that utilize the customer's broadband service to use Voice over Internet Protocols (VoIP), Skype[5] being a good example.

Telecommunication is inherently different from other sectors that have been deregulated.

In comparison to other areas that have been deregulated, telecommunications is inherently different. For example, in the airline industry, customers accept that a bargain airline offers only a limited set of destinations and may use secondary airports in many big cities. For travel patterns, customers may have to use an incumbent airline, or accept the fact that they may need to buy tickets from more than one (bargain) company. Missed connections are at the customer's own risk, as all interconnection problems have to be handled by the customer. Most of these airlines allow the customer to perform bookings themselves on the Internet. There are no standards for these business-to-consumer systems, and the customer has to learn to use each different interface. However, with a large degree of formalization, the few data items that are needed to book a

On the telephone network, customers expect to be able to pick up any phone, at any time, and call anybody, within the country or internationally, independent of which phone company they or the recipient uses.

flight have similar "look and feel" interfaces, and this has not posed a major problem for customers.

On the telephone network, however, customers expect to be able to pick up any phone, at any time, and call anybody, within the country or internationally, independent of which phone company they or the recipient uses. That is, the interconnection problems are a matter for the telecom companies. The network routers of the incumbent telephone companies most often handle any technical issues of this connection, leaving the newcomers to handle, at least, the billing.

However, billing is only a part of the functionality that the software systems must provide. CLECs must have functionality in place for provisioning new customers (often customers that earlier were connected to an incumbent company), or for deprovisioning, when they lose a customer to a competitor. While airline customers must do this "provisioning" on their own, using Web systems for establishing and maintaining a customer profile, the company must do the job for telephone services—at least today. As we shall see, provisioning of phone and data services are not simple matters in the first place and are made even more complex by the lack of strict standards.

While deregulation has opened up competition there are other regulations that are in place and that must be followed. For example, all companies must provide 911 services. This includes the ability to tell the emergency facility where the caller is located. Other services, such as "caller ID" also involve the ability to access and update national databases—an easy task if all the standards are in place, but these services require detailed adjustment to many different formats and processes.

12.4   Back office systems

To perform all these services a newcomer needs reliable back office systems. In principle, these can be developed in-house, or be leased or bought from vendors. In practice, only the latter two alternatives are feasible if a new company wants to be up and running in a short period of time. But the software available today is not very flexible or reliable. The systems are difficult to implement, lack documentation, and do not confirm fully to standards. Competent personnel who understand these systems are in short supply. The issues are further complicated by the fact that the incumbent-run systems do not follow a common set of standards. Thus, a CLEC ends up with an overwhelming number of small and large problems that are difficult and time consuming to solve.

While the "natural monopoly" of telecommunication—the idea that there are advantages to having only one company—has been challenged,[6] the business complexity of having many companies "sharing" parts of a common infrastructure has perhaps not been fully understood. New entrants into the market see the potential for using new technologies to take customers from the incumbents and make money. The number of CLECs that have failed indicates that most of those who are involved with these new companies do not understand the details of the business and consistently underestimate the cost, time, skill, and knowledge that it takes to offer and maintain a wide array of telecommunication services with an adequate quality of service and bound to service level agreements. The complexity of making and completing a phone call, based on current technologies, is astounding, but the activities required to acquire a customer, provision the service, manage the technology that delivers the service, acquire data for billing and legal purposes, and monitor the service and its underlying technology for problems is actually much more complex and changes almost daily.

When a CLEC acquires a customer from an incumbent, a series of formal communications (usually electronic) must take place between the CLEC and the former provider. Since most new entrants utilize some of the network elements of the incumbent to provide their services (for example, a local loop), the new entrant must order these using the systems provided by the incumbent. This requires an interconnection between the incumbent's computer systems and the competitor's. The ordering process requires knowledge of how the telephone business operates, the business rules used by the incumbent, and the special language used.

The ordering of these installations by the incumbent, the installation of equipment at the customer's premises, disconnecting the current incumbent's service, and the activation of the competitor's service must be scheduled and monitored carefully to avoid interruption of service. But that is only part of the story. For example, a telephone service in the United States must provide 911 (emergency) capabilities. This requires that the telephone company maintain a database of addresses where telephone lines are terminated along with the telephone number associated with each line. Since telephone numbers can be "ported" (that is you can take your telephone number with you when you move within a region), there is a national database that must be updated with this porting information. If a caller wants an 800 number, this also requires interactions with other vendors and updating a national database. Likewise, if caller ID is desired, another national database must be updated as well!

In order for a new entrant to connect to the public telephone network, it must establish an interconnection agreement with the incumbent telephone company to connect to their tandem switch, which is connected to the public network. If a calling card service is to be offered to customers, then an agreement with the Centralized Message Distribution Service must be established and call detail records or billing records must be exchanged on a timely basis. Since most customers want a long distance service, interconnection arrangements must be made with the long-distance carriers, and if convergent billing is offered, the ability to acquire and exchange data with the interexchange carriers is a must. Likewise, the equal access regulation requires the exchange of customer information.

A new entrant must establish an interconnection agreement with the incumbent telephone company.

When a customer disconnects, many of the actions that were done to connect a customer must be undone. In addition to these relationships, a central office switch must have a dial plan so that calls get switched or routed correctly. Dial plans are extremely complex data structures that must satisfy a number of rules about the all networks, so that calls get routed correctly.

There is also the electronic exchange of billing data from the incumbent for the components that have been leased. This data must be reconciled with the company's internal inventory of network components and the CLEC's accounts payable system. Although there are data exchange standards for the format of these records, every vendor has its own interpretation or use of various fields within the record which causes back office systems to have many translation software systems for transforming call detail and billing records into a format that their own systems can process.

12.5   Billing

The most complex aspect of all is billing because of several factors. One is that rating calls (determining the class of call and associated billing rate accurately) can be a logical nightmare because a caller can theoretically call from anywhere in the world to anywhere else in the world at anytime, using resources from any company. A call may come from a ship at sea, an airplane, a hotel, a prison, a pay phone, or an educational institution, all of which are rated differently. To add even more complexity to the billing issue, competition has forced many companies to offer special plans, special rates, and special rate conditions. The billing system must not only determine what type of call that was made but also what plan a customer has and how the charge must be computed, for example, was the call on a weekday or weekend, after 9:00 p.m., over a thousand minutes of usage, and so on?

Billing is the most complex part. Calls must be rated, taxes computed, and plans for each customer must be considered.

In addition to the difficulties in rating calls and computing the charge, there are other charges that must be computed as well. Sales and usage taxes as well as special telecommunication taxes must be computed. Then there are the data management issues arising from the large volume of call detail records that are generated for every call which is originated or terminated at a switch. This volume quickly reaches millions of records per month even for a small carrier. These records must not only be processed for billing but also archived for law enforcement agencies. A carrier must have fraud detection software that looks for patterns of abuse. The billing data must be interfaced with the journaling and other accounts receivable functions of the company.

This summary of the business issues only touches the surface of the details associated with the business of telecommunications. The bottom line is that the fractionation of the telecommunication business by lawmakers, regulators, and the incumbents have made it overly complex to the point that making a software system that can function in an integrated, cost-effective, accurate, and stable manner is nearly impossible.

12.6   Costs

How much does all this cost? A lot! But, companies that fail to invest in the resources to guarantee scalability and reliability will suffer greatly when the capacity to handle the next million call detail records is exceeded or the system is not available for sales, provisioning, installation, customers, and management personnel due to a system failure. The loss of revenue because of such failures is serious, but the loss of confidence in the IT department is a severe blow. It can be hard to convince management of a new company about the need for excess capacity and redundancy at startup; however, the cost of upgrading and the potential for downtime at a critical stage in the growth of a company can be a disaster.

One way to mitigate the high initial cost of a more or less centralized system with the required capacity and redundancy is to design a distributed system that can be upgraded in more manageable cost increments. Many of the available software packages on the market do not scale and are not reliable, which in turn, can cause a new company to fail.

12.7   Discussion

The Telecommunication's Act of 1996 and its subsequent amendments created visions of competition, more services, better services, and lower costs. While the need for access, also electronic, to the incumbents data systems were foreseen, the practical difficulties of administering a wide range of services over a complex infrastructure with many competitive companies may have been underestimated. A reliable software system is a necessity for a CLEC, but these systems do not fulfill expectations, the major reason for the failure of new entrants to the telecommunication business.

CLECs fail for a number of reasons, but the complicated issues discussed here all contribute. The fact that a telecommunication company has a software system that is operating does not mean that it is successful. Most systems are incomplete, not integrated, do not match the company's business, do not scale, and are unreliable. In addition, they tend to be inflexible and suffer performance problems almost daily.

The complexity of the telecommunication's environment in the United States contributes to the likelihood of the software systems failing to perform all the necessary functions in an effective, efficient manner at a reasonable cost. Very few individuals or groups of individuals understand the complexity adequately, which leads to incorrect requirements and specifications upon which the systems have been and continue to be built. Likewise, many of professional service personnel lack an understanding of the telecommunication business and, in many cases, do not even understand their own products.

To make competition from new entrants practical and possible, strict and well-documented standards are needed. This will determine the foundation for developing reliable software systems, but will require a major effort in updating both the physical and logical network infrastructure so that each part conforms to the standard.

12.8   Conclusion

We have used the telecommunication business as a case in order to show how the number of details may result in systems that are very complex; maybe even so complex that huge efforts will be required to develop and maintain them.

Terry Winograd presented a theoretical case in 1979.[7] His example was a university president who wanted a scheduling system to assign courses to lecture rooms. This was to be done in a convenient manner, avoiding clashes (a student or lecturer getting two classes at the same time), offering a reasonable amount of time to get from one class to the next, finding practical schedules (for example, with time for lunch), smart utilization of rooms (for example, not putting a small class in a large room), and so forth. Winograd explained that while each part is feasible to implement by itself, building the complete system would be an impossible task. In other words, in practice we have to accept non-optimal solutions. Just as in chess, the number of the possible combinations will be too great for them all to be checked. This was the case in 1979 and remains true today as shown by our example from the telecommunication business. Beware of the details!

Notes

1   This chapter is based on Williams, J. G and Olsen, K. A. (2008). Developing Telecommunication Operation Support Systems (OSS): The Impact of a Change in Network Technology, in Gutierrez, Selected Readings on Telecommunications, Information Science Reference.

2   McDermott, Martin F. (2002). CLEC: An Insiders Look at the Rise and Fall of Competition in the Local Exchange Competition, Penobscot Press.

3   Docket 96–98.

4   My coauthor on this part, Jim Williams, worked as a Central Information Officer (CIO) in a CLEC for several years.

5   A Voice-over-Internet Protocol application, with additional services such as videoconferencing and file transfer. Calls to other Skype users are free, but calls also may be made to phones in the traditional phone networks, both mobile and landline.

6   Perez, F. (1994). The case for a deregulated free market telecommunications industry, IEEE Communications Magazine, December.

7   Winograd, Terry (1979). Beyond Programming languages, Communication of the ACM, no. 7, vol. 22.

13 Cultural Constraints

Even if an application is within the constraints mentioned earlier, which range from formalism to technical considerations, there may be reasons why the application is not accepted in the marketplace. These may be based on issues such as:

- *Legal issues.* The intellectual property rights (IPR) may belong to companies that use existing technologies.

- The problem of *critical mass*, the difficulty of moving everyone to a new technology. Some services require that all—or close to all—have access to the technology.

- *Social issues.* The new technology may be effective within some areas, but may have negative side effects, for example, that they reduce social interaction.

- New technology may force a change to existing *power structures.*

- *Knowledge and experience.* New technology may require new skills.

- *Conservatism.* Users may be happy with the situation as it is and are often not willing to invest time and money in unknown technologies.

- *Threat to privacy*, the risk of losing data, or that unauthorized persons can access personal data.

Each of these constraints is discussed in detail below. Some of these constraints are closely connected to the technological issues discussed in Chapter 11. For example, the skill requirement will very much depend on the user interface, but it is still valuable to look at these areas from a cultural and social point of view.

13.1 Copyright

Is it possible to maintain **copyright** in a digital world, where everybody has access to the dissemination technologies?

We have had recording devices for many years, tape machines, cassette recorders, and VCRs, but the lack of access to source material has limited copying. The possibilities were either to copy from a broadcast signal, radio or TV, or to borrow the source from a friend. The analog medium also had the disadvantage that quality deteriorated for each new copy. This situation has changed in two respects. The Web now acts as a source for all types of material, an abundance of music files, books, and entire movies. Second, what we get from the Web is in digitized formats, which can be copied without quality reduction. We do not even have to store a copy, as items can be streamed from the Web, and the sound quality can be as good as on the CD that we bought in the store for $15.

Many copyright owners see copying from the Web as an infringement on their rights and are fighting numerous court battles. To date they have won several, but they may be losing the war. This is like a Norwegian *Troll*: Cut off its head and three more grow out. Today, the big battle is about music; tomorrow it may be about movies or textbooks. Already, the battle is moving to these areas. For example, some mathematicians have challenged publishing companies for restricting access to scientific papers through very high subscription fees.[1]

The record industry, the publishers, and movie distributors have built their business models and attained market shares based on their ownership of the technology. When the technology becomes available to all, retaining central control is difficult. Of course, record companies and publishing houses offer more than just the printing press. They also select products to publish, give advice, perform marketing, pay contributors, and so on. However, to perform these tasks, they need revenue from the products that is significantly higher than the price of making and distributing a new copy, thus offering the incentive for pirated copies. Case studies related to these issues are presented in Chapter 14.

> Copyright owners are often afraid of Web solutions, as it will be more difficult to protect owner's rights.

13.2   Patents

Patents protect intellectual property. The idea is that a company or a private person who has used time and resources to develop a new product needs protection. The patent offers exclusive rights for a number of years, or more correctly, the right to exclude others from making, selling, or using the idea or product. Property owners need time to profit from their invention, to generate the income that will pay for their expenses and the risks they undertook. If not, nobody would use large resources to design new industrial products, improve designs, or develop new medical drugs or new algorithms.

While this seems reasonable enough, the patent idea is getting out of hand. Today, one can patent very simple ideas, even what we can call natural solutions to a problem. This can be a shopping cart symbol for an online store or a slide button to open or start a touch device. In the 1970s, in a project develop-

> Patents protect intellectual property.

> Can patents be a hindrance to innovation?

ing IT systems for health care, we were among the first, perhaps the very first, to use an OK-button on a screen. Should we have patented this idea?

So although the rationale behind patents is to support research, they may hinder new ideas. Software companies have to use a large part of their income to fight battles in court. Google's purchase of Motorola may have been driven by the desire to get their hands on Motorola's patents rather than their technology. These patents will help Google protecting their Android operating system and other software products.

To invite innovation, regulations are needed to restrict both what kind of ideas can be patented and how long a patent can be enforced. For example, the very first idea of a patent, 2,500 years ago,[2] offered exclusive rights for one year. Today twenty years is often the limit, which seems excessive in a dynamic society.

13.3   Critical mass problem

Many applications do not become efficient before they have reached a **critical mass**, while others demand that nearly all have installed the technology.

The owner of the very first telephone had no one to call. The telephone, like e-mail and many other communication technologies, needs a critical mass of users before becoming efficient.[3] E-mail has a history of more than forty years, and has become the main communication channel for many groups; phone and letters are of secondary value. Although social networks have taken over leisure communication, e-mail will continue to be an important communication channel in the workplace.

Today we expect to be able to contact airlines, travel agencies, and newspapers using e-mail, but we cannot be sure that the plumber, electrician, and local garage will have an e-mail account and read their mail regularly. Many firms still use telephone and fax, although digital services would be far more efficient. But each of these organizations faces the same problem. E-mail becomes efficient when all or at least a large part of suppliers and customers use this medium. Until then, many seem to view e-mail communication as an add-on, and do not establish good routines for handling this form of communication. The same is true for private communication. Should we call, send a letter, write an e-mail or connect through Facebook? A letter can reach everybody, but an e-mail will reach only those who have an e-mail account and who check the account regularly. However, many of us are on Facebook, since our friends are there.

An electronic bank may solve the problem of critical mass by offering service only to customers who have an e-mail account and are willing to communicate electronically. This requirement is more difficult for public organizations that serve the entire population. E-mail can be offered as an alternative input/output channel, but a public organization cannot require, at least today, that everybody use electronic media. For this reason, we may never see Web-based elections for state officials. Even if alternatives were provided for those without an Internet connection, it could be seen as undemocratic that parts of the population had easier access to the voting system than others. In addition, there is the problem of maintaining security, avoiding hackers, and denial-of-access (see Chapter 15).

In his 1999 book, *Business @ the Speed of Thought*,[4] Bill Gates tells us how we can succeed in the digital economy. Yes, he talks about new and interesting applications, but also point out that we should try to utilize e-mail, this more than forty-year-old application. Bill Gates is correct; e-mail is an important tool for many businesses as an inter-business tool, but also has interesting applications in contact with ordinary customers, as it is already replacing other media such as telephone, fax, and paper-based mail.

The applications of the future are here now!

13.4   Social factors

Media may also be characterized by an open-closed taxonomy.

Humans are social animals. We work and live in close contact with others. Virtual contacts can replace some parts of face-to-face meeting, but they clearly cannot replace all.

If we sort different communication methods along a continuum from closed to open, we will find forms (for example, on the Web) at one end and personal contact at the other, with Facebook, e-mail, telephone, and videoconferencing in between. E-mail is an efficient medium, but it is not as "social" as a telephone. That is, if we rely only on e-mail for contact with customers, we may lose the personal connections that may be important in many contexts. In some situations, less personal connection may be an advantage, such as when efficiency is primarily important. At other times, close relations with customers may be needed to convey trust and to handle exceptions and complicated situations. Some see social networks as an alternative, but these may be too private for business. We may be willing to discuss our skiing holiday with a supplier, but may be unwilling to invite him as a friend on Facebook. We acknowledge the merit of different media when we use a Web form to order a movie ticket, use e-mail to send a complaint to a company, send a birthday card through the post office, use the telephone to discuss which restaurant to go to, and meet personally for a job interview.

Even a videoconference, in which sound, images, and documents can be conveyed over a network, is far from a face-to-face meeting, to some extent because of limitations in the technology. In most videoconferences, we can see and hear the person talking, but we do not see what effect the words have on all participants. Are they shaking their heads, nodding, or are they bored or enthusiastic? This problem will change with more bandwidth, more cameras, and larger displays. Still, a video-conference may not provide the options to talk off the record and socialize that physical meetings provide.

Can a **videocon-ference** replace physical meetings?

The limitation of virtual media, compared to face-to-face meetings, may not always be a constraint. In some situations, we can utilize these constraints for our own purposes. For example, in the virtual world users can choose their own person-alities and acquire skills that would have been impossible to get in the physical world. In the virtual world, we can start again, without all our handicaps. We can be stronger, smarter, prettier, younger, and swifter in the virtual world. These possibilities are exploited by providers of sex chat lines, as well as by developers of Internet games.

13.5   Power structures

The incumbent record industry was not the pioneer in using the Web for distributing music; neither were the existing book-stores, banks, or travel agencies. They were happy with the situation as it was, and like many of us, were not very willing to adopt technologies that would turn their world upside down. But there are always techno-pioneers who invent and utilize new technology, and sometimes we are forced to accept change.

The turbulence in the computer industry, with newcomers driving away strong incumbents, demonstrates the difficulty in controlling these new technologies. IBM, which once was the major player in both computer hardware and software, has been forced to relinquish the leader's jersey to others. In opposition to many industries that rely on land, natural resources, or large plants, a symbolic industry, such as the computer software in-dustry or even parts of the hardware industry, can start in a ga-

New technology offers an **opportunity** for start-ups.

rage. On the other hand, retention of power within these industries is more difficult than in many others.

The music industry may try to resist customers' using the Web as a source of material, but this is a technology change that they do not control. Moving from CDs to the Web is not comparable to moving from LPs to CDs. CDs (or DVDs) represent a technological change that is clearly within the business and market models of the record industry. The Web, however, is what is called a *disruptive* technology[5] for the music industry, a technology change that cannot easily be absorbed within the existing structure of a business. Business may resist such changes, but in the end, often will be forced to accept the new technology.

An example is found in some cities at the start of the twentieth century when trucks began to compete with old, horse-drawn wagons. To protect the incumbents, some cities passed laws that limited the speed of the trucks to that of horses. Of course, this did not work, and trucks replaced wagons.

The global economy is an accelerator for technological changes. If unions are reluctant to accept new technology and the layoffs that may result, companies may argue that the competitors will adopt the technology, perhaps in another country. The shop owner that earlier enjoyed a monopoly in his home-town, now faces competition from Internet stores. The European Union has simplified customs between member countries. Together with the euro, the common European currency, this increases competition over national boundaries. However, customers are still not happy with the limitations in Internet shopping. If I, as a Norwegian, want to order something on the Internet from another country, I may have to pay VAT, and perhaps tariffs, in addition to a fee to the postal company for computing these extras. Consequently, the EU is working on schemes to simplify Internet shopping across borders, for example, by introducing systems that will handle taxes automatically.

13.6   Conservatism

Acquiring and using new gadgets is a way of expressing that we are "in" and trendy, and there will always be a group who gets the latest designer smartphone, Internet TV, or other new device. However, at the other end are those more conservative users who are satisfied with things as they are. They are not willing to use time and money to get something new, even

There are **eager beavers** who will try any new gadgets, as well as those **technically adverse** who will never move to a new technology.

when the new technology proves itself superior to the old. For service providers, this makes it difficult to phase out older technology and ways of doing business based on this technology. The analog telephone will be here for many years to come, as will CDs. Years will go by before the last check is written, and even then, many people will never bank online. So while new technology and new services are introduced at a record-breaking pace, the older technology will take much longer to disappear. Some services and devices will not go before their users go. In the computer industry, magnetic tape was supposed to meet its demise twenty years ago, but it is still a prime backup and data transmission media.

Conservatism in technology may be based on sound principles. "If it ain't broke, don't fix it" tells us that the value of something that works reliably is very high. The new technology may be better, but has not proven itself over years of usage. There may be unknown problems that occur when we try to implement the new systems, connect them to other systems, or when some users complain that they don't get the functionality that they were used to. I return to some of these problems in later chapters.

13.7   Conclusion

Cultural constraints can slow down the advance of new technological applications. Introduction of new technology into the real world is more than just a question of technical possibilities and functionality. However, cultural constraints may slow down the dissemination of new technology, but cannot not stop the adoption. For example, if there are legal barriers, there will always be "pirates" that circumvent these. We shall present a case in the following chapter.

Notes

1   A boycott of the Amsterdam-based publishing giant Elsevier was initiated by Timothy Gowers, a mathematician at the University of Cambridge, UK, a winner of the prestigious Fields Medal. In a blog post on January 21, 2012, he criticized Elsevier's high prices and its support of the Research Works Act (RWA), legislation that would hinder access to scientific material.

2   According to Wikipedia, 2,500 years ago, the Greek city of Sybaris offered patents for a space of one year.

3   The usefulness of a communication device is often calculated as the square of the number of users in the network.

4   Bill Gates with Colin Hemingway. (1999). Business @ the Speed of Thought, Succeeding in the Digital Economy, Warner Books.

5   See Christensen, C. M. (1997). The Innovator's Dilemma, Harvard Business School Press.

14 Case Studies: Cultural Constraints

Chapter 13 presented a set of cultural issues that could limit the acceptance of new technology or new services in the marketplace. Here, we examine a set of case studies. These cases seem promising based on our knowledge of the technology, and they also are well within technical constraints. However, cultural and social issues may influence the success of these applications.

14.1 E-music

Downloading **digital music** is an ideal Web application: It is formalized, symbolic, and the technical infrastructure is in place.

Software and music are in many ways ideal for Web distribution. These all-symbolic, digital products can easily be transmitted via the Internet using current compression techniques and connections. Downloading or streaming music files via the Internet has flourished as more consumers have the possibility of retrieving and playing these files. With CDs, music is already represented as bits, and modern PCs have both the ability to play this music, for example, through a hi-fi system, or to store files in compressed form. Or, with good bandwidth, storing files is unnecessary; they can be streamed directly from the Internet to loudspeakers. Several Internet sites exploit this symbolic nature of music, to allow customers to exchange music files, often music that has been captured from CDs and other sources.

Understandably, the record industry has looked upon file-sharing service such as Napster and its followers as a threat to their business. Other, less centralized ventures than Napster are more difficult to fight legally, and if this is not enough—a service may be set up in a country with weak copyright laws. Without a central site, the record industry goes after the users instead, suing students, parents, and grandmothers. To some extent they have succeeded, putting a scare into many.

The web is clearly a **disruptive** technology for the entertainment industry. In the long run, it will be difficult to maintain existing business models when users can get music or movies from the Internet.

The Internet is the natural dissemination vehicle for this type of data. With digitalization the music has been separated from its representation. The industry may wrap the CD in nice packaging and also include a booklet; however, in the long run, the physical formats will disappear as online formats have more to offer. While the music itself is formalized on a low level (as technical binary codes), it is clearly indexed with the names of songs, albums, and artists. Therefore, it is easy to find a piece of

The Internet is **ideal for distributing music**: The data is all symbolic, has limited size, and can be streamed to a variety of different players.

music on the Web or in a customized database integrated into the hi-fi system. Online, one can also take advantage of the possibility of fast dissemination of new songs, and of additional multimedia information, such as music videos, along with the audio. In an all-symbolic form, a new copy costs practically nothing to make, and it can be compacted to a size that makes it practical to stream to the users. The bits are sent more or less directly to the booster, so that only a small cache is needed locally for storing (to adjust for small discrepancies in bandwidth).

The pirates have forced the industry to offer Internet-based services.

Pirates have forced record companies to meet this threat. Several pay-per-song or subscription sites are now available, as the industry has realized that the Web needs different forms of packaging and distribution than traditional channels. Many of these services offer a free service, perhaps with commercials, and a more flexible premium version without advertisements. As prices fall, more and more users go for the premium versions. In many ways, pirates have done their job: They have forced record companies into providing a good service at a reasonable cost to compete with free products. Even if these sites offer a very large choice of tracks and unlimited streaming, total revenues may be as high as those under the CD model. That is, new technologies often require new business models.

14.2   Electronic scientific journals

Scientific papers should be a prime candidate for electronic publishing, with the advantages of a speedy publishing process, hypertext links to references, inclusion of background material, electronic searching, and inexpensive dissemination worldwide. Perhaps most important is the open access to electronically published scientific papers.

Today, a large part of university budgets is used to pay for journal subscriptions, and increasing expenses make it difficult to maintain a wide coverage. Access to information is severely restricted as less affluent universities, especially in underdeveloped countries, cannot afford the $10,000 to $20,000 subscription fees that some of the most well-known journals demand. Paradoxically, the very same universities that provide the subscription fees pay the basic costs of preparing these papers. Most scientific papers are written, reviewed, and edited by university employees.

Historically, scientific papers were offered very cheaply or for free through the research community, first by personal

E-journals, or online journals, are an interesting Web application. All arguments, on a practical, economical, or professional level, favor the electronic version.

communication and then through membership in professional associations. The professional publishing houses entered the process later, to handle administration, publishing, and dissemination. Today, the Internet may return us to the former "ideal" situation.

With new technology, the author can create the paper in a publishable format. The review process can be handled on the Web using software that aids the editor in finding available reviewers, notifies them, and collects evaluations. Reviewers can add detailed comments directly in the manuscript. All correspondence between editors, reviewers, and authors can go through e-mail or the Web. The final, accepted version can be posted on the Web site for the "journal," and the system can send an automatic e-mail notification to all subscribers who have indicated interest in this type of paper. The site may also offer readers the possibility of adding comment or reviews, to vote on interesting papers, or to create a chat group for a paper. That is, through new technology, we may reinstate the personal correspondence and in-person discussion groups from the early days when the number of researchers was low. This system will be inexpensive and offers the opportunity of free access to scientific information. The advantages of electronic formats for these types of publications are paramount, not unexpectedly, considering that Berners-Lee created the Web based on the need for such an application.

From the discussion above, one would think that the advantages of an electronic version would surpass any difficulty in read from the screen. If not, these limited-size papers can easily be printed. Universities may be conservative, but one would expect that the need for cutting expenses should demand a more rational solution; therefore, we should expect that the combination of functional and economic arguments would be a driving force for electronic publication. Why, then, are many journals still offered in paper form (albeit with a parallel online version), and why do so many journals have high subscription fees?

The publishing houses will, of course fight a transition to a new medium. With paper journals, publishing houses are needed to handle printing, distribution, and subscription. With an electronic medium, these parts can be automated, and the publishing houses are no longer a necessary part of the value chain. Electronic journals make it difficult to retain high subscription rates, and "illegal" copying is more difficult to con-

The traditional **publishing houses** are no longer needed to create and distribute a journal, but they own the most valuable asset: the journal brand name.

The Web has removed the constraint on the **size of a volume**—for scientific journals this can be a disadvantage!

trol. As in the recording industry, publishers are trying to bind the new technology to existing business models.

While the publishing houses own the copyrights for previous publications and for journal names, their most important staff works for universities. Therefore, it should not be impossible for the research community to establish new, electronic journals. But perhaps the scientific community is also skeptical; perhaps there are arguments beyond the rational.

While a paper journal is a means of disseminating scientific articles, it is also a symbol. A paper in the right journal can be an important step toward tenure, funding, or a better faculty position. Only the best articles are published because a paper journal has to limit the number of pages per issue for practical reasons. Over the years, a number of high-ranking journals have emerged in every field. These journals are well known in the entire scientific community, and a new electronic journal may take years to establish a similar reputation. Also, the quality of electronic journals may suffer if there is no practical limit to the number of papers that can be accepted. Consequently, readers and the paying institutions may recognize the advantages of an electronic medium, but authors and publishing houses may want to retain the paper versions, even if they often are forced to publish online as well.

This persistence of the hard-copy scientific journal demonstrates the difficulty in gaining acceptance for new media when cultural change is involved. Institutions and people who master the playing field will be reluctant to abandon their positions, and accept a new area where the rules of the game are different.

Most recognized journals still require expensive subscriptions, but alternatives have been established. Most interesting are archives of electronic papers, where everyone can "publish." These sites are especially important for third-world countries that cannot afford the subscription fees of the paper journals and that may also be hampered by inadequate postal systems. These sites offer a possibility of publishing as well as gaining insight into the research results of others. Access to these sites, including publishing, is free. Here we have the interesting situation that third-world countries are forced to use a service that in many ways works better than that found in more developed countries.

Some online sites charge a fee for publishing, but the papers are accessible at no cost, which is a better model than the traditional. However, the problem will be to build the reputation of these sites, especially since there is an economic incitement to accept papers.[1]

Unlike the music industry, academic publishing lacks pirates to force the industry to move to online models with acceptable prices. However, some well-known academics have begun to boycott publishing houses, which may signal the beginning of an open source movement, or perhaps may force the publishing houses to reconsider their subscription fees.

Nevertheless, in the long run, the practical advantages of online media in this area are so great that the subscription versions will disappear eventually. An important weapon for the e-journals will be their availability. Therefore, papers in e-journals may be read and referenced more often than papers published in traditional journals, and references are as important for an academic as the name of the journal. Today, sites such as Google Scholar index a large part of what is published. For many papers, the full-text version is also available for free. All of this can be seen as a transition from expensive journals on paper to more open online journals.

The brand names will still be important, but perhaps the leading universities can establish their own, or force the publishers to accept more reasonable subscription prices?

14.3   Distance education

Distance education offers flexibility both in place and time. It has been an option to students who were willing to study on their own, at home or at work, following their own schedule. These distance education programs have worked with traditional textbooks and other forms of text-based support material and have often followed a plan with a sequence of "letters," in which each letter described a problem to be solved. Answers to these exercises have been returned to teachers using ordinary mail.

Every new technological breakthrough—tape recorders, video players, computers, and CDs—has been predicted to boost distance education, but these hopes have been unfulfilled. Until recently, distance education has been a niche market. Today, the hopes for distance education are based on the Internet and the Web. Both universities and private companies are investing huge amounts in what they believe will become an important market.

To understand the possible impact of the Internet and the Web for distance education, we need to understand the proc-

The Web can handle many of the **closed aspects** of education, such as presenting lectures and material. But what about the open, more social parts?

esses and functions involved in teaching. A traditional college course, for example, will have three major stakeholders: students, professors, and their assistants (often graduate students). The course will be based on a predetermined curriculum, syllabus, and schedule, but the professor is usually given great freedom in the course structure and the material to present. Course topics are covered by textbooks and other written material, such as scientific papers and descriptions of projects and exercises. Lectures are given in classrooms or auditoriums that may seat from a few to several hundred students. Most professors will present lectures using a presentation board or will use a computer and a video projector along with slide presentation software, such as PowerPoint.

Class-based teaching opens a dialogue between teachers and students, in which students can ask or answer questions, give comments, and participate in the lecture or class discussions. The degree of interaction depends on the class size and the culture. Not all students dare to talk in public, and in some cultures, the authority of the teacher may hinder a good dialogue. In addition to participating in classes, students are expected to study on their own, read background material, and do exercises and projects. In many courses, the "learning-by-doing" paradigm is seen as important, and students will be expected to write and present papers, to solve problems, to develop systems, or to do practical laboratory work, depending on the type of course. This independent work may be supported, supervised, and graded by the professor and his or her assistants.

At face value, the Internet and the Web may support all of these activities. The Web can support any type of written material, with the additional advantage of integrating text, animations, sound, and video. With reasonable bandwidth, students can follow the slide presentation on the Web, including the teacher's narrative, and a broadband connection makes a video presentation possible as well.

For many courses, the Web can be used to create a virtual laboratory, for example, with the software development tools that are needed for courses in computing science. We can expect many of the experiments in physics, chemistry, and electrical engineering to be performed in a virtual setting rather than physical laboratories of today. In other areas, such as social science and economics, computer simulation may become an attractive tool. Professor-student and student-student com-

In analyzing the effects of a new technology, try to see what it offers compared to **existing technologies**. This gives us some real data in making a prognosis.

munication can occur through e-mail, chat rooms, newsgroups, or bulletin boards. Simple tests can be performed directly on the Web, even examinations if student identity can be guaranteed.

Thus, we should expect an exploding market for online education. But, before we invest our money and our time, let us play the devil's advocate. We will notice that many of the advantages offered by the Web were also available in pre-Web times. For example, in the mid-1980s and later, with the advent of the CD, it was possible to offer courses that used text, video presentations, and virtual laboratories on a computer. The Web has offered a simpler way of updating and distributing this material, nothing more. This simplicity may be important for some types of courses such as courses offered to very large groups at such a low price that the cost of distribution has an impact. However, if the student base is large enough, satellite TV broadcasts are an alternative (in which the full broadband capabilities of TV can be utilized). While such a system simplifies distribution and the equipment needed on the receiving end, it has the disadvantage of having student input go over a different channel, such as a telephone line. Here the Internet offers the advantage of two-way communication. For the higher-priced courses, the distribution advantage of the Web should have a more moderate impact. Offline media, such as video cassettes, CDs, and DVDs, will be advantageous when technical constraints, such as low bandwidth connection and slow response times from Web servers, limit the functionality of a Web application.

When the computers handle the formalized functions, **humans** must take care of the more open tasks. This "work sharing" must also be reflected in education when it is more important to give students an understanding and an overview of a field than to concentrate on the lower-level details.

One may argue that the Web offers unlimited access to information. While this is true, students at the lower levels do not often go outside the required and suggested readings to get information. For most, the textbook and other required material will be more than enough. Another pro-Web argument is that it allows for online tests, with the possibility of saving test results directly on the server. This takes us back to the early efforts to develop an "electronic teacher" that could give students immediate feedback and grade tests automatically. Such a system will work where the formalization level is high, but not when questions are more open.[2] Paradoxically in education, the computer works best for testing types of knowledge that are no longer needed precisely because of the computer. While a student needs a good understanding of language, spelling can be checked by the computer. Students need to have an understanding of the basic principles of mathematics, but computers can perform detailed calculations. However, higher-level concepts and basic principles cannot easily be checked by formalized tests.

Exceptions may be found in more training-oriented courses, where the idea is to teach students to react correctly to different situations. Here, simulations and scenario-oriented systems may be used to check that the student has the correct response in the right situation, for example, when handling complicated machinery. Not unexpectedly, the more formalized tests will work best for these formalized applications.

Combining Web and e-mail, we get two-way communication that can support the open parts. The question is whether the student can manage without the social learning environment of a physical school, or whether this environment can be offered in other ways.

All in all, the Web alone may not be enough to boost distance education. But the Web, combined with e-mail or a social network, offers a simple system for two-way communication. Now teachers and students have technologies that may replace some of the interaction that they have in class and through personal advice. A teacher can reach all students with one e-mail message or with a comment on a social site, and students can return questions and answers to exercises in the same way. In principle, this is just a replacement of the old fax or letter channel, but is far more efficient. Further, students can reach each other and participate in discussion groups. Thus, chat, e-mail and social networks can replace informal and formal group work at a school or university to some extent. Perhaps the most important feature of online technology in this setting is its asynchronous nature, allowing both students and teachers to retain the time-based flexibility of distance learning.

Will these new methods replace traditional teaching? The answer is "no." Being a student, staying motivated, and organizing work is difficult in the best of circumstances. In the physical world, one can hope to get inspiration and support from professors and fellow students in a good learning environment. Motivation is much more difficult with distance education, where all or a large part of the work has to be done in isolation. The motivation or influence that a professor can give to a student will be much stronger in a physical environment than over virtual channels. E-mail, chat and social network groups may give some support, but dropping out of these is easier than in a physical environment where someone may come and look for you if you do not turn up.

Motivation is a problem with distance education, where all or a large part of the work has to be done in isolation.

For this reason alone, it is unrealistic to expect that online or distance education will replace a physical presence of both professors and students at a school or university. Schooling also has important social functions in addition to formal teaching. In a good educational environment, students learn to organize their work and to interact with their peers. Such an environment offers the possibility for students to build networks, to university professors and to fellow students. This is a major reason to attend a recognized university. If it is difficult to be admitted, one will work together with other students that also have excellent qualifications.

An understanding of the technological possibilities and constraints can help us find the best applications for **e-learning** systems.

Good applications for online education may be found in areas where the motivation may be strong enough to overcome the lack of a physical educational environment, and where the drawbacks of not having such an environment can be minimized.

Such areas may lie within adult education, especially where the intent is to give additional or upgraded information. Here students will have the experience and background needed to get a personal feeling of the topic and to participate in discussions. In addition, many are in work situations and may be unable to follow scheduled classes, which maximizes the advantages of distance learning. Ideally, such courses should be taken at work, where it is easier to establish a good educational environment, for example, by establishing groups of employees who follow the online course. These groups can then provide the necessary social support.

Adult education and training are especially suited for **e-learning**.

Another application may be for schools that want to offer a large range of courses for their students, such as offering basic courses the traditional way and more specialized courses online, hoping that the students selecting a specialized course will have the background and motivation to work online.

Distance education, in spite of all the technology, is often an expensive product. Traditional education, especially at lower levels, can be offered in huge classrooms with streamlined setups. Students who are physically present can use each other as information sources and will often have a similar background. Being together in the same environment also forms students into groups so that, to some extent, they can be advised and treated as a group rather than as individuals. In contrast, distance education students remain more isolated; they may have very varied backgrounds and will need more personal advice, which limits the number of students each professor can advise. In addition, the cost of preparing online courses may be high. Some companies spend large amounts to prepare courses. Clearly, distance education is not a means to make teaching more efficient or to reduce the cost of education. Rather, it is a way of accommodating students who cannot be physically present in a classroom at a given time. This was the case before the Web and seems to be the case also with the Web.

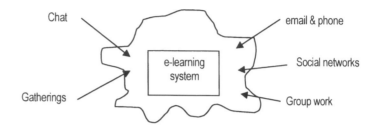

Figure 14.1 Distance education over the Web, supporting open tasks.

A figure used previously can be applied to this more specific setting (Figure 14.1). The rectangle represents all that a distance learning system may provide in services, and the more diffuse boundary represents traditional education. While the electronic system can offer a large set of services, there are parts—such as social environment and physical presence—that are left out. We can expand the electronic service to include some of these areas. For example, if we offer good e-mail contact to teachers who can give personal advice or use social networks, we have a door toward more open services within the electronic system. Or, we may let distance students meet physically at certain times during the term to provide motivation and a sense of community. However, efficiency will be highest when we are able to perform all services within the system, for example, presenting material, performing quizzes and exams, and so on. This will be simplest to achieve in the more formalized training applications, in which the discrepancy between the rectangle and the irregular figure is at a minimum.

14.4   Marketing on the Web

On the Web, many sites try to survive using the TV model, offering free programs and generating income from commercials. Until now, the idea has been to get as many "clicks" as possible, using these data as the Web equivalent of numbers of viewers, listeners, or readers. But, the Web is a very different medium from TV, and experience with ads on TV may not be directly transferred to this new medium. Therefore, I will start this chapter by comparing these different marketing channels.

The user initiates a Web session at a time she chooses herself. Traditionally, from a "cold start" point, she has to turn on the PC, wait for the operating system to load, open the browser, and wait until the connection to the ISP provider has been established. On Local Area Networks (LANs) with direct Internet access, the connection will be set up immediately, but may take a minute or two using a dial-up connection. Here tablets and modern PCs with fast memory have an advantage, as the start up may be nearly instantaneous. And where one is continuously online, as is the case for many smartphone users, no start up is required to get on the Web.

The Web has the advantage that the user has the possibility of selecting what she wants to see. The disadvantage is that it requires a higher **activation level**.

When the home page is displayed, the user needs to be actively involved, both cognitively and physically. The user will be sitting in front of the device through the whole session, hands on the keyboard or ready to touch the display, and eyes on the screen. Each screen involves choices of where to go next, what to read, and what to type. A new screen may be obtained by a simple click on a link, or by entering URLs or search terms from the keyboard. The user will use brain, eyes, and motor operators (hands), and also possibly ears and voice. She needs training and experience to master the medium to satisfy her needs. Even then, the sequence of pages downloaded may include repeats and many pages with little or no value for the user. In addition, there is some overhead involved in this sequence of keystrokes, mouse movements, or screen touches. For low bandwidth connections, response times may be substantial. Thus, through parts of the session, the user may be waiting for a page to appear, a passive phase in an otherwise active session.

In contrast, a medium such as TV may be activated with a single button click. Professional content creators have created or selected the stream of sound and video that is received. Today, a viewer has no way of influencing this data stream, but has the option of selecting a different channel. To watch a particular program, the viewer will have to synchronize her schedule with that of the broadcast, or program a recorder to capture the program at the right time. (For some channels, programs can be streamed from the Internet.) TV viewing, after channel selection has been performed, does not require any active participation from the viewer. She can choose the degree of involvement, follow a program with all senses open or let the TV

With the higher activation level, care must be taken that the **ads** do not come between the user and her goal.

simply be a background activity. She can watch TV sitting down on the couch or walking around. Hands are free, allowing her to do other things while watching.

Superficially, one would expect that ads would have a greater effect on the higher activation Web than the lower activation TV where users are more passive. However, with the higher activation level and the user's clearer focus, ads may come between the user and her goal, risking the user's negative feelings toward the advertisers. Pop-up ads may be especially annoying for the user who is on the Web to satisfy an information need or to perform a service, less annoying for the user who is only "surfing." Many users install programs that remove pop-ups,[3] proving that these are considered annoying and also demonstrating the possibilities available in digital media—removing ads from a TV is not so easy.

Because of the TV viewer's passive participation, advertisers are allowed to capture the whole channel for an extensive duration. This option allows for a stronger marketing influence, but has the drawback that viewers may not choose to spend three hours watching a two-hour movie or to get an abbreviated version. They may switch to other channels during commercial breaks, fast-forward through ads on a recorded program, or select pay-per-view or subscription channels.[4]

Since the activation level of the Web is higher than for TV, users will generally not accept using the full channel for advertisements. Less intrusive than pop-ups are banner ads, which can be compared to highway billboards. Billboards are put up on sites with heavy traffic, hoping to grasp our attention using images, colors, and animation without interfering with our driving. Billboards access "spare capacity," since driving, especially in simple conditions, does not need all our attention. On the Web, we may have some spare capacity when waiting for a download, otherwise all our capacity is used to scan and read pages and to decide where to go next. Advertisers do everything possible to attract attention toward their banners, but users have a tendency to focus on the task—finding a link, entering data in a field, using the browser commands—and ignore the banners.

Perhaps banners and pop-up windows should appear only in a "while you wait" context, popping up in the seconds after we have clicked on a link and until the page is displayed. Even then, they may be too intrusive for an active user. Another alternative is to integrate the marketing in the material that is re-

On the Web, the most effective **marketing** may be the ads that help the user to accomplish her goal.

While newspapers try to make a clear distinction between editorial material and advertisements, not all Web sites and search engines have followed the same **ethics**.

E-mail marketing is so inexpensive that even a marginal response rate can make it cost effective.

turned to the user. Banners try to do this by adjusting to the context. To some extent, this was possible with the billboards (marketing hotels and casinos on the road to Las Vegas), but banners may be set up for the needs of a single user. The question is then, how does one know what the user needs?

This question is quite simple to answer in query situations. When we search for a hotel, the banners or sponsored links display hotel advertisements. For example, when a user gives keywords such as *London*, *hotel*, and *discount*, a smart ad may direct him to a London hotel site, showing bargain hotels only. That is, both the banner and the site that the banner points to can be customized according to user needs.

The ads will have an even more direct impact if they appear in the results from a search engine, especially if they can aid the user in satisfying her information need. While traditional media companies try to separate ads from the journalistic contents, this separation is not so clear on the Web where search engines and portals can give their sponsors a favorable presentation in the result set. From a marketing point of view, this is, of course, an ideal solution. Some search returns result in two different data sets, first a set of paid entries (advertisements), then the results from the open Web, a more ethical alternative.

Ads in newspapers and journals have some of the same advantages as TV. The activation needed from the user (to pick up the periodical) is very limited. Paper ads have a further advantage over TV in that they have a low intrusion factor ("I am here, read me if you want"). Catalogs and (junk) mail advertisements offer some of the same advantages, but do not piggyback on other incentives for reading as in a newspaper. There is, therefore, the high risk that the user will disregard the ads, not even opening the catalog. However, this risk may be even greater on the Web, where the user has to go through several steps in order to access a site. Interestingly, even dot-com companies send out paper catalogs, clearly showing the need to attract non-Web users, or to get the attention of passive Web users. For marketers, the Web has a clear disadvantage because users first have to access a site, while TV, radio, and to some extent newspapers and junk mail put activation in the hands of marketers. Therefore, some sort of initiation—a banner ad on another site or an ad in other media—is necessary.

E-mail offers another channel for direct mail, but with the same risk of a physical direct mail letter, being discarded unopened. Junk e-mail and spam have become a huge problem, especially for users with e-mail addresses that are presented in public where they can be retrieved automatically by spiders. As we have seen, the cost of marketing through e-mail is marginal. In the same way as pop-up windows, these ad messages often come between the user and her goal. While they may be removed easily, junk e-mail messages have the disadvantage that they clutter up e-mail systems and also impose the danger that we delete an important message by mistake.

But there are also advantages to e-mail for marketing—less intrusive than a telephone call and cheaper to send than surface mail. Computer-generated e-mail also offers a high degree of customization. The most effective e-mail offers will be based on a previous customer history, and will give the user an offer that is relevant. If the e-mail comes from a source with whom the recipient has a relationship, it may survive immediate deletion. While too many messages may be annoying, most users will allow a "conversational exchange" of messages. For example, when we have initiated a contact by subscribing to the local paper, we may accept getting an e-mail offer of a Sunday paper extension. Or, if we have bought a book written in Spanish from Amazon, we may find a note about a new Spanish collection interesting. That is, for every message we send, we may accept a relevant message in return.

Push sites do not require activation on the user's part, but can **overload** the user with information if not used carefully.

Many sites allow us to subscribe to news, for example, about new books by specified authors, bargain flights, or technical issues. Subscriptions offer the advantage of moving the activation part from the user to the information-provider (from a pull to a push system); the disadvantage is that we may get overloaded with information. Good systems include an unsubscribe reference in each e-mail (one that works), making it easy to delete or alter the subscription.[5] That is, these systems acknowledge the problem of information overload, and see that there is little point in pushing information on an unwilling user. They may also get more subscribers, when the information to unsubscribe is so readily available.

General Web marketing has several drawbacks compared with other media, the higher activation level of users being the most serious problem. But the Web also allows for more customized marketing that is directed toward the needs or interests of the specific customer. To do this, sites need to be able to retrieve user needs, and, if efficiency is to be maintained, to do this in a formalized manner. This is quite similar to other problems of formalization. With regard to Web searching, a user

The Web allows for a form of "inverse" marketing, where the customer describes needs or interests. It is then up to the system to find or create offers.

must formalize his information needs through a query, and to market itself, the site has to formalize the user's needs or interests. While the precision does not have to be very great, the success of the marketing will be directly related to how closely it matches users' needs. We may capture this information directly by asking the user to describe his needs in a formalized manner.

But the online environment is also changing. With tablets and smartphones that are always connected, with touch displays that make navigation easier, the steps to get on the net have been reduced. If we are on a social site, our interests may be determined from our profiles, and, especially from what we write and comment on in the moment. For example, I may tell my friends that we are planning a trip to Paris, which may be an important clue for the advertizing robots to present ads for flights and hotels. If I write that we are departing next week, ads from restaurants and art galleries may appear. We may view this as an intrusion of privacy, or perhaps see it as an advantage to access more relevant ads.

Thus the social networks are poised to be an important marketing channel. They seek to become a platform for users: Log in to the social site, stay on this site, shop from there, and book tickets from there. The advantage for the user is that one login may be sufficient, as the site can store all administrative information, from addresses to credit cards. The advantage for the site is that they have information that can be used to offer personalized ads, bargains, and offers.

14.5   The electronic customer

Are customers on the Web less loyal than those in the physical world, or is perhaps the word "loyal" not relevant for customer relations? We may be loyal to persons or a higher cause, but are we really "loyal" to a business? Are we loyal to the only airline that services our hometown, or to the bank that gives us the best service, the lowest fees, and the highest interest rate on our savings? Are we loyal to the neighborhood service station, perhaps paying somewhat more for an oil change than at a larger chain because we believe the station will be there the day the car will not start, or is this just an overall strategy from our side? We may be loyal to the local grocer that we know well, but this may be more of a personal than a business relationship. The same may be the case of the deeper relationship between buyers and sellers who may be bound together by mutual trust, some-

Technology changes the **relationship** between companies and customers. Until now, this development has gone from open to more closed relationships.

While the Web offers a formal channel of **communication**, it also allows a company to collect more data on its customers, data that may be used to build a sort of "personal" relationship.

Personalized marketing may raise privacy issues.

times intertwined to the extent that the futures of both rely on the well being of the partnership. However, the word loyal may give the impression that the customer, or the company, will be there whatever happens. This is a dangerous belief to have in any form of dynamic world, physical or virtual. On the Web, the competition can be only a click away.

With increased competition from all sides, contacts are less personal than before, and thus, less "loyal." This is clearly seen in the retail business. Not so long ago we would find neighborhoods and towns where most shopping was personal. Then the business could be carried out with a long-term view and not always on a transactional basis. Customers kept to the same local store, paid the standard price, and got personal service. The grocer would offer free delivery and give you credit if you could not pay. The shop owner knew your preferences ("we got in some really nice cheese today"), your family ("you know the cake that is your husband's favorite, today it's offered at half-price"), and had a fairly good knowledge of your economy.

Then came malls and superstores that could attract customers from far away with lower prices and huge inventories. Without the personal relationship, business had to be performed on a formalized and transactional basis. There was less possibility of using personal customer information or "I-owe-you-one" type of business. Everybody paid the same price and got the same service, formalized by store regulations.

However, in the same way that new technology (cars as a commodity, malls, and large stores) limits the possibility of having a personal relationship with retail customers, a different technology (computers) opens the possibility of building a new type of relationship. Some of the information that the local grocer got from informal channels and had in his head can now be obtained from more formal channels such as point-of-sale terminals and credit cards. Data are available on names, addresses, telephone numbers, and the items purchased. The same information can be retrieved over the Web, with the addition of information about what the customers did not buy. That is, we may retrieve information on what the customer did from the moment he "entered" the online store. We collect information such as what pages he visited, items that were placed in the shopping cart, carts that were left abandoned, and so forth. And, if the customer has a personal Web page, we can collect additional information about family, birthdays, and so on.

The Web offers possibilities for really getting to know the customer. This information can then be used to offer products and services of interest. The more accurate the information is, the more direct the offer. For example, most of us would appreciate this e-mail from our bank: "Last year, you had a minimum of $10,000 in your checking account. This amount would have generated an additional interest of more than $200 on our preferred customer savings account. Please let us know, by a reply to this message, if you would like to open such an account." We may also find the following note from our insurance company useful: "We have been informed that you have signed up for a climbing trip to the Himalayas. Please note that your standard travel insurance does not cover such trips. Would you be interested in extending this policy?" Of course, we may wonder where they got the information. Most of us would be very concerned about our privacy if e-mail marketing from pharmacy companies were customized, offering remedies for all our illnesses.

While there are unlimited possibilities of gathering personal information in an online world, there are rules and regulations that protect our most private data. For other types of data, privacy policies may vary from company to company. But there are also practical limitations. When buying a new car you may be interested in information on all cars that fulfill your requirements. A Web portal may capture your information needs, and offer it to dealers. But from the day you accept the best offer, you will no longer be interested in this type of information. In many ways, it may be irritating to get (good) offers too late. Similarly, there may be a good reason why you want a large amount of funds readily available in your checking account, and you may have obtained your special climbing insurance from another source than your regular insurance company.

The problem is that the formalized sources may only get part of the picture. The local grocer will not offer a cake for the husband if he knows that he was taken to the hospital in an ambulance yesterday with an open ulcer. Can a computer (the formalization) manage these important details? We see that any type of profile information has to be used with care, especially when we do not have the whole picture.

In their simplest form, profiles can be used to customize online ads, to select the most appropriate ads, increasing the chance that they will be effective. In a more advanced form, profiles can be used to augment both Web searches and Web

Creating and maintaining a **customer profile** by formal means is a very difficult task. The system will not have all data available and may not grasp the context.

sites. If the profile shows that a customer is primarily interested in bibliographies and art, an online bookstore can rearrange its display so that these sections are the first the customer sees, and where the new and bargain book displays offer bibliographies and art books at the top. This should be done with care, so that the site looks familiar when the customer comes back, not rearranged completely because she bought two art books. A smart customization policy should ensure a positive effect if the profile is correct, but no negative effects if it is wrong. For example, this goal can be achieved through customizing only the special displays for bargain or new items, but keeping the main store structure intact. That is, we have to acknowledge that our formalizations capture only a part of the picture.

Social networks and search engines may get a better view, especially if the user uses one site for multiple tasks. Imagine that you search for cars through you social site, check specifications, and ask for offers. This information is valuable for advertisers. For example, there may be cars that fulfill all your requirements but which you have not yet considered. The site may also know that you want full coverage on this new car, and also what price you have been offered from your insurance company. The possibilities are enormous if we do everything through the one site, and—of course—if we accept that the site looks over our shoulder to see what we are doing.

14.6   The electronic employee

A job has both **open and closed parts**. The computer can perform some of the closed parts, and can support some of the open parts, but perhaps not all.

Many of us perform our work in front of a computer screen, using software and hardware on the office PC, local server, or the Internet. With a PC and Internet connection at home, some workers may not need to commute to the office. The work can just as well be performed from a distance. This situation was envisaged with the emergence of the first data communication networks. However, most of us still go in to the office every day. Office space is as expensive as ever; the roads and public transportation are as packed in the rush hours as they ever have been. If some work from home, it seems to be very few.

Will cloud computing and new applications change this situation? While this technology does not offer anything fundamentally new, some practical limitations have been removed. But working at home has further constraints. Other parts of work are equally as important as the ability to access office computer files, such as formal and informal meetings with co-workers. While some of the formal meetings may be held using

If all contact is through **virtual channels,** it will be difficult to build and maintain strong bonds between employees and companies, which may be a drawback for both parties.

electronic communication, from a simple telephone or chat meeting to a more advanced videoconference, this may not be the case for the informal meetings. We meet in the hallway, around the water cooler, and at lunch. Even formal meetings have informal parts, when we whisper to the person next to us or continue the discussions during breaks. These people-to-people meeting places are an important part of lubricating the ongoing formal processes. Here we can advocate our view off the record, receive information, discuss policies, solve problems, make decisions, practice diplomacy, and generate ideas. Contact with co-workers is also essential in building a community feeling, the idea of working together for a common goal.

Working at home, alone with the computer, will not provide the same attachments. We may communicate with co-workers using telephone, e-mail, social networks, or videoconference equipment, but this is a far weaker form of contact than face-to-face meetings. In the more formal setting, people play roles, and over the Internet we will mainly see our coworkers in their role as manager, engineer, consultant—perhaps not so much as full persons. This has social disadvantages for employees, but also may be dangerous for an employer. Employees without any strong personal attachments to the company or their coworkers may be susceptible to quit whenever they get a better offer. And they may get one! If the only connection to their place of work is through the Internet, these people can work for any company in the world. They will not be limited by commuting or by social bonds, such as for "physical" workers.

But a high turnover rate may not be the only problem with people working at home via the Internet. All firms face situations in which they may have to demand an extra effort from their employees, for example, to finish a big contract within deadline, to overcome production problems, or to surmount temporary financial difficulties. Then, they have to rely on existing bonds between the firm and its personnel. These may be positive—employees may have a good relationship with the company and a belief in its future—or more negative—employees simply lack any good alternatives for employment in the area. Nevertheless, these bonds may provide what is needed in order to weather the crisis but they may not exist or be very weak among a company's e-employees.

Computer and network technology offer a new way of **organizing work**, especially for the more formalized jobs. But these are also the jobs that the computer can remove.

This model does not tell us that work at home is not an option, but we have to know the consequences independent of being employees or employers. The negative effects can be reduced if work is divided between home and office, and if the company creates additional meeting places and contact points for their employees. In some situations, working at home is ideal and a company can accept the weaker bonds with employees. This is especially the case for employees who do work on a commission or a transactional basis, such as telephone operators who provide information, book tickets, and register orders. This type of work can be done with a telephone and a computer terminal, perhaps in another country, does not require a high degree of training, and can be ideal for part-time work. The formalized nature of the task makes it easy to check both quality and efficiency, but, of course, also makes it easier to develop computer systems that perform the task. We again see the paradox: Jobs that computers make possible can often be replaced with computers.

The editing of this book provides an example of "an electronic employee" in an unformalized setting. I found the editing company[6] on the Internet. I sent the book by e-mail and received the edited material back. It took me some time before I understood that this company was situated on the other side of the world from me, in New Zealand. This shows that, nowadays, editing is a job that can be performed anywhere. The task, "turning this text into good English," is easy to describe, while neither the results nor the task itself are formalized (we continue the discussion of natural language in part 8).

14.7   Replacing travel

Science fiction authors have envisaged a future when humans can be transported through the air, in a form of telecommuting. In *Star Wars,* people were able to be present at other locations through a hologram. Today, with faster networks and computers, three-dimensional movies can be transmitted from one location to another in almost real time and can be presented as a holographic image.[7]

Video conferences come in many forms, from the simple camera on top of the laptop display to special video conferencing rooms with many cameras.

Until this becomes a standard, we will have to do with current applications for telecommuting, such as telephone conferences, simple videoconferencing using a Web camera in the office, or more advanced videoconferencing. The latter will often be in a separate room, with several cameras and a large screen. Participants may be seated at a table, with the other end of the table in a different location—seen on the large screen. Using very high bandwidth and many displays and cameras, we may create a near realistic scene in which we can follow all participants in the meeting. Not only can we see the speaker, but we can also see what impression she has on the audience.

This is a far step up from the Web camera in our office solution, but it still has limitations. First, it can be complicated to follow all participants in the meeting if these are situated in many different locations, not just here and there as with the table metaphor. Second, a videoconference meeting has formal parts only, with no chance to talk off the record. Third, many meetings and conferences have a social component that in many ways can only be realized when participants meet physically. These, such as excursions and dinners, are the glue and lubricant that are so important when people are to work successfully together.

Physical presence often makes a difference.

Therefore, telecommunication will work best for the most formal meetings, among participants who know each other. For example, a company may have seen major budget overdrafts on their earlier projects. To avoid this situation the board has required that the committee handling the budget to meet weekly. With participants in different locations, much time and money will be used for travel. But a videoconference, or perhaps a simple telephone conference, may be a solution. That is, until the day that severe overdrafts in the project are discovered. Then the participants will probably book airline tickets for the next meeting.

14.8   Games

With the Internet we can **play** with and against other people—geographically independent. This is one of the most successful examples of computer-supported collaborative work.

Humans are game players. Since technology takes care of a large part of daily activities efficiently and effectively, many have time to spend on leisure activities. Part of this time may be used for physical games such as soccer, golf, sailing, and basketball; more intellectual games such as chess, bridge, or Monopoly; or more personal, such as role-playing games.

Games create a world of their own, formalized to higher levels than in the real world. The goal is clearly defined for both soccer and chess, as are the rules of the game. However, soccer and most other physical games operate in an environment where there is room for interpretation; referees are needed to tell us if a move is in violation of the rules or not. In contrast, in intellectual games, the operations often are formalized. Playing a card, for example, or making a move in chess may be performed with full precision. The card is played when it is on the table. We select a chess piece by picking it up and confirming the move when we let it go. In principle, no referee is needed to interpret the rules.[8] An exception is the more serious tournaments, where referees are needed to ensure that participants follow the rules.

We should not be surprised to see that games are a major application area for the home computer. A computer is just the place to create virtual worlds, to keep track of rules, and to compute scores. Using the power of a modern PC, these worlds can be visualized using multimedia techniques, with animations, sound, and dynamic input. With simple local area networks or over the Internet, more than one person can participate in the same world, and, for example, we may have car races in which each person steers his own car. Today, we see a tendency for these applications to be moved to more specialized equipment, to game machines designed for just this job.

The Internet offers new opportunities for the game enthusiast, and collaborative "work" is flourishing. While games often are modeled on real-life situations, the higher formalization level (stricter rules, simpler goals) makes it easier to collaborate. Participants from different cultures may have very different values and ways of working, but all have accepted the "rules of the game." This higher formalization level removes the need for personal relations necessary in real life.

On the Internet, more persons can join the game than is possible in the real world. Organizing a game is much simpler when participants do not need to be physically present. We may play chess with an opponent anywhere in the world, or persons from different continents may "take a seat" for a set of bridge. Thousands of people may come together virtually to play against each other. Some games are played synchronously while others are asynchronous. Ongoing games also exist in which we may join at leisure, but are required to find partners who can protect our interests when we are off the game, preferably partners in different time zones, so that we are not all asleep when the enemy forces attack. Games on the Internet may move into a realistic setting, when we receive telephone calls, e-mails or SMS messages from the game system during the day.

The disadvantage of game playing on the Internet is that many games require high bandwidth to produce all the "necessary" effects. However, by running parts of the software locally, the communication lines can be used for compact data only. For example, the central system keeps track of position,

Games let us create visual worlds that are formalized to high levels with well-defined objects, rules, and goals.

Global participation in **collaborative work** requires more than communication technology.

course, and speed of all forces while the local machine performs the actual visualization of the spacecraft.

Perhaps the Internet, developed as it was by a scientist, may have gotten off to a false start. Maybe this is not primarily the medium for serious business or for in-depth data. Instead, it may end up as a medium directed toward entertainment, following the home computer as a game-playing machine.

Notes

1   Interestingly, we find also online publishers that offer nice "scientific"-like layout of papers, but that cheat on the review process and accept any paper as long as the author pay the fees.

2   There are numerous humorous examples of how some of the early systems performed, such as the father who saw that his daughter got a "wrong answer" from a simple math program—"The answer to 3 + 4 is 7, not SEVEN."

3   An example may be the Google Toolbar, which can be downloaded from the Google Web site (www.google.com).

4   With a digital format, it is possible to skip commercials automatically. This may force the advertisers into a different model, integrating ads and programs in a seamless manner (for example by placing products in movies, or shows), just as in the early days of television.

5   Note that spam is seldom stopped by using an "unsubscribe," as this often may be taken as a signal that this is a working e-mail address.

6   http://www.wix.com/jamesedits/jamesedits

7   http://www.wired.com/wiredscience/2010/11/holographic-video/

8   In practice, we should perhaps have a referee to stop fights about the creative words that are created in a game like Scrabble and to interpret the not-so-clear answers in Trivial Pursuit.

15   Privacy and Security

Chapter 10 presented exceptional situations linked to hardware, software, or the way systems were used. As long as systems were stand-alone or connected over private networks, this discussion of exceptions was complete. However, with the open Internet, a new kind of situation has arrived: malicious attacks on the integrity of computer systems, designed to destroy data, to steal computer power, or to take down networks or other systems by overloading channels.

15.1   Hacking

Hacking relies on the openness of the Internet and the Web, but forces the systems in the opposite direction, toward more closed environments.

Some attacks performed by technically oriented hackers to show what they are able to do often have very limited consequences. Still, in many ways these hackers harass the very openness of the Internet and the software platforms that they heavily rely on. Well-known institutions, such as the FBI and Microsoft, are prime targets. Hacking these sites not only guarantees publicity, but also proves hacking proficiency, thus creating an interesting loop of negative feedback—the more security the higher the gains of breaking into the site.[1] Since negative publicity is expensive, these institutions need a secure system that does not allow anybody to tamper with their site, or the sites of their employees. For institutions such as banks or hospitals, the consequences of unauthorized persons getting access to data are so serious that security is a primary concern, in the virtual world just as in the physical. To establish trust, these security concerns go well beyond protecting confidential data because even hacking rather harmless Web pages can reduce customer confidence.

Organized crime may be behind an attack on computer systems and networks.

A more serious threat is hacking by organized crime groups. These may have IT competence and be willing to spend time and resources on an attack. Even more serious are politically or economically motivated attacks by unfriendly countries. The answer is to have more secure systems, with constant supervision of what is happening on the Internet. Most countries today have agencies that perform this form of net supervision.

Society and the military forces depend on the Internet and GPS systems and satellite communication to work. These technologies present an area of vulnerability. The idea of cyberwar-

Nations have to consider the risk of **cyberwarfare**, an attack on their computer systems.

fare where a first attack, or an only attack, is to penetrate, disrupt or destroy a nation's computer systems, is becoming a realistic scenario.

To protect against such an attack, or to have the capability of launching such an attack, a specialized military arm is being established in many countries, a cyberbranch in addition to the army, navy, and air force. To have the ability to fend off such attacks, a country will need well-educated computer security specialists. Their task will be to protect systems, to indentify attacks and to limit the consequences of an attack, very much the same goals of a traditional army unit. However, a problem with cyber-attacks is that the attacker may be hard to identify, and the attacker may therefore be able to launch attacks without having to encounter the consequences.

There are several examples of such attacks. The most known is a cyber-attack on Georgia, timed with the Russian invasion of the country in 2008. China is suspected of being behind industrial espionage over the Internet, and Israel may be behind a virus that caused problems at an Iranian nuclear facility.[2]

With the more complex products that we have today, which are usually produced in a distant country, there is a risk that malicious software may be hidden within the systems, such as software that can capture confidential data, or, perhaps shut the systems down if a crisis occur. These concerns have been raised as Huawei, a large Chinese company, is winning tenders all over the world to establish communication systems. But the situation is not so simple that it can be restricted to this one company, as European and U.S. telecommunication suppliers also produce in China

15.2   Viruses

Viruses exploit unprepared users or loopholes in computer systems.

Earlier, in the childhood of computing, unreliable hardware was a serious problem. But at that time, nobody even had the intention of performing malicious attacks on computer systems. While these attacks may come in many forms, the most serious for ordinary PC users, even smartphone owners, are viruses. A virus is a computer program that may be stored, or store itself on your computer. When started, it may do everything from giving you a "have a happy day" screen message to destroying everything on your hard disk. The program is called a virus because it can be spread from computer to computer on the Internet, in much the same way a virus is spread from crop to crop, or from human to human.

Viruses exploit unprepared users or loopholes in different types of systems, e.g., mail systems, browsers, or operating systems. The virus may be activated by a user that clicks on the wrong attachment or visits the wrong Web page. However, it is quite a dangerous situation when a virus attack is only a click away. Open the wrong attachment and your hard disk may be destroyed, your e-mail system may be clogged, and personal files may be sent to others. In other situations, the virus may use flaws in the underlying software to be able to infect your machine with malicious programs. In many ways viruses exploit the existing formalism and standardization. For example, when many use Microsoft Outlook as an e-mail program, we get a common infrastructure that can be exploited, very similar to the real world in which bugs exploit large fields with the same crop.

The functionality offered by modern operating systems is a part of the problem. Not only do they allow programs to set system parameters, but they also open themselves to the Internet. In most cases, this openness benefits the user, making it easier to install new programs or new components. But, openness also offers a way for a virus to infect and damage a machine.

Simple means of protection are to keep operating systems updated at all times, something that in practice demands a good Internet connection, which also increases the probability of being attacked. Antivirus programs that scan all incoming data to see if they contain the code patterns of known viruses are a must if your computer is on the Internet. However, these need continuous updates to work effectively. To avoid being affected, an Internet browser can be set to the highest security level, restricting the functionality to a minimum. But that solution will block a large set of services that require some control over a computer system to work properly. That is, if we bolt the door we can keep thieves away, but we may also restrict access for others. We can further protect transmissions by cryptography and certificates that tell who we are and that give us control over who we have at the other end. Such systems are used for most critical applications, for example, for monetary transactions.

Not everyone has installed virus protection programs, or has not updated these or the operating system code frequently

Hacking and viruses may be used as a **weapon** against cultures, countries, or organizations.

Attacks on our systems, whether they are physical or virtual, make us move toward a more **closed society**, with locks, limited access, and control points.

As in the physical world, mono-cultures are open for **virus** attacks. The standardization we have for operating systems, Web browsers, and mail programs makes it easier for computer viruses to multiply and spread.

enough. When nonprotected computers are connected to the Internet, they can assist in propagating viruses, just as people without the necessary vaccines can spread diseases in the real world. Perhaps we need a system of "health certificates," where one needs a clear bill before a computer can be connected to the local ISP, where the ISP needs a clear bill before their servers can be connected, and so on.

The seriousness of virus attacks was not foreseen. System development has been focused on positive and open functionality, making efficient systems where everything is possible. For example, a philosophy for the last versions of operating systems has been to move the desktop toward the world, to integrate network functionality to the point that there is no distinction between a file stored locally or on the network. Perhaps we will see a step back in future versions to a clearer distinction between the secure local world and the dangerous world beyond. As with crime in the physical world, the greatest harm may be the indirect consequences that we are forced to exchange open systems for more closed and proprietary ones.[3]

We have seen that viruses, often transmitted as attachments to e-mail messages, are a serious problem. Even when no data is lost, it is quite embarrassing and also a violation of privacy when all our contacts understand that we opened the "I love you" attachment immediately as it was received. A virus may also install software on your system that monitors all activities. In the worst case, such programs may discover user names and passwords; in other cases, the virus may report statistics to its mother site that can be used for marketing.

Just as with hacking, some may send innocent *viruses* for "fun," but others may have a clearer political agenda (to attack a company, the US economy, or the western world) or an economic agenda, for example, to exploit the victim's computer resources in order to send spam messages.[4] To a certain degree this form of symbolic warfare was possible even with older technology, telephone, fax, or letter. However, these action forms had a democratic nature, as one needed many collaborators to block the switchboard of a company or state agency or to overwhelm a senator with mail. Today, only one person armed with a computer and the right software can do this. More dangerous is the possibility of attacking internal systems without using physical force, from a secure position far from the point of attack. This form of warfare is undemocratic in yet another respect—major companies and institutions often have the know-how available to set up adequate protection against virus attacks, but small companies and inexperienced users are often hit harder when viruses are globally disseminated.

15.3   Phising

Phishing is an attack on computer systems in which an attacker fishes for user names, passwords, and account numbers. We have all received these messages camouflaged as a genuine message from a bank, an Internet store, a transportation company, or any other organization. A standard form is to tell that you have to log on to the organization site to renew a credit card or to avoid having your membership cancelled, and the e-mail provides the link to this site. Mail protocols that are too simple aid these attacks, allowing a sender to hide his e-mail address. In addition, the name of the link and the link itself may be different. For example, the link www.mybank.com may really connect to www.swindler.com. Inexperienced users may not see this.

There are countermeasures that can be used to stop **phising**.

Most of these phising attacks are simple enough for most users to detect, but some are more sophisticated, resembling genuine messages. However, even if most users recognize the scheme as a swindle, some users will be fooled and offer confidential information.

Such attacks can be stopped. One way is for the organization that the swindlers are trying to mimic to return millions of false user names and passwords to the attackers. With this spamming the attackers will have a difficult task of separating the few genuine responses from the spam. A more subtle approach would be to recognize the swindlers when they return with one of these false user names. Instead of rejecting their login, one could provide access to a shadow system. This would offer the opportunity to gather more information on the attackers. A bank, for example, could then easily find the account numbers where the attackers wanted to transfer money; an Internet store could find the addresses that were offered for sending the goods.

"**Big brother**" may be implemented without computer technology (Gestapo, North Korea).

15.4   Big brother

The idea of **phising** is to lure the user into offering confidential information.

From the advent of the first computers, there have been warnings that computers can be used to control ordinary citizens. With many types of data in electronic form and powerful processors, government scrutiny of e-mail, tracking of electronic

Not much can be learned from automatic **supervision** of e-mail messages and other transmission channels. There is a large discrepancy between words, their meaning and intention.

funds, and maintenance of registers has become practical. While this is absolutely true, we should remember that the German secret police, the Gestapo, was able to control both their citizens and those of occupied countries during World War II without computers. That is, the threat of misuse of power is independent of technology.

However, with the more complex products that we have today, most often produced in a distant country, there may be a risk that malicious software may be hidden within the systems, for example software that can capture confidential data, or, perhaps, shut the systems down if a crisis occur. These concerns have been raised as Huawei, a large Chinese company, is winning tenders all over the world to establish communication systems. But the situation is not as simple that one can restrict this one company, also European and U.S. telecommunication suppliers produce in China.

Tracing electronic money can be very useful in the fight against crime and tax evasion, especially as we move toward less use of cash (see Chapter 66.4). Electronic supervision may also be used to find criminals and terrorists. However, the belief in automatic supervision methods of e-mail and telephone seems pretty naive. An automatic program cannot grasp the meaning of a text. Instead, one has to rely on the occurrence of words. But ordinary citizens may use words such as "murder," "attack," and "bomb" in their messages, and smart criminals can so easily use code, for example, by replacing dangerous words with more innocent ones. An action plan can then be covered as a discussion of football results; a cryptographic message can be hidden within an innocent budget.

Law enforcement agencies may get a lot of data by studying who's calling who, data that can be collected by automatic methods. However, the new technologies also have offered new possibilities for the criminals. Messages can be hidden within spam mail and distributed to millions as an advertisement, even if it is only meant for a few—the persons that have the ability to decode the message.

The measures needed to capture criminals and terrorists and to fend of terrorist attacks must be balanced with the need to maintain privacy. Some of these issues will be discussed further both in the following chapter and in Chapter 65.

Notes

1   "Brag-walls" on the Web are where hackers can post screen shots of their successes.

2   See *The Economist*, July 3th, 2010.

3   The problem will then be to protect the systems from physical attacks, especially the high bandwidth systems that rely on cables. A cut with an axe in the right place may be enough to take out major communication channels; a bomb within a central telephone office could interrupt service for millions of lines.

4   The word "spam" comes from a canned meat product, and was perhaps given its new meaning when a Usenet-reader reacted negatively to a commercial launched on all Usenet services in 1994 by asking everybody to "send coconuts and cans of spam" to the company involved. The word was also used in a Monthy Python comedy sketch in which a group of Vikings interrupted the story by singing, "spam, spam, spam, spam, spam, spam, lovely spam!"

16 Case Study: Internet Elections

Several countries have experimented with Internet elections. While voters in Estonia could use the Internet in their 2007 national election for parliament, other countries have offered this option for local elections only. The argument in favor of allowing voting over the Internet is that it may increase voter participation, which has dropped in many countries in recent years. Another key argument is that Internet elections can increase access for people with disabilities. Furthermore, some people feel that Internet elections are an inevitable case of allowing democracy to enter the Internet world along with shopping, banking, and many other applications.

One argument against voting on the Internet is that it cannot guarantee the anonymity that a voting booth can offer, which can lead to coercion and the buying and selling of votes. Even more serious is the risk that someone may tamper with the voting or the results. This risk is aggravated by the fact that voting could be performed from a computer that has malware installed.[1]

16.1 Norwegian system

Norway tried to implement a secure e-voting system, using advanced cryptographic techniques and a system to hinder vote tampering.

To overcome such obstacles, the Ministry of Local Government in Norway launched a $40-million project in 2009 to design an electronic voting system to be used in the 2011 local elections. The system is based on experience from other countries, and is comparable to the Estonian system. Experts from academia, research institutions, and industry were engaged to develop a secure system and to check the proposed solutions. To prevent voting errors or coercion, the system allowed repeated voting. The Internet option was closed one day prior to the election, voters always had the option to cast their vote at a polling station, and the voter's last vote would always override any previous votes. To counter malware and other risks, an advanced cryptographic system was employed.[2] An important part of this is a coding system designed to prevent vote-tampering.

This system uses codes to identify each political party participating in the election. These codes are presented on the back of a "voter's card," which is mailed to everyone who has the right to vote. After casting the ballot on the Internet using a

The voter received, on a ballot card, a number of individual codes that identified each political party.

home or office computer, voters receive a confirmation text message. This message includes a code that the voter can compare to the card in order to check that the vote was registered for the correct party. Since these codes only exist on the paper card and are proprietary for each voter, malware would have to break into the central server to find the codes. Tests also showed that many voters do check that the code is correct. Thus, the ministry determined that it would require a "large-scale conspiration and unreasonable amounts of money" to break into the system.

16.2   Breaking the system

As we shall see, there are many approaches that can be taken to attack such a system. While the designers have taken these into account, they have not considered the possibility of "social phishing," that is, designing a system that entices users to offer the secret code.

Our **malware** exploits the most vulnerable parts of the system.

To demonstrate these possibilities, a colleague and I designed a "malware system" of our own. Although we assumed that the server part of the e-voting system is secure, our "malware" exploits the most vulnerable part of the voting system: the voter. After the voter has chosen a certain political party, the official voting system presents a page with the name of the party and the user is asked to confirm by clicking a send-button. Our version is similar, but it also asks for the (secret) party code: "Please confirm your selection by typing in the code for this party. You will find the code on the back of your voter's card." In a test simulating voting on paper, we tested this on 158 college students, including twenty-five IT students. None of the students found any faults with the system. In addition, over four hundred high school students tested an on-line version. All of the students typed in the party code when required by the system, despite the fact that all participants, both college and high school students, were shown an animation made by the ministry that explains the e-voting system and stresses the correct use of the party code as a final manual check.

The system exploits the user's desire to type in PIN codes.

However, in all other situations PIN codes are supposed to be typed into some computer system. Even the e-voting system has a part where a PIN received by a text message is to be typed in during the identification process. Thus, while my malware uses the code as users anticipate, it is the official system that applies the code in an unfamiliar manner.

Once it has the code, the malware can easily send the correct confirmation to the voter and then discard or change the vote. In the latter case, the voter will receive another text message, this time from the ministry, with a different code (for the party that the malware has chosen). With malware also present on the smartphone, this second text message can be discarded. Or, more simply, the user can be warned that additional messages may be forthcoming because of some communication problems, and to "please ignore these."

16.3   Fake URLs

A ministry document on security objectives stresses the risk of such malware: "The insecurity of browsers and operating systems on the client platform will invariably make it possible to subversively install malicious software."[3]

Those with such intent may opt for straightforward solutions. Introducing a fake URL for the voting system is one possibility. Many users will find the link through other Web pages, such as community pages. These sites have been hacked before and can be hacked again. A false Web site will also receive identification data from the voter, and will, at least in the Norwegian system, be able to change the phone number for the confirmation message. Even more simply, a villain could send an e-mail to voters before the election with a "vote here" URL. By targeting the recipients, such as groups that the villain feels vote unsatisfactorily, it is extremely simple to make an e-voting system that mimics the original system, asks for the party code, sends a confirmation message to the voter, and then discards the vote. It took me just a few hours to create such a system.

While someone would certainly notice a large-scale attack, a small-scale attack, perhaps in one community only, could go unnoticed. Even if there is disclosure, what should be done? Should voters be asked to vote again or should the election be considered invalid? Creating such chaos may even be the main intent of the villain. Even in such a case, there may not be an easy fix. As well as changing your vote, malware may also know how you voted. This information, which most people consider private, could be used for blackmail or embarrassment.

16.4   The user is the most vulnerable part

In theory, the Norwegian e-voting system is safe. According to the developers, the risks involved can be expressed mathematically. However, this assurance is based on the condition that voters do what they are supposed to do. We have demonstrated that voters are actually victims of the user interface, and we argue that voting systems are particularly vulnerable. A conscientious voter who participates in all elections will in many countries vote once every two years. This is not frequently enough to get any practice or routine with an e-voting system. In any case, there also may be modifications in the interface from one election to another. So, while methods such as those presented here may, in principle, be used to obtain secret codes from Internet bank users, in practice, most of us would get suspicious if the system broke its expected pattern; for example, if it asked for additional codes. Furthermore, if someone breaks into your bank account, you would at least see that money has disappeared. A changed or discarded vote, however, may never be discovered.

Estonia requires citizens to insert their nationwide ID-card in a card reader connected to the home computer to vote on the Internet, and then offer PIN codes as further proof of identification. This may increase security on the home computer, but the risk of malware or a false election site is still the same.

Postal voting is another option offered in many countries, and some states have this as the only alternative.[4] It offers the same possibility of voting from one's home as the Internet. Theoretically it can be as vulnerable as Internet voting, but it would take more resources to mount an attack. Also, while the Internet offers anonymity to the villains, this may not be the case for those who try to interfere with a postal voting system.

Postal voting, as any system that lets a voter cast a vote outside of a voting booth, still has the disadvantages that voters can be coerced or paid to vote in a certain way. The possibility of repeated voting could reduce this problem. By going to the polling place after giving the Internet or postal vote, one has the opportunity to vote again. However, a patriarch of a closely controlled family could easily restrict his daughter's movements on the final day of the election, just as he could control their Internet voting. For those buying votes it is just a small calculated risk that the seller of a vote will turn up on Election Day.

Repeated voting on the Internet may not offer any solution. Votes can still be bought, not by requiring how people vote, but by taking control over their ID-codes.

Repeated voting on the Internet may not offer any solution. Votes can still be bought, not by requiring how people vote, but by taking control over their ID-codes. This allows the buyer to vote on their behalf. However, the Estonian solution with an ID-card would make it more difficult to hand this over to others, especially when the card is used for other purposes as well.

In Isaac Asimov's science fiction story *Franchise* (1955), the all-encompassing supercomputer Multivac chooses Norman Muller as the "Voter of the Year." In this electronic democracy, a single person is selected to represent all voters. Based on the answers to a set of questions to Norman, Multivac determines the results of the election. Norman is proud that the citizens of the United States, through him, "exercised once again their free, untrammeled franchise." This isn't exactly Internet voting, but the two systems do have something in common: It is impossible for non-experts to verify that they work correctly. The old system with paper ballots may be inefficient, but it does allow any voter to understand how it works, which is also true for postal voting. Trust in such a system is more direct than with any electronic voting application.

Perhaps voting is one task that should not be moved to the Internet. Trustworthy design of an electoral system is critical for democracy; this is a place where no risks, neither practical nor theoretical, can be tolerated. The advantage of running a computer system that is to be used sparingly is also dubious and, as we have seen, creates additional risks since users have no routine. It is also reasonable to believe that electoral participation does not depend on the voting system alone. Perhaps it has something to do with politics.

Notes

1 This chapter is based on the Olsen, K. A, Nordhaug, H. F. (2012) Internet elections – unsafe in any home?, Communications of the ACM, no. 8, volume 55, August.

2 Gjøsteen, K. (2011) Analysis of an internet voting protocol, http://eprint.iacr.org/2010/380

3 E-vote 2011 Security Objectives, Ministry of Local Government, see: http://www.regjeringen.no/upload/KRD/Kampanjer/valgportal/e-valg/tekniskdok/Security_Objectives_v2.pdf

4 Qvortrup, M. (2005) First Past the Postman: Voting by Mail in Comparative Perspective, Political Quarterly, Volume 76, Issue 3, pages 414–419.

PART 3
Usability

More than twenty years ago, the first efforts to develop a universal system of information sharing, the Web, were started at CERN in Switzerland. This gives us many years of user interface experience with the Web. However, the field of human computer interaction started many years before. The work became really important in the early 1980s, when the development of the PC made computer technology available to new user groups, most with no computing experience. The basic rules of creating good user interfaces were then, as now:

- Simplicity and efficiency
- Support the user
- The user should be in control
- Avoid errors

Today most users have many years of computer experience.

Today most users have many years of computer experience. They may use a PC several hours a day, in addition to other electronic devices such as mobile phones, tablets, car navigators, TVs, movie systems, and digital cameras. While the basic rules are still the same, their interpretation may have changed. Today, accommodating the experienced users is as important as accommodating the novice. We may want user interfaces that reduce the time to perform a task, for example by avoiding unnecessary input. It may be just a click, but when we perform hundreds, maybe thousands of these a day, avoiding unnecessary clicks becomes important.

A novice may make an error due to a misunderstanding of the user interface, while an experienced player may perform as many just by trying to be efficient. In both cases, the interface must protect the user, not by generating a long sequence of warnings, but by collecting all the available information and intelligently informing the user whenever there is a possibility of an error.

The interface can be simplified by hiding details.

The interface can be simplified by hiding details. Today we do not have to know anything about the engine to drive a car. We turn a key or push a button to get it started, and all information that we need is there on the dashboard. Connoisseurs may feel that something is lost, but the automation makes driving simpler for most of us. However, loss of control is a danger. Blocking access to low level structures such as files and folders, can make the system more complex to use for general operations such as copying, taking backup, deleting many files at once, and so on.

Automation is another way to simplify systems.

Automation is another way to simplify computer systems. That is, the system performs all the detailed operations without user intervention. But a system may also perform actions that go contrary to the user's objective, leaving him perplexed, and creating errors. One example is automation error in which the user relies on the system, confident that it will do the job. Then, if something goes wrong and the automation relinquishes control to the human operator—the engineer in a train or an airline pilot—the operator may be ready to take over. This problem has caused serious accidents.

All these aspects of user interfaces are well understood. They have been in the user interface textbooks for many years (Shneiderman, 1987; Morville and Rosenfeld 1998; Nielsen, 1999, Dix et al, 2003). With the PC and later with the World Wide Web, interfaces have been "tested" on millions of users. The advantages of good user interfaces have been firmly established, not only to get satisfied users, but also to create revenue. Apple Corporation is a good example. Instead of developing new technology, they have utilized ideas and products that are already in the marketplace to offer excellent user interfaces. Amazon with their "one-click" philosophy is another best-practices case.

User interfaces should offer simple solutions to tasks, automate what can be automated, and let the users be in control.

Today, we should demand that all user interfaces keep up with the state-of-the-art, that they offer simple solutions to tasks, automate what can be automated, and let the users be in control. Alas, this is not always the case. While there are some good user interfaces out there, many if not most, have faults. Some of these have only minor consequences: They may require users to give unnecessary input, lead them down back alleys, select the wrong options, give warnings that cannot be understood, or otherwise waste the user's time and cause irritation. In the more serious cases, a bad user interface may result in loss of data, or an unsatisfactory or erroneous result.

The techniques applied to develop good interfaces are forms, menus, buttons, and wizards. A form offers a way to provide structured input, where every field has a pretext to tell what kind of information is expected. Good interfaces will check the input and tell us if anything is wrong, for example, if we have the incorrect number of input characters for an account number or an incorrect date format. Command buttons are easily integrated into the form, to start actions such as save, next step, add to basket, and so on.

Where the major part of the display is used for text, as in a word processing system, spreadsheet formulas, or photos in a photo-editing program, commands can be organized in pull down menus. This saves screen real estate for the more important components. In systems that require many steps, such as an application that requires many different data elements, a wizard may guide us through the steps.

An undo facility is important, letting the user go back to the situation before the erroneous command was given.

Users often hit the wrong button, enter the wrong characters, or select the wrong menu item. In these cases a good system should offer an "undo" facility, letting us go back to the situation before the erroneous command was given. Many applications offer such a feature. The importance of providing a facility to make corrections is seen from the fact that one of the most used keys on a keyboard is the backspace key, the key that removes the last character entered.

A system should at least give warnings when a user performs an unexpected action, for example, trying to exit a document before changes are saved to disk. However, the most important thing is to avoid errors in the first place, which most often can be ensured when the interface applies the user's terminology and has a logical sequence of actions and messages that the user can relate to.

This section presents these issues in more detail, starting with a discussion of interactive computing (Chapter 17). In the following Chapter (18) we consider general usability issues. In Chapter 19 we look at ideas for developing simple user interfaces. We will see that application makers need to respect their customers, and always put the user in control. This implies respecting the knowledge and experience of the user, for example by avoiding making radical changes to systems that users are comfortable with and by making polite programs that put users in control.

A case of flexible user interfaces is presented in Chapter 20, and Chapter 21 presents two cases of bad user interface design.

17 Interactive Computing

If tasks have both **open and closed parts**, the ideal systems seem to be those of humans working in close cooperation with computers.

In the early days of computing, programs were run without human intervention. Batches were set up with a set of programs and all the data, often represented on punched cards. The stack of cards was read into the computer and the programs were executed one after the other, giving output to a line printer. Most programs are now interactive, communicating with the user during processing. This is true even for many programs that run in devices. For example, a computer in a car takes input from the driver through the accelerator and provides output through the instrument panel or directly to the engine.

Interaction provides for greater flexibility, as the user can react on the basis of previous output from the machine. We go from a predefined command system, "do this job, here are all the data and instructions," to more of a dialogue with the computer. For example, we can ask an airline booking system to present available bargain tickets and then choose the offer we want. Instead of one program doing all the processing on pre-made input data, the program is split into smaller functions that we invoke from the user interface. Data are entered one field at a time, which provides for continuous error control. Input may be simplified if the program can offer default values, and errors can be avoided by letting the program control input and giving a message wherever there is a problem. The system is, of course, still formalized, but the involvement of the user in the process allows for greater flexibility.

The principle of interactivity is manifested in modern user interfaces, which are designed along a "control panel" metaphor. The user is in control. The machine is the assistant that executes the tasks according to the user's instructions, when the user decides. The human being is the expert, not the system. The computer performs the tasks for which it is best suited: computation, archiving, transmission, and presentation of data. The human being makes the decisions and controls the high-level aspects of the tasks, following overall strategies and goals. (At least, that is what we want. However, modern systems have a tendency to take control from the user, something that is discussed further in Chapter 19.2).

Interactive systems can give us the best of both worlds, letting humans handle open tasks and the computer the closed parts.

Interactive systems offer the best of both worlds, utilizing the ability of human beings to do the overall planning and decision making, while the computer is in charge of the formalized

Some systems allow the users to write their own **program functions,** "tuning" a system so that it fulfills all needs.

parts. Most interactive systems offer user control over data, and which processes to invoke. Some systems allow even greater flexibility by letting the user write program functions. This can be done with high-level functions within special domains, such as "programming" formulas in a spreadsheet system or using mathematical programs such as Maple and Mathlab. "Application generators," such as Microsoft Access, offer simple application design, allowing forms, data tables, and database queries to be described visually, adding programming code where needed. Full flexibility is achieved within programming languages, such as Visual Basic, PHP, and Java, which allow for detailed descriptions of what we want the computer to do.

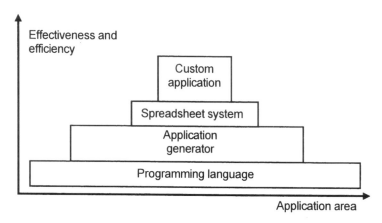

Figure 17.1 Balance between application area and efficiency.

Flexibility can be obtained at the cost of efficiency; it is difficult to get both at the same time.

The flexibility offered by interactive systems and programming languages does come at a cost. The higher-level functions that make a program simple to use also narrow the application area. This contrast between simplicity and applicability is illustrated in Figure 17.1. The systems that are most efficient to use and that require the least input from the user have the most limited application area. Some devices, such as a watch, would have been displayed as a vertical line in this figure because a watch is very efficient, requiring minimum input and performing only one task. Programming languages such as Java can be used for all applications, while custom-designed programs have a narrower application area but with higher-level functions that make these programs more efficient within their specialization. Spreadsheet systems and application generators are somewhere in the middle of the range.

Word processors, spreadsheets, and similar systems are only assistants. They do only part of the job. Their effectiveness comes from the fact that they are each dedicated to an important application area, offering all needed functionality needed within that area.

To clarify, we can compare a pencil and a word processing system. The pencil has very few limitations; we may use it for all fonts and symbols, but these have to be drawn by hand. A word processing system may have a limited font set and drawing capabilities, but is much more efficient to use.

The flexibility offered by programs such as word processors, spreadsheet systems, and Web page editors are achieved because these systems are only assistants. They only do part of the job—editing and formatting text, handling numerical data and formulas, and creating Web pages, respectively. Their effectiveness comes from the fact that they are each dedicated to an important application area, offering all the needed functionality within that area. However, all higher-level tasks are left to the user.

This is just another part of the formalization picture. Formalization to a high level may be achieved within limited domains, but not for general applications. As the application area gets narrower, formalization level can be increased, under the requirement, of course, that tasks can be formalized.

We return to the issue of flexibility in Chapter 20, studying how current user interfaces, such as booking tickets, do not accommodate all user needs.

18 Usability

Humans make errors. These may be caused by anything from a lack of knowledge to merely a slip. Clearly, the design of the interfaces, the part between the human and the machine, is important. A good interface reduces the chances of errors, while a bad interface may increase them.

18.1 User interfaces to avoid errors

Booking Reference 7Q25OP

Flight/Date Class	Route Status		Departure Meal	Arrival	Latest Check-In	Terminal	Baggage allowance
SK4515/10OCT W	Molde - Oslo Confirmed		06.50 Continental Breakfast	07.45	06.20		1PC
Scandinavian Airlines SK4524/11OCT T	Oslo - Molde Confirmed		15.45 Food and Beverages for Purchase	16.40	15.15		1PC

Figure 18.1. A ticket itinerary.

Most user interfaces can be **improved** to reduce the chance of a user error.

Consider the airline ticket in Figure 18.1, which depicts a fairly standard way of providing an itinerary. It is unambiguous and correct, but can it be improved to avoid errors? One improvement is to include redundant information. For example, by including the name of the day—Monday 10 OCT and Tuesday 11 OCT—instead of listing only the date, the user may have a better chance to identify an error in the date. Also, spelling out the month in full would make it more difficult to mix up JUN and JUL.

We could also put an emphasis on the most important times—the departure time, for example—by putting these in a bold font. When the itinerary is long with several stops, there is a risk that the passenger may turn up at the departure airport at the time given for an intermediate stop. Since "terminal" is not used here, this column should be removed. Perhaps we should also tell the passenger that the trip includes one overnight, as some people have mistakenly booked a trip for a week instead of a fortnight.

This airline uses a cryptic booking reference without recognizing that characters such as 0s and Os should not be mixed in random codes. For example, the letter O in the reference number could easily be mistaken for a zero, since two digits precede

Use reference
numbers and IDs
that the user can
understand.

it. A better reference number could be the passenger's telephone number, but because the passenger may have more than
one booking, a phone number will not give a unique identifier.
However, in most cases, such as checking in at the airport, the
context will help the system to identify the correct booking. In
other cases, the system could present a list of all bookings, letting the passenger choose.

18.2   Looking at the complete system

**The user is a part
of the system.**
What we need are
systems where all
parts work, not
only the technical
part.

In the late 1970s, as a part of a university project, we implemented an advanced journal system for a health center. As system developers, we argued that a unique personal identification
number (similar to a Social Security number) should be used to
identify patients. But the doctors argued strongly for a system
based on birth date and name because many patients could not
remember their identification number, or they might be collecting medication for relatives or neighbors. So, we implemented
a simple alternative system in which one could enter a combination of name or birth date, getting a list of the patients who
fulfilled these requirements along with other information, such
as phone number and address. This was not the simple identifier that we had wanted, but it worked in practice. Interesting
enough, today we may have used the formal ID, the personal
identification or the social security number. Over the years, so
many computer systems have required this ID that most persons can recite it offhand (but perhaps not for their neighbor).

The important lesson here is that a computer system does
not work on its own. Most systems have to interface with the
real world, where their success or failure is determined. We
have seen that computers employ the binary system, but no one
will ask users or programmers to use this system today. That is,
the computer systems have to adjust to the world of humans.

This is not always easy to achieve. However, the advantage
is that with modern interface equipment, such as graphical displays, touch screens or mouse positioning, and excellent software packages, one has all the tools necessary to develop good
interfaces.

18.3   Standards

De facto standards emerge, that is, techniques that are established as "standards" because they are used by important systems.

Compared to old-fashioned interfaces with panels, knobs, and buttons, a computer interface offers flexibility. An airplane cockpit is an example. With a physical interface, the most important instruments are placed in front of the pilot. But importance may vary with the situation: preflight check, starting engines, taxiing, before takeoff, takeoff, long distance navigation, landing, and so on. But with computer displays, the relevant instruments can be displayed to the pilot precisely when they are needed. Such a system can also handle exceptions. If there are problems with the starboard engine, all data on this engine can be presented on one of the main displays. Similarly, as ordinary users, we apply this flexibility when we place the application on which we are currently working in front of us, on top of the display.

As we gain more experience using computer systems, de facto standards emerge. For example, we know that a program may be started by clicking on a program icon. We know that we can move files by dragging their icons from one folder to another, and that buttons can be clicked to reveal menus. No organization has formalized most of these standards; rather, popular programs and systems have set them. For example, the GUI (Graphical User Interface) features were first introduced by Xerox Parc research centre,[1] then made popular by Apple on their Macintosh machine, and later used in Microsoft Windows. A similar development today has occurred with touch screens on smartphones. "Standards" are emerging, such as the use of a sliding button to open a laptop, and to move two fingers apart to zoom. (However, patents may restrict the use of some of these best practices.)

Standards allow us to take with us the experience of one system to the other.

With these standards, we can take with us the experience of one system to another. This portable experience is especially the case for Web sites, Apps, and many other programs that are meant to be intuitive, that is, systems that can be used without any training. This is a tough requirement. There are many users, with very diverse backgrounds.

However, with a good understanding of users and their needs, interfaces can be developed that need no training to use. The task must be structured in a reasonable way, and each step simplified by indicating which data is needed. For example, to book a flight, the data needed are the airports of departure and arrival, travel dates, and perhaps a departure time. Input can be

It is, alas, not difficult to find Web sites that violate the basic principles of usability.

simplified by letting the user choose airports from a list and to select dates from a calendar. In this first step, the user identifies available flights; personal details are left until after the user has selected flights. Of course, details on payment, credit card number, and so on, are left until the end, after all information on prices, including extras, has been presented. In many ways, this process mimics the way we booked a ticket in pre-Web times through a travel agency. But with the Web, we are on our own, which means we require very simple-to-use interfaces.

Some Web sites violate these principles, for example, by asking for personal details up front or requiring payment details before the total price has been presented. However, in a very competitive world, these sites will lose customers. With experience, Web "best practices" emerge, and bad sites will have a chance to improve their user interface. The advantage with the Web is that the interfaces are open for everybody; good solutions cannot be hidden from the competition.

Web technology is still not mature. Web user interfaces come in all forms and are often difficult to understand and use. There may be no clear distinction between required and optional data; commands and links may be labeled inappropriately and inconsistently; the user may be asked to provide data that the system already knows; or the system may require special formats for date, names, and addresses. Today, we can go into a brick-and-mortar shop, find the things we want to buy, pay, and then leave. On the Web, many online stores require us to register and provide a lot of personal information. This practice may be useful if we are to become regular customers, but way off the mark if we are one-time shoppers. Companies should be concerned about this practice as well. Tests have shown that a large proportion of potential customers turn away when the user interfaces become too complicated, when they are asked to provide too much data, or when the whole process becomes too cumbersome.

18.4   The Web interface

Interestingly, many companies apparently look at the Web interface as a technical issue, leaving the job to technical experts. Instead, the interface really should be discussed in board meetings because the Web interface is where the customers meet the company, where standards for service levels are set, and where the company profile is presented, just as in physical locations, brochures, or other advertisements. The Web, and any other

The Web interface is not a technical issue, but is the **face of the company** in the electronic world. For many companies, this is the only face.

computer system, should in principle give the same high level of service as with more manual communication. For example, we would not accept that the bank returned our letter because we had used a date format with dots between the numbers instead of slashes, but many Web pages do. Neither would we accept that the travel agent answered "no flights available" to a question; we would expect her to offer alternatives. However, on the Web the "not available" answer is often used.

As we have seen, we cannot expect the same flexibility from a computer system that what we would get from a human. However, it is not difficult to build in at least some basic flexibility, such as decoding different date formats.

Not all systems are meant to be intuitive. Complex graphical packages, engineering systems, even word processors may require training to be used effectively. However, with graphical displays, desktop systems, menus, and help facilities, the systems themselves can help us explore new functions. Modern systems show what they can do through the interface, making commands and data visible.[2] For example, when we choose the "print" command in MS Word, a form is displayed showing all the different options—the form presents what the system can do. Menu- and form-based systems invite exploration. If we make an error or are not satisfied with the results, we can backtrack with the "undo" command.

18.5   New interfaces

In *Hitchhiker's Guide to the Galaxy*, Douglas Adams described how interfaces have changed from pressing buttons and turning dials, via touch sensitive displays, to interfaces where "all you had to do was wave your hand in the general direction of the components and hope. It saved a lot of muscular expenditure, of course, but meant that you had to sit infuriatingly still if you wanted to keep listening to the same program."

Legend has it that everything King Midas touched turned to gold. I have a similar problem when I try to take my ringing smartphone out of my pocket without answering or rejecting the call at the same time. Or when I push the phone to my ear to hear what is being said and disconnect the call when my ear touches this field on the display. On the other hand, the display sometimes rejects my advances; for example, it will not accept the touch from a gloved hand. With novel interfaces that use kinetics, body, and hand movements, we are getting even closer to the situation that Adams described.

Touch-sensitive displays are ideal for many applications, such as surfing the Web, moving through text and photo collections, and for scaling maps. In these cases, the multitouch interfaces, where we can use two fingers, are at their best. However, physical buttons also have their advantages. Pressing a physical button is more explicit than touching the display. The operation can also be performed without looking at the display. For example, with an old fashioned phone it was possible to reject a call without taking the phone out of your pocket. We should therefore expect that future smartphones will come with more physical buttons than those of today.

Similarly, the kinetic interfaces that can recognize body movements may pave the way for a new set of applications, especially for entertainment; however, in many other areas it will be a disadvantage if these movements have any impact on the interface. While science fiction movies have presented speech input to computers for decades, we see that this is used only in very special situations today. That is, there are advantages to using an explicit keyboard, a mouse, and a touch display for communicating with a computer, to retain speech for communicating with humans and to let us scratch our head without the computer recognizing this as a command.

18.6   Help facilities

In practice, **help systems**, often do not provide any help to more experienced users.

Most systems come with extensive help facilities. These may be helpful for the novice, explaining the functionality of the system and "how-to" setups. However, they are often not as helpful when it comes to giving advice for solving specific problems. Help systems simply cannot cover the many different problems than can occur for different configurations of equipment and operating systems, for users with different backgrounds and competence, and for different types of data. But one improvement would be if the help system knew something about the user: The answer that the system gives a novice on a given issue should be very different from what it offers an expert.

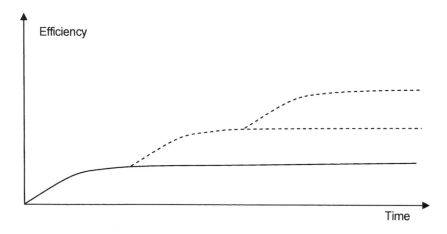

Figure 18.2 Most people use a system at a "convenience" level that is too low.

Most people settle for a "level of convenience" in a system that does not match the system's capabilities, such as using an advanced word processing system as if it were a typewriter. This is illustrated in Figure 18.2. They would be more efficient if they spent some time learning more advanced functions and moving to higher proficiency levels (as illustrated by the dotted lines). Handbooks, courses, and training sessions may be used to elevate users to these higher levels. The system itself can also participate, providing "tip of the day" and help-agents to offer context-dependent advice.

18.7   Usability testing

As with all other types of engineering, user interfaces can be tested before they are offered to real users. The testing can be performed in two distinct phases. First, a test is done to see if the programs work as expected, a phase common to all software engineering. This phase is usually performed by the programmers themselves or by other professionals to find bugs in the system—everything from buttons with no connected actions, code that cannot accept the input that it is given, to errors when connecting to other systems or databases. (We return to program testing in Part 4 on system development.)

The second testing phase is more interesting. Once the system works technically, we need to find out if it works for users. This usability testing can be performed by letting the actual users test the system, or often easier, by recruiting a number of persons to perform the test. Since testing takes time, it is often better to perform these in a lab than in the actual user environments. It is important to select "guinea pigs" with a similar background as the intended users. For Web applications aimed at the general public, we can recruit testers from this group.

Testers will be given a set of tasks to perform. For example, to test the interface of an airline booking system, we may offer tasks such as:

- o You are interested in a round-trip from Pittsburgh International to any airport in New York, leaving on Friday morning and returning Sunday evening.

- o Book a ticket from Washington, DC to Madrid for two persons leaving October 10 and returning October 20.

To see how users perform, we can observe their efforts, or perhaps mount video cameras to capture the interaction. An even more efficient method is to run the program within a test bed where all input is registered.

Independent of the method, these usability tests will find many of the weaknesses in the interfaces, even with only a few testers. However, a fair number of testers are required if we are out to prove something, such as the efficiency of the interface. If professionals made the system specifications, usability requirements may be a part of this, for example, that 90 percent of users should be able to perform a booking within five minutes, or that 98 percent should be able to do so within ten minutes. In these cases, as many as fifty testers may be needed to get a statistical significant result.

Based on the testing, weak points, misunderstandings, and errors will become apparent. Then we need to modify the interface to address these issues. Of course, this will only work if the first version of the interface is inherently good. Testing can only help us "tune" an interface to users needs. If it shows that there are major problems, one would have to start from scratch. However, today we have "standards" for many types of interfaces; in addition to good knowledge of what is needed to accommodate users. However, some important interfaces have not been tested for usability. Two examples are presented in Chapter 21.

When developers are in doubt if users will master a function or a user interface, it seems inefficient to first build a system and then learn later on that it causes problems for users. In these cases, developing a prototype may be helpful, for example, a system with nothing behind the user interface. Usability tests of the prototype will offer valuable information.

18.8   Virtual politeness

Since we now interact with computer systems, perhaps as much as with other humans, we need polite systems.

Computer systems are now an integral part of everyday life. Many of us spend more time on the computer than face to face with other people. Computer systems must be developed to tackle this integration as smoothly as possible. One way to achieve this is to learn from human-to-human communication, which requires politeness to run smoothly.[3]

Many of the polite phrases we use in everyday conversation also have an important use as protocols. We enter a shop and are greeted with a smile from the girl behind the counter. This informs us that we are welcome, but also implies that she has recognized our presence and will serve us as soon as possible. No words need to be interchanged. When meeting people, we say "hello," "*hola*" or "*bonjour*," a polite welcome that is also a code to initialize a conversation. In addition, we emphasize our intentions by using gestures, such as smiles and handshakes. When we leave we say "goodbye," "*adiós*," or "*adieu*," signaling to the other party that we expect our meeting to be at an end.

Without these protocol words, we may miss the start of a conversation, we may not know if our presence is recognized, or fail to see that the other party has more to say before we leave. With gestures, we acknowledge that we receive and understand the other party. Confirmation is given by a nod or by what we say in return. Eye contact is an indication that we (probably) are listening. If we lose eye contact, we expect that the other party may not have heard what we were saying. Giving no response at all would be considered very strange or rude. These protocols are even more important when using the telephone because we cannot see the redundant gestures. Try to avoid the initial "hello" when you take a call next time, and see what happens.

Politeness, both as a form of respect and as a protocol, is as important in the virtual world as in the physical. While we can let technology handle the low-level communication processes when using e-mail, Web forms, or text messages, we must

A drawback with asynchronous communication media is that we do not get an **immediate response.**

explicitly add these functional higher-level "protocols of politeness." As we shall see, this is essential both to show respect for other human beings and to ensure smooth and trouble-free communication.

Asynchronous communication devices have many advantages. We can send e-mail or text messages whenever it suits us, and the receiver can reply whenever it suits her. The drawback is that we do not get any instant acknowledgment that the other party really has received the message as we do in the physical world or on the phone. Therefore, e-mail may cause anxiety. We wonder: Did I send the message; did I have the right address; did they receive it; perhaps it was intercepted by a spam filter; was too big or had enclosed files that were not accepted by their security systems; perhaps there was a technical error? We can check the sent-items box to see that we have done our part, but we have no idea what has taken place at the other end.

Explicit acknowledgment is required, which should be no problem with personal mail. Often we may give an answer immediately, or, if we need more time to give a full answer, a simple reply with a sentence or two can act as an acknowledgment. In more formal situations, politeness is often just a question of setting up the correct routines. For example, every message sent to job@company.com could get an automatic "message received" with a description of how the job application will be handled and when the applicant can expect a full answer. Some companies have routines like these, but many are impolite and do not offer an acknowledgment.

Whatever happens, data entered must never be lost.

Data from customers are often entered in forms, sent to a Web server that uses a back-office system. This setup works fine until the back-office system fails so that the save operation cannot be executed. Still, many Web servers continue to provide the forms, working as if everything were up and running, and thus, leading new users into the trap. Since the error message will first appear after all the data has been entered—when the customer hit the save or continue button—the data entry effort is futile. Frequently, an error message will replace or hide the contents of the form, making it impossible to save even a screen shot of the data. This is especially annoying when the user has used time and effort to collect the data.[4]

In the physical world, we expect to be told up front if our transactions cannot be performed because systems are not working, but few virtual systems are polite enough to do the same. And, of course, this is as simple as letting the Web server check the status of the back-office system before presenting the input form.

Marketing students are taught to speak the customer's language, and interface designers should take this lesson to heart. A computer interface should present only terminology that the user can understand, in the language she has selected. This is not always easy to achieve. Word processors may call it a document instead of the more technical word "file," but in error situations, these programs may still tell the user "file not found." Many Web systems use a confusing terminology, calling it a "booking number" on one page and a "reference number" on the next.

Most Web sites allow the customer to choose a language, but that choice is often inconsistent. When I purchased a PC from Dell, the Web site initiated the process in Norwegian, the technical specifications were presented in English, and the order confirmation came in Swedish. This experience caused me to recollect a strip from Calvin and Hobbes in which Hobbes finds a user manual extremely complex, as it seemed to require competence in many languages to read the whole thing.

One brutal—and arrogant—interface method is to ask questions that cannot be answered. Operating systems do this when a user tries to install programs, plug-ins, or certificates. The warnings may be severe, explaining that data may be lost or the PC may stop to work if the user continues the installation. Still, the user may have initiated the process to access an Internet banking account or to increase the functionality of her PC, and knows that there is no other remedy other than to continue the installation process. We can be glad that we still do not have these systems in cars. Just think what kind of disclaimers and warnings that we would have to go through just to start the vehicle!

System arrogance can also be expressed by asking the user to remember complex sequences, such as passwords or reference numbers. It has been said that usability can be measured as the inverse of the length of the customer identification number that companies provide on invoices, that is, the number that we have to enter when paying bills. Norwegian tax authorities ask me to enter nineteen digits when paying my taxes, this in a population of five million. The tax authority could have received ten thousand payments a day

Use the customer's language in computer systems.

Never ask questions that the users cannot answer.

The user should be in control.

from every person in the world and still have unique IDs for the next three hundred years.

As a guest in a house, we do not rearrange the bookshelves. However, many computer systems love to do this if you give them the chance. When choosing a typical installation of Adobe Acrobat it will insert new menu categories in Microsoft Word and new lines of buttons. These clutter the display and take up valuable space, especially on a laptop where screen real estate is at a premium. An inexperienced user will also have problems removing these items.

Apple has just as bad manners. When installing QuickTime, Apple's video viewer, we automatically get iTunes. This is not a shy program that will hide in a corner on your computer. When installed, it will harass you for questions on updates. We should require a minimum of politeness. Polite systems will ask: Do you want a shortcut on your desktop, a new menu in Word, or automatic updates? At least then we feel we are in control.

Interrupting others is discourteous. We wait until the other party has finished talking or time our interruption as smoothly as possible. This is much more difficult to achieve in the virtual world when context may not be known. While some polite programs understand this, many behave as elephants in a glass store. Messages pop up at the most inconvenient time. We may give a speech using a presentation program and the computer may tell us that new mail has arrived, offer help cleaning the desktop, or worse, require a restart of the computer.

In some situations in the virtual world, a direct interruption is allowed. For example, we appreciate it when the operating system interrupts to warn us that the batteries are running low on our laptops. Nevertheless, as in the real world, the offence of barging in must be balanced with the importance of the message.

Consulting your long-time family doctor, you would be quite astonished if she asked for your name. At some places we expect to be recognized. But only in the movies do they say: "Welcome Mr. Bond—the usual, shaken not stirred." However, polite computer systems can offer some conciliation.

The system should remember data provided in previous "consultations" and not require the user to offer these again.

The airline that you use frequently could show availability of flights between your typical destinations, perhaps already on their home page based on your IP address or a cookie. They should retain all the data that they need and try to seat you in your favorite place automatically. When you call them, their system could retrieve the information needed before they take the call. Thus, we could be met with, "Hello Mr. Olsen, yes, your flight tonight is confirmed."

As customers we seldom experience rudeness in the real, physical world—at least in competitive environments. Often helpful employees are there to offer personal service, a smile, and help whenever needed. This has not come from nowhere. First, most people are polite, but to ensure that customers are treated correctly, companies have standards, offer courses in customer service to their employees, and focus on the importance of politeness.

On the Web or in other virtual worlds, customers are on their own, perhaps with limited experience in using the new technology. The communication channels are more restricted, the system may not know the context, and misunderstandings are not easily resolved. However, from these few examples, we see that programming helpful and polite computer systems is not difficult. As in the real world, when the focus is on service, we can implement systems that reassure instead of frustrate them, that help instead of confuse, that promote efficiency, and that help avoid errors. Since the infancy of computing is over, we must call the companies that do not offer this level of service impolite.

Notes

1   For an interesting story on this research center, see Hiltzik, M. (1999) Dealers of Lightning: Xerox Parc and the dawn of the computer age, HarperCollins, New York.

2   For a more detailed discussion of these issues, see Dix, Finlay, Abowd, Beale (2003) Human-Computer Interaction, 3rd ed., Prentice Hall Europe.

3   Part of this chapter is based on Olsen, K. A. (2011) Programmed politeness, IEEE Computer, July, 2011.

4   I experienced this situation with a tax system in Norway. I collected all the data, made my calculations and entered the result into the tax form. Later on, when I clicked on the save-button, I got an error message from the back-office system. Since the message covered the screen, there was no chance of retrieving the numbers. The system did not offer to store the information in an intermediate location. Apparently, something was seriously wrong with the back-office system, but not with the Web server, which displayed the form again, luring new users into the trap.

    These errors can be reduced or avoided by letting the Web server perform a dummy storage operation on the back-office system to see if these are up and running. And, of course, as a minimum the Web server should offer to store the information until the back-office systems are restarted.

    Some systems do this. While entering data on an insurance policy, I was interrupted by a telephone call that lasted an hour. When returning to the computer, the session had naturally been timed out. However, when starting again, I got the message: "Your previous task was interrupted. Do you want to continue?" That is, the system had saved all the data. They also saved my day.

19 Simplicity

Interfaces for ordinary users should be as simple as possible. A good example is Apple's iPod Shuffle, the music player that came without any buttons on the device itself. With a small control on the ear phone cable one could adjust the volume, and skip the next track. The idea was that the user only put songs on the device that she wanted to hear, so that no selection was needed. Other models have a "click wheel" that offers all the necessary functions, including the ability to rotate the wheel to control volume or to go through menus.

The **simplest interface** is often the best interface, at least for ordinary users.

For ordinary users, the simplest is often the best. A system that the user fully understands and masters can be put to many uses. A good example is spreadsheet systems. The basic principle of a matrix of columns and rows and formulas is quite easy to understand. With some idea of how to define formulas, often supported by an easy-to-use interface, the spreadsheet may be used for very many applications. Sometimes too many! Many use spreadsheet systems for applications that would be better suited for more specialized systems. For example, a spreadsheet may be a good tool for setting up a budget for a new project, but should not be used for routine tasks such as invoicing and accounting. For these applications a spreadsheet that needs user invention is inefficient, and may also be error prone.

19.1 Generic or specialized

Can simplicity go too far?

Sometimes simplicity may go too far. I have problems with the one-button mouse when using an Apple laptop, and find the PC's two-button version very convenient. Here the right button is used to offer a set of commands that are useful in the current setting. For example, clicking with the right mouse button on a file name will offer a list of operations that may be applied to files, such as open, rename and delete. The center scroll wheel is also very convenient when scrolling. That is, while the simple one button device functions well, the more advanced interfaces may be more efficient. Moving to a one-mouse button creates problems. Although Apple users manage with a one-button mouse, in some situations, more complex devices may have their use.

We have this balance between functionality and simplicity in many other areas. There are kitchen tools specialized to cut onions, but most of us still use a knife for this task. The knife is not as efficient as the specialized tools, but can be used for many other operations as well. However, if cutting onions is something that we do often, it may pay to get a tool for just this task. When I perform a small repair job in my home, I use an assortment of tools, all spread out on the floor: several screwdrivers, an electric drill, different drill bits, tweezers, and so on. All are specialized and all are needed for doing a good job efficiently. Some tools are flexible, such as the electric drill, which can take different types of bits.

Generic functions have the advantage that they can be used on any type of data.

This flexibility is much easier to implement in computer systems. For example, a photo may be viewed as such by one program or as a file of binary bits by another. We can perform a large set of operations on files—such as copy, move, rename, and delete—without knowing what they contain. Similarly, we may use the clipboard for any type of data. With a copy (or CTRL-C) command we can put the selected objects into the clipboard, and paste (CTRL-V) these into any another location. In one movement I can use CTRL-C and CTRL-V to copy an account number from a Web page into the Internet banking system; in the next, I can use the same commands to copy text between two documents. Users who have learned to utilize the clipboard thus have a convenient generic device that can be used in many situations.

Specialized functions have the advantage of being very effective.

However, these generic functions cannot perform any task. In many cases we need specialized commands. These may be on a very simple level, or more advanced. The advantage with simple systems is that they often may be used intuitively—no training is necessary. For example, there are many simple programs that we can be used for simple editing of photos, for example, to crop the image, make it lighter or darker, and change contrast. These may fulfill many users' needs. But professionals may find it pays to have a more advanced system, even if this requires some training. More advanced functions will make the professional more effective in the long run and enable him to perform tasks that would be impossible or very difficult using a simpler system.

19.2   User in control

Should the user have access to the **underlying file structure**?

I have a printer at home that asks me to perform a test print, with no option to cancel this request. And, if I submit and start this test it will not work, since the color ink cartridge is empty. I would be satisfied to use the printer as a scanner and to print black and white documents, but the printer will not accept this. It keeps asking for the print test, and ignores all other input. Yes, I can accept a warning that there is no color ink, but not that the printer takes full control.[1]

At one time, our IT center installed a Norwegian version of an operating system on my new PC, instead of the English version that I prefer. When trying to install the similar English version, the system gave the error message that this version of the system was already installed. While a more modest system would offer a warning and leave it to the user to continue, this system took control and blocked the user's action.

There is a tendency today, in the operating systems for PCs, tablets and mobile phones, to take away control from users. One way this is done is to hide the underlying file structures. The idea is to simplify by hiding "technical details." But there are situations where the user needs to work on a more basic level. Modern computer-based devices, such as PCs, phones, and tablets, are designed for wide markets. Since these devices are acquired to make our lives simpler and perhaps more interesting, we do not want to spend a lot of time learning to use them. Interfaces should be intuitive. The techniques that are applied to attain this goal go in two opposite directions: hiding and visualizing.

By hiding technical details, we can reduce the number of objects and processes that an ordinary user needs to know. With visualization, we can represent the more important objects so that the user can handle them. Manufacturers of computer devices, operating systems, and application software have used these principles of hiding and visualizing for decades. Low-level technical parts, ASCII codes, disk track and sector numbers, program code, and system files are hidden. At the same time, care has been taken to visualize more high-level objects such as programs, files, and folders. Based on ideas from Xerox Parc in the late 1970s, the user is allowed to start a program by clicking on an icon or to copy a file by "dragging" the file icon from one folder to the other; that is, to operate directly on the visual representations of the underlying objects. The aim is not only to make interfaces intuitive, but also to empower the user. With control of the data, she can apply the device to all sorts of tasks.

An explorer program, or a file manager, becomes crucial. This program offers the user an overview of all data resources on the PC, often with folders visualized as a tree-structure.

Simplicity can be obtained by hiding and visualizing.

By hiding technical details, we can reduce the number of objects and processes that an ordinary user needs to know.

A file manager gives the user control over all data.

However, on modern devices, from mobile phones to tablets, we see a tendency to hide files and folders. Perhaps the aim is to make things simpler by taking hiding a step further, using application-dependent file locations. For example, when the user takes a picture, the mobile phone's operating system will store the image in a default location. Most users will not be aware of where. The user views the pictures through a photo viewer that shows the contents of the hidden folders. Some devices even come without an explorer program. Where folder and file names are created by the system, an explorer view will be of little or no use anyway. But this development may be counterproductive. As we shall see, there are many situations were an explorer program is necessary to offer the user full control over the device.

Many user-oriented interfaces that try to hide the underlying systems break down in error situations.

The user-oriented interfaces that are built on top of the underlying hardware and software break down whenever a device error occurs. It may be an unreadable disk, a corrupted USB device, a change in the underlying file structure, or lack of disk space. That is, the command, "open document" may result in a "file not found" message. Since we cannot build hardware and software that never fails, it is better to require a basic understanding of important concepts up front than to confuse the user whenever an error occurs. Knowledge of the basic technology is also required to comprehend why a backup is needed. Even when backup is automated, for example over a wireless network, the user would still need to understand that no backup will be performed if the network is unavailable.

A user may have several devices, such as a phone, tablet, camera, and a USB key. At some time, she may also buy a new type of device—X. All can be connected to a PC. The traditional strategy has been to present these devices as generic disks, with similar folder structures as for internal devices. The user can then view this structure through the explorer program, and may use standard desktop operations to move or copy files between the devices. This will also work for device type X. The advantage of letting a user work on low-level objects such as files and folders is that on this level one may use a large set of "generic" functions, such as copying, moving, and deleting. Copying an image is of course similar to copying a document, a spreadsheet, or any other data type. By viewing external devices as generic disks instead of cameras, phones, or music players we can perform similar operations on these, for example moving files, without learning new specialized

New devices can be connected and presented as generic disks.

operations. Of course, any new device—a GPS navigator, an e-book reader, or even device X above—can be handled in the same way.

The alternative, that many modern operating systems apply, is to let an application pertinent to the device type take care of the connection. For example, when a user connects a Nikon D90 camera to a PC running XP, the following alternatives are presented as default: view, edit, and print. But most users would want to copy the pictures to a folder on the PC.

Automatic **synchronization** may go out of hand.

On the iPad, Apple uses synchronization as the default mechanism. When an iPad is connected to a PC, the software will automatically synchronize data such as photos or documents between the two devices. But synchronization is a powerful mechanism that can have dramatic effects. The user may not want to transfer all the images from the PC to the tablet; there may not even be storage space on the tablet for everything. Therefore, synchronization may easily result in an "out of memory" error, leaving the average user in a situation that she cannot recover from. If the user has more than one PC, for example, an office and a home computer, she may get into real trouble. At home all photos from the home computer will be synchronized with the iPad. But if she later connects the iPad to her office computer, for example to synchronize documents, all pictures on the iPad that are not on the office PC will be deleted.[2]

To simplify and hide details, the user's aims must be predictable. This will be the case for a car, but not for a flexible computer system where users can download new applications, modify software, add Apps, and so on. Then it becomes important that the user control the data objects. For example, the owner of a small bakery that offers home delivery may get orders by text messages. The default sorting of messages that his phone offers, with the most recent message at the top, is not what he needs. Instead he may want to have messages ordered on delivery date, or by address. He could have developed an App to move the data to an order entry system, but this will also require access to the data objects. The manufacturers of the mobile phone probably never have envisioned such a use of their device. However, with an overview of the data—the text messages—our baker can use the device for his special purpose.

Even the ordinary user may encounter problems when the data structure is hidden. Most mobile phones offer only one

Even the ordinary user may encounter problems when the data structure is **hidden**.

folder for storing incoming messages. This works fine with a few messages, but navigation becomes difficult when these run into high numbers. Users also will encounter problems when they employ their phone as a camera. With just a few images sequential storing works fine, but when the number of images runs into the hundreds or thousands, user-controlled structures are required.

A user can be amazed when her PC has noted the calendar event that she entered on her mobile phone, when the phone can provide her with a weather forecast for the current location at any time, or when she can "walk" down a street using Google. Many of these application-oriented tasks can be automated and the data hidden with little cost to the average user. In other cases, we have to take the "magic" away. Simplification is important, but should not be taken to the point that users are less effective. Jakob Nielsen said, "Using the system changes the users, and as they change they will use the system in new ways."[3] That is, users evolve with the system, in fact, users and systems co-evolve. Systems may be used in ways that designers never dreamed of. Thus, it can be a good investment for a computer user to learn some fundamentals about the technology. With access to data through an explorer program, users are able to conquer the world; but hiding the data may kill innovation.

Why do companies that have excelled in usability hide files and folders, even when the arguments for visibility are compelling?

Why do companies that have excelled in usability hide files and folders, even when the arguments for visibility are compelling? The professional answer may be that they expect that large customer groups will use the devices only in the most straightforward ways (as planned, restraining the need for flexibility); that users have limited amounts of data (so memory or disk overflow will not occur); that tablets and phones are connected to only one PC (to avoid synchronization problems); that backup routines can be performed automatically, and that users will contact service personnel whenever an error occurs. But, there may be another reason. With access to the underlying data structure, users can exploit standard formats for images, documents, and for all other data types. It does not matter which camera was used to capture the images or on which computer system they are stored. Users are free to move the data to their next PC or mobile phone. But if files are hidden, they can be stored in proprietary formats, thus making it more convenient for the user to continue to use devices from only one.

19.3   Input free user interfaces

The **simplest interfaces** do not require any input from the user.

Some time ago, I stayed at a large airport hotel with six floors and as many elevators, all in the same area. As I left the reception area and approached the elevators, one stood ready with the door open for me to enter and press the button for my room floor. Later as I left my room to go to dinner, again, I found an elevator waiting. By a simple addition to the elevator control program, this hotel was able to offer guests a convenient service—an elevator standing by at each floor.

With some extension, this idea can be used when elevators are busy or when there are fewer elevators than floors. A "here" command for bringing an elevator to the reception floor could be executed automatically when the receptionist hands a keycard to a guest. The same action could be performed when guests retrieve the keycard as they leave their room. Thus, a better service can be offered just by using contextual data. This is the ideal interface—one that does not require any input but takes its cues from the data that are available.

Of course, if we stop to think, there are many examples of input-free user interfaces. Most of us tell the time just by looking at the watch that we carry—no input is needed. Signs are similar; they tell the story without a button click. The dashboard is another example, it gives the data that is necessary for driving, such as the speed, and the amount of fuel left.

The advantage of these interfaces is that the "cost" of using these may be negligible. These examples contrast sharply with many current systems that we navigate by button clicks or by touching a screen, and in which we have to provide search terms and other data by typing or giving voice commands. While touch screens and voice commands make navigation easier, the simplest systems will always be those that do not require any input at all.

While a watch can only tell the time and a sign is a very static thing, input-free user interfaces will have better possibilities on a smartphone, where the systems can deduct what information the user needs from background data and her location. We return to these issues in Chapter 63, where we shall see that the computer can offer interesting data to a user, based on some knowledge of context.

19.4   Changing user interfaces

With experience and a good interface, the tool seems to disappear.

Have you ever watched an experienced operator handle an excavator? The machine seems to be a part of his body. We get some of the same feeling when driving a car; it feels like the steering wheel and pedals become extensions of our own limbs. To achieve this "nirvana state," we need an excellent interface that gives us full control. The excavator has levers and joysticks that are natural to use. While the first automobiles were steered with a tiller, the steering wheel was soon introduced, a natural control for making a turn. Since the basic functions are similar for all cars, we can use our experience for any model. Similarly, the handling of an excavator is simplified by interface standards, ensuring that an operator can move directly from one machine to the other, retaining the practice part. However, in order to reach this stage of operation, one will have to build experience, sometimes by taking lessons, but always by hours of training.

Studies of people using tools show that control of the tool is partly determined by the interface, but also by what we can call routine or practice. The practice part is how we use the tool. It is often idiosyncratic, influenced by the functionality or the design of the tool itself, but also by previous experience and customs. If we use a tool often, we perform tasks efficiently. Often, with a good tool and experience in using it, we may come to the stage where the tool disappears. The operator of the excavator does not have to think about how to get the desired action, neither do we when driving.

Computer applications are similar. Most of us send e-mails, write documents, chat with friends, enter data into a spreadsheet, make a call from a smartphone, and scan photos using computer equipment, all without thinking about the tool. The advantage is that we can fully concentrate on the task. Initially, of course, we had to explore the user interface and at worst read a user manual. But with experience, we reach the stage at which the tool becomes invisible. At this stage, we become very efficient, when all mental resources can be focused on the task; for example, not focusing at the word processor at all, but solely on writing the document. In some cases, a good tool may even help us attain the mental stage of operation that psychologists call *flow*, where we are fully immersed in an activity.

A good interface may help us attain the mental stage of operation that psychologist call **flow**, where we are fully immersed in an activity.

As professionals, we do not want to see the interface; we want the **invisible tool**.

Change in an interface may come at a high cost.

Modern graphical user interfaces, with forms, command lines and icons, help us reach this stage—until they change, that is! While the steering wheel has been with us since 1898, the current user interface of a very important tool, the word processor, has only been around since 2007, at least for those of us who use Microsoft Word. In that year, Microsoft introduced its "Fluent User Interface," which represented a dramatic change for its Office package. It had good reason for making this change. When users were asked what they missed from previous versions of Office, many mentioned functions that were already there. The aim of the new interface was to present, in a better way than before, what the system could do. The drawback was that every function was moved to a new location. As professionals, we had to accept that part of our practice and routine with this tool had disappeared. The invisible tool suddenly became very apparent and obtrusive.

Location is an important organizing tool. We find things—a book on the shelf, a document in the office—because we remember where we put it. The importance of location is manifested in keyboard layout. Even if the Dvorak keyboard layout has proved more efficient, nearly all keyboards have the traditional QWERTY layout. The cost of changing is too great. With larger displays and graphical user interfaces, location also becomes important on the computer screen.

Change may come at a high cost. When using a new interface, we fall out of our streamlined processes. Suddenly we have to stop and think. Where is the print command; how do we select a special paste; how do we change the automatic save options? Commands that were embedded in practice in the old version, which could be performed with a subconscious mouse click, now require attention. Suddenly we concentrate more on how to use the new interface than on what we are writing. Instead of devoting all of our mental resources to the writing task, we have to spend time searching the interface. The fluent workflow is broken, and efficiency is reduced. It is as if someone had removed the steering wheel.

A paradigm of user interface design is that recognition is better than recall. Microsoft would probably argue that the new Office interface advocates for recognition. This may be true, and may be an advantage for a novice user. However, assuming that the user already knows how to perform a task, the display of visual commands will be superfluous. As professionals, we do not want to see the interface; we want the invisible tool. In some cases, this is achieved by giving shortcut commands, such as CTRL-P to print; in others, by subconsciously clicking on the right button.

My Nokia phone requested an important software update. However, after the update, all icons were changed. The new ones may be cooler, but now I have problems finding the right applications. The icons may have changed on the screen, but my memory has retained their old versions. If you want to annoy your customers, this is a good way of doing it. Apple uses the same scheme. The first iPad came with a side button that was used to lock the display in landscape or portrait mode, turning the rotate function on and off. In newer versions of the software, this button has a very different function—it controls the sound. This change was performed automatically with a new update of the software. After many months, I still try to use this button as it was first intended.[4]

Is this just conservatism? Have we stagnated in our old-fashioned patterns and customs and become unwilling to learn anything new? Perhaps, but we do welcome new technology and new user interfaces in many other areas. The mobile phones that we use today are very different from those we had a few years ago. We are using touch tablets for reading e-mail and browsing the Web. In all these cases, we have to conform to a new interface. We even accept that there are situations when we have to accept a dramatic change in the interface, such as when we get new solutions to old problems. For example, we have accepted that the choke lever in many cars has disappeared, and many people now drive cars with automatic transmissions without gear shifts. Graphical displays or touch screens come with new interfaces, but in these cases the disadvantages of having to learn something new are surpassed by the advantages of the new technology.

While the new software is installed on top of previous versions and replaces them, the new "practice" is installed next to the old in our long-term memory. So, in addition to using unnecessary memory, which we don't have a lot of in the first place, we have two competing versions in the brain. At some time, we expect the current version to dominate, but this will not happen until we have made numerous mistakes. We experience something similar when we move into a new apartment. Again and again we pull out the wrong drawer, go to the wrong room, or look for a light switch in the wrong place. Several psychological experiments support this view.

While the new software is installed on top of previous versions, replacing them, the new "practice" is installed next to the old in the user's **long-term memory**.

Our previous experience produces what is called a schematic intrusion. This may be unavoidable when we move to a new apartment, but usually we have something to counterbalance the cost of changing the "interface." We know experienced computer users who go to great lengths to avoid these costs, such as running virtual machines just to retain the old interface of an operating system. This method squanders a considerable amount of system memory, but saves the user's human memory. (I must admit that this book was written using the 2003 version of Microsoft Word.)

We may feel that the tool developers—Microsoft, Apple and the like—are overly focused on making things new and exciting when they present a new version. New and exciting may be a good strategy for new users, but most users these days are experienced. As professionals, we are not interested in the tools per se, but in how we can use them to perform tasks. Is it not the same as with a new car, when we may be fascinated by design and new functions. Even in the case of a car, most of these brand-oriented parts are distinguished from the functional parts. For example, we can rent a car and drive away immediately, perhaps using the car for days without noticing the brand or model. For new versions of software products, we will be thankful for all improvements and new functions, but please do not violate the practice part! Every time a change is inflicted on practice, the tool asks for attention. These interruptions should be kept to a minimum.

There are two solutions. One is to use continuous improvement, which is Amazon's approach. It has brought its customers along from the very first, primitive, text-based interface in 1994 to the advanced interface of today. Most users welcome new functionality and improvements, but developers must take care to let them follow along. The other solution is to let users retain the look and feel of the old interface.

Does this imply that the world will never change? Clearly, we must accept new tools with new interfaces whenever there is a significant change of technology. At one time, we may have had experience using a typewriter, but we cannot and should not take this experience with us into a word processing system. However, in these cases, when the new system is quite different from the old, we will not confuse the two. Experience with each will be stored in our long-term memory, but because of the disparity in usage patterns, these will not conflict.

> As professionals, we are not interested in the tools per se, but in how we can use them to **perform tasks**.

19.5   Discussion

We have introduced simplicity as one way to create easy-to-use interfaces. But attaining simplicity is not easy. Apple made many prototypes and used word-class designers and engineers to design the iPods and iPhones. What is important is to focus on the user and try to address both what the user needs and how to provide these needs. I use the verb "need" instead of "want" because when it comes to new technology, users may not always be able to express what they want. Understanding the user is one clue to a good design, but we also must know the technological limitations and possibilities. In the design of the first iPod, Apple used a small disk developed by Sony, producing a small, simple to use device that could store "a thousand songs."

But simplicity can be taken too far. In the long run it may be in the users' interest to get powerful tools that can provide an advanced and efficient experience. The systems should still hide unimportant details, but not hide the underlying data structure. Knowledge of this structure, such as folders and files, may help the user in error situations, such as when a backup is needed, and also to help her to see new possibilities.

Notes

1   This subchapter is based on Olsen, K. A., Malizia, A. (2012) Interfaces for the ordinary user – can we hide too much?, Communications of the ACM, vol 55, no 1. January 2012.

2   More advanced users will recognize that there is a possibility to set up synchronization. But again, this requires a basic understanding of folders and files.

3   Nielsen, J. (1993) Usability Engineering. Academic Press, San Diego, CA.

4   It is possible to manually set the function of this button, but many users will not be aware of this.

20 Case: Flexible User Interfaces

Is the current system **flexible** enough, that is, can it fulfill all our needs?

We have seen that with the Internet and the Web, the "terminal" can be moved into our homes, allowing us to directly access databases of any kind without going through intermediates. In practice, these business-to-consumer applications have been implemented by building front ends to the old legacy systems. Is this enough? Let's try to answer this question using airline booking as an example. [1]

Many customers who go to the Web to make a booking may be flexible regarding dates and times, where to go, and even if to go. However, the interfaces offered today expect detailed and specific data and do not account for this flexibility. This was not a problem when travel agents, who had a good overview of flights and fares, handled bookings, but flexibility is a problem when the ordinary user is performing the task. We would like Web services to offer the same kind of service as the human travel agent.

Current interfaces allow users to select from lists, choose dates from a calendar, and pay by credit card, just by button clicks and by filling in forms. Anyone with a minimum of computer and Internet experience can perform the process. This works for simple closed request, one that can be mapped directly into formalized terms such as dates, airports, and flights. However, the interfaces break down for the more complex closed requests, in which the customer is flexible with attributes such as destination, and often dates. That is, current systems cannot handle the more open requests that cannot be mapped directly into the formalized terms offered by the Web interface. These are the cases in which the intermediate travel agent used her knowledge and experience to aid the customer.

For example, a request to the intermediate, the travel agent, may be to find an "inexpensive weekend trip from Pittsburgh to New York." Initially the agent can expand this open request by asking the customer what type of hotel—quality and location—he is interested in and on which dates he may wish to go. The agent may use her experience to suggest times of the year when bargain tickets are more readily available, or to suggest airlines that offer discount fares. She may ask what he wants to see in the city, and may even recommend Washington, DC as an alternative if he is interested in taking the kids to museums and benefitting from good weekend bargains at hotels.

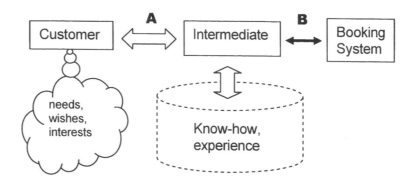

Figure 20.1. Booking tickets through an intermediate (a travel agent).

Thus, the agent formalizes the customer's open request, as shown in Figure 20.1. While the first part (A), between the customer and the intermediate can be open or closed the second part (B) must be closed, formalized to the level of the B2C system. In this process the intermediate will use her know-how and experience, illustrated as a "database," to aid the user. Thus A = "inexpensive weekend trip from Pittsburgh to New York" may be replaced by B = "Search flights 04/12, return 04/14, Pittsburgh-Washington, DC; Washington, DC Hotels 04/12-14."

Current systems support only the case in which all customer data are closed, and most systems support only the simplest of these. The open part has disappeared; the customer himself must formalize request into the terms required. When the customer does not know exactly what he is interested in, the limited flexibility of the B-part becomes a serious drawback. Note that the limitations of the B-part were seldom a problem for the human travel agent. At this point in the process, she would have used her experience to pinpoint the alternatives. She then uses the system to check out availability, to get detailed prices and to perform the actual booking. The limitations first become apparent when we remove the more open part that occurred between the customer and the travel agent.

The customer can work around some of these limitations by trying all alternatives, and then choosing the "best" one. Through extensive searching it may be possible to accumulate some of the know-how and experience of the agent, at least with regard to the customer's special needs and wishes.

However, without the travel agent's experience, the task can be a tedious job without any guarantee of a satisfactory result. The customer will not only have to check out various combinations of locations and dates, but also will have to organize the data returned.

We could try to replace the travel agent by a "virtual intermediate," an "intelligent" system that could embody the knowledge of the travel agent. Here, however, we shall see that by viewing the booking system also as an information system, many of the problems that ordinary travelers meet on the Web may be resolved. The task of the information system will be to provide the user with a general picture that will help with decision making. This overview may be offered based on data from the customer. By allowing him to select a range of alternatives—a range of destinations, a range of departure dates—and to limit the scope by setting constraints—latest return Sunday night, any weekend except—the system can find the best alternatives with extensive searching.

For broader queries, we will have to formalize the intermediate's informal knowledge. For example, to answer a request as to "a place suitable for children," we need a value for this attribute for all locations. This could be set manually, such as with a star ranking, but that will be a major task. However, there are alternative ways to retrieve these data.

Let's use a scenario to describe the requirements for more flexible Web interfaces. Say Joan lives in London and has a friend in Berlin. In her last letter, her friend invited Joan to come for an extended weekend. Joan has some flexibility in her job and can leave London on any plane later than 4:00 p.m. on a Thursday as long as she can return Sunday night, alternatively leaving on a Friday and returning Monday. She tells the system that she can go any weekend in the next six months. Based on these data, the system should immediately give her choices of fares (minimum fare, average economy fare), departure times, arrival times, and so on for different weekends through the next six months. This information tells Joan that she will get the best offer if she takes a Thursday to Sunday trip in October, and that the fares are within her limit. Some current systems can handle part of this flexibility, for example, telling her when she will be able to get bargain fares, but will not be able to handle her alternatives for when to leave.

In the most open case, the user may go to the Web system with "travel" as his only need. However, even the human travel

---

What we need is a system that performs all the tasks that were previously handled by the human intermediate.

At least parts of previous open or unformalized knowledge can be formalized.

agent would be astonished if this were the only specification the user could give. In most cases, the customer will be able to specify more, wishes, destinations, dates, and price ranges.

For example, destination may be given as the name of a city, but also may be more broadly specified as a set of cities, or "a place in the sun," "the Caribbean," a "ski resort." In some cases, there may be no destination, such as when the user simply specifies a "cruise." Further, dates may be specified by day/month/year, by names of days ("leaving on Friday," "returning Sunday"), or left out altogether ("a one-week holiday"). Accommodation may be specified as the name of a hotel, a hotel chain, a class of hotel ("three star"), or a maximum price ("up to $100 a night").

The specification of these requirements and wishes should be offered to the system up front. Because many of the needs would fall into clear categories, this entry process could be performed using a form or by a wizard.[2] Here, the users could indicate places that they wanted to see, for example by checking out the various locations. To simplify, the system should also be able to group locations, such as major cities, historic sites and resort locations. In addition, or as an alternative, the users could select what they are interested in seeing or doing from an alternative list. Here a user may check out "theaters" and "art exhibitions," while another is interested in "swimming" and "scuba diving."

Today, at least some of the Web interfaces offer some degree of flexibility.

Some of the current Web interfaces allow for flexibility regarding dates, for example with the possibility of trying the week ahead or the week after. Ideally the user should be able to specify any possible pattern. In the interface this can be specified by indicating interesting dates in a calendar, by specifying an interval of interests (from/to or next three months) and by setting departure and return days.

By filling out such a form or running through a wizard, the interface tries to simulate the conversation that goes on between the customer and the human travel agent, that is, the phase in which the agent tries to get an idea of what the customer's interests really are. As we have seen, this can imply that the agent offers different alternatives to what the user had initially considered (Washington, DC as an alternative to New York). Of course, this is more difficult to do in the more formal setting of a computer system, but can be partially implemented by letting the user distinguish between requirements and wishes. For example, the user may offer departure, arrival date, and a major city in Europe as requirements, specifying that London is only a wish. That is, the user may accept other destinations than London as long as the requirements are followed.

This can be implemented by letting the system perform a search based on the user's initial data. Since this may encompass a high degree of flexibility, in the worst case all destinations and all dates, major resources in the form of fast servers and efficient databases will be required. Although such a system may seem to be a major undertaking, already search engines such as Google are able to do this on the open Web. The trick is, of course, to gather as much information as possible ahead of time and store the indexes (the inverted database) on fast servers. Compared to Web engines, the booking system has the advantage that it searches in more formalized databases; the disadvantage is that updated information is needed. However, in any query, cut-off values can be used to simplify the searching.

The examples above used formalized data, expressed as locations, dates, and so on. However, if we return to the travel agency situation, the customer also can provide unformalized or open data—asking for a "good hotel," "a place suitable for families," "close to the beach," or "suitable for the elderly." In these cases the human travel agent will utilize her knowledge and experience to find an accommodation that fulfills the user's needs.

On the Web, such request needs to be formalized, such that the system can match the request with the information in the databases. The formalization can be performed by the customer ("not more than two hundred yards from the beach"), by the providers ("family hotel") or by an unofficial or official organization ("three-star hotel," "lifts, handicap access"). However, in practice it may be difficult to get such data for all different types of hotels. Customer's reviews are a good option. A Web-based travel agency may invite customers to offer a review after the trip. Many sites do this today, but the reviews would be more useful if they were formalized to a higher degree. This could be done by letting the traveler click on boxes, for example, marking the hotel as close to the beach. Such review systems are open to possible fraud—a hotel owner enlists family and friends to give excellent reviews—but this problem may be reduced if only those who have actually made a trip to submit a review.

Why should the user need to perform **many searches**? It seems better that these can be performed automatically by the computer systems.

In addition we can get interesting statistics from the system. Where do families with small children go, to which locations and to which hotels? Where do the elderly go? To which places do travelers return most often? This valuable data can be provided to the customer as additional information to close the open case. Such a system would be similar to the "customers that bought this book also bought" functionality of Internet bookstores.

Flexibility and some methods to handle the more open data are especially important in booking systems, as users may not know exactly what they want. However, the same functionality and the same methods described here will be useful in any other situation in which the customer is flexible—anything from online shopping, to queries, to real estate systems.

In addition to the clear advantages for users, a more flexible system offers benefits to providers as well. If I use today's inflexible systems, I have to choose a destination for my weekend trip. When I type "London" the system cannot offer me trips to Berlin. But London may not be a requirement. If I could say "major city in Europe" instead, the system may offer me a bargain trip to a destination where there are plenty of available seats and hotel rooms. That is, there is a cost to requiring the customer to give detailed specifications.

Notes

1 This chapter is based on Olsen, K. A., Malizia, A. (2005). Flexible User Interfaces for B2C Systems, Using Booking as a Case Study, Proceedings HCI 2005, Las Vegas, USA, 25-28.07.

2 A wizard will aid the user through a process, asking questions, let the user provide input, and adjust the process to the user's needs.

21   Bad Systems

The breakthrough, simple-to-use technology and applications that apply touch screens and wireless technology may give us the impression that all systems are up to this standard. Today, the knowledge of system development and usability is high enough that it should be possible to produce only excellent systems. Since many applications—nearly everything on the Web—is open to all, we also have the ability to learn (or steal) interface ideas from others.

Still, there are exceptions, and this chapter presents two cases. The first is taken from a much-used Internet banking system in which a customer managed to type an incorrect account number, thus transferring a large amount to the wrong person. Initially this was viewed as an error of the user, who had to take full responsibility. But, as we shall see, the fault was in the interface.[1]

The second case is an example of an employee service system (ESS), a system that allows employees to service their own needs, typing in travel expenses, overtime, and so on. This system requires users to spend significantly more time on simple administrative tasks than they did using the previous paper-based system. Interestingly, this system managed to do everything wrong, from the aims of the system to the details in the user interface. It is an excellent case for what not to do.[2]

While one cannot generalize from two cases, they are both examples of the low dissemination in development environments of basic concepts of human-computer interaction, or of the unprofessionalism of many organizations.

21.1   Case 1: The $100,000 Keying Error

An ordinary bank customer keyed one digit too many in an account number, and $100,000 was sent to the wrong account.

An ordinary bank customer, Grete Fossbakk, used Internet banking to transfer a large amount to her daughter. She keyed one digit too many into the account number field, inadvertently sending the money to an unknown person. This individual managed to gamble away nearly $100,000 before the police confiscated the remainder. The case received extensive media coverage in Norway. The Minister of Finance criticized the bank's user interface and requested new and improved Internet banking regulations. Suddenly, the risk to Internet banking had become apparent to both the government and ordinary citizens.

Confirmation of the final transaction did not help.

Clearly, the user made a slip. She also had the chance to correct the typo before she hit the confirm button. However, the system had every opportunity to catch her mistake, yet it did not. The system's developers had neglected to build in a simple check that would detect if the input were erroneous.

This case raises questions about what the minimum validation procedures from a banking system developed for ordinary users should be. It also challenges system designers to help users avoid such errors.

Today's users operate alone in front of a computer, with intermediates and colleagues replaced by computer systems. This new reality makes it important to have interfaces that can offer as good as—or even better—error detection than found in previous manual systems. This case is illuminating because the Internet system Fossbakk employed when making her fatal mistake was one common to a large group of Norwegian banks. Reviewing this case provides insight into the types of typos that users make, the psychology behind "confirmation," and the pitfalls inherent in many Web-based transaction systems.

Fossbakk's daughter's account number was 71581555022, but she inserted an extra 5 and keyed in 715815555022. The user interface accepted only eleven digits in this field (the standard length of a Norwegian account number), thus truncating the number to 71581555502. The last digit is a checksum based on a modulo-11 formula. This will detect all single keying errors and errors where two consecutive digits are interchanged. Inserting an extra 5 changed both the ninth and tenth digits.

The average checksum control will catch only 93 percent of the cases in which such errors occur. For Fossbakk, the final eleven-digit number was a legal account number. However, only a small fraction of all legal account numbers are in use. Further, the chance of mistyping the account number so that it benefits a dishonest person without income or assets is overwhelmingly low in a homogeneous country such as Norway. Our user was thus extremely unlucky. The person who received her $100,000 transaction and kept the proceeds has been sentenced to prison, but this does little to help Fossbakk get her money back.

Fossbakk took the case to the Norwegian Complaints Board for Consumers in Banking,[3] which handles disputes between consumers and banks. The board has two representatives for the consumers and two from the banks, with a law professor as

The **complaints board for consumers in banking** found that the user had made an error and that she was to blame.

The **banking interface** changed the (illegal) twelve-digit number into a (legal) eleven-digit account number.

Can we prove that the user typed one digit too many?

chair. In a three-to-two vote, Fossbakk lost. The chair voted for the bank, arguing that "she made an error and has to take responsibility." He also regretted that Norwegian regulations set no limit for a consumer's loss in these cases, as there would have been if Fossbakk had lost her debit card.

Fossbakk took the case to court, backed by the Norwegian Consumer Council.[4] She argued that she typed twelve digits and that the bank system should have given an error message in this case, instead of ignoring all typed digits after the first eleven. She acknowledged she would have no case if only eleven digits had been typed. The bank argued that she cannot prove by any measure of probability that she keyed twelve digits. They further stated that there cannot be different rules of responsibility depending on the number of digits given. Finally, they stressed that she confirmed the $100,000 transaction.

At this point, I was called in as an expert witness for Fossbakk. In my opinion, and I should expect that of most other computing professionals, a system should give an error message when the customer types a too-long number. Clearly, such a test can be inserted with a minimum of effort. In fact, The Financial Supervisory Authority of Norway has required all banks to implement this functionality based on the experience from this case.

Reasonably, we could argue that the bank showed negligence when developing the user interface in question. However, can we prove, beyond doubt, that Fossbakk keyed twelve digits? Since any digits beyond eleven were stripped from the HTML form, no information log exists to show us what happened.

To get an answer, we decided to get our own data by implementing an "Internet bank simulator," a simple interface that had the same look and feel as the system Fossbakk used. Students from a college and some high schools were engaged to enter transactions. After removing some outliers, this experiment yielded data on about 1,800 transactions.

Our student testers got 124 account numbers wrong, 7 percent of the transactions.[5] In 29 percent of the cases with a wrong account number, the number ran too long. In half the cases where this happened, students made the same error as Fossbakk, inserting an extra digit in a sequence of two or more identical digits. Of the abbreviated numbers, the modulo-11 test captured all but three. That is, of the nearly 1,800 transactions, three (0.2 percent) would have passed the banking interface's error-detection routines. Multiply this by the nearly 200 million Internet transactions performed each year in Norway, and we see that this small percentage hides a massive problem. In an improved interface, with a "too long" check, along with the modulo-11 routine, all errors made in our test would have been captured. Given these statistics, it seems nonchalant to code software that lacks a detect-too-long number.

Since none of the people who entered an extra digit or missed one managed to finish with an eleven-digit number by making yet another error, we can state with high probability that Fossbakk entered a twelve-digit account number.

This leaves us with the argument that she confirmed a $100,000 transfer to the wrong account—as did the students in 124 of our test cases. In addition, for every tenth transaction, the simulator replaced the typed number with a similar-looking number before confirmation. For example, it replaced the number 70581555022 with 70581555502. In only 5 out of the 178 cases, 2.8 percent, where this was done, did the users recognize the error and correct the number.

> We should expect that a banking interface would be able to aid the user in **avoiding errors**.

It appears that most people perform the inspection while keying, not when the whole number is displayed on screen. In many ways, this is efficient. While keying, we can concentrate on one digit at a time, and after keying we have a large number. If this seems correct, we hit the "confirm" button.

Psychologist Donald A. Norman explained this behavior in his book, *Psychology of Everyday Things*.[6] Here, a user confirmed deletion of his "most important work." According to Norman, the user confirms the action, not the file name. Thus, the "confirm" part of the transaction, while having some legal implications, has a minimal effect on detecting errors.

Like many new IT applications, Internet banking is effective. As users, we enjoy reduced costs and 24/7 availability. However, transferring real money based on instructions from possibly inexperienced humans who might slip up means we must look to the system for help. Developers must require that it intercept as many errors as possible. If Fossbakk had used the manual system instead—by writing a letter to her bank requesting the transaction—no responsible employee would have removed the twelfth digit of the account number in hopes this would correct the error.

We should expect more. The banking system could offer the account owner's name as confirmation when an account number is entered. In cases where this conflicts with privacy issues, a first name or alias could be used. The system could give a warning message whenever a previous pattern is violated. For example, if we pay a utility bill of $100 to $200 each month, we should get a warning if the reported amount is way off in either direction. Further, e-invoices and other automatic procedures can limit the number of transactions that must be keyed in, reducing the overall error rate.

In Fossbakk's case, the banking system erred. Next time, it might be a weapons system or medical information system that fails. Examples from these areas have already revealed misinterpretations between systems and users that caused serious consequences. All systems must protect users from their own errors, intercept all detectable errors, and give informative warnings when we believe the user might have made an error. The "she made an error and must take responsibility" defense is too simple. We need systems that work in collaboration with the user such that the overall error rate drops to a minimum. Yes, we need responsible users, but a good system can handle most slips and typos they make, as this case shows.

When we asked the bank lawyers about data on usability testing, they returned with data on a market research survey. Sure, if we go to *Wikipedia* to learn more about usability testing we will find a paragraph on market research, but under the section "What usability testing is not." That is, not only had the bank skipped usability testing, but they also lacked an understanding of what this concept implies. Note that this was an interface that was used by 40 percent of Norwegian banks since year 2000, and many foreign banks have been using similar systems.

This gave ammunition to a case of gross negligence. Probably the bank also saw that this could be the outcome. They gave up two days before the case was to be tried in court, returned to Fossbakk all the money that she had lost, with interest.

21.2 Case 2: Employee self-service

Many systems have millions of users; these systems may be commercial and may be used because they offer good services, such as banking or booking, or because they offer pleasure, such as YouTube, Facebook, and online games. Although these systems may have faults in the user interface, overall, they must satisfy users. If not, the user would switch to the competition. However, in another type of system, the users cannot choose an alternative—a system that is used internally in organizations. In this case, the users are employees and are required to utilize the system, and there is no limit to how terrible the system can be.

The case presented here is a fairly new system, Employee Self Service (ESS), which has been developed by the Norwegian Government Agency for Financial Management to be used in all state organizations. The idea is that the system should encompass all administrative and personal functions that an employee may need, such as travel allowance, salary, time registration, leave, and vacation. This example focuses on travel allowance.

Previously, travel allowances utilized a paper–based system. All travel expenses were registered on a special form, receipts were attached, and the form was signed and delivered to the administration. It was then checked for consistency with travel regulations, and eventually the amount paid was returned to the employee. For a national flight, with some buses and taxies, some nights at a hotel, and so on, an employee might take between five and ten minutes to fill out the form. But the paper version had some drawbacks. You would have to get the printed form, do the adding manually, and find the correct amount for some regulation-defined values, such as the standard meal allowance. A simple spreadsheet-based system automated the addition, stored general data (such as name, institution, account number), and in later versions, updated the standard allowances. These improvements reduced the employee's time to complete the form to five minutes, somewhat more for international travel.

Currently, the new ESS system has been introduced in all state-owned colleges in Norway. All employees have to participate in a two-hour user course. There was no mention of what the system is intended to achieve, but according to the Web site, the idea is to give a better "overview of the work situation," and that the system can liberate administrative personnel to do other tasks. As a professor, my work situation consists of research and teaching, and ESS does not cover these parts, thus the "overview" goal cannot be achieved. I would be delighted if introducing more efficient systems could reduce administrative tasks, but not if this implies that the workload is moved from the administration to the professors.

In my college, the ESS system has been used for two years. The data shows that the time used to fill out the travel form has

The new IT system is **less effective** than the previous paper-based system.

increased to at least thirty minutes for a simple trip, much more for complex trips. More personnel are involved in tasks connected with travel allowance in the administration than at any time before. One reason is that many employees need help to use the system, even after two years of experience.

This raises two interesting questions. Why did the system fail and why do we still use it?

ESS is based on a SAP ERP[7] platform, an enterprise software application. It is run on central servers and is accessed using a Web browser. ESS only works with a given version of Internet Explorer, not with any other browser.

The employee encounters problems from the very start. ESS uses a proprietary user name, different from the one that we use on the college system. It also has a proprietary password, which must include digits, letters, and special characters, must be eight characters long, and must be changed every three months—that is, a password that no one can remember. Thus, most users have the password on a yellow tag stuck to their computer displays. Interestingly, if you forget the password, the system will send you a new one using e-mail. Thus the security level is not higher than that of the college computer system (even lower, as the college avoids sending passwords by e-mail).

When every system requires a special user name and password, it makes the life of the user very complicated.

If one is lucky the login process will not take more than a couple of minutes, but the system is often not running (by far the most frequent e-mails I get is one telling me that ESS down.[8]) Inside ESS, we find the travel allowance form, which looks like the old spreadsheet form, although with has several peculiarities. Terminology in the system is strange; instead of *salary,* it uses the term *pay*; instead of asking for the *reason* for a trip, it asks for the *cause*; instead of asking for the *name* of a hotel, it wants a *description.*[9] This makes it difficult for novice or low-frequent users to navigate in the system. Error messages appear in a small line at the bottom of the screen, which most users ignore. The reason for such a modest presentation may be that most error messages will, in any case, be incomprehensible to the ordinary user.

Information architecture in ESS is terrible. As with the paper form, the system is based on the idea that the user should fill in information on all expenses, dates, type of expense, and amount. Normally, when a full form is presented on the screen, a user would think that she can fill out the form as she chooses.

Not so with ESS. The user must start at the top and work her way down. If not, the system will lock up.

ESS presents the overall menu at all times, which implies that you can move to other parts of the system while filling out the travel form, just by clicking a button. We expect this functionality in a modern application, noting that the users may perform more than one task at the same time. However, in ESS you can never get back to the travel form again if you move away. No warning is given, the system just assumes that you have changed your mind and want to disregard everything that has been entered.

ESS implements efficiency in a strange way, forcing the user to work at its pace. In the first version, the timeout was set to two minutes! This has been changed to ten in later versions. If you are passive for a longer period, the system will automatically terminate the session or log you off without saving anything. That is, when working with ESS, the user has to close doors, refuse to take phone calls, and bar colleagues and students—administrative tasks come first.

Clearly, the developers of this system have no idea of how business trips are performed. These may come in all variants. For example, one may combine private and business travel, perform tasks for more than one institution, and recursively, perform a new trip while being on a trip. To handle such a degree of flexibility one needs a very open system where the user is in full control. For example, the user may want to divide the final amount of compensation in two, splitting the expenses between institutions. However, ESS tries to formalize and control the task, and no user manipulation is allowed—not even reducing amounts.

The time you are away is computed automatically, with no possibility of removing additional days used for private purposes (tempting). Amounts in other currencies are computed automatically into Norwegian kroner based on the current exchange rate, ignoring the possibility that the expense may have occurred at quite different times at quite different exchange rates, and neither does ESS include the overhead added by a credit card company. In one situation, where I tried to set a different exchange rate for a conference fee paid in dollars several months in advance, I got the error "More than 10 percent difference in exchange rate." Sure, it may be a problem that the value of the dollar decreases, but I am not responsible.

The developers have not **understood** the tasks they automate.

As with all other systems where the formalization does not cover all situations one has to bend the system into describing reality. For example, instead of dividing the total amount by two and sending a copy to each institution, we have to make up two different trips and try to adjust expenses so that each institution pays what is due. This implies that the dates must be fixed, if not one will get reimbursed twice for some expenses (also tempting). A friend who had a one-month sabbatical at another institution, went of to a conference while staying there and also attended a fully paid overnight institutional seminar, had to make this into six different trips to get it through ESS. On paper, one form would have been enough.

The idea was to **remove paper**, but this has only been partially fulfilled.

The finished form is sent electronically to the administration. So, this is where we get an advantage? No, all receipts have to be glued to A4 pages and put in a mail box. The administration then has to connect the electronic form with the paper receipts, so very little is gained. In fact, since users have problems understanding the system, most forms will have to be returned to the user at least once to be corrected. Many users also will require expert help. After two years, we should expect users to be more experienced, but many travel rarely or may have very few international trips. With months or years since one used the system the last time, the tricks we learned the first time are forgotten.

Thus ESS fails because the developers have not understood the task involved nor the user's work situation. Instead of being creative and recognizing what is possible today, such as retrieving expense data from a credit card company, they have tried to use IT to make the old paper-based system more effective. The meal allowances are a good example. These are quite complex, based on the time one is away, on country, sometimes on the city in which one stays, and on the type of accommodation. Staying at a hotel gives full benefits, while part of the amount becomes taxable if one stays at a friend's house. ESS tries, by requiring extensive data from the user, to compute both the allowances and the tax data automatically.

When designing new systems it is important to study the new possibilities, instead of retaining concepts and processes uncritically from the old system.

However, when designing a new system, developers should stop and think. Why do we have an allowance system; why don't we get reimbursed for the actual expenses? This would be so much simpler, avoiding time, location, type of lodging and all tax issues if one were paid for actual expenses. The answers to these questions are quite simple. Before electronic cash registers and credit card systems, it was cumbersome to ask for receipts for small transactions. Allowances were introduced to avoid requiring the cashier to write a paper receipt by hand when buying a cup of coffee for a dollar. However, by using a credit card today this transaction can be moved to the travel allowance form automatically. That is, we no longer need allowances. These can be replaced by a maximum amount (which can also be taken care of by an automatic system).

Why do we still use a system that has proved its ineffectiveness? This is a very interesting question, especially as private businesses are moving to better systems, those in which much of the data entry is avoided by retrieving expense data directly from credit card companies. With such a system, it becomes possible to create a "one click" expense form, perhaps needing some editing in a few cases. But we use ESS even if it has a performance record that cannot even be compared to a simple paper based system. ESS violates the most basic rules for universal access. It does not work with screen readers; it does not support the users in performing the tasks, it is inefficient and is not robust with regard to errors.

When calling ESS the worst system ever, I have been accused of exaggerating. There are, the critics say, many systems that don't even run because of technical errors. But that would have been so much better!

21.3   Conclusion

It is important to **analyze** the tasks as a part of the system specification in order to determine what is needed to get an efficient system.

Two cases have been presented: a banking system that has not been submitted to usability testing, causing a serious error where one customer risked the loss of a large amount of money and another got a nine-month prison sentence; and an employee self-service system (ESS) in which the basic tasks have been misunderstood and which has an unnecessary complex error-prone interface.

Both systems have large user groups and both show disrespect for their users. We expect that books are proofread before publication, that industrial products are tested, that is, as consumers we at least expect that all organizations have good quality assuring routines. But software seems to be different. Many systems, such as the cases presented here, have faults that could have been found with very simple usability testing. One can assume that the problem is lack of professionalism at all levels. This again may be caused by low-quality educational programs in informatics, or, perhaps more to the point, by uneducated system developers. We also find examples of systems, such as ESS, in which the basic model is wrong. Again, this may be because of a lack of understanding of the problems to solve—a lack of professionalism. It is also possible that the system is based on very different priorities from those that the users have for their work—for example, that administrative functions are the most important.

ESS also tells us that it seldom pays to use IT to make the old paper-based system more effective. To get full benefit of new technology we have to be free from all restrictions inherent in the previous systems. That is, IT not only allows us to run existing business processes more effectively, it also opens up a new way of doing business.

Notes

1 Parts of this example are based on Olsen, K. A. (2008). A $100,000 keying error, IEEE Computer, April, vol. 41, No. 4.

2 Parts of this example are based on Olsen, K. A. (2010). Two cases of bad Web usability: banking and employee self service, UniTech 2010, Oslo, Tapir forlag.

3 Finansklagenemnda Bank (www.finkn.no).

4 Forbrukerrådet (www.forbrukerportalen.no).

5 This error rate is higher than we would expect in a real system. First, since analyzing faults is our initial task, the simulator does not offer any error messages. Second, the testers enter a large set of transactions. Third, the test situation does not involve any real money. We suspect that users would verify transactions more carefully when using a live system. While the overall error rate might be higher, there seems to be no reason why the distribution of different error types should be any different from what we would find in a real system.

6 Basic Books, 1988.

7 From SAP AG, a German software corperation. The company is a market leader for ERP (Enterprise Resource Planning) systems.

8 By the way, one should not send an e-mail to all users warning that a system is down. What if all systems did this? This information should be presented on the Web page of the application.

9 Since they ask for a description, I give it. My travel forms are full of hotel descriptions such as "large white building with balconies."

PART 4

System

Development

In the beginning there was only computer hardware, the electrical circuits. The instructions were entered into working memory by setting switches. The results were displayed binary, with a light telling the value of each bit. The working memory was very limited and the computer could be used only for the simplest programs.

In the next step, programmers could punch their programs on paper tape. Assembly language became a norm. In this simple programming language, there was a one-to-one correspondence between a program line and the basic instruction (see Chapter 2). The assembler's task was to assign locations in working memory, a program that translated the assembly code into machine instructions; that is, a program was used to facilitate the development of other programs.

Later on, more advanced programming languages were developed with which programmers could use a vocabulary and syntax at a much higher level than that of machine code. A compiler, an advanced assembler, converted the program code into machine instructions.

Today object-oriented languages, such as Java, are popular. With these it is possible to create higher-level objects that contain both the data structures and the operations that work on these. Object-orientation allows for very flexible solutions, with few limitations for the user. For example, a modern word processor, developed according to these principles, allows us to insert objects such as tables, figures, and pictures into a document. But we also can have tables within tables within tables, and table elements can be text, numbers, figures, or photos. Since all items are described as objects, this is just the case of allowing objects within objects. But there are also limits to object-orientation, which are discussed in more detail below.

Operating systems also simplify the programmer's task. Instead of building an application on top of the hardware, one can build on top of the operating system, which is just another program, albeit a program with special privileges. However, the operating system offers a convenient platform. It manages machine resources, the processors, working memory, peripheral devices such as disks, and all low-level functions. For example, programmers work with files, named entities, which allow data to be stored on the disk, and the operating system finds space for the file on the actual physical disk. Similarly, the operating system facilitates contact will all other devices, keyboard, mouse, display, printer, and so on. And, of course, it handles execution of programs in such a way that no program can interfere with the running of others.

An operating system has another advantage. When a program works on top of the hardware it can only work on machines of the same type. However, with the operating system between the hardware and the application, the application programs can run on any machine that can run the operating system. This layer-idea is used extensively in computing. With Android, mobile phones are becoming full computers, and these, as the PC, need an operating system on top of the hardware to facilitate application development.

Today programmers not only enjoy advanced operating systems and programming languages, but their programs can interface with a set of software packages, database systems, user interface modules, graphical systems, and mathematical packages. That is, there is no need to reinvent the wheel; there are packages for every standard function. In addition, programmers also can insert premade modules into their programs. Some of these come in precompiled fixed forms; for others—especially open-source modules—the program code may be available. The module then can be adjusted to any special need. (We cover open-source more extensively below.)

Today we also find an abundance of premade programs for all standard applications, such as systems for e-mail, word processing, graphics, and spreadsheets. In many cases, there is no need for development. These off-the-shelf programs will install themselves (plug and play) and can be used directly, often with an intuitive interface so that no training is required. But, as discussed in Chapter 18, some training may be required to use these programs effectively. The advantage of most off-the-shelf programs is that many people use them, sometimes to the extent that the programs define de facto standards. For example, Microsoft Word is used so extensively that we expect everybody to be able to read and work on .doc or .docx files. Another advantage of many users is that the development costs are shared, thus we may get excellent systems for a low price.

This part begins by describing the phases of system development (Chapter 22), and then moves to software engineering (Chapter 23), including how we can handle the engineering process of constructing software. Packages and ERP (Enterprise Resource Planning) systems are covered in Chapter 24. Niche companies often will not find off-the-shelf systems that fulfill their need for software to handle core functions. One alternative is to develop their own core software, something that can be done with the simpler methods introduced in Chapter 25. A case is presented in Chapter 26. A special form of development that has been accentuated by smartphones is the development of Apps, which is discussed in Chapter 27.

22   Developing a System

IT is a **tool**, a means to achieve a higher-level goal.

IT is a tool, something that most often is not important in itself, but is a means to achieve a goal. To develop any type of system, we must clarify the goal, which often can be described as a problem. For example, a manufacturer may call saying that they need a better planning system because customers are complaining about late orders.

The first task for an IT-consultant then will be to understand how the business works, and to get to the bottom of the problem. The business may need a better planning system, but many different factors may be causing the late orders. Perhaps delays are due to missing parts, which again may be traced to a bad inventory system or perhaps bad routines around inventory. For example, if the inventory system does not register every removal of a part, the company eventually will run out of the part. This deficiency may lead to problems in assembly and delayed orders. If such is the case, a new planning system will not solve the problem.

22.1   Needs analysis

All system development should start with a detailed **analysis of the task**.

Thus, all system development should start with a detailed analysis of the task, the current problem, and its causes, which could entail an analysis of the company. For example, developing a new system may not be a good solution if the problem with the previous one was simply a lack of discipline in using it. Such a "needs analysis" will determine what kind of IT systems that a company will need to solve current problems, or better, to see how the company can fulfill its business goals. In this phase, the IT experts need to work closely with company employees who know the business and what kind of problems they have. However, the IT experts often will be the ones who suggest solutions, since they know the capabilities of the technology.

IT consultants must be able to think **outside the box**.

IT consultants must be able to think outside the box. Many of the processes that we have established in organizations are important and necessary, even those that do not seem to have an apparent rationale. For example, rigid testing and accounting practices may have been established after severe incidents in the past. However, many tasks may be part of the former implementation. This is especially the case when we replace manual systems.

Several cases presented here will demonstrate the importance of understanding the system we are building. The example used in Chapter 21.2, in which a complex system for per diem travel expenses was implemented rather than using actual expenses, provides a good background. While the per diem scheme solved problems with the previous paper-based system, it can be replaced with a much simpler system that collects all expenses electronically, based on credit card usage. Therefore, system developers must understand the motives behind the regulations, and see how to fulfill this goal in the best way, given new technology.

Changing regulations—such as from per diem to actual expenses—is a high-level decision, perhaps taken by state officials or company executives. This is why having executives involved in IT projects is vital. The goal is not to transfer the paper-based system to an IT platform, but to develop a new and much more efficient system, which may demand new regulations and new processes.

A needs analysis may conclude that the problem is in the processes around the systems, and that the existing systems are adequate or that a new system is required. If a new system is needed, the next step will be to determine the specifications for the system, that is, formulating a detailed description of what the system should do. These specifications may be presented in a formalized form, for example as something that can be used as an attachment to a contract. We may even use special specification languages to create an overview of the system in a formalized syntax. However, at this early point of systems development, there are many advantages to using natural language so that everyone can read and understand both the "needs analysis" and the specifications. This understanding is important because if we, for example in a manufacturing plant, manage to communicate with machine operators, foremen, and middle- and top-level management we will get important feedback on our reports. This early feedback will aid in developing a useful system. Better to be told up front that this system or this feature will not work, than after it has been implemented.

Using calendar time in these early phases is important, too. When system experts and company personnel have the chance to consider options over a longer period there is a better chance

The **system specifications** can be presented in a formalized form, or often better in natural language. The advantage of using natural language is that this can be understood by all.

that the company will get a successful system. Often we see that initial ideas are replaced with new and better ideas, even quite radical solutions, if the persons involved are given time to discuss and consider.

When specifications are clear one will have to determine if these can be fulfilled with an off-the-shelf system or with modifications or configurations to an existing system. While niche companies may find that they will have to develop a new system to get what they need, larger companies may find that an ERP (Enterprise Resource Planning) system can be tuned to their needs.

An improved development infrastructure, from operating systems to development kits, also makes it possible for independent developers to participate in building applications. We see this with Apps for tablets and mobile phones, some of which are developed by techno-interested kids. (Apps are discussed in Chapter 27.)

22.2   Prototypes

Delay program-
ming until the task
is fully understood.

Independent of the type of system, development should not start until we know what goals the system shall fulfill, and never before the specifications are clear. Making prototypes at an early stage can help us know what we need. Prototypes mimic the user interface, so that users can try out the system long before real development starts. Many packages are suited for making simple prototypes. If we are developing a new device, with integrated software and hardware, such as a check-in automat for an airport, it will be a good idea to build a prototype that also mimics the complete interface, with touch screen, slots for reading a credit card, output for boarding pass, and so on. Prototypes often can be made easily using available standard parts, without having to add the machinery inside the device.

Prototypes can
help us to get data
on unknown parts
of the system.

If we are in doubt of how the system will tackle a heavy load, we can try to calculate response times. Or, often simpler, we can simulate a situation of many users, something that is especially important for systems where realistic testing is not possible to perform. An example may be an election system, in which there is no load until Election Day. All "white parts" on the map should be explored before we start real development, which will reduce, often eliminate, the risk of a failure.

22.3   Divide-and-conquer

Divide-and-conquer, a large system is split into manageable parts.

The final system may consist of millions of code lines. To develop such a system, we use the strategy of divide-and-conquer. For such large systems, we may start by describing the overall architecture, defining the parts that are needed. Later on, each part can be divided into subparts, down to a level in which a subpart can be described as a set of modules, each of these consisting of a set of procedures and data descriptions. At the bottom level, a procedure such as checking the validity of a date is described as a set of programming lines. Thus, by dividing the system into parts, we reach a point where subparts are simple enough to be implemented with a limited number of program lines.

However, a system may be unbuildable even if every part is understood; there may be just too many parts, such as in the case from the telecommunication sector in Chapter 12. There are many other examples of similar system failures because of the complexity of too many details. Therefore, as a part of the needs analysis and specifications, developers should study how the application area may be simplified before implementation starts.

22.4   Models

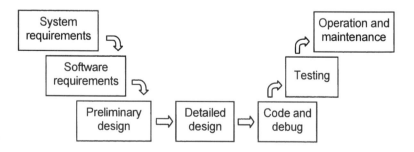

Figure 22.1 The waterfall model.

A traditional model for system development, shown in Figure 22.1, is the *waterfall* model, in which the process is described as a flow between separate tasks, from system requirements to system operation. While this model presents the major phases of system development and is based on ideas from other engineering disciplines, its structure is not realistic for the development of IT systems.

There is a significant difference between traditional engineering disciplines and **software engineering** that is often not recognized.

Traditional engineering disciplines and software engineering are significantly different. This difference is often not recognized. If we compare software development to civil engineering, we will see that the construction of buildings, bridges, and roads are, most often, a copying process in which the same methods are used as in a previous project. There are differences between each case, but the methods applied are designed to handle this. Rarely are completely new types of objects introduced. For example, the suspension bridge dates as far back as 1433, with the modern design dating back to 1595 (according to *Wikipedia*). While all suspension bridges are based on these original ideas, there are several subtypes. Still, an effort to build a new bridge can be based on design and engineering from similar bridges, often using standard calculation programs to determine the dimensions of the various components.

With software the copying process is more or less automatic. Simple programs, such as word processing programs and spreadsheets, install themselves. More complex systems, such as an ERP system, may need specialists to configure the system to its application. But even this major task is a copying process. Most software installations are of this kind, either automatic installation or a configuration. New systems are developed only when no standard program will do the task. This process can be compared to constructing a new type of bridge. Experiences from other projects may be valuable, one may even use components made for other systems, but in the end many software engineering projects launch into the unknown.

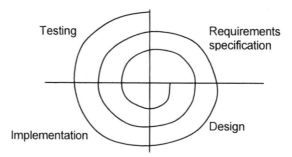

Since nearly all software development involves new applications, it is difficult to have the complete overview up front.

Figure 22.2 The spiral model (Barry Boehm, IEEE Computer, May 1998).

Thus, it is seldom possible—when we design large projects—to have a complete overview up front. One learns as one goes along. For example, during the later stage of programming, the specifications may have to be changed to avoid unnecessary coding, complex user interfaces, or to utilize predefined modules. To include this need for feedback in the process, the spiral model in Figure 22.2 has been introduced, showing that system development is an iterative process.

The weakness of such a model is that implementation and testing are part of the cycle. Changing specifications after programming has started is expensive since this may require a change in the detailed program code. Similarly, if the system is changed after testing, new tests must be introduced because the modifications may influence not only the changed parts of the system but also other parts.

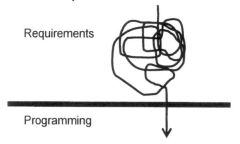

Requirements

Programming

Figure 22.3 A more realistic model?

The "model" shown in Figure 22.3 tries to avoid this problem. The idea here is to have a clear separation between the requirements, above the line, and programming, under the line. This model accepts that the requirements phase is creative and often cannot be structured. In this phase, we try to understand the customer's problems, and to devise solutions, we must have a good understanding both of the problem and the context—the business processes, and also the business environment. We interview stakeholders, study the existing systems, and get a good understanding of all processes to create the foundation for proposing a new system. In some cases these processes may be structured, in others they will be as random as visualized in Figure 22.3.

The programming should not start before we have a clear understanding of what is needed. This reduces the risk that we have to make major changes in the system. However, during programming, we may get a better understanding of the system, encounter problems, or see new solutions. Therefore, some modifications to the requirements will always be necessary as the project develops.

22.5   System specifications

In which form should the requirements be presented? If these are to be used as a request for a tender and later a contact, they need to be very detailed and unambiguous. Terms such as "user friendly" and "simple to use" must be replaced with explicit terms, such as, "the user should be able to perform function X in three minutes."

However, system development often takes us into unknown territory. Even with a model such as the one in Figure 22.3, problems and ideas may come up during programming that require a change in the specifications. Then it is extremely difficult to foresee all problems and to make a full specification. In these cases, it may be better to work in a partnership with the developers, which will allow changes to be made along the way.

Such a process also will take care of changes in the environment, which is especially important for lengthy projects. As the project develops, the company may experience changes in products, business processes, or relations to customers that require a modification of the system.

Therefore, the complete specifications and specific contracts should be used only for cases in which there is a good overview of what is needed. An example could be when one system is to be ported to another platform, from Windows to Linux. In such "formalized" cases, it should be possible to describe the requirements in a detailed contract. In all other cases, the partnership model will most often work better.

22.6   Case: System specifications

Sometimes software development can be as easy as replacing cumbersome paper-based processes with electronic, but often there are more creative possibilities. As an example, let us consider a manufacturer who has a major supplier that delivers relative inexpensive things, such as screws and bolts, as well as more expensive items. The requirements for these components are calculated based on the overall demand for the manufacturer's products. With these numbers and a bill of material, a data structure that shows which components go into each final product, it is quite easy to foresee demand for each single component.

The manufacture turns these requirements into orders that are faxed to the supplier. This process is cumbersome for the supplier because the orders have to be typed into its computer system, which takes time and is prone to errors. In addition, our manufacturer indicates that there never seems to be enough of everything, and he often runs out of screws and bolts.

As IT consultants, our initial solution may be to send these orders electronically, which can be as easy as sending a data file with all the orders. The supplier may then copy these directly into its computer system. With regard to the missing parts, we may be tempted to suggest a higher data discipline, reminding employees to register every withdrawal of additional components. For example, when losing a screw into the drain, the employee must enter the "withdrawal" of an additional item.

However, other solutions may work better. Many manufacturers use a two-box system for minor parts, such as screws and bolts. For each item and dimension, there are two boxes, one in front of the other. When items are needed during assembly, they are removed from the outer box. When that box is empty, it is put aside and the next box is put out front. At various intervals the supplier will fetch the empty boxes, refill them, and return them to the manufacturer. This simple system eliminates the need to reorder these items and also handles the situation when someone loses a screw or when more screws are used than stated in the bill of material. The company achieves significant savings, with very low costs, without implementing a new IT system.

More expensive parts cannot be handled in this way because having many items in stock is not cost-effective. Also, there is the risk that some of these may become obsolete. Orders for these components should be sent as a data file.

An alternative that can be applied in some cases is to give the supplier access to the company's IT systems. Now the supplier will know exactly what is needed each day and can deliver accordingly, eliminating the need for orders and perhaps also invoices (if there are fixed contracts with suppliers). Many industries, such as car manufacturers, implement these ideas.

As we see, specifying system requirements is not an easy task. To find creative solutions, calendar time is often needed. Hopefully, in the discussions between IT experts and users, the right solutions will then appear. When developers know just what to do, they pass the line in Figure 22.3 and start programming. In many cases, with today's tools, programming is often a much simpler phase than determining specifications

With a **two-box system** one can avoid administration of simple parts.

Perhaps we can eliminate the need for orders and invoices?

and can often be performed in much less time. I have been engaged in projects in which it took six months to get the requirements right, but just a couple of weeks for programming.

22.7   Basic tools

The **database system** handles storing and retrieving of structured data.

All application programming is built on top of the operating system, which offers convenient access to system resources. While disks are organized as tracks and sectors, programs can access these on a higher level as files and folders. A file is a named entity and can be viewed as sequential storage. In practice, this may not be the case. One part of the file may be stored in one location on the disk, while other parts are stored in other locations. However, the operating system takes care of this; it puts a layer between the physical environment and the application and gives the application a much simpler view of the resources.

In many cases, however, a file is too simple a mechanism for an application program. Often there is a need to store *records*, such as information on individuals. These may have many attributes in different formats, for example, name and address as text, income as a decimal number, or dates in special formats. In addition, mechanisms are needed to retrieve this information. An application can build this functionality on top of the file concept, but it will be much easier to use a *database system*.

We build **layer upon layer**, starting with the hardware, adding an operating system, database systems, and applications.

A database system lifts the disk storage to a higher level than the file system by implementing a layer between the file system (the operating system) and the application. With this layer, the application can operate on structured data, with a record for each object. For example, a system for handling a vehicle registry may have records for vehicles and owners. A vehicle may be described by license number, manufacturer, model, engine type, and size. To simplify, one may define types of vehicles, such as buses, trucks, and cars, where each type is described as a record. For a bus it will be necessary to have an attribute giving the number of seats, for a truck the maximum load, and so on. Similarly, vehicle owners may be described as organizations or private persons. In addition we may need records to describe emission standards, emission control, and payment of vehicle tax. We will end up with quite a complex structure, not only with several record types, but also with links between these. For example, we will need a link from vehicle to owner and from owner to vehicle. Multiple links will be needed because an owner—organization or a private citizen—may possess several vehicles.

The database system will handle all of this, enabling us to describe the structure in a simple way and then automatically implement this structure. In addition, it will offer functionality for handling errors, such as maintaining backup routines and ensuring the integrity of the system in exception situations. For example, we may store a record both for a new vehicle and a new owner in the vehicle registry system. The integrity of the database requires that both records are stored, that every vehicle has an owner. If an exception occurs, such as a power loss, after we have stored the first record but not the second, we have a database that does not follow requirements. However, when power is resumed and the system restarts, the system will delete the vehicle record and give a warning that the registration of the new vehicle (and owner) will have to be repeated.

Modern applications have often a graphical user interface (GUI) consisting of menus and forms. As with the database system, every application does not have to develop the user interface from for scratch; premade systems also can handle this part. We can get these basic systems as software packages that can be integrated with the application programs, or we may use a tool that embeds all that we need. Microsoft Access is an example. This simple system has a GUI that allows the programmer to "draw" forms with input fields, buttons, and so on. An example is presented in Figure 22.4.

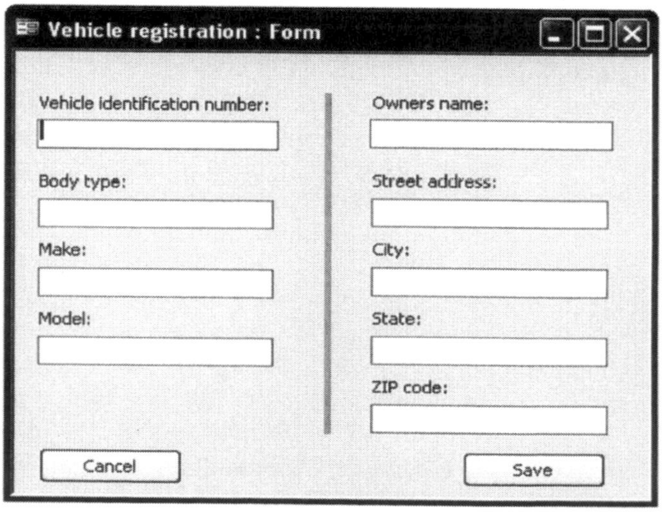

Figure 22.4 A simple vehicle registration form.

A wizard may aid the user in inserting program code for standard functions, such as retrieving or storing data. For nonstandard operations, Microsoft Access offers Visual Basic, a standard programming language. With Access, or similar systems, system development can be simplified. This is especially the case for small and medium-sized organizations, in which issues of security and resource requirements are more relaxed than in larger firms. Thus, smaller companies may achieve a higher-level of IT employment than larger ones. We shall return to this issue in Chapters 24 and 25.

Often we find that others already have developed the modules we need. Many premade modules are offered as a part of development systems, usually in a binary version, that is, in a machine form, which ensures that developers have full control of the product. The disadvantage is that users must take the modules as they are. There is also the risk that the developers may no longer want to maintain the code.

Often a better alternative is to get the premade modules as source code, as a program. Then the code can be integrated in the system, as if it were developed in-house. One is free to make changes and is, in principle, independent of the programmers that developed the original module.

The **open-source** movement offers an abundance of both premade modules and full systems. The *open-source* movement offers an abundance of both premade modules and full systems. The idea behind this movement is to promote free distribution of software, and to advocate a cooperative development style. Open source is behind a large set of very important software products, such as Linux and Android operating systems, the Mozilla Firefox browser, the OpenOffice.org program suite, the Apache Web server, and the PHP programming language. These systems are widely used today, both by nonprofit organizations and commercial companies.

Other tools include Application servers, that provide services to run applications in a secure and load balanced environment and Web servers that deliver Web content. The primary function for a Web server is to return Web pages that are requested by clients (the browsers). Most Web servers support server-side scripting, i.e., the possibility to execute scripts before returning a Web page to the requesting browser. I shall return to these issues in part 5.

22.8 Programming

While the internal low-level representation in a computer is in the form of bits, programmers and system designers are free to use any form of higher-level symbolic structures to represent data and processes. We have programming languages that can represent data as integers, floating point numbers, text strings, or images. They offer statements for formulas, selection, iteration, and all the other basic operations that a computer can perform. These languages have unambiguous syntax and semantics. While natural language, such as English, allows us great freedom in how we construct sentences, programming languages have a fixed command vocabulary and a strict grammar. We can introduce new identifiers for variables and processes, but there are clear methods as to how this can be done. In this way, the meaning of every statement—the semantics—is under control. There is nothing unclear and ambiguous about a computer program; there is only one way to interpret it correctly, just as with mathematical formulas.

As tasks and programs get bigger, the emphasis is on constructs that allow us to use even higher-level concepts, to organize the millions of code lines into symbolic structures that can be developed and maintained in an orderly manner. Such constructs are found even in the very first programming languages. Here higher-level operations could be described in the form of procedures (subroutines, functions) and data could be structured in the form of records. The idea is to make new, custom operations out of simpler basic operations. For example, we may need the ability to sort a sequence many places in a program. Instead of adding the code wherever needed, we instead define a procedure *sort* that does the job. To make this procedure applicable to different types of data, we will define *sort* so that it can work on abstract data, to be replaced by actual data whenever we need sorting. In this way, we can build a hierarchy of higher-level operations. Similar constructs exist for creating structured data; for example, we can define an employee record that contains all the attributes that define a person (name, Social Security number, salary, and so on).

The first programming languages had only these two constructs—procedures and records for building program and data structure. Later on, additional constructs were needed, such as a modular structure that could contain both procedures

Classes can **inherit** methods from other classes.

and record descriptions. Today, object-orientation is a common technique for organizing operations and data in a computer program. Here data and the procedures (methods) that work on these data are described as a class structure. A basic idea is the principle of encapsulation. The class presents itself to the outside through the methods it can perform, while the detailed implementation of these methods is "hidden" within the class. For example, a class may offer a method for sorting a file. To use this method, we need a description—for example, that it requires the name of the file with the data—but we do not need to know just how the sorting is performed.

An "interface" describes an abstract type that contains no data. The behavior of the type is then described through the methods. The interface can be implemented as a class. For example, we can define a class that works on lists. A list is a set of connected objects, and the methods offered can be to insert an object in the list, delete an object or to search through the list for an object. The idea is to describe this class without having to say anything about the objects. Thus we have a generic implementation that can work on any type of data.

An object-oriented approach develops a set of building blocks that can be reused many times. For example, in a college archive system, there may be a class describing students and another for employees. While the first may have a method for registering an exam, course code, year, and grade, the second may have methods for calculating salary and taxes. However, since both students and employees are persons, we may find many common features in the two classes, both data and methods. For example, each class may have attributes for name, address, and Social Security number, and perhaps methods for presenting and changing the address. To avoid duplication of code these common attributes may be described in a third class, a class person. We can then declare that both the student and employee classes should inherit the properties or attributes from the class person, such as name, address, and a method for checking Social Security number.

In designing these program-structures care must be taken to make them both efficient and flexible. This is easiest when we control the application area.

Classes describe a mold or template for making objects. Whenever we have a new student we create a student-object based on the generic class. Now we can enter the attributes that describe the individual. In this way, we build an organized structure in the computer that can perform all the operations that the user needs.

The idea of **reuse** is to make classes and modules generic, so that they can be used by many different applications.

In designing these program-structures care must be taken to make them both efficient and flexible. This is easiest when we control the application area, for example, when we design software for virtual worlds, such as software tools for user interface development, graphical systems, mathematical packages, and so forth. Here we are in full control. In real-world applications, however, we may find that the foundations on which we built our class- and object-structure are not as solid as expected and that changes in the environment or organization may force a complete restructuring of the program. In some cases, we may even find that a less structured program will be the most flexible.

System development and programming is expensive. The idea is to bridge the gap between the needs and requirements of the real world on one side and a generalized machine on the other. Our task is to convert a general machine into something that can solve problems, into a word processing system, a manufacturing planning and control system, a flight guidance system, and more. Even if all of these applications are different, there will be common parts, and one way to reduce development costs is to explore commonality, to reuse software components. Object-oriented techniques are interesting here. Classes can be reused at a programming level; for example, the general Java classes developed for application A also can be used for application B. Or, we can use object-orientation at a tool level. Visual Basic, for example, offers system designers components for Internet access, for presenting a video clip, or components used to design an input form, such as text boxes, radio buttons, and menus. If one needs to provide the ability to play movie clips to a program, a standard component simply can be added to the user interface of the program.

Components and other forms of basic software help us to narrow the gap between the general computer and the application.

If we are in the process of constructing a Web site, for example, an online bank, we will find that several of the functions we need, such as those for checking a credit card and for transferring funds, are available as premade components. These may be included directly in our system, or perhaps they can be used as a Web-service, a service that can be accessed over the Web (we shall return to Web services in Chapter 53). In practice, we will only have to design a small part of the system ourselves, such as the user interface and special functions. Components and other forms of basic software help us to narrow the gap between the general computer and the application.

Whatever programming language is used, it is important to write programs that are easy for other programmers to understand. The code will only be written once, but it will be maintained and extended over many years, which means it is important that any programmer can read the code. If not, modifications and extensions will be difficult to perform, and the risk of introducing errors will be high. Since systems may run into many thousands, perhaps millions of code lines, understandable code can only be achieved with a good program structure. I return to these issues in Chapter 25.

While we are free to choose the internal symbolic representation of our system there are two requirements: It must be possible to translate the structure into bits, so that it can be run on a computer. Language translators or compilers perform this task, converting the class structures from a high-level programming language, such as PHP or Java, into binary code that the computer can execute. The other requirement is that the internal structure must be presented in a form that is suitable for the user, for example, a graphical user interface with menus, command buttons, and forms. What we get is a formalized "pipeline" of data and commands all the way from the user interface to the low-level bit representation inside the computer, moving through different symbolic structures.

23 Software Engineering

Many software systems today, such as those for finance, business, or military applications, have become enormous systems of ever-increasing capability, interdependencies, and complexity. The only reasonable way to create these huge, complex systems is to use thorough and rigorous software engineering practices—system architecture description, modularization, object-oriented modeling, encapsulation, reuse, version control, strict testing procedures, and highly automated deployment procedures. These concepts and practices have been included in software systems as the software development field has matured, going from "ad hoc" processes to the development of very large systems. The idea is to make software development as foolproof as other types of engineering.

The standard textbook ("correct") approach to system development is characterized by:

- Software as a product
- Strict requirement specifications
- Three-tiered architecture (user interface, application and database level)
- Model according to code by using techniques such as object-orientation, and tools such as UML (Unified Modeling Language), a modeling language, and Java, an object-oriented programming language.
- Reuse of code, development of highly structured programs and generic modules
- Rigid testing procedures
- Version control
- Deployment procedures
- Maintenance plans
- User support and help systems

Absolutely nothing is wrong with these methods, and they are a necessity in many cases. A strict requirement specification is a must if we want to set up a legal and binding fixed-price contract with the developing organization. The three-tiered architecture, that is, the separation of a system into user interface, application programs, and data layers, offers flexibility, especially regarding the user interface and the database, essential if the system is to be implemented on different platforms.

Taking a programmer's view of a system may be correct for code intensive applications in which the programs themselves are considered the most important part of the system. Here object-orientation offers the promise of well-structured programs that may foster reuse, and consequently, a reduction of the code needed. From an academic point of view, object-orientation also offers a more theoretical and better structured approach to programming than early languages such as Fortran and Cobol. As we have seen, object-orientation is ideal for modeling artificial and closed worlds and in other situations in which we are in full control of the environment. It has given us flexible operating systems, drawing packages, system development toolkits, and word processors. In these cases, we can start by modeling the underlying reusable "building blocks," use polymorphism to let these work on many types of data, inheritance to let attributes and methods propagate to other modules, and encapsulation to separate the inner part of a module from its interface.

Strict testing is important for developing code that is to be used in different systems or perhaps for different purposes. Strict version control procedures are a necessity when one has different versions running on different platforms, perhaps at the same time as the programs are being revised. With many installations, it is important to ensure that the right systems and modules are installed at each location. Therefore, a system for widespread deployment is needed.

Taking a programmer's view of a system may be correct for code intensive applications.

23.1   Maturity levels

The methods described above are sound software engineering practices. The theories and practices have evolved over time to offer high-quality software using these principles. In some ways they are summed up in the first Capability Maturity Model from the Software Engineering Institute.[1] Here five levels of software maturity are defined, from an initial ad hoc approach, via an intermediate level of defined processes to an optimized managed level.

The five levels are:

1. Initial (ad hoc)
2. Repeatable (with sufficient documentation to be able to repeat the process)
3. Defined (use of standard business processes)
4. Managed (the development process is managed according to agreed-upon metrics)
5. Optimizing (the development process is optimized)

For each level there are five important concepts:

1. Goals
2. Commitment
3. Ability
4. Measurement
5. Verification

The detailed model tells how an organization can move incrementally from one level to the next. This model was initially developed to evaluate the ability of governmental software contractors; however, many successful software companies do not follow this model.

As noted, software development distinguishes itself from other types of engineering. Since making another copy of a system is an automatic task, most software development is for quite new systems and has an aspect of moving into the unknown, where experimentation and creativity play a role. This will especially be the case for companies, such as Microsoft, Google, Facebook, and Apple, which provide quite new products and services. Then it becomes difficult to start a process by detailed specifications, or to follow well-defined and optimized processes. In fact, many of the processes of developing the successful software products from these companies could best be characterized as being on level 1 and 2 above.

23.2   Agile methods

The rigidness and bureaucracy of the traditional approach leave little room for creativity and individuality. As one of the ideas is to develop software independent of individual programmers, programming may become a more uninteresting job. That is, excellent programmers, some of whom see the process more as

Agile program-ming offers simplicity, fast development, and a focus on pro-grams, not docu-ments, and team-work.

art than engineering, may choose to work in companies that use less strict methods.

A movement has been underway since the millennium to advocate for simplicity, with a focus on producing working software rather than documents, concentrating on self-organized teams and customer collaboration. This more flexible approach offers developers the means to react to change. That is, instead of limiting change, agile methods offer a way of handling change. The ideas are summed up in the Manifesto for Agile Software Development.[2] The central comparative values are:

- individuals and interactions over processes and tools
- working software over comprehensive documentation
- customer collaboration over contract negotiation
- responding to change over following a plan

The manifesto does not imply that the authors do not value processes, documentation, contracts and plans, but that they have different prioritizes and values. Agile development covers methods such as Extreme Programming (XP), Adaptive Software Development, Feature-Driven Development, Dynamic Systems Development Methodology, Scrum and Kanban. These methods emphasize people and communication. The application of agile methods has been widely discussed in the literature. While many offer compelling arguments for the new methods,[3] others see this as a way to make hacking respectable.[4]

Many of the methods that may be categorized under the agile-umbrella are oriented towards programming. For example, instead of working out detailed specifications ahead of programming, XP, for example, stresses the importance of early prototypes and rapid feedback from customers. This is to be done while maintaining quality through extensive and constant testing. While some compare agile methods to ad hoc or cowboy coding, this is certainly not the case. According to Boehm,[5] agile methods may be a way out of these coding practices: "Another encouraging trend is that the buzz of agile methods such as XP is drawing many young programmers away from the cowboy role model and towards the more responsible agile methods."

The people factor has been an issue in the debate on agile methods. Constantine said that all of the "agile methods put a premium on having premium people...."[6] Boehm stressed "that agile methods derive much of their agility by relying on tacit knowledge embodied in the team..." While high-capability people are needed in all software projects, it seems reasonable to believe that the less structured agile methods need more experience in the team players than the more traditional software engineering methods. However, agile methods are finding their way into software engineering curriculums, and even if the experiences are not always encouraging, there may soon be available candidates who know how to use these methods.

Agile methods are said to work best where there are turbulent environments and when rapid change is the norm.

Agile methods are said to work best where there are turbulent environments and when rapid change is the norm. Most of its advocates find that agile methods work best with smaller teams and not life-critical software. However, few discuss the type of system that is to be developed, whether generic or specific, whether developed to be installed for many customers or for only one.

As the ideas of agile software development have spread, several methodologies have been devised, fulfilling the function of frameworks for organizing agile teams. In addition to XP, some of the most well known are Kanban and Scrum:

Kanban stresses incremental and continuous (evolutionary) development.

- *Kanban development.* Kanban is known from Toyota, which used it to implement Just In Time (JIT) manufacturing. The idea was to go from a push development, where subparts are manufactured based on an overall plan, to a pull system, where parts are manufactured when they are needed. For software, the Kanban method stresses incremental and continuous (evolutionary) development, leaving the organizational structure as it is. As for its parent, Kanban in the manufacturing plant, the method stresses the importance of workflow, to visualize and manage flow and to offer JIT delivery of software based on pulling work from a queue. The idea is to achieve a basic understanding of the workflow. Based on this, it is expected that a team will reach a common understanding of what is to be done and what is to be prioritized.

With **Scrum**,
development time
is partitioned into
small units called
sprints.

- *Scrum development*. The word Scrum is taken from a way of restarting a game of rugby after an interruption. The basic ideas are also taken from manufacturing. With Scrum, development time is partitioned into sprints. These start with a planning meeting, where one determines what to do during the next sprint. Tasks are defined based on the product backlog, a prioritized list of requirements. Each sprint lasts for a period of weeks, during which time the development teams will retrieve and develop code to fulfill these requirements. This is followed by a new meeting to review progress. Scrum is based on the recognition that requirements may change during development. The customer can have new ideas about what it wants and the development process may give new insights.

There are differences between the proposed methodologies, but they share the values outlined in the agile manifesto and the value placed on small, quick-moving teams and the process of breaking down every task into manageable chunks. Documentation is only produced when needed.

23.3   Testing and Test-driven development

Testing is an
important part of
software engineer-
ing.

Testing is an important part of software engineering. However, testing in agile methods differs from testing using traditional approaches. As each task is small, taking hours or at most a few days to accomplish, the number of implemented features grow steadily as the project progresses, allowing for rapid feedback from users as the task is completed, or to quickly bring a potential problem to the attention of the team if it is taking longer than expected. In this setting, testing is a continuous process throughout the lifecycle of the project.

Testing starts by checking each unit, often by automated tests. These run on small sections of code, often a single call of a method, verifying that the results of the call are as expected. Test-driven development (TDD) takes this process a step further, with the idea of repeating very short development cycles. The cycle starts with a test case; that is, defining the conditions that determine if an application is working correctly. Often, one may also define a negative test case, which is the conditions that define whether a test has failed. Based on this, a program is developed that fulfills the test conditions, and then

A **"test-first"** approach forces a developer to specify exactly what the effect of the implemented functionality should be.

the process is repeated with a new test. In many ways, test-driven development can be seen as a new way of handling requirements. The advantage is that these are now focused on the conditions that have to be met in order to succeed. In practice, this means that the test case must be formalized. Note that with TDD, no functionality, however small, is developed before a corresponding test has been written.

A "test-first" approach forces a developer to specify exactly what the effect of the implemented functionality should be before he or she starts thinking about how to implement it, and this approach ensures that the percentage of code that is checked by automated tests is high. If code added to one module conflicts with the behavior in another, the corresponding tests will fail and the issue will quickly be brought to the programmers' attention. An application is never deployed unless all tests are executed successfully.

Even if every unit test in the project library passes with flying colors, there might be still be problems with the code. The test coverage may not be complete or, worse, tests may be missing or the tests can be looking for the wrong problems. As discussed in Chapter 22.8, it is also important that the code is readable.

A high level of code quality can be accomplished if all code committed to source control is **checked** by at least one other developer.

A common technique for accomplishing a high level of code quality is to ensure that all code committed to source control is checked by at least one other developer. If there are missing components, poor tests, missing tests, or if the reviewer has problems understanding the code, changes may be made at an early point, before there has been any consequence to the system as a whole. Automated systems are often used to assist this process. There are also fully automated ways of reviewing code, such as checking whether the code conforms to an agreed-upon style.

23.4   Source control

In its simplest form, a source control system can be a collection of source files kept on a common file share. In fact, this is the state of affairs for many smaller projects. But as systems become more complex and the number of teams working on the same source code grows, a more refined solution is needed.

All source control systems support the concepts of versioned files; that is, they can find the current version of the file, and any previous version. They track changes, when it was performed, by whom, why the change was made, and so forth.

Modern source control systems support branching and merging. This enables the project to maintain several versions of the same codebase. A common strategy is to keep one main branch of the code (commonly known as the "master" or "trunk"), which reflects the code as it exists in the production version of the system. Changes made in preparation for a new release are made to a "development" branch, which is branched to "test" before finally being merged into the master branch when the release is ready to go.

The technique of continuous integration, performing small and incremental changes continuously, leverages modern source control in order to ensure that the project has a working code-base. This is accomplished by encouraging frequent commits, submitting the latest changes to the code repository. Each commit will trigger a build on the project's integration server, alerting the developers to any problems that might have developed.

Rigorous automatic testing is necessary in order for this strategy to be truly effective. The first line of defense against unforeseen problems caused by a change is to automatically perform unit tests. If all units pass, we move on to the next phase, which is integration testing. These are large-scale tests, which require a full infrastructure to run. The type of tests vary, for example to test if a Web service responds, if creating a new user through the Web interface results in the expected changes in the database, or that the right numbers show up in a specified report. The key concept is to test large slices of the application with each test, as opposed to unit tests.

23.5   Release management

Release management has traditionally consisted of separate phases. The changes that go into a release are planned, specified, and submitted to developers, who implement and perform automated tests. Then acceptance testing is performed, either by end users or specialized testing personnel, before the code is delivered to the operations team, which deploys it on the production servers.

In many organizations, this is a large and complex process, and just deploying a release to the production environment is viewed as a high-risk activity, planned months in advance. This makes for long release cycles, as many projects will at least have six months between each release. However, this implies that the users may sit around for months waiting for requested

Frequent releases of the system are an advantage.

features. While this is obviously not desirable from a user's point of view, it also slows down the feedback cycle: developers wait for feedback, users wait for adjustments made by the developers based on the feedback, and so on.

A slow cycle is also a risk in itself: when a process is performed sparingly, the organization is slow to learn about and improve the process. If there have been substantial changes in infrastructure or personnel since the last time the process was performed, it may have to be rediscovered, and it is likely that mistakes made then could be repeated now.

An obvious solution to the above problems is to speed up the frequency of releases. The users will then receive features more rapidly, feedback is quick, and the organization learns faster. In order to accomplish this goal, the organizations must leverage the tools discussed above.

Agile development offers the dynamic development teams that are necessary, automated unit testing decreases time spent to ensure that the system works as expected, while continuous integration followed by automated testing reduce the risk of nasty surprises. A fully automated system for deploying can make this task much more robust. Further refinements are often added. Using multiple production servers running in tandem in combination with load balancing enables the organization to upgrade one server while the other is still serving requests on the old version, or even roll out a release gradually, starting with a small selection of users and let this increase gradually.

Today, we are building **systems out of systems**.

This is especially important today when system development is as much about setting together modules than it is about programming. Parts of a system can be available either as open source, to be bought in the public software market, to be found within the company's or its partner's software archives or, for example, be available as a service on the Web. In other words, we are building systems out of systems. This process is complex enough in itself, for example when already pre-existing components are to be used in quite new systems. However, the Internet makes it possible for development to often be performed by a distributed and decentralized group of organizations. If this is not enough, complexity is added by the fact that many systems are in a continuous cycle of development, testing and deployment, as described above.

To help in mastering these processes, release management has become an important part of modern software engineering. Someone, often called a release manager, will oversee this

Release management has become an important part of modern software engineering.

process. A central task is to ensure that the various development groups and business units are synchronized, that the modules are delivered on time, and that they will work seamlessly together. This requires that dependencies between components be clearly understood.

As we have seen, for more mundane tasks like compiling, linking, and testing, build automation is applied. The idea is to make scripts that automate several of the tasks in this process. The scripts may also handle version control and documentation.

While scripts simplify the process, reducing errors and make the complete task much more efficient, there are now several tools, both commercial and open source, that can automate these processes to an even greater degree. For the more complex systems, automation is the only answer, as the complexity will not be manageable by manual methods.

With explicit and formal definitions of how the full system is defined into components, with formalized specification on interdependencies and a description of the location of each component (often on different servers), such a system can manage the complete software release process. That is, it can build systems based on components, perform automated testing of the system, and deploy these to customers, adding the necessary documentation.

23.6   Discussion

Software Engineering is a complex process. This chapter and the previous one have provided a short overview of both traditional methods and modern, agile methods. However, all methods address the same issues; namely, how to manage a complex process, how to reduce risks, and to deliver on time. All methods offer ideas about how a large system can be split into smaller parts, and how to ensure some flexibility during development.

In Chapter 25, I introduce my own agile method and present a case in Chapter 26. But let us first look at the possibility of avoiding system development (at least some parts) by using premade systems, separate packages, or larger Enterprise Resource Planning (ERP) systems.

Notes

1   Software Engineering Institute (SEI) is a research and development center at Carnegie Mellon University (Pittsburgh, USA).

2   http://www.agileAlliance.org

3   For example, see Beck, K., Andres, C. (2005) Extreme Programming Explained, 2nd ed., Addison-Wesley; Cockburn, A. (2002) Agile Software Development, Addison-Wesley; Cockburn, A., Highsmith, J. (2001) Agile Software Development: The People Factor, Computer, November, 34

4   See for example Rakitin, S. (2001) Manifesto Elicits Cynicism, IEEE Computer, December.

5   Boehm, B. (2002) Get Ready for Agile Methods with Care, IEEE Computer, January.

6   Constantine, L. (2001) Methodological Agility, Software Development, June.

24 Packages and ERP Systems

Many standard systems, such as office suits (word processing, spreadsheet, and mail system), browsers, and accounting systems are available as off-the-shelf-programs. Some of these are free; for others we have to pay a license. However, since these systems are sold in many copies, development costs are spread, which keeps costs moderate.

24.1 Customization

Most of these systems offer some flexibility. For example, a word processor can be adjusted to the user's own language. A Norwegian using Microsoft Word can set up the system with commands, help texts, spelling checker, and dictionary in Norwegian. The system also will accept the three additional characters in the Norwegian alphabet (æ, ø, å). In addition, the word processor can be used for languages with quite different character sets, such as Chinese, as well as languages in which the writing direction is not from left to right, such as Arabic.

In addition, modern software also will allow the user to customize menus, button lines, autocorrect options, and so on, to her needs.

24.2 Macros

Some systems allow the user to program functions in the form of macros. For example, Microsoft offers Visual Basic for Applications (VBA) as a macro programming language for its office package. For example, a company that has its own special needs for word processing may start with Microsoft Word and build its own code on top of this.

This box is inserted by using a **macro**.

As an example, consider the boxes in the margin of this book. These have a fixed width, and should all have the same horizontal position (0.42 cm from the margin), and a vertical position defined by the line where the concept is explained in the text. Within the box, a 10-point Arial font is used. This box can be created using the standard command in Microsoft Word, and then offering data on width, position, and font. But this process can become tedious, and also risks placing the box out of position. To avoid this, a macro can be developed, which is easy to do with Word's macro recorder. The user turns on the recorder, which generates code for all the operations that the user performs. So we create one text box manually, set size, horizontal position and the font that we want and the recorder generates the code:

```
Selection.Font.Name = "Arial"
Selection.Font.Size = 10
Selection.ShapeRange.left = CentimetersToPoints(0.42)
```

With **macros** it is possible to tune a package to one's own needs.

We can now customize the word processor by putting a new button on the command line, or better, by defining a shortcut, such as CTRL + B, for the macro. A click on the button or CTRL B will run the macro and insert a text box in the left margin. To get the vertical position we invoke a system function, which will return the position of the cursor. With macros, it is possible to customize many off-the-shelf products with just a minimum of programming knowledge.[1]

The Turbokforlaget,[2] a publishing company, is a good case. Pictures play a central role in the company's visual hiking guides. With the guide, hikers can tell which path to take from a picture of every intersection, which includes arrows to indicate direction. Instead of buying a general typesetting system, and learning to use this, the company chose to write their books using Microsoft Word.

Because Word is not a typesetting system, the company extended the program with macros, adding some thousand lines of code on top of the standard system. Macros provided functionality to place pictures on the page, to insert arrows and text boxes on pictures, and to check the final product.

24.3   Covering all needs

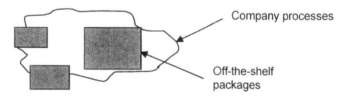

Figure 24.1 Trying to satisfy requirements by standard systems.

Customizing by macros is seldom enough to cover all of an organization's needs. Figure 24.1 shows a situation in which a company tries to satisfy its IT requirements with a suite of standard systems. As shown, some parts are not covered by the

Using standard systems with manual operations can lead to errors.

systems. These are usually handled manually. This process offers flexibility, but has three main drawbacks: It is expensive and time consuming, and there is the risk of errors.

As an example consider a manufacturer which stores product specifications in a spreadsheet. One day a customer wants a modification of the product. The employee will then open the spreadsheet, perform the modifications and hit the save button. But this spreadsheet was not only used to make new products, but also as an "as-built" description of previous products. Now this description has been lost. Such incidents can be avoided when a system has full control of the data, for example, to retain previous versions.

Another problem with using separate packages is that the same data may be stored in more than one system. This violates the principle of "store once, use many times," and may lead to errors, for example, when a data item is updated in one system and not the other.

24.4   ERP systems

ERP systems are mostly used by large companies.

To avoid these problems many companies, mostly large, go for an ERP (Enterprise Resource Planning) system. These are huge systems that will integrate all management information within a company—finance, accounting, manufacturing, sales, service, and customer relations. These systems embed best practices that are the vendor's idea of how each business process should be performed.

The advantage of an ERP system is that there is one system for the whole company and data will be available to all. The disadvantage is that the system may end up being a lowest common denominator. That is, instead of programs adjusted to the needs of each division, all divisions must now use the same system. In homogenous companies this may not be a major problem, but for those in which divisions perform very different tasks, the company may end up with a system that suits nobody.

Installing an ERP system is a major task. First it is important to understand how the company functions and what an ERP system can offer. There have been many failures, and good advance planning is one way to achieve success. During installation, the company will find that it has to adjust its processes to those of the ERP system. Since the ERP system incorporates best practices, this adjustment may be a good idea in many situations. However, if the idiosyncratic functions reflect the business ideas of the company, the system must be adjusted or configured to their special needs, an extensive and costly process.

Today, large companies that apply more standard business processes are better suited for ERP systems than smaller more idiosyncratic companies. Also, large companies that operate in many countries may take advantage of all the functionality that is embedded in ERP systems, for example, to adjust to accounting regulations in each country.

Notes

1   In writing this book, I have programmed several other macros. For example, using "CTRL R," I ask the system to remember the current page and cursor position, with "CTRL G," I can go back to this position. I could have used the function in Word to return to the last change, but this is not what I need.

2   www.turbok.no (in Norwegian).

25 Simpler Software Development for Niche Companies

Software development remains a **costly process**, even if the development tools are far more efficient today than in the pioneering days.

Independent of maturity level and rigid processes, software development remains a costly process, even if the development tools are far more efficient today than in the pioneering days.[1]

Thirty years ago, when developing systems for the early PCs—or microcomputers, as they were called in the 1970s—we had to write everything ourselves. Today we are in a very different situation. We have a suit of excellent tools that let us describe the data model in a high-level language, perform database operations through a standard language (SQL),[2] create user interfaces by "drawing" forms directly on the screen, and use ready made modules or components for every standard operation. Equally important, we have a set of standards that let us interconnect packages and program components almost seamlessly.

At the same time we have an abundance of premade systems and large ERP systems, which many companies can use. When niche companies cannot find off-the-shelf packages to suit their needs, an ERP system can be a solution. These large packages, with their standard business processes, can be customized to the company. However, there are some problems. First, the typical generic software modules that are a part of the ERP system may not directly implement all the necessary functionality or in a manner that fits the company's business model. Second, most companies exist in a dynamic world where changes are frequent in business activities, such as production planning routines, how products are manufactured or sold, or how customer relations are maintained. In a changing world, the software must be changeable as well! But when installed in a company, the typical generic ERP system is more or less unchangeable, in all practicality.

In-house development of core functions is an interesting alternative.

In-house development of core functions is an interesting third alternative. If one can develop IT systems that are better suited for an organization than the general, packaged software, a strategic advantage can be achieved. This advantage is maximized if we can do this at less cost than installation, customization, and licensing fees for a standard, packaged system. Given the tools and standards we have today, this can be a good alternative for many customers, especially small and medium-sized niche companies. However, as we shall see, in order to really simplify the development process, a different software engineering process is required, avoiding all unnecessary tasks. We achieve this by ensuring system integration at the database level, avoiding interconnections between program components on all other levels, and modeling business rules at the user interface level, using off-the-shelf packages for all standard parts.

While traditional methods of software engineering stress the importance of rigid procedures for developing software, simplification is often needed when working with small and medium-sized companies that do not have the resources to pay for a costly development. Then we develop proprietary systems or add-ons to existing systems using very fast and efficient processes with a minimum of effort. In doing this, we break the rules and skip most of the phases that distinguish good software engineering. We bypass the extensive requirements and modularization phases; avoid version control by having only one version for development and production; and use simplified testing methods. That is, we revert back to the pioneering days of developing proprietary systems, but with the tools of today.

> While traditional methods of software engineering stress the importance of rigid procedures for developing software, **simplification** is needed when working with small and medium-sized companies

25.1   Proprietary development

Breaking away from the traditional path of system and software acquisition and development is difficult and may involve greater risks. However, the opportunities for getting a strategic advantage materialize because most organizations follow the main-street approach of adapting and tuning the business functions to the system rather than adapting and tuning the system to business functions. The generalization and formalization of business processes that is a consequence of the commoditization of software offers opportunities for those that are willing to try something different.

> Breaking away from the traditional path of system and software acquisition and development is difficult and may involve greater risks.

Of course, only companies that can and will use IT to do business in a different way than everybody else should take this approach. Not all companies have this opportunity. Many businesses are "standard" in the sense that they rely on a market defined by their location more so than their products or services. For these companies the default and often correct solution, is to use the standard, off-the-shelf software developed for their business to reduce IT costs and risks.

Nicholas Carr argues that IT (2003,[3] 2004[4]), like other technologies, follows a typical life cycle of introduction, pioneering period, and maturity. When mature, a technology becomes part of the essential infrastructure and no longer has strategic importance. When everybody uses the same hardware and the same software, it is no longer possible to get any competitive advantage out of IT. As Carr pointed out, even usage patterns become standards when companies install an ERP system such as SAP[5] ("company in a box"). In this situation, said Carr, one should concentrate on reducing costs and risks such as buying only the computer power that one needs, relying on open standards and open source code, and avoiding unnecessary updates. The same applies to the more mundane applications within a company. Most tasks such as word processing, spreadsheet and accounting can be performed perfectly well using off-the-shelf products.

For specialized companies or for special functions within companies, there may be advantages in developing **proprietary software**.

However, for specialized companies or for special functions within companies, there may be advantages in developing proprietary software. Here we leave Carr who dismisses the possibility of developing proprietary software. His arguments are that software development is a costly and risky undertaking and thus the costs have to be shared by many customers. But, as we shall see, by implementing their own core systems, organizations can offer better, more dynamic, and more efficient services. This will be the case, especially, for niche companies and highly specialized companies that serve focused markets, and can be done with moderate costs, often comparable to that of using standard software.

What we propose is really quite simple. Today IT is used to implement business models, business rules, and business processes. IT is no longer seen as a tool for isolated functions. Standard, packaged software provides nearly all the standard business process capabilities. If one wants to do something different and create proprietary business rules or processes, then these can be implemented using proprietary software.

25.2   Reducing risks—the use of standards

In-house development is only a viable option if the risks can be kept to a minimum. In practice, this means keeping the development costs low enough to minimize the risk. This is achievable if one employs modern development tools, uses standard system platforms and existing software whenever possible. Here standards, such as SQL, VBA, HTML, HTTP, XML, SOAP, to name a few, make it possible to interconnect different systems, programs or software modules, and let these use the same database or communicate with other programs over a network.

We try to make as few **interconnections** as possible between the different parts of the system to minimize complexity and dependencies.

We also propose a new perspective for this type of software development. Instead of focusing on strict modeling and reuse techniques, we try to make as few interconnections as possible between the different parts of the system to minimize complexity and dependencies. This opens the way for simpler development and easier maintenance, for what is called "change-oriented" software, which is achieved by modeling the system according to the user's point of view, not from the programmer's perspective or the standard business model. At the same time, we strive to reduce bindings between components of the system. The idea is to offer customers the necessary functionality with minimum time and cost, and to also ensure that the customer gets a system that can evolve with the changing company and business environment, that is, a system that can be easily maintained and enhanced to meet new business requirements.

There are several software engineering methods for agile development, as presented in Chapter 23.2, and these methods have clear similarities with what we have discussed here. However, we break with the reuse idea of mainstream software engineering.

25.3   Core functions

Using these methods it is possible to develop complete systems for a single customer very efficiently. The idea is to focus the development on core functions, using off-the-shelf systems wherever possible. While development is an important issue, we also focus on life-cycle development. We do that by developing a change-oriented system.

The methods presented here may be used for many different types of applications; however, we are primarily focused on developing user-oriented software of strategic importance for small and medium-sized niche companies. In these cases, there are often only one customer and probably only one installation. As we shall see, this allows us to take the agile methods several more steps towards simplicity. We shall also see that proprietary development for core functions may have many other advantages for the customer, even in these days where there are an abundance of generic systems available.

A solution is to develop proprietary systems for core business functions, and then use existing standards and the openness of many off-the-shelf products to interconnect the various parts. I have used this process with success in several cases (one of which is presented in Chapter 26). Of course, when the complete system consists of parts from different suppliers, the same consistency will not be achieved as when a single system is employed. However, since most systems today share a commonality in "look and feel," the differences are often minor. In many cases, users only employ a few systems, so that the differences are relatively easy to handle.

25.4   Database

When each system has its own database, which is often the case, the open standards allow us to insert and retrieve data from these databases as if they were one. That is, multiple databases do not imply that we have to break the rule of storing data only once. In practice, these cross-database operations can be isolated to the core part of the system, that is, to the proprietary software.

This approach has several advantages. First the company gets an implementation of the core functionality part that is developed just for its needs and that is under its full control. Second, since we integrate on the database side and not on the system side, the company can keep the systems that are already in use, as long as these support the standards of interconnectivity, for example, SQL, ODBC, or XML. This approach is very different compared with the "all-in-one" philosophy of the ERP systems, in which the new system is to take over the functionality of all or most existing systems. When needing a new standard package, the organization can, similarly, choose freely in the marketplace as long as the new package supports the standards mentioned above. Third, this approach will most often reduce cost compared to a full ERP installation.

25.5   Developing proprietary software

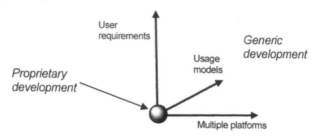

Figure 25.1 Dimensionality of software development.

Software development today is often performed within a three-dimensional space, as illustrated in Figure 25.1. That is, developers of systems that are planned with several installations must take into account three aspects: the union of user requirements, multiple platforms of operating systems, and architectures and different usage models (the customization) of their system. However, with only one customer, one installation and perhaps only one platform, the process is much simpler than in the generic case with many customer organizations and IT environments. That is, we may reduce the 3D space above to one point! This is the case when we provide an organization with an IT system that supports its core business functions tailored to include its proprietary business practices, within limited costs and risks.

This process is characterized by:

- Nonbureaucratic organization of system development
- Software as a process
- Focus on customizing core functions
- Use of standards to integrate off-the-shelf software packages
- Two-tiered architecture (user interface and database)
- Database as the common denominator
- Often only one installation
- One user organization
- Proprietary code
- Independent components
- Reuse only on the database level

- Change-oriented development
- Use of modern system development tools
- No need for strict systemwide testing
- Minimum of user training

As seen, the agile software development movement shares many of these factors. However, the focus that we have on developing proprietary software for small and medium-sized firms, allows us to add factors that simplify development even further.

25.6   Organization of system development

The task of developing a new system or add-on system requires modeling the system according to the user's needs. These are expressed by a general requirement specification or a needs analysis document as we prefer to call it, as discussed in Chapter 22. However, the specification document describes only the overall needs of the user and is not necessarily complete. For the purpose of efficiency, we can leave many details to the system developer. The idea is to:

- Avoid unnecessary specification work
- Accept that many details are embedded within the tools and standards that we employ
- Be able to utilize the ideas that emerge during the development phase
- Recognize that users will not have a full understanding of the system before it is actually implemented
- Exploit the experience and knowledge of the development team

A consequence of a loose specification is that development must be done without a strict, fixed-price contract. However, in our experience, strict contracts are of no use when developing strategic core software for an organization. Since all organizations are dynamic, the software must also be dynamic and must be adapted and tuned to the organization at all times. To develop the system under a strict contract, and then establish a new maintenance contract with the one contractor who knows both the system and the organization is not a sound approach. Instead, we follow the basic principle of the agile movement in stressing the need to establish a partnership agreement with the software developer from the very start. The best approach will be to develop and maintain software in-house. If our business approach is to have better software than our competitors, it is an advantage to keep development close to the chest—just as other core functions.

25.7   Software as a process

Software that implements core business functions needs to be under **continuous** development.

Software that implements core business functions needs to be under continuous development. When new functionality is needed, it should be implemented as soon as possible, preferably immediately. That is, the software must change along with the company. Only then can the software fulfill its strategic obligations. This simplified view of changes is made possible by reducing the dimensionality of the development from a 3D space to a point, and to have a user- and change-oriented view of software development.

Such a process-oriented view of software is not compatible with using off-the-shelf packages for core functions. With a standard package, suggestions for improvements have to go through a process of first convincing the user community and the vendor that such improvements are beneficial, then waiting for the generic modifications to be implanted in the next version of the package, and then parameterizing these according to the needs of the company.

The dynamic view we propose may be difficult to embed even if the software is developed in-house, that is, if traditional methods of software engineering are used. Object-oriented modeling and reuse principles may create an efficient first version of the software, but also produces a system with so many interconnections that maintenance will be complicated and expensive. Therefore, we suggest a simpler architecture that is more conformant with the flexibility needs in proprietary systems.

25.8   Two-tiered architecture

Standard architectures have been one-tiered (an application program only), two-tiered (application and database code) and three-tiered (inclusion of a user interface part). Today the three-tiered architecture is predominant. We use a two-tiered architecture, but without the application (program) part that has been central to all architectures until now.

The new tiers consist of the database and the user-interface parts. All application code is embedded within these parts. The idea is to model the system according to the following priorities:

- The database as a common denominator for all applications, modeled to fulfill current needs and extendable to fulfill future needs.
- Applications modeled according to the user's view; that is, we embed all other functionality within the user interface part using a forms-based approach.
- Change-oriented view; that is, we try to incorporate as few bindings between modules as possible to simplify modifications and extensions of the system. Reuse is not a priority.

We shall explore each of these principles below.

25.9   The database as the common denominator

The database, as the **common denominator**, is central to our development approach.

The database, as the common denominator, is central to our development approach. The database serves the needs of the organization today and must do so in the future, even if we cannot predict the business functions that will use the database. What we do know is that the database will be modified and extended as time passes. A new or revised function in the system can use the data structure already available and must eventually deliver data to the database in agreement with the data model.

The relational model[6] is ideal for this. Its flat structure offers the possibility of modifying existing data tables and creating new with few side effects. The stability of the data layer is further enhanced with an extensive use of database views. If the application code is accessing views only, a change in a base table will be hidden for all functions not directly affected. There are, of course, a large number of excellent database systems that support this model.

Our approach requires integration of proprietary and standard packages. This integration can often be implemented most easily on the database level. Modern packages offer an open database structure that is typically well documented. While single software components and modules may be changed frequently and often replaced by quite different versions, the database will be much more stable. That is, the developers of the standard packages have good reasons for keeping the database structure as it is. Further, data may exist in many forms in the program, but will be normalized when stored into the database.

25.10 User interface part—forms based development

With the database structure established, we can proceed to implement the user interface that offers the functionality that users require. We will model this part using a forms-based methodology. That is, we shall structure the system using forms and implement all functions as forms, relying heavily on modern development tools that allow us to design a form by "drawing" it on the screen.

This approach has several advantages. First and foremost, users understand forms. Often the initial requirements may be presented as forms, which may be sketched by hand or copied from previously used systems or from Web pages, often with modifications performed directly on these samples. When we have developed the initial prototypes for the users, this process is reversed. We show users the system prototype, which may be only a collection of forms, and we get an immediate response. We are talking their language!

Forms in modern development tools are, of course, also implemented using an object-oriented approach. Forms encapsulate data and methods on these data, typically implemented by input fields and buttons that associate business functions with actions in data systems. The code is organized as event handlers for the objects making up the form, which leads to very small code units with strong cohesion. A typical event handler has less than a hundred lines of code. This natural "divide-and-conquer" approach allows for straightforward development and maintenance of code. In fact, whenever a user wants a new form that is somewhat similar to another, we say copy instead of reuse. By limiting the bindings and connections among forms, we can have many components and still maintain an overview of the system.

25.11 Change-oriented development

Business systems are open-ended, reflecting a reality outside themselves, and will be confronted with the need for changes continuously. Users will ask for modifications to forms, for new forms, and for the implementation of new business rules. If we model our system according to program code, perhaps relying extensively on object-oriented techniques, we risk that requests for new functionality will create havoc to our structure. In contrast to artificial constructs, real world systems must be prepared for sudden and dramatic changes. The simpler the structure, the easier it is to handle change. At least, by using a forms-based modeling approach, users will appreciate the work that has to be done to implement their wishes. Also in this respect we are talking the same language as users.

With few bindings, the maintenance of existing forms, and the deletion and insertion of new forms, we may focus on one form at a time, independent of other forms.

The disadvantage of the copy-approach compared to reuse is that we may get similar code in many forms. Of course, if these use identical methods, we may put them in a common module. However, in general, the advantages of duplication of code override the disadvantages. We now have complete freedom to modify code within each form, without thinking of side effects. This is a huge advantage considering a dynamic system under constant modification. In the real world, we often see that the similarities between two forms, reports, or other modules that are used to implement the users' needs may be superficial and perhaps time-dependent. In the next system update, these modules may move further apart and soon they may be on completely different logical paths. The disadvantage of copying is that we may need to perform a change in more than one place. In most cases this is a minor problem, especially since we most often copy from modules that have been in use for a considerable time and which are stable.

> The disadvantage of the copy-approach compared to reuse is that we may get similar code in many forms.

25.12   Version control and deployment

When developing proprietary software, we frequently can avoid version control by having only one version. Yes, in many cases we use the same version both for production and development. Most modern development tools allow this. The advantage is that changes are available immediately without any deployment phase. In many cases we may find ourselves extending or updating a system as it is being used by company employees. Within small organizations this works fine, and most systems will keep other users away from modules or forms that are under revision.

But what if we have more than one installation of our software package? Well, our approach is based on proprietary software. If two customers need a similar system we would, in most cases, take a copy and maintain two different systems. The argument is identical to the one we used above with forms. The similarity across organizations is often superficial. It is much more probable that the two organizations, if independent, will move in different directions than that they will need the same extensions to a package.

25.13   Testing and maintenance

Testing can be reduced to a **minimum** in our case.

Testing can also be simplified. While many agile methods, such as extreme programming, rely heavily on testing, this phase can be reduced to a minimum in our case. With independent modules, testing can be isolated to the one new or modified module. With only one installation, the software can be tested with the data that the user provides. That is, instead of having a three dimensional test situation:

1.   The generic module,
2.   interconnections between modules,
3.   many installations,

there is only the first part in a simplified version, often as an object rather than a generic class. This allows for very simple maintenance and testing situations. Testing is performed on the fly, with real data. With the users involved in the testing, the risk of unwanted side effects is reduced to a minimum.

25.14   Training

With proprietary development, training can be reduced to a **minimum**.

In general, training can be a costly process. With proprietary development, training can be reduced to a minimum. This is possible because the organization gets software that is customized to its particular situation. If the developers have done a good job, users should immediately feel at home with their new system: Forms should be structured according to well-known tasks and the terminology used should be familiar. That is, instead of training the users for a generic system, we now have developed a system that conforms directly to their needs. The system reflects the user's world from the text on a command button to the structure of processes.

25.15   Conclusion

For IT to be used to gain a competitive advantage, a company must have a strategic plan and associated processes, practices, and policies implemented through dynamic software in which changes can be performed when needed. Standard software, such as an ERP package or off-the-shelf systems, often will not provide such a strategic advantage, since the software is available to competitors as well. However, through programming, a computer can offer unlimited flexibility, that is, the possibility of implementing functions tuned to the company's needs. Still, most companies accept the much more limited flexibility offered by the ERP packages, which, in many cases, is not enough to get a strategic advantage in a dynamic world.

To be applicable, proprietary development must be achieved at a low cost, in minimal time, and with minimum risk. Based upon my experience in developing software for various types of organizations, I have described an "ad hoc" process that acts as a starting point for discussing methods found to be highly successful in developing software to meet specialized application needs for business processes. This is a two-tiered methodology with only the user interface layer and the database layer. It is based on ideas from agile methods, but methods for simplifying the development effort are taken a step further to utilize the fact that a proprietary system is being developed, a system for only one customer, only one group of users, and often with only one installation.

Proprietary development of core functions opens a way for a business to continue using "standard" functions such as accounting or payroll, while at the same time instituting new processes and procedures that provide a competitive advantage. It requires less time, cost, and risks than acquiring a whole new core system or having the vendor integrate specialized components into the core system.

For software to be of strategic importance, I believe it must be controlled by the organization, must fulfill the organization's needs, must enable the organization to be more efficient, and must allow the organization to be dynamic and flexible. Proprietary development involves the IT people as well as the users in the development process so that together they can maintain the software without the need for long-term contracts with consulting firms or vendors.

I stress that only kernel functions, functions that give a strategic advantage, should be developed in-house. For all standard functions, word processing, accounting, and so on, off-the-shelf packages can be used, of course. However, these can be integrated with proprietary systems using existing standards.

The ideas presented here have much in common with what Eric Evans calls Domain-driven Design.[7] His ideas are to match software design with the developers and users mental model of the problem domain, stressing iterative development and that developers and domain experts have a close relationship. In many of the cases I describe, developing systems for small and medium sized companies, there will not be any domain experts, this role must then be shared by developers and the users.

These ideas for simpler software development been applied in many cases, one of which is presented in the next chapter.

Notes

1   This chapter is based on Olsen, K. A., Sætre, P. L., Williams, J. G. (2007). Breaking the rules—proprietary software development for small and medium sized organizations; University of Pittsburgh Press, Toni Carbo and James G. Williams, Editors, Perspectives on Information, A Festschrift in Honor of Anthony Debons, School of Information Sciences, Pittsburgh, PA, USA, 2007.

2   SQL (Structured Query Language) is a programming language for relational databases. In these, data are structured as tables. A table *product* can, for example, include fields for product number, product name, and price. To retrieve a price for a certain product, identified by a product number 1234, one can use expressions such as:

SELECT price FROM product WHERE ProductNumber = 1234

That is, SQL will perform the necessary data base operations, and return the value of the price attribute.

3   Carr, N. G. (2003) IT Doesn't Matter. Harvard Business Review, 41–49.

4   Carr, N. G. (2004) Does IT Matter? Information Technology and the Corrosion of Competitive Advantage, Harvard Business School Press, Boston.

5   SAP (Systems, Applications and Products in Data Processing) is the most used ERP system. It is developed by the German firm SAP AG.

6   In a relational database, data are organized in tables. For example, we may have a table vehicle with fields (or columns) for each attribute that characterizes a vehicle in our system, such as license number, type, model, and production year. Each vehicle will then occupy a line (record) in this table. Data on vehicle types may be stored in another table, this with fields for type name, number of passengers, total load, and so on. A record in the first table may have the type as "bus." Then, we can lookup "bus" in the second table to get data on buses, or we may *join* the two tables to create a *view* with details on every vehicle, including detailed information on type.

7   Evans, E. (2004) Domain-Driven Design: Tackling Complexity in the Heart of Software, Pearson Education.

26   Case 1: In-house Programming

In house programming lost its attractiveness in the 1980s. Ever-raising costs and overdue projects discouraged businesses from developing their own systems. As an alternative, many small and medium-sized companies went for off-the-shelf packages, some for larger ERP systems. If one views IT as a commodity, this may be a correct move. However, for many businesses, especially niche industries, good opportunities may be lost if they are satisfied with being just as good as everyone else with regard to IT. Improving competitiveness is possible with IT in general, and even more so for companies that develop their own software.[1]

26.1   A foundry

This case uses a foundry as an example, but the argument will hold for all **niche** industries.

This case uses a foundry as an example, but the argument will hold for all niche industries. By using IT extensively, automating everything that can be automated, offering users power tools that enable them to handle complex jobs efficiently, we shall see that a company can gain a strategic advantage.

Our case company manufactures propeller blades for ships. These are cast in a nickel-aluminum bronze based on design specifications from customers, which are companies that produce complete propeller systems. Propellers are designed for each particular vessel, which means our foundry must handle a large set of different propeller geometries.

The process is as follows: An inquiry from the customer is most often followed by an order specifying the propeller blade design, the pattern or model to be used. If this is a new design, the propeller geometry will be specified. A model is then constructed, machined into a casting pattern in a 3D CAD/CAM process utilizing a five-axis milling machine. The foundry will place the pattern in a sand fixture in a molding box. Molding boxes come in different sizes, and the foundry will try to accommodate the model in the smallest box possible. Different parts of the box are joined to define a mold for the nickel-aluminum. After solidification, the casting is machined and measured according to an ISO[2] standard.

On a scale from one to ten, the castability of nickel-aluminum bronze is determined at level eight, being one of the most challenging alloys for the foundry engineer. Therefore, not many foundries can produce propeller blades, which is why our case company can be called a niche company. However, the company is "niche" only in casting propeller blades; in all other areas—such as finance, human resources, billing, and tax—it is a standard company. So we can divide this company in two parts, the standard and the niche part, and employ different IT strategies for each.

26.2   Standard part

The IT needs for the standard part can be met with off-the-shelf products. The aim is to get the necessary functionality with low risk and low cost, that is, the commodity view. An abundance of packages are available from which the company can chose freely. However, we require that systems have an open database solution, that is, with a well-documented data structure, which makes it possible to connect in-house programs with the standard packages, as we shall see below.

Some off-the-shelf packages offer a macro language, an option in which the customer may program functions, with access to the data structures and basic operations of the package. This feature is often an advantage, and will make it possible to seamlessly integrate different programs. (Macros are discussed in Chapter 24.)

26.3   Niche part

For the niche part, we are more ambitious: We will develop proprietary software and get the strategic advantages. To simplify program development, an application generator is employed—Microsoft Access, in our example. Access offers a form design language, a simple visual query part, a relational database and VBA (Visual Basic for Applications) as programming language. The advantage of using Access is that it comes with the Microsoft Office package (professional version) and is fully integrated with this. The advantage of using an application generator is that new functionality can be implemented with limited effort.

Some of the proprietary parts are straightforward, still particular enough to demand custom designed solutions. Order entry, data on models, documentation needs, and e-business functionality are all handled by this system. Most data entry is performed on the shop-floor, using touch sensitive screens. The system is used by all employees. Since this is an in-house system users find well-known terminology and processes that feel natural. It is also important that the users have been actively involved in the specification process and constructive suggestions are implemented right away. This gives ownership to the system which simplifies both training and acceptance.

The system handles all the different methods and electronic formats that customers may employ for describing propeller geometry. There are, alas, no standards. Even one particular customer may use many different coordinate systems, often one for each company with which it has merged over the years. Some may have an electronic format for new blades, while the propeller geometry for an older vessel may be only available on paper. Therefore, the system must provide an input routine for each format. However, all are converted to a standard internal format. These conversion routines are very straightforward, set up by a visual definition of each coordinate system. Still they allow the company to use one, and only one, standard internally. These simple routines, needing only a couple of hours programming, save many man-hours each day.

An in-house IT system can be adjusted to changes in **business processes**.

The great advantage of an in-house system is that the IT system can move along with the business processes. In-house programming offers flexible solutions, something that is easily forgotten in a world in which off-the-shelf products are becoming the norm. For example, propeller data may arrive in a new format, and a routine is then set up for input and conversion. When the rapid changes in metal prices require a new price mechanism, this can be implemented straight away. IT also may influence new business ideas or processes. That is, if IT is going to have a strategic significance the systems must follow along with the company, as well as influence management in improving processes and products. This flexibility is only possible when the company has full control over the software.

26.4   Smart solutions

It has been astonishing to see how often "smart solutions" are the answer. Planning, for example, is quite complex in this company because it is dependent on the size of the mold boxes that can be used at one time. This decision is determined by a table offering allowed combinations, which leads to an NP-complete integer programming optimization problem. Heuristics are used to find a near optimal solution.[3] This

Brute-force algorithms can find the optimal solution.

program alone packs the production plan, reducing delays by 15 to 25 percent. In other words, math produces money.

Programs for the measuring machine are generated automatically based on geometry data, which allows for accurate and efficient measuring. The results are used to see if the blade fulfills the ISO requirements, basically a set of formulas that describe the tolerances that are allowed for pitch, thickness, and a set of other attributes. If the blade data are outside these tolerances, material has to be removed from the blade by grinding—a cumbersome process. The task is then to calculate how much to remove at each coordinate point. Formerly, an experienced manager would find the corrections that were needed at each point, using a spreadsheet to see if the resulting blade were within the tolerances. This process could take hours, and became practically impossible for the most complex blades. Today, a very simple brute-force algorithm runs through all possibilities and offers the best solution, the one that requires a minimum of grinding. This system, complete with the measuring part, ISO control, and documentation reports, was estimated to have paid for itself after three weeks back in 1998—and it is still running!

Brute-force is also applied when a blade is to be milled to nominal values. Milling is used instead of grinding when an exact blade is required. Then the problem is to find the optimal position of the nominal blade within the casting. There are six degrees of freedom (translation and rotation along the three axes), but a brute-force algorithm finds the optimal solution within a few minutes on a powerful PC. Again, simple algorithms solve tough problems. Brute-force also has the advantage that it makes zero assumptions about the blade geometry, and thus, it can be used for all blades.

This company has won a huge contract for a set of large and very complex blades for British Royal Navy destroyers. Casting knowledge was, of course, an important part, but IT also mattered in winning the contract. The simple brute-force program was essential in quality control and for documenting each blade.

The alloy holds 1,300 degrees Celsius when it is poured into the cavity in the sand fixture. Since it shrinks when it cools off, the model has to be made larger than the nominal blade. Traditionally, this was done by increasing all nominal attributes by a given percentage, but that method had the disadvantage that a lot of excess material had to be removed to get the blade within ISO tolerances. Today, a table for each type of blade, based on experience, provides the allowance that is to be added to each part, for example, more at the periphery (where the shrinkage is higher) than at the center.

These allowances are added to the nominal geometry, and a new geometry is constructed. The software smoothes spline curves, as well as generating additional geometry information at the top of the blade. The final results are used to mill models that produce castings that can be adjusted to the ISO requirement with very limited grinding. Here IT has influenced business ideas, opening for marketing this "shrink-to-fit" process.

26.5   Costs

Change-oriented programming simplifies modifications to systems.

Interestingly enough, the software costs of the niche part are comparable to the standard part. The company pays as much in licenses for the off-the-shelf software as it does for programming, partly because it uses an effective development tool and partly because it has developed robust systems. Since our users talk about forms, we also structure our programs around forms. Instead of reuse, we copy, that is, we advocate what can be called "change-oriented development" (see the previous chapter). If the user wants a new form we create it; if they do not need an old form, it can be deleted devoid of consequences. There are no bindings. The common denominator is the database, which is fairly stable because of the number of data records alone. New fields and tables may be added, but there is no incentive to change huge amounts of data. Thus we end up with a simple two-layer model—user interface and database—and the application part is hidden within the GUI.

Testing can be limited.

Testing has been the one great issue of software engineering. Even the "agile group" that advocates rapid prototyping, stress testing. While NASA must be quite sure that their software is bug free before a launch, the consequences of a software error are seldom severe in small and medium-sized firms. The few errors that occur are fixed on the spot. At the worst, a few work hours are lost. Clearly, errors could have some significance if the programs produced erroneous output, but checking all data for consistency reduces this possibility. We should also acknowledge that the processes rely not only on correct software, but also on all other machinery and employees doing the right thing. From my experience, software is the least likely part to fail.

26.6   Merging of niche and standard parts

Off the shelf packages can be **integrated** with the in-house developed parts.

After splitting the company in a standard and niche part, we merge the two. When an order is fulfilled, the kernel software enters all data for the invoice, customer ID, reference numbers, prices, and so on directly into the database of the off-the-shelf accounting system. When run, the software will find the new invoice record and handle this in the normal manner. The accounting system will perform all further processing; that is, from the accounting system's point of view this company delivers from stock. But from the point of view of the kernel system, blades are shipped to the customer and nothing happens after that. It is not a fully integrated system, but data are stored only once. The open database of the standard system makes this possible.

The recipe for gaining a strategic advantage requires some simple mathematics, programming experience, a good development environment, and creative employees who are interested in trying new processes. The case company has increased the production volumes by a factor of four in the last ten years in their different departments without increasing the number of employees. New machinery and an improved casting process is partly the answer, but this increase would have been impossible to achieve without IT and proprietary systems.

Can the competition follow suit? Of course, but our foundry has now moved part of the game to another arena. It is as if we played the first round on the soccer field, and then—compensating for a tie—forced our opponents to the tennis court for the finals, over their strong protest that they cannot play tennis. This is not allowed in sports, but in business it may be advantageous to play part of the game in an arena where the opponent may lack competence.

Notes

1   This chapter is in part based on Olsen, K. A. (2009). In house programming is not passé – automating originality, IEEE Computer, April.

2   International Organization for Standardization (ISO).

3   See Nonås, S. L., Olsen, K. A. (2005). A MILP formulation for a common scheduling problem in a foundry: Optimal and Heuristic Solutions, Computers & Operations Research, Volume 32, Issue 9, September, Pages 2351–2382.

27　Case 2:　Developing Apps

Many large companies encourage exploration and invention, to develop new products and services. Here we shall discuss some of these efforts, and then present the idea of Apps—independent applications for smartphones and tablets.[1]

27.1　Everything invented

"Everything that can be invented has been invented"—this infamous 1899 quote has been attributed to Charles H. Duell, director of the U.S. Patent Office. But he never said such a silly thing. What he said to the U.S. Congress was something quite different—that America's future success depends on invention. This is clearly the case today, not only for America, but also for most countries. And invention and innovation seem to prosper, not least in the software industry. The last decade has given us new tools and new ways of disseminating applications, from Apps to cloud computing. As a consequence, we have been offered an abundance of new applications, to the degree that we may fall into the trap of thinking that everything in software has been invented.

Some time ago, I had a creative idea for a new App—a location dependent "reminder," which could attach a message to a location, instead of to date and time. With this, the next time you went near a hardware store, your smartphone would beep and tell you to get a new hammer, a message you may have input some time ago. Or, when you read about a famous restaurant in Madrid, you store the URL of its home page in the "reminder." A year later, when you leave the train in the center of Madrid, the restaurant information will pop up on the phone.

To develop this application, I got some information on how to build Apps, searched the Web for relevant information on APIs, and started programming. But then I found a similar App already available for Google's Android operating system, which had not been there when I got the idea. Very annoying! What has happened? Has everything that can be invented been invented?

The answer is clearly no. However, the possibility of coming up with a new App may not be so great. There are already half a million applications on the Apple's App Store, and two hundred thousand on Google Play (Android Market). Facebook is also opening a similar store.

27.2   Models of innovation

Traditionally, large companies have offered a centralized model of innovation. Bell Labs is a good example, called a "scientific Valhalla" for researchers and engineers working there.[2] They are free to pursue their own areas of interest with the resources needed. This model comes from a time when companies maintained control over innovation with a centralized approach. In these companies, AT&T being a good example, the innovation was delegated to an internal research center, often the pride of the company. Companies were willing to invest heavily in the hope that at least some of the projects would be a success. But delegating innovation to a separate research center may have drawbacks, especially in getting the inventions to the marketplace. A good example is Xerox's failure to exploit the GUI-research at Xerox Parc.

The open-source movement is an interesting alternative for software development.

The open-source software movement is an interesting alternative. While the big companies adopt a monolithic approach, open source is based on a decentralized model. Here entrepreneurs with good ideas may set up a development project. Then, the rest of the world is invited to participate. While the open source movement has demonstrated its efficiency in large systems and software modules, it may not be as effective for developing applications for the end user. The problem may be the marketing—how to get applications to the customer.

Google uses another model.[3] Promoting innovation, Google invests in a kind of internal entrepreneurial model in which employees are encouraged to innovate. The company, with its flat organizational structure, supports innovative employees by offering services, data resources, and tools. They offer free time for entrepreneurship and additional resources for the most interesting projects. Most important, through Google Labs and similar facilities, they offer a place where new products can be tested in the marketplace.

Hewlett-Packard was born in a garage as early as 1939. Many other electronics, computer, and software companies had similar humble beginnings in which the entrepreneurs themselves put in the time and money to get a company working. Today we have moved from the physical to virtual garages, which are furnished with extensive toolkits in the form of operating systems, development packages, and open-source code. In this way, device manufacturers have opened their systems up to third-party developers, giving them access to all the underlying functionality of the PC, tablet, or smartphone.

Thus, implementing my "reminder" application is no big deal. An entrepreneur with a Java development tool will have access to all the necessary smartphone resources, including keyboard, display, files, and location coordinates—everything needed to develop the App. In principle, there is nothing new here. Apple invited third-party developers for the Macintosh thirty years ago, and other manufacturers have followed suit. What is new is the support that is offered for getting new applications to the end user.

27.3   Sandbox environment for Apps

Traditionally, in engineering terms, a sandbox environment consists of a controlled set of resources with which a new application can be tried without the risk of damaging critical parts of the system. As an innovation model we can take this further, including the phase of getting the product on the market. Google offers this to their employees—a tight-coupled extended sandbox, as the entire process is internal to the company; entrepreneurs take advantage of the infrastructure already in place for the company itself, and "extend" the environment to the market.

For Apple, the sandbox innovation environment is its App Store, together with the developer network and all the tools that go with it. The App Store mechanism controls the quality of published Apps and also provides a platform to reach the end user. Moreover, Apple provides easy integration with iAds, a framework for advertisement, including a payment mechanism for iPhone and iPad Apps. This is a loose-coupled sandbox; Apple owns the infrastructure, but the entrepreneurs may be you or me or anyone else. The marketplace for Android Apps offers similar services.

The short time from idea, via implementation and quality control, to the market is crucial.

For all these models, the short time from idea, via implementation and quality control, to the market is crucial. This short time frame may explain why we feel that "everything has been invented." Earlier, many of us may have had ideas for new applications, but most ideas stayed in the head of the inventor or never came out of the lab. Even if a new invention reached the market, many were noticed by only a fraction of the potential user community.

Programming environments make it simpler to develop apps, and the **marketplaces** make it easy to distribute these.

Today, with all the available tools, development is simpler, and nearly any application can be put on the market immediately. Marketing is an important part. Through centralized channels, such as iAds or Google Play, it is easy to find what one is looking for; it is only a matter of time before the App is on the market, and before the world at large knows what we have invented.

Clearly, the sandbox environment has a lot to offer developers. The tools, APIs, and other resources simplify development. The marketing support and predefined tools for downloading and installation help with the last and most crucial part—reaching the customer. The models also may offer an opportunity for revenue. But, if we exclude the few success stories, making money on Apps may not be so easy in the long run. With the large number of Apps, newcomers to this market may be forced to offer them for free just to be recognized, thus reducing the potential for revenue for all developers.

27.4   Sustainability of Apps

This development environment may also be unsustainable in the long run from the users' perspective. For a given function, the user must choose from an overwhelming number of applications. For example, there are about 400 wakeup applications and 2,500 calendar applications in the App Store, and around the same number on Google Play. Though the most popular Apps are presented first, popularity may not be a very good indicator of quality.

After choosing an App, the user must agree to let the application have access to phone resources. Few users will be able to evaluate the security risks and most hit the OK button without thinking. Then, the App must be downloaded, perhaps paid for, and installed on the device. When moving to a new device, especially if the native operating system is changed, the user must locate the Apps (or similar ones) in the store, choose, pay, and download all the Apps again.

On a particular smartphone or tablet, there may be many different Apps, each presented with an icon in an application window. It is now up to the user to remember which App did what, to be able to locate the icon, and to remember how it was used. It will be her task to update her Apps. Even if the Apps are developed under the same guidelines, they may have different user interfaces.

Are apps just a
test-bed for the
major companies?

Thus, while many enthusiastic users have welcomed the App idea, it may not be a good solution for the less technologically oriented. The App market is perhaps only a test-bed for the major companies, an implementation of a digital ecosystem in which the Apps can compete, using a survival-of-the-fittest scheme to find the most interesting functions and the most popular approaches to them. By letting third-party developers create the initial versions, and offering these to the market, the major companies have a very simple and profitable way to determine the functionality to be included in the next version of the basic software. They can then use the resources of the company to ensure that each of these "Apps," or each function, is offered in a high-quality version.

An even more competitive approach than including App functionality as a part of the native operating systems is offering this functionality through browser-based systems.[4] The advantages of centralized dynamic applications, true platform independence, ubiquitous access, and no local installation or update of software may be the demise both of "Apps" and of large native operating systems.

27.5   Conclusion

Looking at a clear, dark night sky we will see a myriad of stars. As yet, there are not as many Apps as there are stars, but each one may shine as brilliantly, showing the extent of human invention and covering every "dark spot," every possible function. But in the long run, numbers and brilliance may not be enough. In our everyday work, we seldom take the time to look at the stars. Instead, we focus on functionality, practicality, and effectiveness. While the stars will always be there, we are not so sure that the Apps will survive in a practical world. In the software world, perhaps the browser—the dinosaur that can do everything—will be the survivor.

Notes

1   This chapter is based on Malizia, A, Olsen, K. A. (2011) Has Everything Been Invented? On Software Development and the Future of Apps, IEEE Computer, September 2011.

2   Wu, T. (2011) Bell Labs and centralized innovation, Communication of the ACM, May, pp. 31–33.

3   Savoia, A. and Copeland, P. (2011) Entrepreneurial Innovation at Google, IEEE Computer, April.

4   Mikkonen, T. and Taivalsaari, A. (2011) Reports of the Web's death are greatly exaggerated. IEEE Computer, May.

PART 5
Internet and WWW Basics

In this part, we discuss the underlying technology for the Internet and the Web. Chapter 28 presents HTML and XML, the first as a layout language for Web pages, the latter to describe the contents of documents. Internet protocols, the standards that are used to let computers communicate over the Internet, are discussed in Chapters 29 and 30. While these chapters are somewhat technical, an understanding of the basic concepts is needed to see the possibilities, the limitations and, as important, to avoid being overrun by experts and their jargon.

Next we present a set of interesting applications, and study what ramifications these will have: e-mail in Chapter 31, Web browsers in Chapter 32, and the World Wide Web itself in Chapter 33. We continue with a presentation of Web searching in Chapter 34, in which we introduce important concepts such as precision and recall, and discuss problems of information overload and filtering.

In Chapter 35, we discuss portals, or how we can develop an index for the Web that can help us satisfy a need for information. This problem is discussed from the opposite perspective in Chapter 36, that is, how we can be visible on the Web or promote a Web site. The ideal of a democratic Web where everyone can be a publisher is not easy to implement in practice, as being "seen" is difficult among billons of other Web pages, some of which are heavily marketed through other media.

Will the world of computing change when we go wireless with mobile computing? We discuss this issue in Chapter 37, along with a presentation of these new technologies. Will the problem of usability be solved if we implement automated solutions in which Web pages push information to the user? We discuss this technology in Chapter 38, but also return to these issues in Part 9. In Chapters 39 and 40, we go into details on more advanced topics such as dynamic Web pages and embedded scripts. These chapters also are somewhat technical, but they explain the development of more advanced Web pages (such as pages that allow for user input through fill-in forms).

An introduction to peer-to-peer computing is given in Chapter 41. This technique exploits the unstructured Internet, and creates networks where all participants are equal. Peer-to-peer computing opens for new and interesting applications, for example, file sharing. Social networks are presented in Chapter 42, while we discuss the concept of Web 2.0 in the last chapter of this part, Chapter 43.

28 HTML and XML

The first version of **HTML** was designed by Tim Berners Lee at CERN in 1991.

Most data on the Web is described as HTML or Hypertext Markup Language. Tim Berners Lee at CERN, the European Research Facility, designed the first version of this computer language in 1991. His idea was to use HTML as a format for scientific papers, with links between papers as the most important function. HTML is inspired by the Standard Generalized Markup Language (SGML).[1] Instead of in-text references, hypertext links, automatic links, can take the reader directly to the paper in question. On the Web today, we find pages in many other formats, such as PDF (a standard for presenting documents), doc and docx (the formats used by Microsoft Word), and XML.

While HTML, PDF, and the doc-formats present the layout of a document, XML offers the possibility of describing the contents. The formalization aspects of HTML and XML are presented below. In addition, we will discuss more formalized applications, such as Internet banking and booking, in the next part. (For a more detailed description of XML, see Chapter 52.)

Data on the open Web is most often described using HTML. The basics of HTML are a set of tags that describe the layout of a document (in a few cases also contents). The standard way of using tags is to set these in brackets (< >) and to have a start and a stop tag. For example we can set a text in bold by the <b> tag:

HTML is a **tag language**.

<b> The browser will set this text in bold </b>

The slash is used to describe a stop tag. Thus we turn off bold by </b>. Similarly we can start a paragraph with <p> and end it with </p>. To describe the title of a Web page we use the <title> tag, e.g.:

<title> University of Bergen </title>

Note that this tag describes contents. However, since most HTML tags are used to describe layout, we may call HTML a layout language.

The great advantage of HTML is that it is simple. In fact, you start with a blank "sheet," a blank Web page, and can fill it out as you want. Therefore nearly everything can be put on the Web.

The task of the browser—Internet Explorer, Firefox, Safari, Opera and others—will then be to generate the page according to the layout instructions. Since HTML pages are made for humans, the browser will do its best to present a page, even if there are errors on the page. For example, a page may have the <b> tag but without the accompanying </b>. In this case, the browser will boldface everything until start of the next paragraph, a heading, or similar. The user may perhaps recognize that the bold is kept on for too long, but she can still see the page, and that is what is the most important. It would be cumbersome if the browser gave an error message instead of presenting the page.

These kinds of problems are reduced when computer programs generate pages instead of humans. While it is possible for the human page creator to add the HTML tags explicitly, most pages today are generated automatically. The program may take the data—for example, a list of employees from a database—and add the necessary tags to present this list as a Web page. We will discuss these issues in detail in later parts.

HTML pages have a low formalization level.

The disadvantage of HTML pages is that they have a low formalization level, close to formalizing on characters only, which is apparent when we search. Given the keyword "apple," a search engine will return documents that describe both fruits and computers. Similarly, a search for "Scarecrow" will return documents on the thing that is used to scare birds, a movie, the publisher, and many other documents based on all interpretations of this word.

We may have a discrepancy between our information need and the results returned by the search engine.

The problem that we face when searching in the open Web may be a discrepancy between our information needs and the formalization level of the data. We may want to know more about apple as a fruit and may be overwhelmed by documents describing the computer company. When searching, we can avoid this problem by adding more keywords, making our information need more specific. A search for "apple fruit" will then give us what we want, but this requires that each document on apples also contain the word "fruit," or better, that the pages on apples have a keyword named "fruit."

In HTML, we can add keywords in a meta-statement, such as in this example.

```
<meta name="Keywords" content="apple, fruit, tree">
```

That is, we can raise the formalization level of an HTML page by adding keywords. These keywords will aid search engines to find the documents that are of interest to the user.

We can also reduce the disadvantage of the low formalization level by using smart methods for searching. (These are discussed in Chapter 34.)

While there are advantages to the simple layout-format of HTML, we often need to raise the formalization level, such as when we want to send documents between companies, like an order. The buyer's system can generate these automatically, based on the need for parts, and send them over the Internet to the supplier. The supplier then can enter all data on the order directly into its production planning system. HTML would not be a good choice for describing these documents because this works on a layout, not a content level.

XML, eXtensible Markup Language, will be a better solution here. Like HTML, XML is a tag language, but one in which we create our own tags. The buyer and supplier can agree on a tag set, or preferably, use a set that is a standard for the whole business, if such a standard exists. An order then could be formalized as:

```
<order>
    <order number> 12345 </order number>
    <from>Computer Company Ltd</from>
    <to> Battery supplier Ltd. </to>
    <date> 12. December 2012 </date>
    <order line>
        <product id> B12345 </ product id >
        <number ordered>100</number ordered>
    </order line>
    <order line> .....
</order >
```

That is, all data items are described on a high level, which is necessary when the data is to be used directly by computer systems. If there are errors in the XML documents, the document must be rejected. That is, we cannot risk misinterpretations because these could have serious results.

If we had used XML for all data on the Web, it would have been easy to distinguish between apples and computers:

```
<computer manufacturer> Apple </computer manufacturer>
<fruit> apple </fruit>
```

Here, we have tagged the word "apple" to give the correct interpretation in each case. Now a search for the fruit "apple" will first find all fruit-tags and then check if the contents are "apple." No pages concerning the computer company interpretation of this word will be returned.

However, there is a cost to raising the formalization level. Not only will we have to tag all concepts, but it will often be difficult to find the right tag to apply. For example, the page on apples may be on apple trees. A search for "tree" will not find this page if the <fruit> tag is used instead of a <tree> tag.

In practice, we will use the formalization of XML when there is a requirement to have a high formalization, such as sending orders, invoices, or other formalized documents between computer systems. In other cases, we may choose the simpler, low-level formats, such as HTML. That is, the blank-page concept of HTML not only allows us to describe nearly every type of content, but it facilitates creating the page in the first place. This mix of flexibility and simplicity is often a winner.

Note

1   The idea behind SGML was to develop a generalized language for creating and describing documents, with a clear separation between content and layout. The first working draft of the SGML standard was published as early as 1980, and the standard was accepted by various bodies about five years later. Early applications were within the publishing industry for book and article creation, and for manuscript interchange between authors and their publishers.

29 Internet Protocols

A **protocol** is used to administer communication processes.

Communication is controlled by protocols. On a one-way radio system this may be performed by keywords such as "roger," "over," "out." Computer transmissions need more elaborate systems, but the idea is the same. Machine A tells B that it wants to send a message. After the initial "handshake" process in which contact is established, the message may be sent, most often divided into convenient packets. Packets have a header that includes address, number of bytes, and additional data that B can use to determine if the package was successfully received.[1] If there are errors, B can ask A to retransmit the package, or A will do this automatically if it does not get confirmation from B that the message was received.

Divide-and-conquer: On the Internet, messages are split into small and simple packets that are sent individually through the network.

The Internet is a packet-switched network (really a *collection* of networks with a set of protocol standards). Messages are converted into a number of fixed-size packages that can be transmitted over the network. This strategy is typical within all computing applications; complex objects are divided into smaller and handier objects. For example, if we get a transmission error within a packet, only this packet must be retransmitted, not the complete file. The drawback is that the system must be able to handle a large number of objects (many packages instead of a few files), but high volumes of simple objects do not constitute a problem for modern communication technology.

The important part of the Internet is the open, **standardized protocols**.

The Internet uses an addressing protocol called IP, Internet Protocol. This protocol is used to provide the routing function for the package transmitted across the networks. This implies that the IP protocol not only has to be part of the end systems, but also of the intermediate *routers*. A router is a computer that connects two networks, receiving packets from the one and transmitting them to the other.

The IP header has a 32-bit source and destination address, in addition to other parameters. That is, the Internet address is defined in a number that can hold 32 binary digits. In theory, this can be used to identify more than four billion Internet addresses. When the protocol was designed, this number was considered more than enough; however, with the explosive growth of the Internet, 32 bits is becoming insufficient to address all machines in the network. Therefore, a new standard, known as IPv6, has been developed, offering 128 bits for both the source and destination addresses.

With a 32-bit number, the **IP addressing** scheme uniquely addresses any computer on the net.

The 32-bit IP address is usually presented in a format called dotted decimal notation, for example, as 158.38.10.00. This address identifies the networks and the hosts, in a hierarchical addressing scheme. Numeric IP addresses are acceptable for computers, but not for human beings. Therefore, a textual address was introduced, and a name server (a table of network servers) is used to translate this name into the numeric IP address. Names are organized into domains indicated by a suffix, for example:

- *com*, for commercial organizations
- *edu*, domain name for US educational institutions
- *no*, the Norwegian domain
- *org*, domain name for nonprofit organizations

Name servers map the numeric and computer-oriented IP address into a format that is better suited for humans, and vice versa.

Domains are organized hierarchically. On the next level, *pitt.edu* is the domain name for University of Pittsburgh, *uib.no* for University of Bergen (Norway), and *ibm.com* for IBM. On the bottom level of this naming tree, individual hosts are assigned Internet addresses. A "table," called a DNS—domain name server—will perform the name to IP address translation. This DNS is distributed via the Internet.

IP address space allocation, protocol parameter assignment, domain name system management, and root server system management functions are today handled by the nonprofit corporation ICANN.[2] ICANN is now offering new suffixes, for example, by allowing addresses such as @marketing.pepsi, @support.microsoft and @hotels.norway.

When an e-mail is sent, the local host will query the local domain name server for the IP address corresponding to the name, the e-mail address. If the name is known at this level, the IP address is returned; otherwise, the name server queries other available name servers, until the address is found.

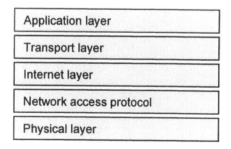

Figure 29.1 The TCP/IP layered architecture.

Layered architectures are used to simplify the complexity of the communication protocols.

While the Internet and Web technologies introduce their own standards, they rely on **accepted standards** for the underlying levels, such as TCP.

New standards can easily be built on top of TCP/IP, allowing us to send e-mail with or without attachments, retrieve Web pages, and so on.

The communication task is organized into a layered architecture (Figure 29.1). On the bottom layer we find the physical connection, the twisted pair (telephone), coax, optical, or wireless communication lines. The next layer, the network access protocol, handles the connection between the computer and the network.[3] The transport layer, here consisting of the TCP (Transmission Control Protocol), built on top of the Internet layer with its IP addressing scheme, will split messages into packets and offer reliable interchange of data between hosts, including error checking and retransmitting of lost packets.

If this sounds complex you are right. It is! On the top level, we want to send e-mail, access Web pages, and communicate over a social network. On the bottom level, we may have a simple twisted pair wire, for example, a telephone line. The gap is too wide. So, to simplify, we define these layers, with every layer performing part of the job. Ordinary users seldom have to think about the lower levels, except when they break down.

While there are many protocols for data transmission, the great advantage of TCP is that it has been generally *accepted*. Virtually all operating systems can read and create TCP packages. This standard is one of the foundations of the global acceptance and use of the Internet. With TCP, data is put into packages, each of which is assigned a TCP header. The header gives the address of the source and destination, the sequence number of the packet, a checksum, and several other bits of control information. The receiver uses the sequence number to acknowledge the receipt of the package and to check that all packages are received. Note that TCP does not guarantee that packets are received in sequence. Packets may take different routes through the network, and may appear out of order. The destination machine fixes this by organizing packages in accordance with the sequence number before they are presented to the user application (for example, a browser or an e-mail system).

Finally, we have the application layer that provides support for the various user applications. Several applications have been standardized to work on top of TCP/IP, among them:

- Simple Mail Transfer Protocol (SMTP)
- File Transfer Protocol (FTP)
- Internet Message Access Protocol (IMAP)
- Multipurpose Internet Mail Extensions (MIME)
- Hypertext Transfer Protocol (HTTP)

SMTP provides a basic protocol for the exchange of e-mail messages; FTP is directed toward file transfer between machines (using commands such as GET <file> or POST <file>); IMAP allows a client to access and manipulate electronic mail messages on a server; and MIME allows for "complex message bodies," enclosing files, graphics, audio clips, and so on.[4] HTTP is the protocol for transmitting Web pages (discussed in the next chapter). Each of these application protocols serves a special purpose, as mail or file transfer, but they all use TCP/IP as the foundation for carrying out their task.

Such layered architectures are used in all areas of computing. The idea is to capture and isolate the characteristics of each level. For example, there are many different types of networks and different types of low-level protocols. Since this information is isolated within the network layer, the transportation layer can work independently of this lower layer, if the interface between these two layers is standardized. The transportation layer will build a package, including header information, and ask the network layer to do the transmission job. On top of the transportation layer is the application layer, which consists of e-mail systems, Web browsers, and so on. These applications will use the transport layer to transmit messages, using higher-level protocols that include the requirements of the application program.

Another way to view the layered protocol architecture is to see it as different levels of formalizations. The physical layer operates with electromagnetic signals; the network layer understands terms such as packets and machine addresses; the transport layer understands terms such as file; and the e-mail program understands concepts such as e-mail addresses, messages, and attachments. The word *understands* is used on purpose because the protocols really have a conceptual understanding of these concepts that allows them to handle the objects in very different ways. For example a good e-mail system can filter messages, send automatic replies, handle attachments, or archive messages manually or automatically, as well as perform actions such as forward and reply. The e-mail system will define a message as a document—a sequence of characters, with a header. The header includes the addresses of the receiver and sender, a subject field, and other information. The user provides

A layered architecture implies the idea of formalization on **different levels**, from physical signals to e-mail messages.

On top of all the layers is the **user layer**, in which concepts and protocols are defined socially.

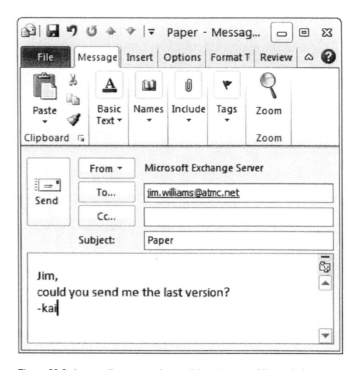

Figure 29.2 An e-mail message (example) as shown in Microsoft Outlook.

some of this information, as shown in the example in Figure 29.2, and the e-mail system collects other data from information given at setup.

The e-mail system will pack the header and content information into a package defined by the SMTP protocol. The sender will then open a TCP connection to the receiving machine, expecting an acknowledgment that the receiver is ready. The message itself is sent using a MAIL command to identify the originator of the message, one or more RCPT commands that identify the receivers, and a DATA command to transmit the actual message text. The destination address includes the textual IP address of the receiving mail server. This keeps track of all accounts at (@) the server. For example, the mail server identified by *mail.himolde.no* recognizes the account *kai.olsen*.

Note that the conceptual understanding of a message by the e-mail system does not include the content of the message. If we replaced the text in Figure 29.2 above with "tjbjhj hnjhn" it would still be a message for the e-mail system. (However, if the e-mail system has a spelling checker, it would state that the words are not in the dictionary.) The writing and reading of messages is performed on a higher layer, a *top layer* or *user layer*. This layer also has its protocols, but these are not formalized to the same extent as on the other layers. I may sign my messages as above, but it will be no problem if I forget, since the e-mail system will include my e-mail address in the information sent to the receiver. I can include a title, leave it out, or, if I reply to an incoming message, I can let the system retain the title text. In a long conversation, the original title often will still be used, even if the conversation has moved to new topics—not really a problem, since human beings rely on context information to understand a message, but out of context, many e-mail messages would be incomprehensible.

Modern e-mail systems rely on the MIME protocol. The purpose of MIME is to address limitations in SMTP. Most important, MIME enables the user to attach files of different types to e-mail messages, for example, text-, image-, audio-, and video-files. For communication, MIME has been a very important step forward.

A drawback of the current mail protocols is that they do not give adequate protection. For example, it is quite easy to forge the sender's address. We see examples of this in many spam messages.

Notes

1   A simple mechanism is to add up all the data in the packet, using the underlying data codes as numbers, and store this "checksum" in the packet. The receiver can then perform the same calculation and compare results to the checksum. If the two are identical, there is a high probability that the received packet is correct.

2   The Internet Corporation for Assigned Names and Numbers.

3   This may be implemented with protocol standards such as X.25 (packet switching) or Ethernet (for local area networks).

4. For a more detailed review, see Connected: An Internet Encyclopedia, http://www.freesoft.org/CIE/

30 Development of Web Protocols

The most important feature of HTML is its **simplicity**.

Tim Berners-Lee first developed the World Wide Web as an Intranet for CERN, the European Center for Particle Physics. He based his development on a set of basic ideas (see his book, *Weaving the Web*, 1999):

- *Simplicity.* It should be easy to create Web pages, and to implement the browsers needed for retrieving, presenting, and creating pages.

- *Hypertext.* The page structure and connections should be based on links embedded in the text, where the user could go to another page just by clicking on this hypertext link.

- *Everybody* should be able to create Web pages (very different from other media such as TV or newspapers in which the creative part is reserved for the few).

- *Universal.* The Web should be a universal system, open for everybody everywhere.

- *Distributed.* There should be only a limited need for centralization.

Berners-Lee worked hard to propagate these ideas, and hypertext was the important foundation. Initially, Berners-Lee distinguished between internal and external links. Later, he saw that this was more a technical than a fundamental distinction, and a general link scheme was adopted. Today, we see that Microsoft and other companies follow the same path in new releases of their operating systems, in which the distinction between data stored locally on the server or globally on the net is removed.

Since the Web soon was envisioned as something more than an Intranet for CERN, it was natural to build the transmission protocol for HTML pages, the Hypertext Transfer Protocol (HTTP), on top of TCP/IP.

The URL offers a **unique identifier** for every page on the Web.

HTTP defines a set of commands that browsers use to request HTML pages, one of these being the GET-command. The GET-command requests a specific file from a particular server that resides on the Internet. The server and file are identified by a Uniform Resource Locator, a URL. A URL consists of the IP address of the server (often given as a name), and information to identify the Web page within the server. For ex-

The Web protocols are **stateless** (it does not remember that you have been here before). Every access is the first.

ample, the URL http://www.ii.uib.no/persons/index.html identifies a page (or a file) *index.html* within the folder *persons*, on the server identified by *ii.uib.no* (a name server will replace this name by the numeric IP address). It also indicates that the HTTP protocol is being used. When the browser sends a GET-command, the HTTP server on that host will retrieve the Web page and return it to the browser. HTTP is a stateless protocol; that is, after the transfer has been made, the server can forget everything about it. In principle, there is no recollection of the transfer and no data is stored.

A stateless protocol simplifies the administration of tasks, as each transaction is performed as an atomic (self-contained) unit, making it easy for a server to handle a large number of requests and avoiding the problem of non-terminated sessions (in which a user gives up in the middle of a process). But what if we need more than one request to do the job, for example, to successively select the next page of results returned by a query? Such a session can be simulated by including the historical data needed in each step. Thus, what is a logical transaction, as seen from the user's point of view, may have to take place through a series of atomic transactions, in which each transaction must offer the complete transaction history up to the present. For example, when you request the second page (or twentieth page) of search results, all data from the initial search is sent to the server with the additional information that the second page (or twentieth page) of results are wanted. The server now performs a completely new search, disregards the first page of results, and returns the second page.

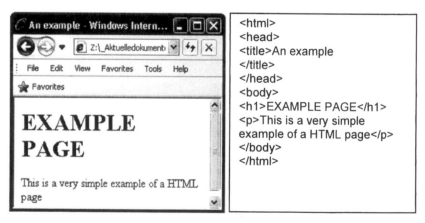

Figure 30.1 HTML page example (browser presentation and source).

Tags are used to add layout information, and, in some cases, structural information.

The role of HTML in this process is to describe the layout of a Web page. A simple example is presented in Figure 30.1, showing how we use this markup language to describe fields and effects. For example, by enclosing the page title in <title> and </title> tags, the browser can identify that title. Similarly a major header is enclosed by <h1> and </h1> and a paragraph by <p> and </p>. A markup language has the advantages that the "program" is a standard text without any special characters. Therefore, it can be stored as a text file and edited by a text editor.

Markup languages are, in principle, easily extendable: New tags can be added at any time. Of course, these additional tags will not take effect before new versions of the browser can be programmed to handle them. HTML browsers are usually programmed to ignore any tag that they cannot recognize. This has the disadvantage that tag errors may not be found (a tag such as <tittle> will just be ignored), but has the tremendous advantage that old browsers can display pages that include new tags. However, since these new tags are ignored, users with old versions of the browser may get a different page, really a layout, from those users who have a new version. Therefore, page designers must be careful when new constructs are employed.

The **href** tag allows us to embed one-way links in a Web page.

One of the most important HTML constructs is the *a-href* tag which defines a hypertext link to any other Web page. This tag defines an anchor and the *href* attribute defines the URL to the linked-to Web page. For example,

<a href="http://www.uib.no/index.html">University of Bergen</a>

will create a link to the page defined by this URL. The actual link will be hidden by the browser, which will display the text "University of Bergen," usually presented with an underline and/or a special color so that the user can easily identify it as a link. When the user clicks on this link, the browser will create a GET-command for the page, retrieve it from the Web server identified by the URL, and present it on the display.

The author of a Web page is completely in control of the links. She can choose freely **where to link** and how to present the link on her page.

To Tim Berners-Lee's credit, he managed to keep HTML simple. Designing a more complex link system must have been very difficult to avoid. For example, the one-way HTML links have the disadvantage that all of us experience: They may refer to a page that has been removed, deleted, or perhaps never existed. These situations could have been handled by a two-way link system, or by linking through a central register. More advanced links, however, would demand a much more elaborate system, and would generate a huge administrative load—perhaps making the explosive growth of the Web impossible. With the Berners-Lee design we can link to any page, without asking permission or changing the destination page. Since the link is only represented in the from-page, there is no limit to the number of links that a system can handle. Other KISS (Keep it Simple Stupid) effects are the fact that HTML files are also text files, and that browsers ignore tags they cannot recognize.

HTML pages were intended to be produced by programs, not humans.

Tim Berners-Lee never intended HTML to be a language used by human beings. His idea was that the editing functions of the browsers would insert the necessary HTML tags, in the same way as a word processing system inserts format instructions in the text. When we select a sentence in MS Word, for example, and click the "italics" button, MS Word will automatically include the necessary tags in the underlying representations that users never see. However, the HTML tags were so simple that many users created HTML pages directly, using Notepad or a similar text-editing tool. This process was simplified by the "View Source" command of a browser, in which the underlying HTML representation of a Web page could be viewed, studied, and copied. In the pioneer days of the Web, people were even hired based on their ability to write basic HTML.

It is quite possible that if the HTTP protocol and the HTML language had been designed by a committee instead of by Tim Berners-Lee, we would have received a much more complex and elaborate system. His great achievement was not to develop new advanced technology, but to offer a simple system that made it easy to create Web pages and to implement browsers. HTML is inspired by SGML, but while SGML offers the possibility of defining very elaborate markup languages, HTML is extremely simple. At the same time, it offers satisfactory functionality. Of course, the HTML of today is much more than the initial standard, but the major KISS functionality has been retained.

XML (Extensible Markup Language) is another important offspring from the initial SGML. Its idea is to offer what HTML lacks, such as functions for structuring document content. We return to XML in Chapter 52.

31 E-mail, Chat, and Text Messages (SMS)

The most important aspect of e-mail is its **asynchronous** nature.

In principle, e-mail is asynchronous; that is *A* can send a message when it suits her and *B* can read it when it suits him. This is similar to ordinary mail and fax, but very different from telephone or video conferencing. You can send an e-mail to a busy person, perhaps a person working in a different time zone, without interfering with this person's schedule, which is the basis for an efficient communication system. Each of us follows our own schedule, even as we collaborate with others over a fast and efficient medium.

Thus e-mail gives us the best of both worlds. While standard e-mail is asynchronous, it can be used for more synchronous two-way communication, utilizing the fact that e-mail transfer is fast. Chat or instant messaging programs can set up such a direct link between the parties. While social networks are replacing traditional e-mail for private communication, e-mail is still one of the major communication media within business environments.

31.1 Text-based

Basic e-mail is **simple** and works on all platforms.

E-mail is text-based.[1] Text is standardized, can be presented on any type of display, printed on any printer, does not require much screen space, and can be created, edited, and represented efficiently on most computer devices. Text does not require high bandwidth, and therefore, e-mail can be used efficiently with any type of equipment or connection. In an age when we marvel about novel technologies such as powerful processors, high-definition TV, interactive video, and visualization, it is easy to forget the flexibility, expressiveness, and compactness of text.

A global communication system cannot expect everyone to be equipped with the latest models. But the simple text-based world of e-mail can be handled by any computer, any operating system, and transmitted fast over any type of network, even on the simplest dial-up connections. That is, e-mail works on all platforms. The strength of this medium is manifested, as we utilize new technological advances in mobility and miniaturization, such as the mobile telephone, instead of going for only power and capacity. While most e-mail messages are in plain text, many e-mail systems also allow different fonts and images. However, the receiver needs the same system, or a system that accepts the same protocol, to be able to see more than the plain text (this is often solved by using HTML to format more advanced email messages).

31.2   Text messages (SMS) and Tweets

Text messages, also called SMS (Short Message Service), are simple and work on most mobile phones.

Telecommunications companies in Europe have been surprised by the enormous popularity of the short text-based SMS messages, a popularity based on the nature of the message itself—the convenience of being in contact all the time is more important than the layout. Text messages have the advantage that they can be created and read by most mobile phones. The simplicity of the technology and the limited bandwidth needed makes it an inexpensive way of communicating. If we are critical, we may argue that widespread use of these 161-characters messages is a symptom of a lack of literate skills in the younger population, but another likely explanation is that the numeric keyboard does not allow for heavy prose. And perhaps texting is just what we need to make those sharp and witty statements that we hear actors utter in the movies. Twitter, "the SMS of the Internet," has success with the same type of messages, called tweets. However, while SMS is often directed toward one person, twitter messages go to all "followers" of the sender.

We may say that the need to be in continuous contact with friends shows a lack of planning and organizing skills, but this need also may be viewed as a way of socializing. Text messages and tweets show clearly that the mobile phone companies have an important market in the younger population, as much for entertainment as anything else. But other groups are coming along. For example, text messages are also a simple way for businesses to keep their customers informed: "The book you ordered has arrived;" "Flight is thirty minutes delayed;" "$1,000 has been deposited in your account."

The low **formalization level** of SMS, e-mail, and HTML offers flexibility.

Text and Twitter messages, along with e-mail, retain the low formalization level of a blank sheet of paper. The only structured information is in the address fields (phone number, ID, or e-mail address), the note itself can be composed as one likes. While the early e-mail protocols were based on 7-bit ASCII characters, newer protocols use more bits to represent characters, which opens the way for special letters and national language characters.

31.3   IP-based

E-mail is based on the IP, Internet Protocol. An e-mail address identifies a person (a person's e-mail account) uniquely in the world; it is simple and often easy to remember, especially where a syntax of <first name> . <last name> @ <institution> . <country or type of institution code> are used (for example, kai.olsen@himolde.no).

E-mail offers data in electronic, computer readable format (the data received is in electronic form). This enables the receiver to store messages on disk, to edit messages, and to copy content into other applications. Messages can be forwarded to others, and replies can be sent just by a button click. E-mail messages can be printed, but the system itself is paper free.

E-mail may be handled by **automatic procedures** that perform actions based on the formalized part of messages.

Many e-mail systems offer automatic procedures for handling incoming e-mail. We can, for example, specify that messages from a given address be transferred directly to a folder, or that messages with a given word in the heading be forwarded to another mail address. It is possible to specify a message that will be returned automatically, as a response to all messages ("I am on vacation…"), or to messages from a given address ("Bill, you can call me at …"). Perhaps more important, we can ask the system to block messages from a list of sites, "junk" mail that we do not want to see.

31.4   MIME protocol

The MIME protocol opens for **attachments** to e-mail. With MIME, we can exploit the de facto standards of documents, spreadsheets, and other applications.

E-mail systems using the MIME protocol can attach files to the messages. These files can be of any type: computer programs, data files, databases, text files, images, word processing documents, spreadsheets, and so on. To a large extent, this simple-to-use, extremely useful function replaces the more cumbersome FTP (file transfer protocols). What makes MIME so important is that it allows us to utilize the de facto standards that have emerged over the last ten years, such as the .doc/.docx and .xls/.xlsx formats. Whether I work with colleagues in Pittsburgh, Rome or Madrid, papers are exchanged as MS Word documents. In industry, data can be exchanged in a formalized manner using Excel spreadsheets, using the spreadsheet as a standard vehicle for data transfer. At the receiving end, programs can then retrieve the data directly from the spreadsheet system.

In the example of the foundry presented in Chapter 26, the detailed geometric specifications of the propeller blades were offered as Excel spreadsheets, transmitted as attachments to e-mail messages. These spreadsheets are then imported automatically into the company's administrative system.

PDF is a standard for distributing documents in a read-only form. Word and other document files can easily be converted to PDF, which can be stored on a Web page or distributed to readers as attachments. The PDF file can be read using a simple viewer program, available as a free download. When the Turbokforlaget, a publisher of picture-based guidebooks, want ten thousand copies of a book, the complete PDF file is transferred to the printers, using FTP file transmissions or as an attachment to an e-mail. Since the PDF gives an unambiguous description of the complete book, no proofing is required. The printers can, in principle, start work right away.

31.5   Computer-generated e-mail messages

The sender, and sometimes the receiver, of an e-mail can be a computer program.

A sender of an e-mail message can be a computer program. An event can activate a program that creates an e-mail message based on data retrieved from a database, for example, offering bargains seats three days ahead of a flight or notifying a customer that the book he wanted can be picked up at the library. But not all computer-generated e-mails are as useful as these. As many users with public e-mail addresses have experienced, spam, or unsolicited e-mail, is a major problem. Most of these unwanted messages can be deleted just by looking at the header or sender, but some come so well disguised (for example, faking a sender's address, perhaps an address from your own organization, using a general header) that we may be far into the message before we know its purpose. The costs of handling spam can be enormous. If we use ten seconds to identify and delete a spam message, a message sent to a million people will take one and a half work-year just to have it removed from all the inboxes.

Spam, unsolicited e-mail, is a major problem. It can be handled by legalization (best) or by software filters.

E-mail is so inexpensive to send that it may be worth the effort if only one out of a million accepts an offer. Many institutions try to remove spam at an early stage, for example, by letting the mail server filter out messages from suspected sources, where there is an incompatibility between name and IP address or messages that can be identified as spam by their vocabulary.[2] The latter case is potentially dangerous, as genuine messages may be removed along with the garbage. However, most organizations manage to remove most of the unsolicited mail today utilizing a set of various methods.

While the EU and some US states have passed laws to ban unsolicited e-mail, that is, enforcing the same rules for e-mail as for fax,[3] others are moving toward a system in which one can ask to be removed from distribution lists.[4] The latter solution is not so good. Not only do we collectively waste years in sending removal messages, but we have no guarantee that these will have any effect. Probably the unsubscribe mail is just a confirmation that we have a working e-mail address that can be used for further spam messages. Even if we are removed from the e-mail distribution lists of the first company, we now can be legally spammed by all others.

In some cases, the receiver of an e-mail may be a computer.

In some cases, the receiver of an e-mail may be a computer. For example, we may send a message asking to be included or excluded from a mailing list. Some of these messages have the disadvantage that they require a strict format, which to some degree violates the openness of e-mail messages. Therefore, in most cases, it will be simpler to provide this type of formalized information using a Web form.

31.6   Comparison

	E-mail	SMS	Mail	Telephone	Fax	Videoconf.
Asynchronous	Yes	Yes	Yes	No	Yes	No
Synchronous	Partly	Yes	No	Yes	No	Yes
Computer readable text	Yes	Yes	No	No	No	No
Images	Yes	Limited	Yes	No	Yes	Yes
Data files	Yes	No	Yes	No	No	Partly
Fast	Yes	Yes	No	Yes	Yes	Yes
One to many	Yes	Limited	Yes	Limited	Yes	Limited
Costs	Low	Low	Medium	Low–high	Medium	High
Forward	Yes	Limited	Limited	Limited	Limited	-
Automatic handling	Yes	Limited	No	Limited	No	-
Automatic generation	Yes	Yes	Yes	Limited	Yes	-

Table 31.1 Comparison of different communication media.

Table 31.1 shows a comparison of different communication media. E-mail clearly has advantages in many areas, making it a strong competitor to the telephone, fax, and ordinary mail. However, for private communication, many prefer the more open and flexible communication platform offered by social networks (see Chapter 42).

The **asynchronous** nature of e-mail and its other advantages make it a formidable tool for creating more efficient businesses.

The asynchronous nature of e-mail and its other advantages make it a formidable tool for creating more efficient businesses. In most situations e-mail is more efficient than the telephone, not only because of its asynchronous nature, but because it leaves a text copy, which can be used as a reminder, forwarded to others, or stored in an archive. The send-to-all feature may have drawbacks. Often messages are forwarded or sent to all employees, instead of distributing to a more limited list. This just-in-case philosophy leaves us with what we can call "internal spam" in our inboxes.

However, the requirements for efficient use of e-mail should not be forgotten. Users need a computer, which may be everything from a mobile phone to a desktop machine, an Internet connection, and an address. They need typing and writing skills, although we do not require messages to be literary works of high quality, the medium requires the abilities to put thoughts into writing in a clear and efficient manner.

E-mail does not offer the same chances of second thought as a traditional letter.

In some cases, the ease of the e-mail system—sending a fast reply not only to the sender but also to all recipients—has resulted in misunderstandings, dissemination of private or confidential information, or anger among recipients (colleagues, customers, or managers). An ordinary letter gives us some time to think before sending, a telephone conversation allows us to make amends, and a statement in a personal conversation can be given with a smile, but a fast and short e-mail may be efficiently brutal. Some of the advantages of e-mail may become a disadvantage in these situations. The angry message we send a colleague or an employee can be forwarded to others and may be read out of context, leaving the recipients with a written statement that we cannot easily explain away. Compared with a letter, e-mail does not offer the same chances of second thought; the message may be sent immediately. Therefore, before hitting the "send" button, go through this checklist:

- Do I want to send this?
- In this form?
- To all these recipients?
- Will it be forwarded, to whom?
- What will the effect be?

We can develop human protocols for communication on top of the technical protocols.

However, as people get used to the medium, e-mail may go as smoothly as telephone conversations. After more than forty years with e-mail, the greatest problem with this technology seems to be its *advantages*. E-mail and its likes are so efficient that it has become the number one communication channel for very many people. Individually addressed letters by ordinary mail or nonprivate telephone calls are often exceptions for many businesspeople.

Can e-mail be too efficient?

While we still use the telephone or personal visits to handle complicated cases, many of the tasks previously organized using personal visits or the telephone are now handled over e-mail or perhaps a social network. The disadvantage may become apparent—communication becomes less personal. While a telephone call and a personal visit open the way for more than shoptalk, an e-mail message is often short and down to basics. The asynchronous nature of e-mail does not provide for a conversation in the same way as a telephone chat in which we inspire each other and the conversation may flow freely from one topic to the other. That is, with e-mail, we find that the focus is on the closed parts, leaving out the more open parts. At the same time, the need to meet with others in person is reduced, as all routine tasks are handled over e-mail. Recognizing this drawback also allows us to compensate for it, for example, by setting up personal meetings with customers, colleagues, or employees regularly.

Social networks are more open and are more suited for personal communication than e-mail.

Social networks are more open and are more suited for personal communication than e-mail. The idea of a "wall" where one can post notes, communicate with many, and use other media than text are all important. Today social sites, such as Facebook, can be an alternative to using e-mail within a group. The advantage of social sites is that it opens for free communication within the group. Therefore, many companies have experimented using Facebook to reach their customers. However, this implies that one is interested in a two-way communication and can accept the risk of starting uncontrolled discussions. Not all see the implications of moving to a social media. Some users view social media as just that, a way to communicate with friends, and do not welcome intrusion from others with different values, such as marketing. That is, when using Facebook to communicate with customers, one should be careful to stay within the "social" context. Perhaps it is a good idea to use e-mail in business environments, and retain social networks for the private sphere.

Notes

1 Most e-mail programs can also create and render messages in HTML format.

2 One of my employers decided to do something about the spam messages that cluttered the mail system, and a novice was set to define the keywords that were used to identify spam. Encouraged by early successes, more and more words were added to the "bad word" list. After "sex," "spicy," and "credit card" were included, nearly all spam disappeared. However, so did many other e-mail messages. For example, a colleague did not receive an e-mail from his travel agency because he had ordered a "spicy Asian" in-flight meal.

3 This is the "opt-in" option, in which we explicitly have to express our wish to be on a mailing list.

4 This is the "opt-out" alternative, in which we explicitly have to ask to be removed from a mailing list.

32 Browsers

In addition to displaying Web pages, most browsers have a system for creating and modifying pages. The first browser was a simple line-based, text-only program developed by Berners-Lee, and available on the CERN server from 1991.

However, the Web did not really take off until the National Center for Supercomputing Applications (NCSA) at the University of Illinois at Urbana-Champaign offered the more advanced Mosaic browser in 1993. Marc Andreessen and the rest of the design team worked hard to incorporate requests from early Web users in Mosaic, which was both a browser and an editor. The most important new feature was the img-tag, which made it possible for the first time to have images as a part of a Web page. This opened a whole new world of layout and applications. Later on, the Mosaic team founded Netscape, while Microsoft bought the company that licensed Mosaic.

The **img-tag**, making it possible to embed images in HTML, opened a new world of Web applications.

32.1 Display HTML pages

Figure 32.1 Browser window (Firefox).

The main job of a browser, such as Firefox or Internet Explorer, is to retrieve and display HTML pages. As discussed in Chapter 30, a page is retrieved based on the URL. URLs can be entered

The browser is our **window on the world**.

Web **surfing** works best when response times are small.

With **forms**, the browser can be used as a terminal to specialized applications. HTML is moving toward a full **user interface** language.

by users directly in the address field, retrieved from a bookmark or "favorite" archive, or extracted from a link. The page is then presented, as shown in Figure 32.1. To simplify navigation, the browser offers forward and back buttons, as well as a list of previously visited sites.

The browser uses the HTTP protocol to request and retrieve pages, for example, by using the GET-command within this protocol. HTTP works on top of an Internet protocol, and defines an envelope for the transmission of Web pages, with fields for source and destination URLs, size of the page, the HTML version that is used, and so on. The browser strips off this header information before the page is displayed.

For the user, the browser is the window to the world. By navigating among URLs, the user can point his window in any direction, at any source. Behind the scenes, the browser will issue the GET-command, retrieve the HTML pages, and display them. Ideally, we want immediate feedback, especially when we are "surfing the Web," moving from page to page in our quest for interesting data. We do not know exactly what we want, and may only spend a few seconds on each page before we follow another link, replacing the contents of the browser window. In many ways, Web browsing resembles scanning more than reading, something that we should acknowledge when we design Web pages. Ideally, Web pages should be efficient to download, and the main contents of the page (title, abstract, and important hypertext links) should be presented in the browser window using a layout that gives a good overview, without the need for scrolling.

The layout of the page is controlled by HTML, which has changed dramatically over the last twenty years. Not only do we have an image tag in the standard, but modern HTML also recognizes a larger variety of layout commands, offers image-maps in which input can be given by clicking on a map or image, defines simple animations, and so forth. An important feature is the form-tag, allowing the user to enter input data that can be sent to a Web server for processing.[1] Thus the original concept of using the Web to retrieve information has been replaced by two-way functionality in which the browser can get data from the user and send this off to the source. In fact, HTML is moving toward a full user interface language, with not only passive layout functions, but also all the features we expect such as text boxes, radio buttons, and command buttons.

32.2   Embedding scripts

A browser is a
virtual computer
that can run
simple programs
(scripts).

Today HTML can describe dynamic pages that have embedded
scripts in the page source. The script, a small program, is recognized by the browser and can be executed directly or by an
event such as a button click. In this respect, a browser acts as a
virtual computer that exists on top of the physical computer and
its operating system. For reasons of security, the virtual computer may have limited access to local resources, for example,
not being able to read and write to local disks.

The advantage of this approach is a high degree of portabil-
ity. A script or an applet (a small application program, often
written in Java) can be downloaded from the source and run
within the browser, independently of the computer and operating system used.

The disadvantage is that processing may be slow; running a
program in a virtual computer on top of a physical computer is
not efficient. However, newer versions of browsers may be able
to use local resources, such as graphics accelerators, to speed
up processing. In addition, all resources that the program may
need (such as mathematical functions, fonts, images) must be
downloaded from the source. The browser can store data only
temporarily, and any permanent storage must be on the server.
These issues are covered in more detail in Chapters 39 and 40.

32.3   Plug-ins

With **plug-ins** we
can give our
browser new
functionality.

Plug-ins is a program module that can be downloaded, embedded in the browser, and executed on the local physical machine
(not in the virtual machine as an applet), in the same way as the
browser is executed. A plug-in offers a flexible way to extend
the browser's functionality. For example, we can download
plug-ins for playing music or video or for giving 3D capabilities to the browser. New versions of plug-ins can be obtained
without having to get new versions of the browsers, and users
with limited resources can stick to the original browser, avoiding allocating extra space for resources that they do not need.

However, users may be reluctant to download additional
software because of the risk of viruses or to avoid filling up local disks. Thus, for designing ordinary Web pages, avoid requiring plug-ins and use only functions that are a part of the
standard browser. Since modern browsers include a large set of
modules and possibilities in a standard version, there is often no
need to require additional software in the form of a plug-in.

32.4   Stateless

The transfer
protocol for HTML
pages, HTTP, is
stateless. It has
no memory of
earlier transac-
tions.

HTTP is a stateless protocol, meaning that each request is treated as a single discrete entity, not as a part of a longer sequence. The browser requests a page from a server by issuing a GET-command, and the server can forget about the transaction when the page has been returned. The drawback is that it becomes difficult to implement services that are performed as a sequence of commands, for example with login and logoff functionality.

However, a Web server may store state information in separate variables. Another option is that a server can assign the browser to store a "cookie," a small text file, on the browser's local system. A cookie usually includes an identifier that the browser will return to the Web server on its next visit. In this way, the server can recognize you and connect requests. For example, if you provided your name and address in the first visit to the site, this information can be retrieved upon subsequent visits, based on information from the cookie.

Cookies will aid
the server in
identifying the
user.

32.5   Privacy and security

Extended functionality has made browsers more vulnerable to attacks that can violate privacy. Cookies can give away information that you considered private; an applet should not be able to access permanent storage on your computer, but because of the complexity of the software, loopholes in the security system could allow applets to delete or create files. One mechanism for avoiding these problems is to provide systems in which the user can select the level of security wanted, or the level of service.

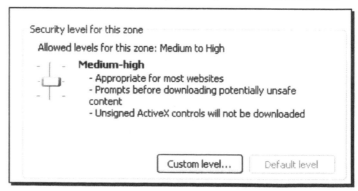

Figure 32.2. Setting security levels in Internet Explorer.

As shown in Figure 32.2, Internet Explorer allows Web sites to be cataloged into different zones, each with their own security level. For example, we may accept a lower security setting on our local Intranet and on trusted sites than we do on the open Internet. We can specify restrictions at each level, as shown in the right part of the figure. For example, we can tell the browser not to accept downloads, or, to give warnings in given situations. The disadvantage of a high security level is of course that the functionality of our Web browsers will be reduced and that some sites become unavailable—or that we will have a high administrative overhead by cataloging sites and setting security parameters. Thus, most users run their browsers with a low or medium security level, choosing functionality over security or, as is perhaps more common, never thinking about the security risks at all.

For example, for a secure transaction with an online bank, it is important that:

1. The browser can determine that the bank site is secure and genuine.
2. The bank server can determine that the customer is genuine, and that he is who he says he is.
3. The data communicated cannot be read or changed by unauthorized persons.

Secure transactions can be handled by the HTTPS protocol.

These secure transactions can be handled by the HTTPS protocol, which codes transmissions using a secure cryptography system and uses a secure identification of the network Web server. Thus, HTTPS can provide a level of protection, even if only one side—the server side—is authenticated. This authentication is based on certificates issued by a trusted agency. To authenticate the server, a certificate is sent to the browser that has the ability to check if it is valid. To authenticate the user (the client), the site administrator creates a certificate for each user. This can be loaded into the browser. But this may not always be simple, given that many types of equipment and many different operating systems are in use.

The certificate, which acts as a signature for the site or the client, is implemented as a complex digital code, with a public and a private part. I give the public key to the bank that uses this key to encrypt messages they send to me. The coding system is so clever that only I can decrypt these messages, using my private key.[2] Thus, if the message is intercepted on its way from source to destination, it cannot be read without the private key. Any tampering with the message will immediately be detected at the receiving end. This may seem complicated, but the browser takes care of everything: storing the certificates, offering public keys to the parties that we are communicating with, coding and decoding messages, and so on. However, to avoid installing certificates at the user's site, many systems offer a certificate only on the server side. This simple version offers authentication of only the server, but works in most cases.

The only way we may notice that the transaction is secure is that the URL starts with "HTTPS," indicating a secure http, instead of the common HTTP. While an Internet bank will require a HTTPS protocol, some sites may use HTTP until one proceeds to checkout, and then switch to the more secure HTTPS. Other sites, such as Facebook, allow users to choose if they want to use a HTTP or HTTPS connection. (When using Facebook on a public network, as in a restaurant or an airport, it may be very smart to use the secure option.)

Online shopping requires the user to enter personal information, such as name, address, and credit card information. To simplify these transactions, the browser can offer to save this information in a password-protected *wallet*. A site can then retrieve this information directly from the wallet, and we avoid reentering it.

Security on the Internet, as elsewhere, is a relative issue.

When discussing transaction security on the Internet and the Web, we often forget that security is a relative issue. We can put two locks on every door in our house, but the burglar can enter through a window. We can put alarm systems on all windows, but to no avail if we forget to activate the system when we leave the house. By using the security mechanisms that are implemented in the browser, we can decrease the probability of fraud, making it more difficult for a hacker to break in, but as in the physical world, a completely secure system is impossible. The highest risk is not in the hardware or the software, but in the users themselves. The passwords we use may be too simple or not changed often enough; we may leave a password on a piece of paper or simply forget to log off.

Crime on the Internet may be detected and investigated following electronic tracks.

The advantage of a computer system in such cases is that if fraud occurs, it may leave a digital track to the criminals. The only thing a hacker can do if he gets access to a bank account is to move money to another account. From here he may get access to the money, but he leaves a trail behind that increases his risk of being caught. However, the bottom line is that security is expensive, and that a complicated access system may scare customers away. Therefore, most banks and credit card companies are willing to take the risks, online as well as offline.

The browser gives us the possibility of accessing information and services from a myriad of sites, but also provides a way in for those with malicious intents. As in other parts of life we have to find the right balance between openness, functionality, and efficiency on one hand and the need to protect our assets and privacy on the other.

In many cases it comes down to a matter of thrust: Do we trust this Web site? Luckily, we are not alone. Others may have suggested that this is a good site; we may have found the link on a trusted site; and there may be reviews that are of help. If in doubt, we can always try to Google the site. On the Web, news travel fast, and if others are dissatisfied we may find their complaints easily.

Notes

1   We will return to these issues in more detail in Chapter 39.

2   Private-public key system utilizes the fact that it is difficult to factorize (for example, 8 into 2*2*2) huge numbers. The public key defines the creation of these huge numbers, and the private part shows how they can be factorized (decrypted).

33 World Wide Web

The Internet has had an **explosive** growth, but so have many other communication technologies.

Some have argued that the adoption rate of the Internet has exceeded that of earlier mass communication technology by several orders of magnitude, but few real data have been presented to prove this claim. Radio and television also had fast adoption rates, and we must not forget that the Internet, in some form or other, has been here for more than forty years. But, if we view the Web as a separate technology, it has had a tremendous impact in just a few years. Tim Berners-Lee opened the Web initially with an almost blank page; today there are several billion Web pages.

We find all kinds of contents on the Web, from amateurish pages with very simple layouts to pages created by professional graphic designers and Web journalists. The Web has become a medium for nonprofit organizations and for global industries. Most sites are open and free; others are hidden behind passwords, certificates, and cryptography. We find answers to primary school exercises, official reports, and scientific papers. Some sites are an explosion of multimedia techniques; others look as if they have been printed on an old-fashioned typewriter. Pages may not have been changed since the day they were created; some are updated every few seconds.

The Web is like a combination of white and yellow pages, with each and every one having a virtual presence—a home page with pictures of friends and family, professional interests, or our hobbies; a place to present our views, organization, or political party; a place for marketing and selling; a place to disseminate documentation or to meet with others in a virtual room.

However, as we see, the movement is from a general Web, where pages most often are described in HTML, to more specialized applications, sites for searching, booking, banking, shopping, or for socializing. As for any other technology, general products are replaced with specialized ones.

33.1   Global village

In 1962, Marshall McLuhan noted, "The new electronic interdependence recreates the world in the image of a *global village*."[1] Since then, many have reused his term to describe the way we use the Internet and the Web to make the world smaller or to create virtual or electronic communities. While the government and other large organizations can use the Internet as a tool for more efficient communication, the new medium offers unprecedented possibilities for very small organizations or groups. Since these small entities may be spread over wide areas with only a few persons at each location, contact between group members may be difficult to implement. Suddenly, with the Internet and the Web, there is the unprecedented ability to keep in contact with very low costs.

As with other technologies, the Web has positive and negative sides.

On the positive side, the Web makes it possible to create virtual networks of people who may share a particular disease, a special job, an interest, or a hobby. Immigrants can keep in touch with their own cultures, read the local paper from their hometowns, keep updated on minor and major events, even participate in local discussions. On the negative side, subgroups such as Nazis, terrorist organizations, child pornographers, and criminals use the Internet to organize their activities. Electronic communication provides the means of keeping transmissions secret, such as by using cryptography to hinder insight into e-mail messages. In this respect, the Internet and the Web provide an additional advantage for such groups, so instead of supporting cross-national and cross-cultural exchange, the Internet can support polarization and fragmentation.[2]

Tools for personal communication include e-mail, distribution lists, newsgroups, chat rooms, and Web sites, and now social networks are replacing these. Instead of having a personal profile on a Web page and using e-mail or chat to communicate, social networks, such as Facebook and other systems, offer everything in one place. Users don't have to just hope that someone will come to their Web pages; they can have groups of friends on a social net, all of whom can follow updates, comments, and photos. (We return to these issues in Chapter 42.)

One clear "global village" effect of the Internet and the Web has been that information is now instantly available all over the world. Earlier, marketers could launch a product in the United States one year, in Europe the second, in Asia the third, keeping up production over many years. Today this is impossible, and, movies, books, CDs, and toys are launched all over the world on the same day. Norwegians who had to wait months and perhaps years to see a new movie, now can see it in their hometown theater before it is launched in Los Angeles (the nine-hour time difference working in the Norwegians' favor here). Of course, this is also supported by digital cinemas: One no longer has to wait to get a copy.

33.2   Formalization level of HTML

The **low formalization** level of HTML (layout) lies behind the high degree of flexibility offered.

We have seen that the simplicity of creating HTML pages was behind the explosion of content on the Web, but this explosion would not have been possible without the low formalization level of HTML—its "blank sheet of paper." HTML is only a layout language, and therefore, can be used for any type of text. The structure requirements are extremely simple, and most browsers will display pages even when we break the rules, for example, by inserting missing tags or ignoring tags that cannot be recognized. Just as we can use a word processor for any type of document, all types of information can be saved in HTML. HTML sets no requirements to the contents or structure of a page, which are both a strength and a weakness. It's like the boomtowns of the West in the nineteenth century: Anybody could build because there were no regulations, no central plan, no permissions to obtain, no bureaucracy. Whole towns could emerge in a few months.

The low formalization level is also a **weakness**, as the Web is created without any formal overall structure.

Today, most HTML pages are created by Web design systems or other computer programs. For more structured information, dynamic pages, pages that are created by programs on the fly, have replaced static Web pages. Dynamic pages have the advantage of being able to extract information from underlying databases. For example, instead of having a static HTML-based telephone list that must be updated separately from all other archives, the telephone list can be created when needed based on a human resources database. (We will return to dynamic Web pages in Chapter 39.)

Hypertext is the ideal tool for the Web, enabling us to link to the source instead of copying or rewriting information. That is, we can create the context for a Web page just by linking.

With the URL, each page has a unique identifier; the HTTP protocol ensures that information can be transmitted via the Internet and HTML that it can be presented on a screen. While the hypertext idea has had limited success (except for manuals and help systems), the Web has really become *the* hypertext application. Of course, hypertext is an ideal technique for the Web. For example, when we create a "home page," describing persons, institutions, or special interest groups, these "objects" do not exist in a vacuum, but are highly connected to other objects. Our personal Web pages can link to the Web pages of friends and families, to the company where we work, to our alma mater, to the portal of the city where we live, etc. The advantage is that we can provide complete information, where we only have to enter and maintain a fraction of the data ourselves.

The simple link system of HTML cannot guarantee that a link goes to a live destination.

The drawback of simple, unidirectional links is that links may go nowhere or page contents can be changed in a way that violates the semantics of a hypertext link. In practice, these problems can be reduced by careful consideration of which links to include. For example, a link to another institution should go to the relevant home page. This page may be changed repeatedly, but the "idea" of the page, to act as a port to the institution, should remain stable. We should also expect that the URLs themselves will stabilize, as the expense of changing a well-known URL will be as high as changing the name of a company. Even where the URL is changed, most institutions will leave a link at the old address, redirecting users to the new site.

33.3   Web site development tools

Today, few people design Web pages using HTML because there are an abundance of tools that can aid in Web page development, for handling both the static and the dynamic parts. These systems offer complete content management functionality, that is, for publishing, editing, and modifying content. Drupal, a free and open-source system written in PHP is an example[3]. It can run on any platform that supports PHP, for example on a Web server such as Apache, and can access databases such as MySQL and Microsoft SQL server.

With such tools, it is easy to set up a full Web site, as well as sites that retrieve information from databases, even with no programming skills.

33.4   Information

The Web is easy to adopt. It is also easy to be an information-provider. But most of the traffic goes to a very limited number of sites.

The Web, like radio, TV, and newspapers, is easy to adopt. But unlike other media, on the Web everybody can be information-providers as well as consumers. In this way, the basic structure of the Web can be called democratic. However, to a large extent, the frequency of hits on a page is determined by the influence of the organization behind the Web site. Today, most of the traffic goes to a very limited number of sites, those created and maintained by professional organizations. So, on one hand we talk about Web diversity and the billions of pages and on the other hand we talk about Internet usage—knowing that the traffic is not as diverse as the pages.

Social networks have changed this situation. Instead of posting a Web page, a profile, to the whole world, we post it for our friends. And since they have the same possibility, we create an active group in which all are both readers and writers.

On the Web, a user has a higher possibility of selecting the information she wants, by using portals, search engines, or going to certain sites. Some people have raised the concern that if every individual targets only the information he wants, we will no longer share a common ground, and the Web will pose a threat to democracy. For example, a person can decide to look only at sport sites, not getting any other news. But this concern may be attacked from several directions. Information selection is not connected only to the Web. Some TV channels, newspapers, and journals also have a very limited scope. People may live in a place or a culture with little or no contact with outsiders. Further, the most successful information Web sites are often sites like those of newspapers, TV stations, and portals that provide headlines and news on a large set of topics, just as in the physical world.

When the Web emerged, it promised empowerment to its users. No longer would we be in the hands of the TV or newspaper editors. On the Web, we could go directly to the sources to get in-depth information on candidates, the economy, the environment—a nice thought, but not very realistic. TV has established its role as the main communication channel in competition with other media that provide in-depth information, such as newspapers, books, and libraries. We find a good example in elections, when citizens have an abundance of in-depth information on the candidates (newspaper articles, books, political programs, and reports), but many seem to form their opinions based on political ads or superficial TV debates. While the Web may offer more convenient access to the information sources, it does not provide the user with the time, skills, and motivation for utilizing these sources. Probably TV news presents what viewers seem to want, a superficial selection of the most interesting stories, compacted to a few minutes.

Is the **medium** the message or do we retain usage patterns independently of the media?

We can use the Web to broaden, narrow, or deepen our horizons. We can get in-depth information, but most of us end up by getting just the **headlines**.

33.5   Web as an interface

When accessing a bank or a travel agency system, we are within a **closed domain**, separated from the open Web.

When we access the site of an Internet bank or an online travel agency, the Web is used only as a standard interface. Within the site, we are really navigating a database structure— the bank accounts, the flight information, or the hotel database. These data are formalized at a high level, as a record structure with well-defined fields. The tools that we use within the site, for example, a search tool, are designed to work on this database structure and in this way are very different from the tools that work on HTML formatted pages. In these sites, hidden from the rest of the Web, most of the HTML pages will be generated on the fly, based on input from the user and resulting from database queries. Thus, the advantages of two worlds are combined: The Internet standards and availability of browsers can give everyone access to specialized and closed databases with a high formalization level.

Using the browser as an interface has been a smart solution for all systems open to the general public. Now, the same scheme is used within companies, avoiding local installation of customized software. If you lean over the airport counter and look at the display the airline representative uses, you will see something similar to the Internet booking system that you use yourself. That is, instead of using a client-server system, in which the software is installed for each client or each office PC, modern systems use the browser as the client. Now all proprietary software is on the server, making installation and maintenance much easier. In many cases employees may use the same systems as the customers, albeit with a set of additional functions. But, even in cases where a system is to be used by employees only, a Web-based interface often will provide the best solution.

33.6   Discussion

The disadvantage of the "boom town" creation of the Web is that the billions of Web pages that exist today are highly unstructured, with exception of the closed databases. But this is only a small problem when a page is to be studied by a human being. Our capabilities of pattern recognition and understanding text based on context are so flexible that we can get information out of nearly any page. And, as we have seen, the Web standards can be used to access closed databases where we can work on more structured data.

Ideally, we would like to be able to access many of these closed systems at the same time, for example, to have a search tool, or an "agent" that looks for a cheap hotel, a best bargain on a book, and so forth. Then, a higher degree of formalization, standardization, and page structure would be welcome.

Notes

1   McLuhan, Marshall. 1962. The Gutenberg Galaxy. London: Routledge & Kegan Paul.

2   See Cass R. Sunstein. 2001. Republic.com, Princeton University Press.

3   http://drupal.org/

34 Searching the Web

One of the great advantages of having data in electronic form is that it can be subjected to automatic searching. This is of special interest on the Web because of the sheer volume of data. However, as we shall see, Web searching is not always easy.

34.1 Precision and recall

Precision =

$$\frac{\text{\# relevant returned}}{\text{\# returned}}$$

Recall =

$$\frac{\text{\# relevant returned}}{\text{\# relevant in total}}$$

When a bank clerk needs a list of accounts with a negative balance, she will expect an answer that is 100 percent correct—if the computer does not include all the customers with a negative balance, and only these, there must be an error either in the programs or in the data. But is a Web search 100 percent correct? No, very often we get many irrelevant references returned from search engines, and we have no guarantee that the most interesting documents are included in the list. Sometimes, we have to give up, without a relevant answer to our query.

Within information retrieval, the terms *precision* and *recall* are used to describe the quality of a document retrieval result.[1] Precision is a ratio of the number of relevant documents (references) in the result set over the total number of documents returned. For example, if five out of every ten returned documents (references) are relevant, the precision will be 0.5 or 50 percent. In the bank example, precision will always be 100 percent, as only accounts with a negative balance are returned. On the Web, precision may be much lower, as the results are often "polluted" by irrelevant references.

Recall is defined as the number of relevant documents returned, compared to the number of relevant documents in the database. That is, if the search engine returns two hundred relevant documents out of a potential of a thousand, recall will be 0.2 or 20 percent. Recall on the Internet will be very low; in fact, for most search engines, recall will be small, independent of the query because the engines index only a fraction of all Web pages.

However, for many users, recall is unimportant. As long as our information need is satisfied, we do not care if other pages could give us the same or similar information. We may go to the Web to get information on a country or a city, and will usually be satisfied when we find a site, perhaps from the local tourist bureau, that provides what we want. Of course, we know that there may be other pages with this information, even better pages, but since we have satisfactory results, we do not need to probe further.

For a lawyer looking for similar cases in preparation for a lawsuit, a high recall is paramount. The only way to achieve this result will be to use special databases with an improved data structure than those on the Web. Still, it will be a challenge to find all relevant cases. Recall is also important when we try to find the *cheapest* hotel in Rome or the *best offer* for a weekend in New York. A journalist searching the Web to find data on previous airplane accidents also will appreciate good recall.

Why can we expect 100 percent precision and recall using the banking system, and not with a search engine on the Web? We know that both the data and the functions of the bank and Web applications are formalized; otherwise, we could not apply the computer. However, the key to the discrepancy in the reliability of the results lies in the fact that the data are formalized on different levels,[2] as discussed in Chapter 5.

In the bank, we will find a database with account records. Each record has a unique account number, a reference to the account owner and a number giving the balance. The bank's administrators have determined this structure as they have specified the attributes (fields) of an account, the length and format of each field, and so forth, keeping in mind the functionality needed from the banking system. They have defined the term *account* in a formalized manner. When the clerk enters her query, the computer will retrieve all records where the number in the balance field is less than zero. We get 100 percent results as the query and the data are formalized on the same level (that is, the computer or database system knows the terms used, balance, account number, name, address, and so on). This result indicates that the database administrators did a good job; they defined the terms needed for the type of queries that are presented to the database system.

However, if the bank clerk tried a different type of query, for example, to find all customers with red hair, the database would not be able to give an answer because hair color is not an attribute of a customer that is stored within the system. If the clerk wants a list of all *good* customers, this may not be easy to provide, even if the basic data may be available. She could try to formalize the term "good customer" as customers with more than $10,000 in their account. But this simplification may miss customers who have spread their money over several accounts,

100 percent recall and precision require that the data have been **formalized** to the level of the queries.

customers who by chance have a low balance at the moment, reliable customers who pay high interest on their bank loans, and so on. On the other hand, a customer who only uses the bank to cash checks, moving the money to another bank later on, may be included in the "good customers" list. The clerk can try to elaborate the specification to handle some of these flaws and create more complex queries. In the end, she always would have to expect a recall and precision below the 100 percent level, as there is no direct way of formulating her high-level query.

A remedy will be to define explicitly the term "good customer," using only formalized terms (for example, in the way some airlines give you a frequent flyer update to silver or gold cards based on the mileage points you have collected). Then the database system will give a 100 percent answer, determining accurately which customer should have which type of card. Of course, this only moves the problem one step up, since we now may have a discrepancy between the common understanding of "good customer" and the mileage point definition. However, this formalized definition has the advantage that the discrepancy with the real-world term of a good customer will be open and known by the whole organization, and not hidden within lower precision and recall.

34.2   Search engines

As we have seen, HTML documents are formalized on a layout level, as characters and words. A page may have a few meta fields, such as title and keywords, but these are not required. In practice, search engines rely on low-level data, expressions, and words that can be retrieved from each page during an indexing phase. In an isolated form, these will not be a good representation of the author's communicative intentions, but there is no other remedy for search engines. These indexing programs store the URL for each significant word in the text, which makes it possible to find the page based on one or more words. Search engines use spiders, programs that traverse the Web to find pages; or, if a Web master does not want to wait for a spider to come along, she can explicitly submit a page for indexing. While the number of indexed pages is impressive, it represents only a fraction of the total number on the Web, which grows too fast even for the most efficient spiders.

Another problem is some data may be hidden from the spiders, such as data stored in databases that require logins, pass-

Spiders are used to find and index Web pages described in HTML, XML, and perhaps also PDF format.

words, or other user input to be retrieved. Data also may be stored in other formats than HTML—an "invisible" Web that is not covered by all search engines.[3] Updates create another problem. Many Web pages are highly dynamic, and some need to be reindexed every day. In practice, even if most engines try to reindex the most popular pages quite often, it can still be weeks between each update. If the page has changed in the meantime, the last indexing may no longer be valid.

34.3   Discrepancy between user's information need and the query

The search engines operate on a string or word level, with no understanding of higher-level terms such as address, account number, balance, or flight number. There is no date of publication or a formalized field for "author." Even where a title and keywords are provided, there is no common ground for understanding these words because the Web covers many languages and topics and authors come from all professions and categories.

The concept of **"information need"** may be described as a collection of terms—the query.

The problem is to map our *information need* into one or more keywords, perhaps using the Boolean operators—such as **not**, **and**, **or**—to better express our need. The success of this mapping, and retrieval results, will depend on:

1. The formalization level of the query
2. The connection between the higher-level concepts in the data and the query terms
3. The specificity of the terms

Let us start this discussion by looking at the simplest queries, for example, finding the home page of the School of Information Sciences, University of Pittsburgh. In this case, we have a high level of formalization. The task of finding a given home page and the "concepts" are simplified by the use of names. While there may be many "Schools of Information Sciences," there is only one at the University of Pittsburgh. Similarly you should be able to find my home page directly or indirectly by providing "Kai A. Olsen" to a search engine. In other cases, polysemy—the fact that a word may have many meanings—may cause problems. Golf is a sport, but also the name of a car, the name of cities, and the communications code word for the letter *G*. However, often cases of multiple meanings can be narrowed by adding additional terms, for example, "Volks-

Web searching is complicated by the fact that the Web itself is a very inhomogeneous collection of documents.

wagen Golf." But then, we will not find the American version of this car, which goes under the name of Volkswagen Rabbit.

The diversity of the Web not only encompasses topics, but also the nature of the documents. While a bibliographic database normally consists of only one type of document (for example, scientific papers), all categories of documents are found on the Web. If we formalize our search for a description of the Rabbit by querying "Volkswagen Rabbit," we will get an abundance of sales advertisements, names of dealers, and, if we are lucky, also one or more pages giving specifications of this model. However, the search engine's scheme to identify the most important pages may help us. For example, Google, with its PageRank algorithm, prioritizes pages that are linked to many other pages, especially if the linked sites also are important. Thus, the official Volkswagen pages may come up first in the result set. Many other sites naturally will be linked to the company's official pages, and these other sites, in turn, may be linked to many other sites.

This ranking system works fine in most cases, but tends to make the practical Web more static and less dynamic, maintaining the existing structure. What Google does is really to use the Web to index the Web. When there are competing pages, it may be difficult for a new page to be seen among the incumbents; initially the new page will have only a few links, and the search engine will list the other pages first. Therefore, to promote the Web site of a new business or just your home page, make sure that many other sites recognize your site (that is, ask others to create links to your site).

Names are a great help in searching, helping us to identify persons, places, brands, and products, but some names are more specific than others. It is easier to use the Web to get an overview of hotels in Nome, Alaska, than in Los Angeles, where hotels abound. Similar, it is easier to find a person with a special name than one with a common name. Knowing where the person lives can narrow the search—a great help if the person lives in Nome, population 3,598, but not so much if the person lives in the Los Angeles area with twelve million people.

34.4   Natural language

When names are not available, we have to rely on natural language, coping with synonymy, polysemy, and the imprecision of terms. Because of synonymy, we may miss some interesting institutions in our search for "computing science" education,

The open nature of natural language reduces search effectiveness.

Sublanguages can aid searching in homogenous databases.

since these may use the synonym "informatics." Perhaps institutions within "information science" would be of interest, but these home pages may not use our keywords.

While these problems occur in all bibliographic systems, they are worse on the Web because of the inhomogeneous nature of the documents. For example, the word "plasma" has one meaning for a medical database, another for a database in the field of physics. That is, when we search a medical database we may utilize the sublanguage of medicine to formalize queries, using terms for diagnosis, treatments, or medicines, expecting that we share a common vocabulary with the authors of these documents.

Further, the nature of the data may provide additional search clues. In a database of scientific papers, we will have the option of limiting a query to words in the title, the keywords, or the abstract. Perhaps we can ask the system to give added weight to documents where keywords are found within headers. Here we profit by our common understanding of the form of scientific papers.

On the open Web, no such common understanding exists. The pages will have authors from all fields, amateurs as well as professionals. Here "plasma" may have all four meanings found in an English dictionary (blood, protoplasm, a green translucent variety of quartz, and an ionized gas), and perhaps also others, if we go beyond English. The documents may be in any conceivable form—notes, memorandums, reports, letters, minutes of meetings, product description, brochures, or scientific papers. On the open Web, we will have all the disadvantages of a natural language search, with few possibilities to enhance queries with context.

However, we may encounter problems even before we submit keywords to a search engine. Often it may be problematic just to find the words that describe our "information need." For example, we may want to buy a new, inexpensive car. Our information needs can be to get a list of the various models available. This task is fairly clear to a human being, but not so easy to describe to a search engine. We may try "inexpensive cars," or perhaps "car **and** (inexpensive **or** cheap)." But inexpensive and cheap are relative terms, often used as a default in marketing. The search will include pages that describe cars for sale, rentals, maintenance, and so on, and may exclude pages where cars are listed with their price. In such cases an experienced searcher may try a different approach, for example, to

Are the words **precise** enough?

Boolean operators are not always intuitive.

finding an auto magazine on the Web, and searching within the magazine for an overview of inexpensive cars.

An alternative would be to include more terms in the query, perhaps using the keyword **not** to exclude pages, which is not always easy in practice. More specific terms may improve precision, but will reduce recall. In addition, many ordinary users have problems using Boolean operator terms correctly, especially when **or** and **not** operators are included because of the rather informal way these terms are used in natural language. The waiter may give you a choice of "Italian, French, *and* blue cheese dressing," whereas a mathematician would use **or**.

We get a more common understanding of Boolean queries if we use only the **and** operator, asking the search engine to include only pages that contain all the query terms. Most search engines assume that we imply an **and** when we give more than one keyword, but this is really not a Boolean **and**, since the engine will list references (farther down in the result set) where only one of the keywords occurs.

34.5   Information overload

Information overload—too many references returned with no possibility of narrowing searches without losing important references.

While computer technology has given us efficient ways for creating, storing, and disseminating information, our ability to read documents is as slow as ever.

We can use Boolean operators to limit the size of the result set, reducing the problem of information overload. Information overload occurs when we get too many documents back and irrelevant documents make it difficult to find what we want. This is a problem may happen when we need a good recall, for example, when we search a scientific database for papers on a given topic.

Of course, the basic problem is that computer technology has given us efficient ways for creating, storing, and disseminating information, but our ability to read documents is as slow as ever. While a search engine may return thousands of references, we may have the time to examine only a few, perhaps not more than twenty or forty references for an average query.

Table 34.1 (next page) shows the number of references returned by a bibliographic system in a test performed some years ago on the topic of information overload.[4] Most of these queries, even the quite specific queries shown in numbers 4 and 7, resulted in information overload—an unwieldy number of documents (the quotes are used similarly to most search engines, e.g., that "information retrieval" indicates a search for the exact phrase). By narrowing the queries, as in query 5 and 8, we were able to reduce the return set to a manageable size (forty). All of the forty documents returned in queries 5 and 8

No	Query	# returned
1.	information **and** retrieval	80,000
2.	"information retrieval"	20,000
3.	full **and** text **and** information **and** retrieval	10,000
4.	"information retrieval" **and** "full text"	2,000
5.	"full text information retrieval"	40
6.	information **and** overload	10,000
7.	"information overload"	4,000
8.	"information retrieval" **and** "information overload"	40

Table 34.1 WWW queries and results.

We can increase **precision**, but often have to pay with a reduced **recall**.

are relevant, showing that it is possible to get high precision in large inhomogeneous databases by giving very precise queries. However, the price is lower recall, which the results of alternative queries describing our information need confirm. Thus, it seems that each precise query yields only a fraction of the relevant documents on the Web. If we repeat the same queries today, with even more papers in the system, we will find that information overload is even worse.

While the documents returned are relevant in the sense that they cover the topics of interest, they do not necessarily fulfill our information need. Some of the information may already be known to us, some may cover aspects of information retrieval that are not of interest, and some may be in an "unpublished" or unedited form that makes it difficult to rely on the information. While formalizing the information need with a set of words or a Boolean expression is complicated in any system, the inhomogeneous nature of the Web makes it difficult to use when high recall is of interest.

Search engines use different schemes to weigh search results, giving us the most **relevant** references first.

Search engines may try to help us cope with information overload by listing the most relevant links first. For example, priority can be given to pages that include our search terms in their "keywords" tag, pages where the terms are included early in the text or perhaps more than once, or pages that are linked by many other pages (as Google does). Although these schemes cannot guarantee a reasonable order, they are important. Without relevance rankings, Web search engines would be unusable in most cases. However, if these schemes are too transparent, Web authors can use countermeasures to avoid their page getting a low priority, for example, by expanding the keyword section.

Instead of using the open Web, we can search more specialized bibliographic databases. If we get too many results, we can limit the search to well-known scientific journals. That is, we can define "importance" by a selection of journals in which we believe the best papers will appear. (We may be criticized for ignoring a paper in these journals, but not in many others.) This shows that in a world with an unlimited number of products— scientific papers, golf clubs, mobile phones or anything else— brands become an important selector. However, the Internet may also dilute brand names, for example, when we use a general site to find a car rental agency or a hotel.

34.6   Filtering

We face the same discussion when we have the inverse problem—that of filtering out unwanted (for example, pornographic) material, from the Web. Such filters can be based on:

1. An automatic analysis of the Web page, for example, excluding the page if it includes words such as "sex," "porn," and "tits."

2. A manual categorization of a Web site by a "filter" agency.

3. A manual categorization of a Web page by the page author.

All of these methods have drawbacks. An automatic classification of pornography may remove pages that are nonpornographic, but still includes the filter words. For example, in Swedish, the number six is spelled "sex." There are also pages that discuss pornography or that give sex-advice, which can be removed by these filters. Some filters try to identify skin color to exclude pages with nude pictures. They may pass through more than the burka-dressed Afghan women, but, in practice, such a filter can never work. The information gap between the "skin color" algorithm and the goal of removing pornographic pictures is too great, just as it is difficult to evaluate the semantics of text by looking at individual words.

A 100 percent **filter system** is impossible to achieve. At best, we can develop filters that remove some of the unwanted pages (but with the risk of removing pages of interest).

A manual categorization is simpler, but also implies some form of censorship. However, the censor element may be reduced if there are many categories and if the browser user herself chooses what to exclude (setting the filter on or off, or determining the filter level), based on a categorization set by the page authors. This requires that everybody follow the standards, which may be difficult to achieve considering the Web's global inhomogeneous nature. The censorship element becomes more troublesome if we leave categorization to a special agency, and the enormous number of Web sites will make such a solution impractical anyway.

34.7 Quality

With all the unedited material on the Web, we have to be **our own editors** to evaluate the correctness and quality of the information we get. This is perhaps more an advantage than a drawback.

We cannot always take what we get on the Web for granted because everyone has the option to be a writer and most pages are not reviewed at all. We can find everything on the Web—high-quality scientific documents, school papers, propaganda, correct information, incorrect information, advertisements, official and unofficial sites, company sites and personal sites, and more. Today, we let schoolchildren access this repository, while not many years ago, we had a very careful screening process of textbooks and other material in many countries.

However, we can choose to see this as an advantage. Because we know that we cannot take what we find on the Web for granted, we have to be critical, review the source, and perhaps try to get confirmation from other sources. That is, with the Web, we can train our children to be critical, instead of allowing them to accept everything in the textbook at face value.

We face another problem if we want to publish information found on the Web. Most often information on the Internet and Web is presented without any copyright notice, and we have no guarantee as to where it came from in the first place. Text and images are cut from copyrighted Web pages, scanned from newspapers, magazines, and books, and put on the Web without any reference to the source. In many ways, the Web is used in the same way as oral channels, but while an oral story is never told with exactly the same words as in the original, on the Web we can get an identical, perhaps illegal, copy.

If we cannot trust the information itself, neither can we expect that search engine results will be presented in any fair order. The advantage of coming up on top of a search list (a Google search on "hotel London" returns more than 300 million hits) is so great that businesses are willing to pay a premium to be prioritized.

An honest, but often expensive, way of implementing this is to add relevant ads (sponsor lists) to the search results, making it easier for the user to distinguish between the commercial and noncommercial result set. Still, the search engine must ensure that these ads are relevant for the query, which often is not the case. If we try "package tour to the moon," Google will offer a sponsored ad for a travel agency, which has trips to many places in the world, but, alas, not to the moon.

Notes

1 Introduced by Kent, A., Berry, M., Leuhrs, F. U. & Perry, J. W. 1955. Machine Literature Searching VIII. Operational Criteria for Designing Information Retrieval Systems, American Documentation, 6 (2), 93–101.

2 Yet another problem may be that search engines produce biased results, where sites can pay to get a high ranking, where links to the competition are removed, and so on.

3 Google, for example, also indexes files in PDF format.

4 Olsen, K. A., Sochats, K. M., and Williams, J. G. 1998. Full text information retrieval and Information overload, The International Information and Library Review, No. 30, pp. 105–122.

35 Organizing the Web—Portals

Today, after ten years with the Web, there are so many Web servers that even the 32-bit IP address scheme needs expanding. Each of these servers can be filled with many thousands—perhaps millions—of pages. With all this information, organization is important. General portals try to provide organization, offering a "table of contents" for the Web. These are presented hierarchically, often in a tree structure[1] and using hypertext links from one level to the next. For example, on the home page or the root page, we may be offered the generic term transportation; clicking on transportation yields a new page with airlines, trains, boats, and so on. Hierarchical menus are a traditional way of organizing material. They are simple and allow users to navigate a predetermined structure. The overall task is broken down in steps, with a simple choice at each step, until the user gets to the "leaf" nodes, the Web pages with the information he seeks.

A menu hierarchy works fine as long as it follows our needs. Restaurant menus are a good example of logical ordering. The appetizers are presented first, followed by main dishes, and with desserts last. Main dishes may be categorized into meat, fish, and poultry, and perhaps with subcategories to satisfy vegetarians. Such an organization supports the ordering process for most guests, but is not helpful when our needs do not follow the standard approach. In a restaurant this is no big problem: We can ask the waiter to tell us which dishes satisfy a salt-free or celiac diet. On the Web, there is no human being to handle these exceptions. If we are looking for a cheap airfare from Paris to Pittsburgh, we may not be satisfied with a travel → air → airlines organization, as accessing every airline's site will be impractical. If we try to find a hotel in a large city, we may be overwhelmed by the thousands of sites that a portal may offer. Here a subdivision into locations or prices would be welcome. The general search engines do not provide this option, but the specialized booking sites do.

While a hierarchical structure may have unlimited depth, navigation in large structures is often complicated. We use menu terms on each level as a link and header for the next subsection. The problem is to find discrete terms, with each term describing a distinct subset of the information space. For example after hitting travel, this subset may be divided into new subsets such as transportation, lodging, and insurance. Transportation may be further divided into air, boat, train, and so on. The disadvantage of a deep structure is that we may have problems finding sites that are covered by more than one menu item, for example, packaged tours or cruises with airfare included.

To some extent broad menus, cross-structural links, filters, and search engines may address these problems. A broad menu offers more choices on each level. For example, a user will get a better overview of the alternatives if all travel-related links can be offered on one page, such as different forms of transportation and lodging, package tours, cruises, insurance and other travel-related services.

While a hierarchical structure is a simple way of organizing material, it has the disadvantage that related sites might end up far apart in the structure. For example, a hotel in London may be cataloged under travel and perhaps under the subcategories of lodging and hotel, although the city itself may be cataloged under a country header. Then it will be convenient to have a link from the hotel to the city site, and vice versa. Such cross-structural links may violate the tree-structure organization, in which there is only one path from the root to the leaf nodes, but they are convenient when more than one organizational strategy is implemented. The disadvantage is the increased possibility of getting "lost in hyperspace," as there may be many paths to a given node.

Filter queries, which provide a means of limiting information, work in formalized areas. When we have to extract meanings from word occurrences, filters may break down—as with most other natural language systems.

Filter queries offer the possibility of limiting information, for example, to show a restaurant menu with only salt-free dishes. Here computer-based menus have clear advantages over their paper-based counterparts. A list of used cars can be shown initially with all cars. Then the user can set up a filter query, for example, to limit the presentation to cars less than five years old, that have four-wheel drive, and cost less than $12,000. For each new filter term, the list can be redisplayed, letting the user decide if more terms are needed.

Ideally, we would like a system that could organize the world according to our needs, but that would require the computer system to have a semantic understanding of both the information that it classifies and our needs. This is not the case with general Internet portals, but may be achieved for more specific portals where the underlying data have the necessary formalization level.

As with search engines, portals only index a small part of the Web. A site can be submitted to a portal, giving the URL

Portals try to make a living out of the traffic that goes through their site.

and the most logical location within the portals' hierarchical structure. General portals try to make a living out of the traffic that goes through the site, which can be achieved by selling commercials in the form of banners, very similar to billboards on a busy corner.

The initial purpose of portals was to organize the Web, but the traffic generated to these sites has opened the way for other business models. Today, we see that portals try to offer all types of services to users, from traditional indexing services to online sales and auctions of both symbolic and physical products. This business model may be valid for some sites, but clearly not for all. Traffic may disappear if a site becomes too similar to other, perhaps better, sites. Many TV stations and newspapers have tried to use their customer base to create general portals, without success.

The most successful have connected portals to their main business, for example, newspapers that offer classified ads online, general TV channels that offer background information on their programs, or shopping-channels that sell goods online as well as through the traditional TV/telephone channel.

Note

1   In a tree structure, each page will link to a number of "children," each child will again link to its children, and so forth. A typical tree structure is the family tree. On the Web, we seldom see these true tree structures, in which each node has only one "mother." Theoretically, Web pages are network structures because every node can link to every other. In practice, however, if we overlook these odd links, we will find that most Web pages are ordered in a hierarchical structure.

36 Web Presence

One of the basic ideas of Tim Berners-Lee, the inventor of the Web, was that everybody should be an information provider, not just a consumer of information. He foresaw a network of scientists who could access each other's papers and scientific data. Of course, the Web expanded early to other user groups on a worldwide basis, not only in geography but also for applications.

36.1 Creating content

Web users exploit the possibility of being information providers, as seen by the **billions of pages** that exist on the Web.

The democratic nature of the Web contrasts with most other media content, which is created by a privileged few. Berners-Lee implemented his ideas by keeping the structure of the Web pages simple, formalizing only on the layout level. With one-way hypertext links, anyone can link to anyone, no permission or central link storage is needed. Thus, anyone can create a Web page, using HTML and a text editor, a Web tool, or just saving MS Word documents as HTML.

Many people have an incentive to create content, to present ideas, opinions, or hobbies. They call in to radio and TV programs and write letters to the newspaper editor. However, radio, TV, and newspapers have practical limitations on what and how much they can and want to publish of customers' responses. On the Web, there are no limitations. Berners-Lee's simple syntax and the lack of formal requirements have removed usability problems, and robust and cheap technology is in the process of reducing technical limitations. A clear incentive combined with few barriers has yielded billions of Web pages. We create home pages and profiles on social networks, Web sites for firms and institutions, professional organizations, nonprofit organizations and so on. Many spend much of their time writing blogs or commenting on other blogs. There are no editors, no consultants. The author alone determines what is to be published. When the page is stored on the server, it is automatically accessible for the whole world.

36.2 Disseminating

Earlier, only wallboards and flyers offered the opportunity for inexpensive, unedited publishing. One can reach quite a few readers with leaflets, good organization, and enough volunteers

Theoretically our home page can be seen by the world; in practice, most of us get very few real "clicks." More than 50 percent of traffic goes to sites controlled by a few major companies.

for distribution. Still, as with bulletin boards, there are practical limitations both in volume and geographical locations. In contrast, the Web has no geographical limitations and no theoretical upper limit to "circulation."

In practice, it is not so easy to get genuine "hits" on a Web page or a blog, that is, visits from actual users and not from spiders and other robot programs. There are billions of pages and perhaps as many authors as readers. In fact, if you want to hide confidential information, it might be a good idea to put it on the Web. The chance that someone will access your page, and actually read the contents, is pretty remote. In principle, any Web user who has a page's URL can retrieve that page; however, to get visitors, the URL must be made public. As we shall see, this is where we depart from the notion of the democratic Web. In practice, we are no more equal on the Web than anywhere else. Money and power have as much influence on the Web, as in any other media. A few major companies control most of the traffic.

If we want **hits** on our Web pages, we must advertise the page's existence.

36.3   Personal information

People who know us can easily find a link to our Web page by using a search engine, providing name and other **formalized information**, such as address and position.

I have a personal home page that lists my background, professional interests, and publications, along with a picture and address information. My page has been submitted to and has been indexed by some of the major search engines, and can be found by searching for my name. Alternatively, it can be located through a link from the list of employees at the institutions where I work, or from home pages to my courses. With this I get some hundred hits a year, mostly from students following links from course pages, but also from visitors to the institutions where I am affiliated or perhaps from scientists or newspapers readers that follow up on my papers and articles. That is, access to my home page is based on my "popularity" in the real world, although perhaps only a fraction of the people who are connected to me in some way find their way to my home page.

However, this is just what we have to expect, and perhaps what most of us want to achieve. When you find out that your old friend, Bill, from college has been hired by one of your customers, and will be in on the next meeting, it is very convenient to be able to gather some updated information. You have no problem finding his official home page at the customer's Web site, and from there, a link to his personal page. You find that he is still married to Jane, that his children are now in high school (oops!), and that he is a local representative of the Republican Party (no longer a radical). The picture will certainly help you to recognize him (even if Bill, like most of us, does not update his home page picture—the exception to the rule that updated information is the better). Of course, Bill also will use the Internet to find out about you. We avoid embarrassing situations, and get information that would have been very difficult to get without the Internet.

However, all of this is much easier through a social network system, such as Facebook. Here one can present the same type of information as on a Web page—profile data, text, and pictures—but the site will have tools to make this very simple. In addition, the site allows you to administer a list of friends, easily access your friends' information, and comment on their posts.

The drawback is that you must invite Bill to your list of friends. Then, you have to decide if the contact is business or pleasure, that is, you may not want to invite Bill, your business associate, into your private life, or you may view this as an opportunity to reestablish contact with a former classmate. An alternative for many is to reduce the "private" parts in the social network account, thus making it easier to accept friends of different categories. That is, we may limit our comments on what we do to, for example, holiday celebrations, music that we listen to, or books that we read (or want people to know that we read). More personal information can be left to more private channels.

While I still maintain a home page directed towards my profession, all personal information has been moved to Facebook. Since many of my "friends" are coworkers and former classmates, the pages are not very private. However, parts of the professional-oriented Web page, such as my CV, could be moved to a business-related site such as LinkedIn, where users can maintain a professional profile and a list of "connections." Such business-related sites are useful for employers seeking potential job candidates, and job-seekers can point to this site for background information. Facebook, LinkedIn and other such sites are examples of how we formalize the Web, replacing general systems with more specialized ones. I return to these issues in Chapter 42.

Facebook, LinkedIn and other such sites are examples of how we **formalize the Web**, replacing general systems with more specialized ones.

36.4   Organizations

A nonprofit organization can present its URL in the letters or newsletters they send to their members. If they have been smart

In the physical world, location sets a context for many names. This context is removed on the global Web and names get **overloaded**.

and lucky, they have been able to get a Web site name that describes their organization, such as www.cancer.org and www.aids.org. These are addresses a person might typically use to search for these organizations. In the private sector, firms have been willing to pay quite a lot to get such "topic" addresses: www.bank.com, www.tv.com, www.loan.com. As long as the extensions, such as dot-com and dot-org, clearly categorize the type of institution, a topic name can be an advantage. The downside is the issue of trust. Are we willing to go to a "generic" site such as bank.com, or is it easier to follow the well-known brand names. All in all, the effectiveness of these names may be exaggerated. Why should we go to tv.com?

Some well-known companies and institutions can rely on the knowledge of their real-world name as a basis for their URL, expecting users to add the necessary extension. Thus, it is easy to find IBM on www.ibm.com, MIT on www.mit.edu, the engineering organization IEEE on www.ieee.org, or the White House at www.whitehouse.gov. The advantage of a well-known name extends to the Web, especially if the name is short and easy to spell. Foreign names, long names, and names containing special characters may cause a problem, even if the name is well known. In most cases, a wrong guess gives an "unknown page" message; but sometimes the visitor may get something different from what he expected—another institution or at worst a page that tries to mimic the intended site.[1]

The global URL naming scheme is not without problems. There may be many Joe's restaurants and many businesses that use an acronym such as SAS, but there is a place for only one joe.com and only one sas.com. In the physical world this is seldom a problem. We use the local directory when we want to call Joe's to reserve a table, and may be unaware of the other Joe's in the world. Similarly, directories help us distinguish between SAS the airline, the software company, and the others. But the Web lacks this context. The extension may help us distinguish between company X, university X, and the nonprofit organization X, but within a domain there can only be one of each.

A physical world presence and a well-known **brand name** are important when establishing a Web site.

To promote their Web site, organizations and companies have to rely on existing channels to their customers. This could be through marketing, or they can hope that a search engine will offer a link to their site. Marketing a URL through existing channels can be as simple as providing a URL on product packaging, buildings, cars, trucks, or airplanes and including the URL in all advertisements. On the Web, the site can be submitted to search engines for indexing, so that the link will turn up in a search for the company name, and perhaps also in a search for products. A firm can include links on their Web page to their major customers' and suppliers' Web sites, and hope that everybody else will do the same for them. If this does not help them to get on top of the search engine results page, they can always pay to get in the sponsor section.

36.5   Startups

For new Internet startups, heavy marketing may be needed to reach customers, if one is not lucky enough to get media attention.[2] Some companies, such as Apple, have clearly managed to get media attention for their new products. Other companies have used traditional marketing channels, TV, radio, newspapers, and junk mail, in addition to marketing on the Web.

These campaigns are a heavy expense for start-ups, and in many cases, have been the cause of their downfall. There is also evidence that continuous campaigns are needed to keep interest high for a site because users turn away as soon as the marketing stops. Here, existing brick and mortar companies have a clear advantage. They can use their well-known name as a URL, use existing channels to promote their Web addresses, and avoid or reduce the amount spent on additional marketing.

Some new companies have managed to be well known through their product alone. Facebook is a good example. However, for a social network, this is perhaps the only solution, that is, that users recruit their friends. There are also other successful examples of this "jungle telegraph" method of introducing a new product or company.

In the long run, we should expect the URL to have less importance. For example, the URL field in new versions of browsers is also a search field. If the words we type there identify a page, that page will load, but if not, a search will result. That is, this feature makes the difference between an URL and a search term less distinct.

The Web has given us a tool for presenting our companies or ourselves to the world, but we will have to compete with many others for attention. Globalization, accelerated by the Web, intensifies the difficulties. Visibility is not a big problem if we establish a store in a small town, but it is likely to be a challenge when our market area extends beyond local or even national boundaries, as is often the case for many businesses today. The Web is both the solution and the problem.

Notes

1   It would be a good idea for any company to obtain the most common URLs that people use to find their site, including common spelling mistakes. Some institutions also go as far as to get control over the addresses that could be used by their critics, such as hateX, noX, and so on.

2   For example, the search engine Google managed to establish itself without marketing. Their search results were so good that several newspapers, among these USA Today and Le Monde, wrote about them. A top ranking by PC Magazine did not hurt either. See http://www.google.com/corporate/history.html

37   Mobile Computing

Usability is to a large extent coupled to a large screen, good pointing device, and keyboard— not available on all portable devices.

Until recently, a mobile phone was just that, a phone without the limitation of a wall plug and a cord. But today, a mobile phone, at least the smartphone variant, is a full computer, although very different from a PC. We should remember that in the 1980s, the ease of the Apple Macintosh, one of the first computers with a mouse and a graphical screen, made it possible to introduce PCs to nontechnical user groups, by:

- *Minimizing short-term memory load* by presenting all the data the user needed for performing his task, on the display

- *Using forms* to structure output and input, informative captions, default values, selection from lists instead of typing, menus and buttons to help the user find the right command

- Allowing *direct manipulation*—the user could move a file by clicking on the icon, dragging the icon to the receiving folder, and releasing the mouse button

Remove the mouse, reduce screen real estate to a minimum, replace the full keyboard with a set of function keys and a small numeric keyboard, and you have something very different from a usability point of view. That is, until now a mobile phone could have the processing power of a computer, but not the easy-to-use interface.

Touch displays have made it simpler to use a mobile phone.

Touch displays have changed much of this. Even if limited in size, these high-resolution displays can present an icon for each function. One can use forms for additional data and offer extensive menus or buttons for selecting the correct subfunction. That is, we can get a user experience on a mobile device that is similar to that on the PC, albeit with a smaller screen. Touch input is ideal for surfing, clicking on links, looking through photographs, starting applications, and scanning and reading documents. "Natural interfaces" allow for easy panning and zooming by using two fingers on the multitouch display, excellent for viewing maps or photographs, for scrolling through a document, or for selecting objects out of lists.

With these improved displays, the mobile phone becomes a full computer system, which is demonstrated by the fact that the earlier phone-oriented hardware and software have been replaced by general operating systems, such as Android from Google, iOS from Apple, and Windows Mobile from Microsoft. The Apps discussed in Chapter 27 are built on top of these systems. Thus, Apps can access all resources on the phone—calendars, contact lists, documents, GPS device, storage medium, display, and keyboard—in a simple, standardized manner, albeit with one version for every operating system.

The advantage of a computer in a mobile phone is that you carry it along at all times, which provides you with continuous access, not only for calling but also to the Internet. The problems are that the displays are small and there are limited possibilities for data entry, for example, through an on-screen keyboard. The best applications are those in which the mobile advantages are important and the disadvantages can be reduced. Examples include using the phone as a music player, a book reader, a calendar, an address book, and as a device for sending and receiving short messages.

For some functions, such as showing maps, the small display is clearly a disadvantage. While the full-sized paper map simultaneously offers an overview and a detailed, "zoomed in" view, a small display necessitates choosing one or the other. However, the mobile phone has an advantage because it can use GPS to pin the current position on the map. The lack of overview also may be less important with good route-finding capabilities, for example, when the smartphone can offer a detailed view of each intersection along the route. Thus, after accepting the choice of route, we no longer need the overview.

To make up for the limited display space, output can be given on the audio channel instead. A Web site with a speech generator could give customized information on the local weather and driving conditions, your stock portfolio, expected delays on your flight this afternoon, e-mail headers, and so on. Similarly, voice commands can provide input, using speech recognition software if we can get the necessary quality.[1]

An example is Apple's Siri, a speech recognition and interpretation system with which one can give voice requests using natural language. The system will direct commands to a set of Web services, providing the answer as voice output. The advantage of this approach is that we utilize the mobile phone as a voice device; the disadvantage, that voice is only effective for small pieces of information. However, one has come up with many applications for speech recognition over the last thirty years, although the technology is still not mature. The user has

The advantage of a computer in a mobile phone is that you **carry it along** at all times.

With a **text-to-voice** generator, we reduce the burden on the display, and also make it easier to use more advanced functions when we are mobile.

to speak very clearly and without an accent to be understood. In addition, background noise, as when riding in a car, may cause problems.

Mobile devices, from smartphones to tablets, can be used in conjunction with a PC, with a facility to copy or synchronize files between the two devices. With Bluetooth technology, the synchronization of data between devices is done automatically, without the need to connect the devices physically.

However, with more bandwidth for mobile units, either though Local Area Networks (WLAN) or through using mobile networks, connecting to a PC will no longer be necessary. Amazon provides an interesting example. Their Kindle e-book reader has a mobile network connection; thus, readers can buy and download books in nearly any location with just a button click—no complex user interface, no PC.

Note

1   Speech recognition has been a hot topic for many years. With fast dictionary lookups as we speak, these systems may get good enough accuracy to
be useful for dictating. However, extensive training is necessary to teach
the system your way of pronouncing words, and the system will easily fail
for persons with an accent, a cold, or when there is a low-quality channel
or background noise. Today, systems directed toward general users (that is,
situations without training), can be used only in the simplest of cases, with
very restricted vocabularies.

38   Automated Web and Push Technology

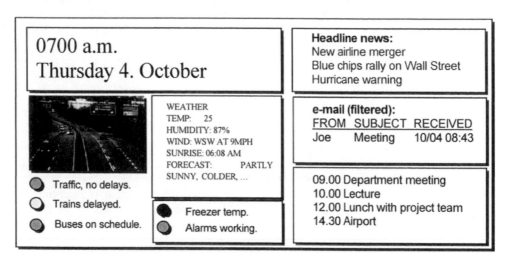

Figure 38.1 A mock-up of a personalized "wake-up" display.

Push technology can offer a personalized news-paper.

Figure 38.1 presents a mock-up of a personalized "wake-up" display, a screen that provides all information that we need at this point of the day—information on weather, commuting, calendar, and e-mail. The screen is personalized, that is, the user determines what kind of information is pushed down from the server, along with the layout of the display.

This technology is already available. Modern devices, such as cameras and sensors, can transmit data over a wireless network. These devices are identified by an IP address, which makes it easy to set up a sensor system and to retrieve any type of data, such as photos or weather data. Different agencies, from road authorities to news corporations, provide an application program interface (an API), in which an application program can call such an interface and provide parameters and retrieve results, for example, in XML format.

The display can be shown on a tablet that can be carried around in the house and connected to the Internet using wireless technology. During breakfast, the display may change to show the agenda for the workday. On the way to work, the user can get updated traffic information through the mobile phone or a wide-area wireless system. Now voice input and output can be used. Input will go to a voice recognition system, so that the user can select the information needed, and similarly, output is sent through a speech synthesizer. When the user arrives at the office, the display will receive an updated version of the agenda, and other information needed to start the workday, which the user can scan while in the elevator. Arriving at his desk, the user will have the same information on the display as on the office computer.

Push technology is ideal when we get unexpected but important information, for example, on a cancellation, delay or change.

While the information itself is dynamic, updated perhaps several times a day, the page structure can be more static. However, we may need alternative information when roadwork or special events change traffic patterns or public transportation schedules. The solution may be to subscribe to *push* services, allowing information sources to push important information to our devices. For example, many airlines and other transport authorities can push data on cancellations or new schedules by sending text messages. If we are connected to the Internet at all times, as with a tablet, this information could be pushed directly to the device. Similarly, we could subscribe to information for the roads we use when commuting.

The disadvantage of push technology is that it may move into spam, that is, messages that we are really not interested in. Therefore, it is important for the user to be able to control both the type and the number of messages sent. For example, we may be interested in messages notifying us of bargains from a bookstore, but perhaps not every day.

I will return to the idea of pushing information to the user in Chapter 63.

39 Dynamic Web Pages and the Form Tag

HTML pages contain text, images, and layout tags. We request these pages by clicking on a link, and the browser will then find the URL hidden in the link, and use this identifier to issue a GET command. This is sent to the appropriate server, identified by the IP address part of the URL. The server uses the additional folder and file information to find the HTML file, and return this page to the browser. These simple mechanisms implement the basic idea of the Web, and describe functionality that does not require any other input from the user than button clicks.

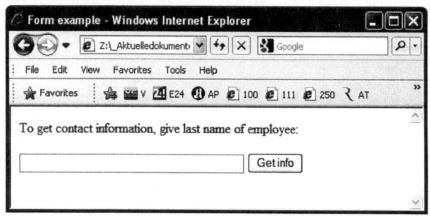

Figure 39.1 A simple HTML form (example).

An important extension from the basic Web is the form-tag of HTML. An example is shown in Figure 39.1. HTML offers quite a selection of field types for creating forms: text fields, check and radio buttons, command buttons, and combo or list boxes for selection. These features enable us to make quite sophisticated user interfaces using HTML.

To study the inner workings of the form concept, I will use the simple form presented in Figure 39.1, a part of a directory system. Instead of providing a static HTML table with name, telephone number, and e-mail address of all employees, we will implement a more dynamic system, in which this information is provided by a "lookup" system based on data from the form. This simple system will use the employee name provided to do a lookup in the employee database.

HTML forms allow us to use a Web browser as an interface to applications, online banks, travel agency, shops, and so on.

```
<FORM name="input"
 action="http://www.firm.com/employee.asp"
 method="post">
        <p>To get contact information, give last  name of
        employee: </p>
        <input type="text" name="lastname" size=40>
        <input type="submit" name="Info" value="Get info">
</FORM>
```

The form lets us provide **formalized input** (for example, with different data separated in different fields).

The source for the form is presented above. The form is identified by a <FORM> tag, which gives the URL of the server page that is to receive the form data. Note that the URL in this example has extension *asp*, not the customary *html*. This tells the server that this file should receive special treatment. Active Server Pages (ASP[1]) is a technology developed by Microsoft. This is only one of several different methods of creating dynamic pages—a good alternative could have been PHP.

Within the form-tag, we have defined two input fields: The first is a text field (for the employee's name) and the second a definition of a "submit" button. When the user hits this button, the browser will generate a command to the server, including the current value of the input fields. If we had used a GET-command, the values would have been appended to the command, for example, as

http://www.firm.com/employee.asp? name=Olsen&Info=Get+info.

However, the POST-command used here, sends the input values to the server in a separate HTTP transaction.

If the URL had indicated a file with extension *html*, the server would have retrieved this file and returned it to the browser. However, since the file in question has the extension *asp*, the Web server will expect to find a *script* in this file. A script is a simple program that can be interpreted by the server, that is, the server reads line after line in the script and performs the operations specified.[2]

The contents of the employee.asp file are shown below. This script is based on Visual Basic, but could just as well have been written using other programming languages, such as Java or PHP.

```
<%@ Language=VBScript %>
<%
set DBObj= Server.CreateObject("ADODB.Connection")
DBObj.Open "Employee"
%>
<HTML>
<HEAD>
<TITLE>Directory</TITLE>
</HEAD>
<BODY>
<H2>Contact information for
<%=Request.Form("lastname")%> </H2>
<%
set stdset=dbObj.Execute("SELECT * FROM employeeTable
  WHERE name = '" & Request.Form("lastname") & "'")
if stdset.eof then
  Response.Write("<p>No persons fulfilled search
  request</p>")
else
  Response.Write("<p>Phone:" & stdset("phone") & "</p>")
  Response.Write("<p>Email:" & stdset("email") & </p><br>")
end if
stdset.close
dbObj.close
%>
</BODY>
</HTML>
```

As seen, the script is a mix of program statements, embedded in <% and %> brackets and HTML. While the details are of little interest here, one may identify some parts. The interpreter will execute the script from top to bottom. All code outside the brackets will be copied directly to a result file, while statements inside the brackets are instructions to the interpreter.

This script starts by identifying the script language and opening a connection to the employee database. The following HTML code defines the heading part of the result page. The *Request.Form* command is used to retrieve the value from the form data (here the value of the name field), so that this can be included in the heading. We then specify a database command using the SQL query language, a standard language for database operations. This SELECT-statement is executed on the employee database. Here we request the database system to return telephone and e-mail address from the employee table, for an employee with a name equal to the input name parameter, which is the name the user provided in the HTML form.

Server side **scripts** are simple programs that can retrieve data from forms, and generate a new Web page based on these input parameters and data from a server side database.

If the database system finds this employee, a simple HTML page with employee data is generated; if not, a message is returned (as HTML) stating that an employee with the given name could not be found, achieved by the *Response.Write* statement. In the first case, the headings "Phone:" and "E-mail:" together with the phone number and e-mail address from the database are sent along with the necessary HTML tags. In the latter case, we generate the message: "No persons fulfilled search request," including the HTML tags for starting and ending a paragraph.

Figure 39.2 HTML page with contact information.

When this script is executed, a complete HTML page has been generated, which is then returned to the browser. Note that the browser gets an HTML page back independently of what happens, either the page shown in Figure 39.2 or the page giving the "not found" message. For the browser, there is no difference between static or dynamic pages; in all cases, it will receive an HTML page.

An overview of the communication between user, browser, and server in this example is shown below. Note that there are numerous steps involved, many of which imply that HTTP messages go between browser and server.

1. The user is on the home page of an organization and clicks on the menu item (link) for "contact info."

2. The URL of this link is sent by her browser to the server indicated by the URL.

3. The server will find the HTML file with the form description, and return this to the browser.

4. Browser displays the form (shown in Figure 39.1).

5. User types the name of the employee and clicks on "get info."

6. The browser contacts the server, now with the URL of the asp-script, and also submits the employee name.

7. The server identifies this as a script (due to the asp-extension) and executes the script.

8. The script generates a new Web page, partly by embedded HTML code and partly by information (on the employee) read from the database.

9. This Web page is returned to the browser, which displays the page (as seen in Figure 39.2).

There are several advantages to replacing static with dynamic pages. It can be done as shown here, using a form to indicate what information one needs, or by presenting full dynamic pages with updated information. For example, an alternative would be to present a dynamic list of all employees. This would be simpler, as we then avoid the form interface. The script would be fairly similar to the one above, but we would need to retrieve data on all employees to create the complete list.

Dynamic Web pages allow us to keep information in one place, in the database.

By generating the Web information directly from an underlying database, we avoid storing the same information in many places. Updates are simpler and new information will be available on the Web, and everywhere else, the moment it is stored in the database. In our example, dynamic pages also have the advantage that names and e-mail addresses may be hidden from spiders trying to collect addresses for unsolicited mail. The simple form-based system that we have programmed here is scalable, as it will work independently of the number of employees.

While basic HTML is a stateless protocol, ASP allows us to declare variables that live as long as the application is running or as long as the user *session* is active. Sessions are administered by the Web server, a program that can create and terminate sessions, keep track of session variables, and handle all different sessions (users) who are accessing the Web site. A session may comprise several requests, making it possible to create state-dependent systems. For example, with these techniques, we can easily implement a log-on function to our directory system, in which a user who has provided a correct username and password will be identified by a session variable. A script similar to the one above will handle this log-on functionality, telling the Web server that a new session is established

With **session variables** we avoid the disadvantages of the stateless Web protocol.

and then creating the session variable. When the user accesses subsequent scripts, each script can include code to check if the session variable for this user has a legal value.

Session data will be deleted when the user quits the application, for example, when he executes a log-out command. Alternatively, passive users can be thrown out of the system if they have been idle, that is, not giving any command, within a pre-defined time frame (ten minutes is often used as a default). In this way, we avoid storing much useless information, and solve the problem of Web users who leave in the middle of a session.

The example I have shown here is simple, but it shows the principle of dynamic pages. It is not difficult to improve the directory system, for example, to store more data on each employee (such as first name, position, address, mobile phone number), to allow alternative search criteria for finding an employee (for example, by first name or abbreviated names), improve form layout (such as inserting the various fields in an HTML table), or provide alphabetic lists of employees.

Web forms offer a **standard** way for accessing an application, using HTML and HTTP as the basic protocols.

The amazing thing about the Web is not that it is possible to construct form-based systems and to perform database lookups, as computers have performed these operations for the last fifty years; rather, we now have a means of accessing a database in a standard way, from everywhere. With the Internet, HTML, HTML forms, and a standard browser, we have the fundamentals for universal database access. Before the Internet and the Web, access to central databases required special software and special networks. If a travel agency wanted online access to a booking system, it had to lease lines for network traffic, install custom-made software to access the booking system, and, in some cases, utilize special terminal equipment. With the Internet, we have standard protocols for communication, and with the Web, standards for input and output; an airline now can offer online booking to everyone just by:

1. Designing *HTML forms* for inputting departure and destination cities, dates, times, fare types, and so on
2. *Developing scripts* that retrieve this information, access the booking database, and output HTML pages with timetables, availability information, prices, confirmations, and so on

Since all user communication is by standard HTML, no installation is needed on the customer side. The customer can use

With a browser, the form concept, and an Internet connection, we can replicate the **terminal** in the bank, travel agency, or in any type of business on our computer screen.

her standard browser and her Internet connection to access the booking system.

This is really the second Internet revolution. With simple techniques and strong standards, customized terminals in travel agencies, banks, and in public institutions can be "moved" to our office, home, PC or mobile phone. For many applications, we no longer need an intermediary, which makes for greater availability, banking twenty-four hours a day, seven days a week, fifty-two weeks a year, if we want. We do not have to call or mail letters to our bank, or make a visit personally to perform a transaction; we can do it ourselves. We get immediate response, a balance sheet that is updated to the moment, and a much better overview of our account. A more detailed analysis of the applications that are opened up by these techniques is given in the next part on business-to-business applications.

We have seen that the low level of formalization of Web pages limits the effectiveness and type of operations that we can perform. But this is not the case when we use the Web protocols as an interface tool to a database. For example, after we have given our user identifier and password by the means of a HTML form, the banking system can provide a set of scripts that gives access to the system. Now we are in the subworld of banking where we can use high-level concepts such as accounts, balance, and transfers, knowing that we will be understood. We input data, such as amount and account numbers, in forms, and the script will then execute the necessary operations within the banking system, in much the same way as in the directory system discussed above. In this world, precision and recall are 100 percent. When we ask for a list of all deposits we know that the answer will be 100 percent correct. That is, we have the same functionality as if we were operating a terminal in the bank itself.

When we use the browser to **access** a database application, we are not on the Web. Only the Web protocols are used. Within these applications, we have a high level of formalization.

At the same time, we have lost some of the advantages of the basic Web. Information in these databases is not open to everyone as user names or passwords restrict access. When we ask the airline booking system to give us the cheapest fare, we can expect a 100 percent correct answer; however, the system has only considered fares within its own database, flights for this airline and its partners.

Notes

1   Not to be confused with Application Service Providers, service centers are
    used for outsourcing computer functions, which use the same acronym.

2   With the Microsoft.net software, ASP scripts can be compiled, that is,
    translated to a more efficient form. In older versions, these scripts are in-
    terpreted (that is, the system will read a line at a time and then execute the
    instructions given by this line).

40 Embedded Scripts

As discussed in the previous chapter, the simple idea of dynamic Web pages makes it possible to use the Web as a standard interface to database systems, where HTML is used for getting input (in forms) and for presenting results and HTTP for data transmission. The disadvantage of such a system is that all processing has to be performed on the central server, increasing communication requirements, and making the server a possible bottleneck in the system. In many ways, handling all the processing on the server seems a bad allocation of resources, as the clients may be idle waiting for the next page. Furthermore, while using standard HTML can take us far, we will soon meet limitations. As an example, consider the form presented in the previous chapter. It is possible to hit the submit button without providing any data. The server script will probably catch this mistake and return an error message; however, it would be more convenient if we could perform the error checking directly in the browser.

Figure 40.1 The interior of a cabin. By touching the furniture, the user can select colors and materials (courtesy Maritime Møbler AS).

Scripts are also useful for implementing more advanced interfaces, for example with maps and images in which users can clicks on various parts of images. An example is presented in Figure 40.1. This application presents a dynamic furniture brochure for maritime applications. By touching an object, such as a chair, a menu will be presented. The user can now select material and color, and the cabin will be shown again, with the new variant. This "hot-spot" system is implemented by using standard HTML, combined with scripts that handle the input.

On the **client side** scripts can be inserted in the HTML code to increase the functionality of the user interface.

Client side processing can be achieved by the same script technique, embedding script commands in the HTML code. In this case, the whole page, including the script commands, is transmitted to the browser that performs the commands. With client side scripts, we can implement a more advanced user interface than with standard HTML. For example, we can change the form layout according to input values, allow users to control a presentation by using sliders, validate the values before these are sent to the server, or implement a hot-spot system as described above. To avoid the complication of adjusting to different hardware and operating systems, scripts are executed within the browser. The browser defines a virtual standardized machine on which the scripts can be interpreted.[1] As on the server side, the client side offers many script languages from which to choose, for example, the general-purpose scripting language PHP, Java, or Visual Basic.

As an alternative to scripts, we can use a Java applet, a program written in Java. The applet is presented in machine-like code, written for a Java virtual machine, and then can be run in the browser. An applet will run many times faster than a script, but a Java Runtime Environment (JRE) must be installed on the machine. The applet can capture mouse movements and can control the display. Applets are executed in a sandbox environment (see Chapter 27), that prevents them from accessing local resources, such as the file system.

For reasons of **security**, client side scripts have a limited command set.

The difference between a server side script and a client side script (or applet) is that the latter has only a limited command set. On the server side, the software engineer will know what resources the server has—databases, program components, and so on—and can utilize these to a maximum. On the client side, she does not have this information, and anyway, access to local resources is restricted for reasons of security. Clients may be powerful or weak machines, may run on top of Windows, Linux, or any other operating system, and may have a diversity of peripheral equipment, but software engineers are usually interested in making scripts that can run on all of these clients. Even if we could demand a standard client configuration of machine and software resources, it would be dangerous to let a script access local disks, as this would allow a malicious or criminal page designer to embed scripts that could destroy local data or steal identities or local passwords. Therefore, client side scripts are limited to performing calculations, receiving input data from mouse and keyboard, opening new windows, and controlling window presentations. Even then, some scripts have found loopholes in security systems, enabling them to gather confidential information, to change system parameters, or to destroy data.

However, new browser versions may be able to use some local resources. For example, the dynamic brochure application above will run very fast in Internet Explorer version 9, as this can utilize the graphics card on the client to speed up the application.

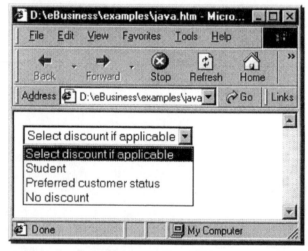

Figure 40.2 List box (example).

With scripts, it is possible to give **direct feedback** to the user, without having to access the server.

As an example, let's study a client side script in more detail. Figure 40.2 shows a simple form, in which the user is asked to select a discount type. If she asks for a student account, we want the program to warn her that this option will require a valid student ID. We can provide this functionality by a simple Java script.

```
<form name="discount" action="../user.asp"
  method="post">
  <select name="discount"
    onChange="checkDiscounts(discount);">
    <option value="">
      Select discount if applicable</option>
    <option value="S">Student</option>
    <option value="P">Preferred customer
      status</option>
    <option value="NO">No discount</option>
  </select>
</form>

<script language="Javascript">
  function checkDiscounts(discount)
    {if (discount.value == "S")
        {alert("Note that a valid student
        id will be required")}
    }
</script>
```

The HTML source with the embedded script is shown above. The details are uninteresting, but let's take a closer look at the main parts of the script. Within the form tag, we have defined an input field, a combo box (select statement) with four options. The value of the student option is "S." Whenever the value of the combo box is changed, the browser will call the script "checkDiscounts," defined in the last part of the script above. If an "S" is given as input value (for discount), the function will present an alert box on the screen (Figure 40.3).

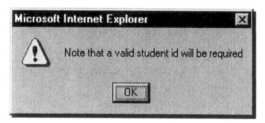

Figure 40.3 An alert window.

Cookies are small text files stored on your computer that aid the server to identify you.

Although Java scripts cannot read or write to the local disk in general, they have the possibility of storing, reading, and editing cookies. For example, after a user has provided a correct user name and a valid password for a site, a Java script can store a cookie on the client computer with a date and a user ID. The next time the user accesses the site, the cookie information can be retrieved and used to determine whether to allow the user direct access, without bothering him with the login procedure. This method may not be as safe as requiring a new login, but may be a good alternative when we prioritize convenience over security.

Cookies can be used to identify and track Web users.

Cookies may persist for days, months, or even years. Many Web sites use cookies to track user profiles. At the first visit to a site or a group of sites, a script instructs the browser to store a cookie with a unique identifier on the client's computer. This cookie is read at subsequent visits, and the site has the information necessary to connect all these visits to the same client, making it possible to draw a more complete profile useful for direct marketing. A client can tell the browser not to accept cookies, to give a warning every time a cookie is stored, or to delete all offline information, including cookies. However, many sites will not function if they are not allowed to store cookies.

In the last two chapters, we have seen how forms and scripts extend HTML, which was created to define a common layout format for documents. While these new constructs are rather primitive compared with the functionality of many development systems, they allow us to use a standard browser to access computer systems. Here forms are used for input, standard HTML for output, server side scripts to access databases, and embedded scripts to improve the usability of the interface. In practice, these constructs have opened the way for the many Web-based businesses we see today—Internet banks, online shops, and booking systems.

Note

1   A browser is a piece of software that runs on top of the operating system (for example, Firefox running on top of Windows). If we use Unix or the Linux operating system, we need a different version of the browser, which is not a problem as the browser is installed only once. However, if we design a Web page with embedded scripts, it would be complicated if we needed different versions of the script for every possible operating system. To avoid this problem and to increase security, a script runs within a virtual machine. This "machine" is really only a piece of software within the browser that can interpret and execute the script commands.

41 Peer-to-peer Computing

The idea of the **PC**—one user, one computer—reduced response times and increased usability.

The mainframes of the 1970s were huge machines, accessed from dumb terminals. These time-sharing machines had the clear disadvantage of increased response time as more users logged on. Then came the PC with local processing power and a local disk, practically eliminating response times, at least for the simplest operations. The disadvantage was that a stand-alone PC did not offer the possibility of sharing programs and data archives with others. Client-server computing was the solution, connecting the local PC to a server, which provided a platform for common programs and databases, while the client provided a platform for fast local computing.

As we have seen, the Web has embraced this model. Locally, we run a browser that displays the pages retrieved from a Web server. But in contrast to traditional client-server computing in a local area network, the Web is biased toward the server. All data is stored on the server and most processing is performed there. The advantage is that programs are installed in one place only and data is stored in one location only—at least in principle (copies may be stored for faster access). In addition, since nearly everything is on the server, we can access and use the Web from all types of devices, not only a PC, but also tablets and mobile phones.

To achieve a secure and standard platform, browsers only occupy a fraction of local resources. The local disk—if present—is used only as a cache for previously retrieved pages and for storing cookies. On the server side, at least for the more popular sites, scalability is a major task (that is, serving all accesses with a reasonable response time). Here huge investments are made in server farms (sets of servers) and database replication (copies of a database on different systems) to handle increased traffic. For many applications this works well. (I return to these issues in Part 8 on cloud computing.)

A set of many **interconnected** PCs can be viewed as a virtual machine with superpower.

However, it is possible to use more local resources by connecting PCs in peer systems, something that has been done within scientific communities to solve large computational problems. Peers access a central site to retrieve their small part of a big problem, along with the software needed to do the computation. The process then will run on the client machine as a low-priority background job, utilizing idle time on the processor. Results will be returned automatically to the central site.

Today, distributed computing companies are soliciting members by offering payment, prices, or the ability to support a good cause. (For example, members offer their accumulated computer power to solve heavy algorithms within medical research, biology, or economics.) This is a much cheaper solution than renting space on a supercomputer, at least for jobs that can be run effectively in this distributed environment.

While these examples are controlled by a central server, using local machines only as low-level assistants, we can envisage more "democratic" systems in which local machines get a more important role. This can be done by keeping just a register on the central server or by eliminating the need for central processing altogether. The latter is termed a true peer-to-peer (P2P) system, while the former is a P2P enabler. Napster was perhaps the most well-known P2P enabler, a system for sharing files of music. The idea is as simple as it is smart: a central site with an archive of all music files and their locations along with downloadable software for the client. Music files (today often in MP3[1] format) are stored on the clients that also had a role as servers in the Napster network. After installing the client software, a user would access the central registry to search for the files she wanted. From here she would get a list of clients/servers that had a copy of these files, with an indication of the type of network connection (bandwidth) for each. Probably she would then choose to download the files from a client/server with a high-speed connection. After this process, the files would be stored on her local machine, and could be made available to others.

As seen, P2P incorporates the democratic ideas of the Web, in which everybody is both a consumer and a provider, at least in the technical sense. While some of the music files organized by Napster were without copyright, most were MP3 files that had been captured from copyrighted material, for example, from CDs. Since the actual copying of files was performed on a peer-to-peer level and no files were stored centrally, Napster hoped to be on the right side of the copyright laws, but the courts did not agree. But, there were many other alternatives for the pirates.

One legal bypass could be to establish the central register in an international zone or in a country with more relaxed copyright laws. This may not be necessary, however, as there are P2P implementations that do not need the central register. An example is Gnutella,[2] a site with a set of P2P programs that can

P2P applications can be controlled by a central server, or operate autonomously.

Napster, the first P2P enabler, supported a system for sharing files of digital music.

P2P incorporates the **democratic** nature of the Web, allowing free access to data.

When running, the P2P program will scan the Internet looking for hosts.

be downloaded. When running, the P2P program will scan the Internet looking for hosts, finding thousands in a short time. When a user initiates a search, the request will be forwarded to these hosts; if the file is not found, the hosts pass on the request, and so forth, until a successful result is achieved or until all hosts within the "horizon" have been tried. When a file is found, the address of the location will be passed back along the line, to the originating hosts that will download the file. With these systems, recording companies have had some success in going after the users instead of the hosts that offer the P2P software.

Gnutella and similar systems work for any types of files. The drawback of these highly distributed systems is that they rely on each individual user to label the files correctly. That is, all the problems with regard to differences in language, vocabulary, background, and so on that we discussed regarding keyword searching (Chapter 34) will show up here. The exception is for files that may be labeled according to de facto standards, such as music files (artist, album, song), movies (title, year, actors), books (author, title, ISBN), and software (name of program, version, producer). But even here, one has to rely on the accuracy and good intentions of other peers. A problem may be malicious individuals who propagate data viruses or offer their files with a false description. For example, pornographic material may be labeled as fairy tales, amateur music as Rolling Stones, and Nazi propaganda as textbooks.

Magnet links identify a file by content.

Newer P2P programs use *magnet links*. These identify a file by content, that is, by running the content through a formula to get an ID, in this case a cryptographic hash value.[3] An advantage of these content IDs is that they ensure that the resource retrieved by the link is the one intended.

BitTorrent[4] software enables a user to search for content and to download from many hosts simultaneously. Data on each target file is stored in a torrent. This file is divided into chunks, and the torrent holds information on the location of the different chunks, which may reside on different hosts. A BitTorrent tracker will assist in this process. Large files may be downloaded quickly and simultaneously, as downloading is independent of individual hosts. If one host goes down, the chunk can be found at another location. When all chunks are downloaded, the client can assemble these into a full file. Many institutions use BitTorrent software, from the state-owned Norwegian Broadcasting Company to the Pirate Bay,[5] the in-

A true P2P system is the **combined** product of all participants.

famous Swedish Web site established by the anti-copyright organization Piratbyrån. Pirate Bay hosts magnet links.

On P2P networks, the collective content of all machines is at the control of each individual machine. Since these true P2P systems do not have any central register, they are very robust. If one part of the network falls out, the system will just pass searches on in another direction. They also are more robust regarding legal action, as there is no central organization than can be attacked. However, the Swedish appeals court found that "the Pirate Bay service makes possibly illegal file sharing in a way that entails a punishable offense for those who run the service," and two founders and a financier were sentenced to several months in prison and ordered to pay a fine of forty-six million Swedish kronor, approx $4.5 million. Similar cases are now fought in courts in other countries.

A P2P system requires that most users are willing to be producers (that is, to share their files with the user community). They also must be willing to offer part of their bandwidth for uploads (for other users who are copying from their machine). Still, P2P sites have attracted large user communities that seem to be willing to take the risk and to offer processing power and bandwidth for the good of the user community. These groups have been established without any marketing at all, just by use of the jungle telegraph, which is very interesting at a time when we often see that dot-coms fail because of heavy marketing costs. Can commercial sites be established in the same ad hoc cost-free manner? Perhaps not. The Pirate Bays have an aura of illegality and offer some sort of group feeling—"let us get together and make fun of the big companies." It is, of course, also important that they offer something for free that had been rather expensive.

P2P has proven to be a threat to the music business, and as more content is available in electronic formats, these systems may make it difficult to sustain copyright laws for other media such as movies and books. While some may talk about the end of the publishing business as a whole, we will certainly see big changes. The answer lies in meeting the technological challenge with new systems instead of trying to maintain the old through legal actions.

An autonomously P2P system—a set of computers connected on the same level— poses a threat to **copyright** laws, as the "responsibility" is spread over the whole network.

The music industry has used the legal approach, closing down sites, even going after individual users. However, its greater success may have been achieved through providing legal online services, such as iTunes, Spotify, and Wimp. For example, Spotify allows free access, albeit interrupting the stream with some commercials. However, for a modest fee, the commercials are removed and one receives a premium service. After a slow start, Spotify and other sites have seemed to manage to move more users from the limited free access to the full-pay option. The advantage for users is good quality, large repositories, site overviews, excellent search systems, powerful servers, high bandwidths, and much better security than with P2P. Since the tracks may be stored at very low cost and since the user already pays for the distribution (over an Internet connection), these sites may offer unlimited downloading for a fixed subscription fee—the new model for everything that is digitally stored. Since costs are independent of what we consume, a subscription model seems to be the natural solution.

Notes

1   MP3 (MPEG-1 Audio Layer-3) is a standard technology and format for compressing files of sound. MP3 manages a compression rate of 12 to 1 while preserving the original sound quality.

2   http://www.gnutella.com

3   A hash algorithm generates a bit string of fixed size by running a set of data through the algorithm. This can be as simple as adding all the bytes to get an eight-bit number (ignoring overflow). However, in this case, since there are only 256 different hash values, there may be a high probability that different data streams get a similar ID. To reduce this possibility, larger bit sizes are used.

4   www.bittorrent.com

5   www.thepiratebay.se

42 Social Networks

Humans are social: We rely on the "flock." Perhaps we all are descendants of a group of some hundred people who left East Africa sixty thousand years ago. Of course, in earlier times the group was a way to survive. Together we had protection from enemies, and the group provided the robustness necessary for survival in a dangerous world. Most important, to avoid inbreeding, one had to be able to choose a mate from a fairly large group. In addition to the tribe, families provided strong social bonds. Both tribe and family were important for individual welfare.

Today, other institutions have assumed many of these social welfare mechanisms. In modern countries, the state offers benefits such as health care, pensions, and unemployment support, or these types of security can be obtained with private insurance. Therefore, groups and families are less important for the physical well-being of each individual. But we still need groups in a social setting—that part is clearly as important as ever.

However, there are some problems maintaining social groups in a modern society. Not many years ago, it was not unusual to live an entire lifetime—from birth to death—in the same location. At that time, group contacts were mostly physical—meeting at the shop, church, at work, or in the homes. Today, people move more often, and go to new places for school, university, or to get a better job. Also, crossing national borders has become quite common.

Social networks are a means to retain contact with friends in a dynamic world.

In this setting, social networks provide the tools to maintain contact with friends, independent of geographical location. Old friends from school can be found and contacted. We may join special interest groups or chat with our coworkers. The systems offer the tools that we need for this interaction: a profile for each user; a "wall" on which to post comments and upload pictures; and, most important, a list of "friends."

Some consider these systems shallow, and of course, there is a difference between contacts on a Web site and those in the real world. But this difference provides an advantage for social network systems: The barrier for contacting an old classmate physically, even by calling, is much greater than inviting him as a friend on Facebook.

The ease by which one may add friends may pose a threat to social systems. As the number of friends increase, the site will become less private. We have to take into account the multitude of friends. Many youth see their freedom to post what they like severely restricted when their parents are on their friend list. Similarly, we have to consider the effect of our postings when coworkers or employers may see them. This again, may make the site less interesting for closer friends. Probably we will learn to apply a balanced policy here, limiting the number of friends and being somewhat careful of the information we provide. (I discussed some of these issues in Chapter 36.3.)

The virtual and the real world can be connected through social networks.

An interesting possibility that several social networks are beginning to exploit is using social network data to facilitate contacts in the real world. For example, some airlines can seat you next to persons who share your interests. Using Twitter, you can broadcast to the world where you are—at an airport waiting for a delayed flight—in the hope that some of your followers may be there also. Facebook offers "Live Feed" for streaming users' activities in real time. Other systems allow users to check in at a location or use GPS to pinpoint other users, making it possible to connect with friends.

Can the systems be too intrusive?

The disadvantage of such systems is that they may be intrusive, or seem to be an implementation of "Big Brother." But as long as they are user controlled, this risk may be reduced. In some cases, however, social systems and Apps seem to exploit data, such as contact lists, without the users' explicit knowledge. Privacy settings are often complex and perhaps not studied careful enough by users.

For example, I was astonished to get an e-mail commenting on the tracks I played on Spotify. I probably had overlooked the privacy setting that made it possible for the site to present my choice of music to my friends on Facebook. Now, broadcasting our musical interests may not seriously violate our privacy, but we might be more concerned if a system broadcast the Web sites we were looking at. Or, what happens the day sites such as Spotify start offering streaming videos? Would we like to have also this information presented to friends?

Facebook, and other social sites, seek to become a platform for the Web. That is, they want us to log in to Facebook, stay with Facebook and perform all our Web activities from here. The advantage for users is that the one login for Facebook may suffice and that the system can track our activities. The advantage for the social site is that it will know more about our needs

Social networks, such as Face-book, are trying to be a **platform** for all Web-related activities.

and priorities, knowledge that can be used to offer more relevant advertisements.

More relevant advertisements also could be an advantage for the user. However, at one time Facebook tried to present to your friends what you were buying, a version of an automatic "recommendation" system that could enhance sales. The feature was removed after heavy protest from users. The feature not only was a clear violation of privacy, but also eliminated every possibility of surprise gifts. Now your wife would be told what you bought her for her birthday, or perhaps she would be surprised when she did not get the expensive necklace that you bought on the Web!

These mistakes may be simply examples of new companies' pushing creativity too far. In the long run, we can expect solutions that do not violate privacy. If not, users will probably disappear. I shall return to these issues in part 9.

43   Web 2.0

Web 2.0 is a buzzword coined to describe an emerging Web that supports collaborative work and information sharing. Web 2.0 examples are social networks, blogs, wiki sites, photo and video sharing services, "mashups," and "folksonomies." A *mashup* is a site that combines data from different sources to offer a new service. The word is taken from pop music, where DJs mix two or more songs to produce something new. In the Internet world, a good example is a site that combines data from a map source and a hotel directory, pinpointing hotels on a map. A *folksonomy* is a system that allows users to tag and categorize content such as photos, videos, or articles. These tags can then be used for searching.

Some of these concepts are discussed in more detail below. (Note that social networks were covered in the previous chapter.)

43.1   Collaborative work

Collaborative work has been a topic of discussion for at least a couple of decades, and the Internet seemed to be the medium to leverage such work—a place to join forces to write a document or to perform a project. Good examples are easy to find to show how the Internet has played an important role in projects with many geographically dispersed participants. The Linux project, an international collaboration to develop a free Unix-type operating system, is a well known.[1] Wikipedia[2] is another. The Internet has simplified efforts to organize international research projects and to administer large projects with many different participants. Some companies manage projects twenty-four hours by engaging employees in different time zones using collaborate systems.

However, despite these examples, we have not seen the large increases in collaborative efforts that many envisaged with the Internet. There are personal, cultural, and other barriers against participation as well as many open questions: Who does the work? When do we work? Who gets the praise or the criticism? The interpersonal relations that we have with coworkers help to overcome difficulties in ordinary projects and in cooperative work. This common ground among participants is usually a prerequisite for successful collaboration in a virtual environment. Social networks may provide a platform for establishing this level of communication, or perhaps we really need the physical meeting places to handle conflicts. As yet, we do not have enough experience to determine if social networks can take this role.

However, as discussed in Chapter 14.8, computer games seem to be the one big exception: People from all over the world play together collaboratively. But, in spite of the fact that games may be very complex, here we have formalized and artificial environments with clear goals.

43.2   Blogs

Politicians, celebrities, and ordinary people use blogs (Web logs) to express their views. These are sites that provide tools for writing, editing, and presenting "posts"—short articles—on the Web. Blog posts usually are presented in reverse chronological order, the most recent posts first. Most blogs are interactive: Visitors can leave their comments, usually stored under each post. Both blogs and social networks provide similar functionality; however, while everyone is equal in the level structure of a social network, one person or group will be most active on a blog.

A blog may be a **personal diary**.

Some blogs act as personal diaries; others comment on a topic, from wine to politics. A few blogs have attracted a large number of visitors, opening the way for placing ads on the blog page and generating revenue through clicks. Companies such as Google offer tools to establish and maintain a blog, and can also put commercials on the site if desired. Product placement—commenting and reviewing products—also can generate income. While this may be against ethical rules for established media, a personal blogger may not have any inhibitions in this respect.

In some cases, bloggers have been able to correct information reported by other media. A well-known case is the presentation of documents on the television program *60 Minutes* that were critical of President George W. Bush's military service record. Within just a few hours, bloggers showed that the documents presented here were fake.[3]

Some successful blogs are written by ordinary persons.

It's not astonishing that celebrities' blogs attract visitors, but interesting enough, some of the most popular blogs are written by individuals who are known only through their blog. A few of these have readerships comparable to those of online newspapers.

A few companies have established blogs as a new way of marketing to customers. However, blogs are a new type of media that need careful consideration. On a blog and on social networks, one needs to master the language and the processes. This is not the place for formal press releases or broad discussions before answering a comment. The problem is, of course, that an official blog is just that, and posted comments may have legal and economical consequences. Perhaps a better idea is to let an unofficial user group take care of these informal media.

43.3   Web mashups

Mashups **combine** information from one or more Web sources to create something new.

Mashups combine information from one or more Web sources to create something new—real estate listings placed on a map, photos on a map, or new views of data within a business environment. [4]

The travel site Trabber (trabber.com) serves as an example to illustrate how this works. Trabber provides data on searches performed by other users. To make a mashup, a system that dynamically presents the information from Trabber, we can use a very simple Web-based "programming system" called Yahoo pipes. [5] Yahoo Pipes is a visual and interactive framework that enables the combination of different data sources like Web pages or RSS (a format for sharing content among different Web sites), into an integrated view by using a visual language. Pipes allows users to filter, combine, and mash-up these sources into a uniform content established by the designer, often a person developing the application for her own purposes but sharing it on the Web.

Let's say our user is a frequent traveler between Madrid and Rome. Many airlines have flights between these major European cities, and finding the cheapest tickets can be quite a task. Trabber offers an interesting feature: It can present the results of queries from other users between given destinations within a given price range. But our user may have to access this site many times to keep up with these dynamic results.

As an alternative our frequent traveler can use Yahoo pipes to set up a dynamic query to the travel site, and to process the results. The pipe "program" asks Trabber for the results of other users' queries for flights between Madrid and Rome that have a price lower than a given maximum. The results are piped into an e-mail that is sent to the traveler, providing a real-time dynamic system that will tell him whenever any user finds another (cheap) trail between these destinations. The pipes are presented in Figure 43.1.

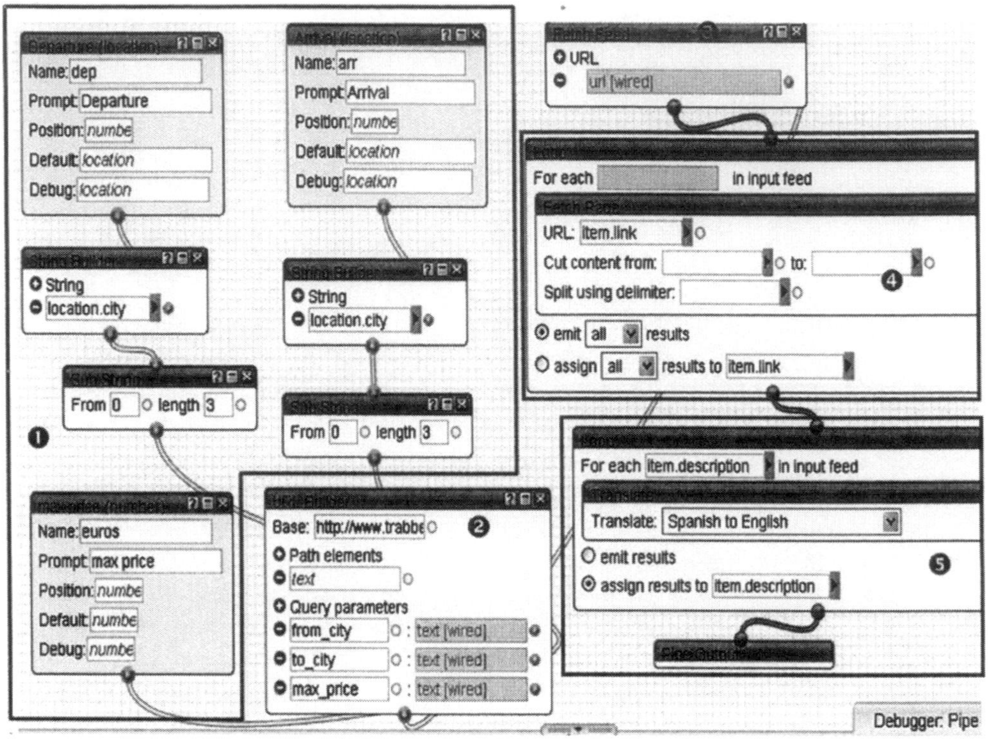

Figure 43.1 A Yahoo pipe used for extracting information from the trabber.com travel system.

The first part on the left (1) is used to build a form asking the user the city of departure and arrival, along with the maximum price he is willing to pay for a flight. A URL builder module is presented in the bottom center (2). This module takes information from the form (1) and builds the URL-string to invoke the Trabber Web site with the right parameters ("from_city," "to_city," and "max_price"). The Fetch Feed module retrieves results from the Web site in an RSS feed (3). Module (4) loops through the results to extract the information desired, while module (5) automatically translates the results form Spanish to English, using the Yahoo translator.

The results of invoking the "program" will be a list of other users' queries, which the program captures and presents to the traveler in English. He can click on each link to go directly to the Web page offering the flight.

Most users can set up pipe programs; the main idea here is that instead of going to a Web site and looking at the information, we make a system that retrieves the information that we need and present it in the form that we want.

43.4   Folksonomies

The term **folkso-nomies** is made up of folks and taxonomies, that is, a labeling system with which ordinary users can tag information.

The term *folksonomies* combines the words folk and taxonomies to indicate a labeling system with which ordinary users can tag information. Examples of such colloborative tagging systems are the del.icio.us system, with which users can tag Web pages, and flickr.com, a photo site where users can tag photos.

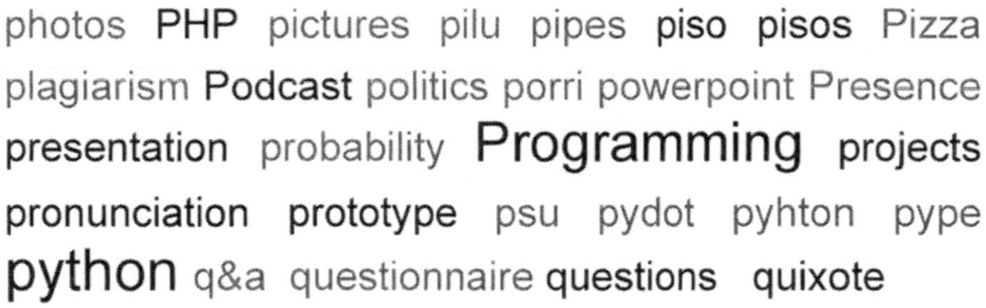

photos **PHP** pictures pilu pipes **piso pisos** Pizza plagiarism **Podcast** politics porri powerpoint Presence **presentation** probability **Programming** projects **pronunciation prototype** psu pydot pyhton pype **python** q&a questionnaire **questions quixote**

Figure 43.2. An example of a tag cloud from the del.icio.us system.

The sum of these tags can be presented as a tag cloud, shown in Figure 43.2. Here the most frequent tags are shown in a bold and larger font.

The advantage of folksonomies is that feedback from very many users—at least the users willing to tag—is incorporated. The disadvantage is that there is often no controlled vocabulary, and users may use quite different terms when tagging a Web site, a photo, or any other object. To some degree this drawback will be reduced when there are many tags because some tags will stand out, representing the average or majority "vote."

Many reviewing systems can be described as folksonomies, especially when these are quantified, for example, using a star or a number system to present averages. Today we have the opportunity to rate nearly everything—hotels, movies, books, and so on.

When each individual review can be identified, they can be compared with each other and personal preferences can be

Compared with professional encyclopedias, Wikipedia may have a few more errors, but these are most often corrected very quickly.

taken into account. For example, say you are considering buying a movie that has received a high ranking, indicating it is a good buy. However, a more advanced system would show how others who share your tastes had ranked the movie. Similar taste could then be measured by how coordinated earlier reviews have been. There may be a group of persons whose reviews correlate strongly with your own. This groups' rating of the movie would be more interesting than the average score. (I return to these issues in Chapter on crowdsourcing.)

43.5   Wikis

Wikis are Web sites where ordinary users provide most of the information.

Wikis are Web sites where ordinary users provide most of the information. The best example is Wikipedia, which today is the most used encyclopedia. The English version has four million articles, and there are editions in nearly all languages. The strength of wikis is they grow fast with their open invitation to participate, and, of course, growth attracts more visitors, creating a positive feedback loop. Wikipedia includes articles on most issues, at least in the English version, and since it is simple to edit, the articles are updated.

However, Wikipedia is more the exception than the rule. Most wikis have just a few providers.[6] Not everybody is willing to invest the time to participate, and there is also a start-up problem. In the beginning, a wiki is only an empty site, open for input. Another disadvantage is that many people write the articles, each with an individual style. Without editorial restrictions, the articles tend to be more verbose than in professional encyclopedias. Since amateurs or semiprofessionals (students) write many of the entries, they may not have the same in-depth coverage as those written by professionals. However, there is always the opportunity to get more information on the Web by following links to scholarly articles. Also, the main idea for an encyclopedia is to offer a general presentation of a topic. In this respect, it is probably more important to cover many topics and to offer updated information, than to provide in-depth coverage.

One would expect many errors in articles written by many persons, but comparisons with more professional encyclopedias have shown that this is not the case. Wikipedia may have a few more errors, but these often are corrected quickly. That is, it seems that the idea of open editing really works. If we see an error in an article we can correct it ourselves—now.

The open nature of wikis makes these systems susceptible to virtual vandalism. Also various editors may battle to establish their version of controversial topics. However, the success of many wikis has shown that these disadvantages can be controlled. The remedies may include identification of editors (such as through an e-mail address), restrictions on editing operations until a new editor can be determined trustworthy, and to establish some central oversight of editing. For example, a central editor can lock an article if there are too many changes and disallow editing on very controversial issues.

In practice, wikis also have some self-censorship. For example, the information department of a company may want to create an article presenting the company and its products. The company would know that an overly positive, marketing-oriented article, probably would be deleted or severely edited; therefore, the information department would tend to write a more balanced presentation.

Usually the structure of a Wiki is determined by the initiators, the persons who set up the site, provide the computer resources, and offer the software for searching and editing. The MediaWiki[7] software application, developed by the Wikimedia Foundation, is often used. It powers Wikipedia, is used by many other Web sites, and also is a content management system in many companies.

Wikis may be especially interesting for public administration. Many communities offer Web sites to provide an abundance of services to their populations. Many of these services are official, such as handling school applications, but some could be available to the general public. For example, my city lists things to do, although because of limited resources, only a few topics are covered, and these very superficially. But this area could be open to the public through a wiki system, which would make it possible to have detailed information on all topics, from the history of the soccer team to detailed descriptions of hiking trips. There will certainly be individuals in the community who are willing to provide this information.

Notes

1   www.linux.org

2   www.wikipedia.org

3   Wikipedia (see Killian documents controversy) presents an interesting account of this case.

4   This chapter is based on Olsen, K. A., Malizia, A. (2010). Following Virtual Trails, IEEE Potentials. Volume 29, Issue 1.

5   pipes.yahoo.com

6   Kraut, R., Maher, M. L., Olson, J. (2010) Scientific Foundations: A Case for Technology Mediated Social Participation Theory, IEEE Computer, November.

7   www.mediawiki.org

PART 6

Business-to-Consumer Applications

Traditionally, Internet applications are categorized as either business-to-consumer (B2C) or business-to-business (B2B).

Traditionally, Internet applications are categorized as either business-to-consumer (B2C) or business-to-business (B2B). With B2C we expect that in the normal situation we have a computer at one end of the communication line, a person at the other. Of course, this person also will use a computer device to access the Internet, but output from the Web site is presented for human beings. This simplifies applications, as the human beings can read and understand nearly any layout or format, at least when it is well organized. It also implies that objects and actions may be formalized on any level, as characters or as higher-level concepts. It is no problem for us that the online bookstore requires an e-mail address, the airline an account number, and the newspaper a user name for identification. It is no problem that some sites ask for our name in one field, while others have fields for first, last, and initials. That is, no rigid standards are needed for a B2C application; the flexibility of human beings allows for nearly any type of interface. Of course, the interfaces will be easier to use if they use familiar terms and commands, and imitate the look and feel of other systems and interfaces that the user may know.

As we have seen, in some situations, the user interface does not provide the needed flexibility, for example, for handling exceptions. Then the B2C model usually can be replaced by a person-to-person correspondence, by allowing the customer to call in, send e-mail, use instant messaging, or complete a Web form. That is, the Web system can be used to handle a large number of transactions efficiently, but we can move to a more flexible (but less efficient) medium, such as chat or e-mail, at any time. In this respect, B2C systems give us the best of both worlds.

The Web system can handle a large part of the transactions in an efficient manner. Exceptions can be handled using more flexible media, such as chat or e-mail.

Note that the person at the other end of the communication line may be a private citizen using the Web from his home computer to buy Christmas gifts, or an employee operating on behalf of her company. There is no fundamental difference if the purchases are paid for privately or by the firm, if the Web sites are open to the public or only to employees. What is important is that there is a person at one end of the communication line. Applications can be formalized to a higher level when the person communicating is an employee, rather than an ordinary citizen. In the employee situation, the items ordered through the B2C site will be limited (perhaps to office stationery), and shopping usually will be performed under predefined contracts.

B2B is defined as communication between computers.

Communication between computers requires higher-level formalizations when higher-level functions are to be performed.

B2B is defined as communication between computers (that is, the "end users" are computer programs). B2B sets up efficient processes that can be automated, without the intervention of humans. B2B applications need a common vocabulary and a common format for data to communicate on a semantic level, for example, to send an order form from one computer to the other. The format of the order, for example, the number of data fields, the types of fields, field identifiers, and so on, must be clearly specified to avoid misunderstanding and errors. Data has to be provided in a way that both computers can interpret. For identifiers, such as a bank account number, some sort of global identifier will be needed, for example, prefixing the account number by a country and routing code.

B2B is not only a matter of transferring bits, it is also a question of elaborate standards. No human beings are in the loop, which makes it more difficult to jump to a more flexible medium to handle exceptions. To maintain efficiency, the computer system should be able to handle all common exception situations, which makes these systems more elaborate and more expensive to build. (I return to B2B in Part 7.)

In this discussion of business models for B2C, I will start with the completely symbolic applications and present these in order of formalization level, starting at the lowest. After presenting information providers in Chapter 44 and online services in Chapter 45, I discuss the "long-tail" issue in Chapter 46, that is, how digital representation allows storing and selling an unlimited number of different products. I then move to applications that have a physical part, products that have to be distributed by other channels than the Internet, in Chapter 47.

In presenting these applications I focus on the formalization part, showing that the formalization level of each area will define the level of efficiency for the applications. Naturally, the Internet and the Web can only handle the symbolic part of an application. The physical parts—for example, the transportation of goods—will have to go on other channels. As we shall see, this will restrict the practicality of many applications. In presenting examples, we will see where we can reap the greatest benefits of Internet technology.

This part concludes by showing in Chapter 48 how important it is that systems handle both the open and closed parts of a task, that is, that they can cover the whole range of users' needs.

44   Symbolic Services—Information Providers

Completely symbolic services can be performed exclusively via the Internet, making it possible to move from physical distribution of information to electronic, reaping all the advantages of the new technology.

With a very small investment, companies and institutions can have a presence and be an information provider on the Web. The information can be stored in static, premade HTML pages or be retrieved from databases using dynamic pages. It can be offered to the public, or be limited to customers and employees; it can be provided free or sold based on a pay-per-page or subscription model.

Revenue seems easier to obtain from providing infrastructure (equipment, communication lines, ISP-provider) than from content.

Pay models have been difficult to implement. Many view the Web as a free source, similar to broadcast TV, and are not willing to pay for content. There are some exceptions: A few newspapers have managed to establish a subscription model, and providers of special information, such as scientific papers, have retained the pay model when going online.

Even if the site has free access, this does not make the Web a free medium. The user has to provide the equipment, the computer hardware and software, and the connection and will have to pay the ISP (Internet Service Provider) for access. There are many valid business models in this chain, for example, computer manufacturing, ISP services, network installation, and maintenance. However, this chapter concentrates on content and the other services that the technology can provide, not on the technology itself.

In addition to paying for the equipment and access, users spend time, skills, and energy to find what they need on the Web. While the Web can provide information on almost everything, it may not always be easy to get what we want. Therefore, in a job situation, retrieving information may be quite expensive, even if the source is "free." However, when the Web is used for entertainment, the fun may be in the process itself, in "surfing" for interesting stuff.

Internet/Web services offer customization (the user chooses what she wants to see), but requires a higher **level of activation** than other media.

Compared with other media, such as TV, radio, and newspapers, the Web requires a higher activity level from the user, which is both an advantage and a disadvantage. On the Web the user is in control: She can follow the links she finds interesting, provide her own keywords for searching, and go to the sites she likes. During sessions she has her eyes fixed on the screen,

hands on keyboard and mouse. This is very different from the
TV viewer, where the only input required is a button click for
channel selection.

44.1   Web presence

The Web can be used to present a company, an institution, or
an interest group. The cost of creating and maintaining Web
pages is often very small compared with other means of dissemination, such as using brochures, direct mail, or advertisements. The Web also has other advantages, such as integrating
many different media, easy updates, and nearly unlimited storage space. While small organizations may choose to develop a
minimum site, perhaps creating the site as an in-house job, larger institutions often will use professionals—graphic and Web
designers—to create a quality site with high functionality.[1]

For a small institution, a Web presence, done in the right
way, will be very inexpensive marketing—a simple way to
provide customers with information such as address, maps, and
employee directories. While some of these pages will be static,
other pages can be created based on information from company
databases. For example, instead of maintaining a separate telephone directory on the Web, a directory can be created on the
fly, based on information in the employee database, as mentioned in Chapter 39. Access can be public (Internet), mainly
provided for users within an organization (Intranet), or only to
users with a password (Extranet). Users can access the site by
giving the URL, using a preset bookmark, following a link on
another Web page, or using a search tool. To simplify access,
institutions try to acquire simple URLs, for example, the company name with a .com suffix, and to present this URL in advertisements and on products.

While such a site will be read-only, simplifying security,
some sites provide a way to send data to the company with an
e-mail address or by using HTML forms to provide more formalized input. If a mail address is embedded in a "mailto" tag,
the browser will automatically open a mail message to this address when the user clicks on this mail link. Forms can be embedded in HTML pages, and form data can be retrieved and
stored by a simple server script (see Chapter 40).

While a Web presence will not give any direct revenue, it
has several advantages for a company and its customer:

*For a small institu-
tion, a Web pres-
ence, done in the
right way, will be
very inexpensive
marketing.*

The data on the page determines the necessary **update frequency**; more general data requires fewer updates than specific data.

- *New customers can be attracted*, perhaps finding the site through a search tool or a portal.

- *Reduced switchboard load* is accomplished as customers may get information directly from the Web page.

- *Customers get faster access to information* over the Web than over the telephone.

- The Web can provide *more detailed information* than brochures.

- *Easy updates*, a new version is available the second it is stored.

- Since information from a Web site is in *electronic form*, it can be forwarded to others, stored on a computer, inserted into other programs, or printed.

- *Need for advertisements is reduced* in printed catalogs, such as yellow pages.

- Customers can create *hypertext links* to the site from their own Web pages.

- *Other advertisements can be simpler*, as additional data can be offered on the Web site, for example, by giving the URL in an advertisement.

For some companies, telephone, fax, and letters may still be the principal means of communication. Still, the Web's advantages are so clear compared to the costs that most companies and institutions have and should have a Web presence today. In fact, customers expect companies to have a Web page, just as they earlier expect a listing in yellow page directories. We also should expect electronic contact to be the norm.

The Web site is the **virtual face** of the company, and care should be taken to provide a look and feel and a level of service that conforms to the company as a whole.

A Web site is the face of the company, perhaps the only face for many customers, and the same care should be taken with the site as is taken to keep the brick and mortar offices clean and inviting. Each company has its own "look and feel," which may be simple or functional, traditional or modern. The Web site should convey the same impression as other interfaces to the customers, whether they are offices, brochures, advertisements, products, or services.

However, the simplicity and low cost of establishing a Web site may be a trap for many small firms. If detailed information is provided, the site will need to be updated often, and many firms have not established routines for this. That is, they order a Web site as they would a brochure, forgetting that a site should

Internet/Web technologies are ideal for government agencies and other organizations that want to provide **information** to citizens or a large number of members.

If a firm needs only a minimum Web presence, care should be taken to design a general and static Web site, where dynamic information is retrieved from company databases.

be a living thing that is accessed today as well as in the future. In contrast to information on paper, the customer will expect the display to provide fresh, accurate copy every day. If price information is provided, the Web page must be updated with every price change. If names of employees are listed, persons that have left the company must be removed.

Managing updates is not always easy. My college, for example, replaced the standard term-oriented schedule with a daily version, but without establishing a system to track changes. All courses were listed using the predetermined schedule, in addition to special events marked for each day. However, the students now expect all information to be updated daily. Students ignore my early e-mail warnings that lectures are cancelled or moved because they expect these to be overridden by the new daily itinerary; that is, they expect (reasonably enough) that the latest version is the one that counts. This was not a problem when the itinerary was given for the whole term. The remedy is either to track all changes, offering a correct daily schedule, or to list course itineraries and special events separately.

If a firm needs only a minimum Web presence, care should be taken to design a general and static Web site, where dynamic information is retrieved from company databases. If there are no routines for regular updates, one should avoid the section with "news" or all other forms of dated information (the news-section could be avoided anyway, as very few go to the Web site of an organization to get news). Detailed data can be generated from the company's database, for example, data on employees retrieved from a human resources database. As soon as new employee data are entered here, that information also will be available on the Web site. This is especially important, as new data often are accessed more often than old data (naturally, as no one knows the phone number of the new employee).

It is reasonable to offer an e-mail address on the "contact us" page, but this implies that one needs routines for handling messages. Tests have shown that the response times for e-mail are often very long, or that some companies do not answer at all.[2] Since many use the Internet as a "yellow page" directory, it is also smart to provide information on how the company can be reached by telephone, fax, and mail and to list all physical addresses.

In many ways, Internet and Web technology is ideal for many public organizations, from interest groups to governments. The Internet and the Web provide ideal tools for these organizations to meet their general goal of offering information to their members and to the public.

Traditionally, mass-distributed mail has been the channel for outgoing information, while these institutions have received telephone calls or letters from the public. With the Internet, one can be more efficient. Updated information can be presented on Web pages, and members or the public can be offered direct access to information archives. Information that earlier was accessible only to employees, now can be offered to everyone. In this way, interest organizations, covering topics from arthritis to zoos, can provide their members and the public with vision statements, background information, information databases, links to other organizations of interest, archives with member input, chat rooms, contact to professionals, and more. Official organizations, working under public information laws, can save reports and research studies "as HTML," making them available at very limited costs.

Do not expect that everyone is interested in **in-depth information,** even when available over the Web.

Of course, few of us are interested in reading governmental reports. It is usually much more convenient to "hire" a journalist to go through the report and prepare a summary for us in the newspaper, adding the background data needed, interviewing the right people, and so on. However, in special cases (for example, when a new road is proposed through our neighborhood, cut-downs are proposed in local schools, or when we need a building permit), we may be interested in more in-depth information. Making this data available on the Web is very convenient for the public and is at the same time, extremely cost effective for government. Now people can do their own searching, often satisfying their information need without any manual support.

It is easy to overstate the importance of these information sources, advocating a new arena for democracy where everybody has access to everything. But we should remember that all of this information was available before the Internet and the Web—the difference is easier access. This may be important in many cases, but the real work is often more in studying the data than obtaining the data. Today, we can get a thousand-page report online in minutes, while we earlier had to order it by mail. Still, the big task is to transform these data into information and that means reading and studying—clearly not a task for everybody.

Information must be well organized on large sites. This is simpler with formalized identifiers. For example, a university can organize its data according to courses and research areas, and offer an interface that is organized according to the user's needs. For example, the home page may have links for students, for potential students, researchers, visitors, and so on. A telephone company may distinguish between private and business customers in the first step, use technology on the second tier, and perhaps services on the third.

Often Web pages are organized according to the organizational structure of an organization. This is not always a good idea as the structure may not be obvious for the outsider accessing the site (for example, a university organized into schools and departments). However, a computer system allows us to organize according to several principles at the same time, so while a departmental form may be suitable for an Intranet, the Internet section should be organized according to other principles.

44.2   Product information on the Web

The next step, after presenting an institution or a company on the Web, is to present product information. Here we can utilize different types of product identifiers, such as ISBN numbers, author names, titles, and publishers for books. Table 44.1 offers some examples.

Business	Formal variables
Car dealer	Model, year, price
Real estate	Location, size, type, price
Booking (air)	Airport codes, flights, date, time, price category
Bookstore	Author, title, ISBN numbers, category
Music store	Artist, album, category
Software store	Program name, operating system
Perfumes & Cosmetics	Brand name, product type
Hardware store	Product type, size

Table 44.1 Formal variables for different businesses.

These formal classifiers also are often preferred in the real world to the more informal ones. For example, most perfume and cosmetics shops organize products according to brand name, although one could imagine organizing perfumes according to smell. However, in the latter case, there are few words to distinguish between different smells, and such a classification would be highly subjective. Bookstores may have a shelf with recommended books, sometimes what each employee has recommended, to flag the choice as subjective. But most often, a best-seller list is used, which is the more objective, formal way of presenting recommendations.

Product information can be organized in product classes, by usage, technology, and so on.

Product attributes can be presented in both an open and a closed form. For example, while book abstracts and reviews can be presented as text, it would be natural to offer product identifiers and attributes such as price, number of pages, type of book, type of binding, and language, in a more record-oriented notation, simplifying both product presentation and searching. For example, with price tagged in this way, we can search by price or sort by price.

Interestingly, when real estate advertisements have been put on the Internet, agents are often still in the traditional culture of paper ads. Often one sees that the routines are sloppy—irrelevant listings are not removed, or a house is listed having zero bedrooms. Of course, in a manual system, the zero will have few consequences, but for those who have initiated a search for all listings with a number of bedrooms this house will not come up. When presenting a flat on the twelfth floor, the agent may expect the customer to take for granted that there is an elevator. However, a search criteria of "elevator" will not find this apartment if "elevator" is not included in the listing description. That is, in going from paper to an electronic media, one has to ensure that the routines also change.

Not all companies can rely on established formalizations as those shown in Table 44.1. For example, a gift store will have problems finding useful formalizations. Here product description must rely on text and images to a greater degree, and classification may be more creative, such as "gifts for him/her," "Christmas gifts" and "new items." In the physical world, these stores are designed for browsing, using much space to present their items. A Web presentation of these products probably will have to follow the same lines.

Product attributes can be presented in both an open and a closed form.

If there are many products, search tools may be necessary to limit browsing, which presents the same formalization problems as above. While it is easy to search for a book or a movie, it will not be as easy to find the right search terms for our gift store. A textual description of each item may be highly subjective, and the user may not apply the "right" keywords when formalizing a query. This situation is similar to searching the

Web sites can provide information that was difficult to present using traditional media.

The Web has some limitations compared with **product presentation** in brick and mortar stores, but also open the way for new ways of presenting products.

open Web. Of course, most products can be identified with item numbers, but these internal product identifiers will most often be unknown by the customer. There are exceptions, however. When needing service, a customer may have the type number of the item as well as the serial number. We also may have the ISBN when ordering a book. In these situations it will be efficient if the site allows us to provide such unique identifiers, shortcutting the more flexible but less efficient search options.

In its simplest form, product information may be displayed on static Web pages, perhaps based on information from paper brochures and fact sheets. However, with many products, it may be easier to build these pages on the basis of information in company databases, if available. The HTML pages can then be created on the fly, based on information from the database, or one could save some processing power by creating all the pages up front. The latter solution implies that pages are regenerated whenever there is a change in the underlying data.

The Web is more than a brochure. With creativity, it can be used for "try me" demonstrations, at least for some types of products. While information on a book will be sufficient in certain cases, we may want to scan the pages of a textbook or dictionary, to see what kind of detail is provided. We can do this in the brick and mortar store, but not always on the Web where unsolicited copying may be a problem. A solution may be to let the user see the complete table of contents, the index, and only selected sections or pages. For the dictionary, the user should be offered an interface for providing words for translation. This may not be as good as a visit to a brick and mortar store, that allows you to see the actual copy that you will buy, but is a surrogate that reduces some of the disadvantages of buying online.

Applying creativity to utilize the new medium, where this has advantages, is also important. Amazon does this by offering customers' the opportunity to write book reviews, a feature that in practice can be provided only online. The multimedia Web capabilities can be used to present music online, by offering snapshots in MP3 or other music formats. In addition, on the Web, it is possible to provide extensive background information on the performer and the music, for example, by showing music videos.

A Web site for a do-it-yourself store cannot let the user handle the products and materials, but can mitigate this drawback by giving color pictures, videos, and full documentation.

The Web medium can further be exploited by offering complete instructions, with checklists for what you need, and perhaps a consultant service available over e-mail. One could establish a chat room for customers and allow customers to enter their own advice about handling tools or materials. The site also may offer to keep a record of all the materials that you buy, for example color codes for paint, so that you can find the right product when you need additional materials for extensions and repairs.

To sum up, presenting product information online has many advantages. While a good Web presentation is a must for online stores, it may provide an additional marketing channel and marketing efficiency for a brick and mortar store:

- The Web allows for very *detailed product information*, in the form of text, tables, images, animations, and videos.

- Customers will have *easy access* to this information, and can print it out if necessary.

- The Web allows the user to *compare* products.

- *Manuals* can be downloaded from the Web.

- Customers can *find a product* by a search, for example, by product characteristics.

- The information is *easy to maintain*. Insertion, deletion, and modification can be performed at any time.

- *Store once, use many times*. The same data source, the product database, can be used both for providing information to customers and employees, while the user interfaces—the views of the database—may be different.

- *Information needs of customers and employees* may be satisfied just by linking to other sources.

- *The load on other and more expensive channels*, such as letter or telephone, will be reduced as information on new and old products can be obtained automatically from the Web.

Today, many companies and institutions see the advantages of providing all this information online.

A disadvantage of providing product information on the Web is that this information will be available for the competition also. Although this is also the case for product information

A disadvantage of providing product information on the Web is that this information will be available for the **competition** also.

on paper, there are differences in quantity, speed, and simplicity of obtaining information. Using spiders and other programs that access Web sites, a competitor can get an immediate and complete notice of new prices, new items, special offers, and so on. A company that is open to its customers is also open to everybody else.

44.3   Archive access—sale of text-based content

What it sold is usually **data**, leaving to the customer to convert data into information. This is an open process, and the "information value" of data is often impossible to calculate at the outset. At the same time the process of converting data into information is expensive.

A market for the sale of information, for example, credit checks on firms and private citizens or stock market trends, has always existed. With the advent of fast computers and cheap, high-capacity disk storage in the 1970s (that is, better means for storing, organizing, and retrieving information), a boom in this market was expected. But, with a few exceptions, selling content was not an easy task. Then, with the advent of the Internet and the Web, direct access to content archives could be offered to a much larger audience without intermediaries or special software and hardware. All the technological and practical barriers for disseminating data in any form were removed. Still, with a few exceptions, the market opportunities have not emerged. It seems that there is an unwillingness to pay for content outside of entertainment.

This unwillingness to pay may have several explanations:

- Since storing and disseminating electronic data is relatively inexpensive, there are *many information providers* on the Web, most of which provide information for free. This competition from free sources makes it difficult to establish pay-for-access sites ("Why should I pay when I can get information for free?").

- Since everybody can be a *content provider,* the Web is viewed as a free medium, where everything is and should be available without restrictions.

- It may be difficult to get people to accept having to pay just for the *right to access information*. Physical media, such as paper and CDs, have a form that symbolizes value. For example, software providers use unnecessary and expensive-looking packaging to make it easier for customers to accept a high price.

- The difficulty of *assessing the quality* of information, just by a description. For example, we may get the title and a short abstract of a report for free, but this is often insufficient in order to evaluate the value of the report.

- For *general information* the Web competes with other sources, such as TV, radio, and newspapers.

- Accessing the source is only a small part of the work; the information also must be found, read, and organized. The user may be *unwilling to pay* up front just for access, when it is so difficult to put a price on the end result. On the contrary, organizations seem to be willing to pay a lot more for consultants, but then these provide more than just the data.

- The *information need* may be very specific, and may not be served by a general archive. The data may be in the wrong form, too general, incomplete, or too old, and so on.

- *The infrastructure is not yet in place for all forms of information.* For example, online video requires more bandwidth than many networks can provide.

- Information-providers may be afraid of *copyright infringement* if information is provided in electronic form (see the discussion on scientific journals in Chapter 14.2).

- *The problem of paying.* While large amounts, such as subscriber fees, can be paid by credit card, we still lack a general system for micro payments, for example, paying a cent for a downloaded page.

The most serious problem with information as a product is that its usefulness is difficult to evaluate (that is, it may be difficult to convert into some form of "revenue"). While this may be easier with formalized information, such as stock prices, credit ratings, weather forecasts, and directions, evaluating usefulness is more acute with more open information.

For example, some newspapers offer free access to their Internet edition, but ask for a very moderate fee, say, one dollar, for access to their online archives. However, in the end this may be too high a price! Let us assume that only one out of five articles that we access (based on title and abstract) is of interest. Let us further assume that we use information from only a small fraction of these, perhaps one in ten (the other articles are dismissed because they tell us something that we already know, they do not provide enough information, or the information

Closed information is easier to utilize than open information. In many cases closed information may be used as it is, for example, as input to an automated process. With open information, the process of converting data to information is more complex.

does not fulfill our need). In the worst case, we would need to read or scan at least fifty papers returned by a query to find one that is useful. Are we willing to pay $50 for this information? And are we willing to spend time finding the articles, reading or scanning all the fifty papers to find the one of value?

This discrepancy between theoretical and practical relevance is also found in bibliographic databases of scientific papers. It may be a valid business model to sell archive access, but a good model may require access to be so cheap that the amount is low even after we have multiplied by fifty. Of course, an alternative model is to use subscription, where one can access everything by paying a fixed amount per month or year. Some newspapers try this model, often in a combination of providing general information (what all the others provide) for free and more special information for subscribers only.

Interestingly, sale of pornographic material has been the big exception. Sex-related keywords are some of the most common used in searching the Web, and pornography is one of the largest revenue sources. Clearly, the Web offers several advantages compared with other media for this kind of business:

- *Privacy*. Family, friends, and neighbors cannot see what one downloads over an Internet channel. Downloaded material can be stored securely on the hard drive, protected by a password.[3]

- *Availability*. Pornographic material is of limited availability in the physical world; sex shops are only found in the largest cities and in many countries pornographic material is strictly regulated. The Web offers unlimited availability.

- *Diversity*. Sex is a strong drive, and takes many forms. The Web can offer something for everybody.

- *A wide range of media can be supported*: text, images, sound, video, live video, chat, and so on.

- *Inexpensive* storage and dissemination.

Unsurprisingly, these businesses flourish on the Web, even if competition is intense in this market, which also includes a wealth of free sources. The biggest surprise, however, may be that few other businesses have managed to build a valid business model on information sale via the Internet.

44.4   Intranet

Intranet/Extranet applications **limit access** to a group of users, but functionality can be increased by utilizing common-alties within this group.

Strangely enough, one of the most useful applications for the Web is the Intranet, *limiting* information to those who work within an organization. While business information systems have been available for decades, the Web offers a simple, generic, and inexpensive way to implement the same functionality:

- Use of *standard software*, as browsers and office tools (all employees with access to a computer will have the basic software installed).
- *No additional training will* be needed, as standard tools are used.
- *Common format* for internal and external information.
- Data previously stored and maintained internally can in many cases be replaced by a *link* to an external source, such as a phone directory.
- The information is *accessible from everywhere.* For example, employees can access company data when traveling.

An Intranet solution becomes especially important for firms and employees who are geographically dispersed. Access to information now becomes independent of location. The foreman at a distant construction site can have access to the same information sources, the same tools and administrative facilities as those working at the head office.

Since Intranet applications limit access to information, "sublanguages" that exist within an institution can be used to offer a higher formalization level. (We previously discussed how sublanguages that exist within a profession could be used to make more formalized queries.) Sublanguages may be everything from product numbers to special vocabulary used within the institution. In a college Intranet application, for example, course numbers, course descriptions, departmental structure, and topics of interest can be used to formalize data to higher levels and to facilitate organization of information and searching. In a business environment, examples to increase formalization may include product names, product attributes, order numbers, names of customers, organizational structure, processes, and methods.

The **advantage** of having an information system on an Intranet platform is that everyone has access—from everywhere.

The advantage of having an information system on an Intranet platform is that everybody can access the system. Universities have been pioneers in offering such systems to their students, making available online course materials, syllabuses, exercises, slides, and even videotaped lectures. Many universities also allow this information to be open to the general public. For example, anyone can (try to) follow an MIT lecture online—free. Similar, Intranet applications can offer many advantages for the university administration, offering global access to data and allowing students to view and update their own records.

This simple Intranet structure works as a common memory for the organizations, a common archive where everything can be stored and retrieved. Within W3C,[4] the World Wide Web consortium, the saying goes, "If it is not on the Web, it does not exist." Other organizations should follow. When everybody has access to the same data, there is no need to go through others to get access and there is no excuse for not having access to the latest information. Of course, access may have to be limited for confidential data, but in principle the "put it on the Web" slogan is right.

The Intranet application offers a **common memory** and common experience base for both company employees and their customers.

Today, the Intranet provides employees not only with static handbooks, minutes of meetings, and regulations, but also with access to systems for ordering office supplies, booking systems, payroll information, and so on. On the Web, a common experience can be created for employees. This can take the form of "best practice" databases, dynamic handbooks, or databases of frequently asked questions. In this way the experience of each employee can be added to a common company experience. While this was also possible in the precomputer world, using handbooks and memoranda, the Web offers much better possibilities for entering, storing, updating, and disseminating the information. The Web has given us a common interface that can be accessed from anywhere by anybody, making it more practical to enter, update, and retrieve information. Wiki solutions, as discussed in Chapter 43.5, are especially useful here.

A formalized database of "best practice" procedures will have the advantage of structured information, and the use of high-level concepts for retrieval. For example, one could be asked to provide in a form information such as date, part numbers, and identification of materials used. In the cases where these data are relevant, the form will support the input process, by structuring the input and, for example, letting the user choose between predetermined alternatives instead of having to

Formalization comes **at a price**. It is tedious to fit information into predetermined forms. It is so much easier to choose the blank sheet of paper and tell the story using our own words and our own structure.

type in data. In this way we ensure a common vocabulary and get a structure that can be processed automatically.

Of course, not all cases can be put into predetermined forms. All of us have experienced the painful situation of filling out a questionnaire and trying to fit our opinions into the standard responses listed (remember our discussion in Chapter 6). The remedy can be to provide more forms or to add a type that fits the new class of descriptions. Still, we need a more open form, "a blank sheet of paper," for the problems that do not fit a standard case. Even in the latter case, items such as date, name, department, title should be in structured fields, leaving the "best-practice" description to an open text field. Thus, all kinds of information may be given, at the same time as basic, common data are in a structured form.

The disadvantage of open alternatives is that these may often be chosen for convenience, even in cases where more closed forms could have been used. With a lack of organization and structure, we risk having the same data entered several times. This creates unnecessary work, makes it very difficult to maintain the data collection, and prevents consistency of the data. With unstructured descriptions, the disadvantage is that we have only low-level concepts (strings or words) for searching the description field. However, text-based searching will function much better here than on the open Web. Within an institution, we will find a sublanguage that can aid the process, as we have seen.

44.5   Extranet

Extranet is often used to describe internal systems that customers also can access.

A limited access Internet application, often implemented by password protection, is called an Extranet. Such systems can be used to let customers follow their own orders through production and distribution as well as other functions. That is, we provide the customer with a window into certain parts of the company database. In this way, the customer can follow the status of orders, track packages through the postal system, and can be allowed to follow the process of his insurance claim or loan application. An extranet allows a customer to be better informed and prevents companies from having to give the same information manually. The hope is that when customers get the same, or nearly the same, information available to company employees, they will be drawn closer to the company.

Access can be restricted to read-only, or customers can be allowed to update parts of their records. Read-only has clear se-

We can **connect customers** more closely to the company by offering access to company systems, but it may be necessary to give customers a different *view* of these data than what we offer to employees over the Intranet.

curity advantages. The "Web window" of an Extranet can be implemented by using scripts or programs that retrieve the data from a company database and insert these in an HTML page that is returned to the user, as explained in detail in Chapter 39.

Normally, some form of transformation is needed before the data can be presented to the customer. There may be information that we do not want the customer to see, or other types of information may have to be translated to make sense to an outsider. The internal formalization may have to be mapped to a more general formalization. For example, a product may be identified internally by a number but externally by a name. In these cases, the Web interface must perform the necessary transformations. A hospital may decide to give patients access to clinical information, but may want to add information that makes the data easier to understand, such as giving an explanation if lab results are within or outside a normal range, or translating diagnosis codes to more common terms. While the formal parts of a medical record can be "translated" automatically, the less formal parts must be presented in its original form or handled manually.

Since the kind of information and reports that we want to give to customers may vary, a flexible system is needed. Users within the company need a simple tool to describe data and layout of customer reports, and should also be able to determine which customers have access to which reports.

Figure 44.1 Virtual Web database.

The information provided to customers can be viewed as a virtual database that exists between the customer and the real company database (Figure 44.1).

The interface can be provided by a B2C system. This works fine as long as there are few data, for example, the case where a customer wants to follow a parcel through the postal system. However, for businesses there will be the need to for B2B solutions, for example by providing an API (Application programming interface), allowing the customers programs to access the

Administering data will be simpler when everything is available online.

system. An example would be the online store, which will program its system to follow every packet sent to customers through the postal service.

Many institutions are offering customers these windows into their internal systems. The natural next step is to allow customers to update this information directly. For example, instead of calling a newspaper or sending an e-mail to change a subscription, the customer could directly access his records, to change address, update telephone numbers, e-mail addresses and other information, and change the method of payment. Of course, the newspaper may restrict access to some items, for example, the "amount paid" field. The advantage for the customer is that she gets 24/7/365 immediate access and does not have to provide data over the telephone or through an intermediary; the newspaper saves administration costs as the customers assume the maintenance of these archives.

For the customers extranet systems have the advantage that the data is available online, and there are no more letters received through the mail to be archived. In the future organizational links to all our contact points—to utility companies, banks, insurance companies, newspapers, journals, and other organizations that we support—should be available through one personal Web page. This should give us all the information we need, directly from the original sources, not from more or less well organized duplicate paper-based archives in our home.

As seen, Extranet systems have several advantages, both for the customers and the companies:

- Information is provided *automatically*, thus telephone calls to company employees are avoided.

- Customers get *updated* information.

- Data are only *archived* at the source.

- *Historical data can be provided automatically*, perhaps with tools that let you present time series of data in visual form (for example, to show a curve of electricity usage over the recent years).

- A good information system may *tie the customers more closely to the company*. For example, from an information perspective it will now be an advantage for a customer to have as many orders as possible with the company (to get complete overviews).

- Customers can get more *detailed information* in a more flexible way than by telephone, fax or letter. For example, information on current orders can be presented in a table on the screen, printed, or provided as a spreadsheet for further processing.

The disadvantage for many companies is that the new Web based access points will come in addition to phone, letters and service over the counter. However, by moving customers from the expensive channels (such as counter service and phone) to the more efficient (where the customer do the job using the extranet), there will be significant savings in the long run.

44.6   Handling customer input

Automatic systems can handle the closed part of customer communication. For the open parts, other channels (e-mail, telephone) must be provided.

A disadvantage of a Web service may be that as customers go from other communication channels, such as physical contact and the telephone, to the Web the connection may become less personal. As discussed earlier, care should be taken to strengthen these personal relationships by other means. For example, connecting with a customer representative through email or telephone should be easy, but these more expensive channels should be restricted to tasks where they are really needed, for example, to solve problems that have occurred.

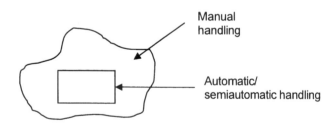

Figure 44.2 Unformalized and formalized parts.

E-mail offers the opportunity of having a **semi-automatic** dialogue with the customer, in which a human can edit the computer-generated messages.

This is just another implementation of our basic ideas on formalization. When the formalized part of a transaction, the box shown in Figure 44.2, is handled automatically, channels for the more open parts (exceptions) also should be provided.

Input from customers may be a good opportunity for a sale. Since the user has initiated the dialogue with his first message and will await a reply, there is an opportunity for including additional, but relevant information. For example, when the user requests spare parts and service on her old lawnmower, we may provide a trade-in offer on a new model *in addition* to giving her the information she requests. The effect of this marketing will be dependent on how relevant the offer will be to the customer's current situation (that is, how natural the answer will be in the context). To offer a new model when the old lawnmower has broken down may be part of a natural dialogue, but to offer a snow blower may not. Neither should we offer a trade-in if the customer has a new lawnmower, or if her message is a complaint on the repair that we have just performed. To some extent a smart program may be able to offer this type of response, but a program never can be expected to understand the context in the same way as a human operator. As in other situations, the ideal solution is a semiautomatic system in which the computer performs the secretarial work and a human being controls the final results.

We have earlier discussed the advantages and disadvantages of using forms to formalize e-mail messages. The disadvantage of this approach is that it is less flexible than using open (blank) forms. However, in setting up electronic customer contact points, we may at least let the customer choose a heading for the message. This can be done through a simple Web form in which the user selects from a set of alternatives. For example, when sending an e-mail to a newspaper, it might be natural to offer headings such as, subscription, advertisement, letter to the editor, or news tip. Incoming mail can then be sorted automatically based on this information and forwarded to the right internal e-mail address. The advantage of this approach is that we have established a layer between the customer and internal mail addresses, which can now be changed without consequences for the outside world. The additional formalism required on the customer's part is negligible, and if we provide an "other" alternative, flexibility is maintained.

Customer input may be as unformalized as an e-mail, but also may be in a more formal manner, for example, as exact specifications for a product. The Internet/Web provides the solution for the specification part of such products. Here we can provide interfaces that can lead a customer through a detailed specification process.

Customized products can be physical or abstract. A kitchen manufacturer can offer design programs online, where the user can specify overall measurements and functionality, and the program can calculate the need for basic modules, print list of items needed, calculate prices, and so on. Such a user interface can be implemented by a downloaded script or by a server side

> Web interfaces combined with flexible product description and manufacturing processes allow for **customization,** so that products are tailored to the individual customer.

solution. The Web site of an insurance company cannot give you the same personal service as a brick and mortar office, but may instead offer customized insurance in which the premium is based on detailed information about your needs. For example, the insurance company may give you a rebate on your car insurance if your employer has an attended employee garage, if you drove 486 miles less than expected last year, or if your son, the youngest driver, is over age twenty. This interface will allow you to choose between different options, and will immediately show how your choices affect the premium.

There are certain drawbacks with using the Web for customer contact, which means it is important to also exploit the **advantages** of the Web.

The important message here is that there are certain drawbacks in using the Web for customer contact as compared to more personal contact points, such as over-the-counter or a phone call. Therefore, trying to move current systems and products directly to the Web is sometimes not a good idea. Instead, one should exploit the advantages of the Web, for example as described here, to offer customized products. It would not have been possible to offer these using the traditional interfaces, as the ordering process would have been too cumbersome; however, when the user does the job herself, this becomes an option.

Notes

1 For example, see sites such as www.gucci.com, www.dior.com, and www.louisvuitton.com. These design companies have managed to combine interesting Web pages with simple-to-use interfaces.

2 This offers many interesting legal issues. At times we must notify organizations of changes, such as a cancellation of a subscription, a change of address, or a new mileage limit for car insurance. In some countries simple building permits (for small modifications) can be given in the form of a notice. If the organization involved offers an e-mail address, it should be sufficient to send an e-mail message in these cases. But what if the organization does not have routines for handling e-mail, or if our message is removed by the spam filter? Can we distinguish a cancellation notice as spam, and receive additional numbers of a journal? Or, from the organization point of view, if they provide an e-mail address, they also need good routines for handling incoming mail.

3 It is interesting to note that within this business, customers appreciate the apparent privacy of the Web, while Web privacy is a concern in all other areas. However, the privacy offered on the Web may be a wolf in sheep's clothes. With cookies, the information provided in one situation can be linked to sites accessed in other sessions, IP and e-mail addresses can be registered and sold to others. Browsers usually store historical information, so that it is possible to review what has happened in previous sessions.

4 http://www.w3.org/

45 Online Symbolic Services—Case Studies

Web protocols and Web browsers offer tools for creating **standardized** interfaces to databases formalized at high levels.

With the Internet, the end-of-the-line for electronic information is in our office, home, or mobile unit. We have a standard user interface toolkit for all applications with the Web. As seen in Chapter 39, on the server side it is quite simple to open a database system to the Internet. On the client side, no additional installation of hardware and software is necessary, since the customer uses his Internet connection and standard Web browser.

Note that this is a somewhat different application of the Web than was envisioned in the beginning. When we use the Web to connect to a banking or travel agency system, the basic ideas of the early Web: open to all, everyone are invited to be both readers and writers, hypertext as an important ingredient, are no longer important issues. The Web standards, HTML and HTTP, now have a role only for implementation of the user interface. Beyond this point, we are in the realm of the application. This has the advantage that the formalization level within each application can be much higher than on the Web. As we have seen, the banking system "understands" concepts such as account, balance, and interest, allowing us to perform high-level operations using these concepts from the terminal in the customer's home.

In this chapter, I discuss the effect of such a personal terminal with respect to services that are completely symbolic (that is, those in which the complete transaction can be performed on the Internet). There is no lack of these application areas within our modern society: banking, insurance, stock market, and booking tickets, to name a few.

45.1 Retail banking

The advantages of offering customers access to their own records can be enormous. A retail bank, for example, may process millions of transactions each day. Some of these transactions originate on paper (checks, deposit notes, letters, fax), or orally, for example, when the customer provides transaction data to a cashier over the telephone or by a personal visit to the bank. Entering these data in the bank computer system is a major effort, especially as care has to be taken to ensure correctness.

The **Internet bank** permits the customer to do the job on his own equipment, letting him pay for the connection. With the Internet the computer is the bank. Due to the high formalization level, most operations can be performed automatically.

Internet banking may be offered as an alternative service to traditional banking, or by new banks that base all their contact with customers on electronic services. These banks try to offer a full suite of functions, similar to traditional banks. Personal contact with customers is through e-mail, chat systems, or by telephone. Paper is used only when required by law (for example, for the initial account setup contract). Customers access their accounts directly, using the Web as an interface to the banking system. They perform their own transactions, check balance, pay bills, print account statements, and so forth.

An Internet bank does not need branch offices, human tellers, cash or check handling, or printing and mailing of statements. In fact, the daily operations of an Internet bank are in many ways just a computer, a server. The customers themselves have replaced the tellers; the branch offices are replaced by the customer's home and office. Customers use their own hardware and software to access the bank system. They pay their own communication fees. Since the customers themselves handle the manual part, all other services can be performed automatically by the banking software. Thus Internet banks can (should) offer higher interest and lower fees.

But there are also additional advantages for the customers. They can access their accounts 24 hours a day, 7 days a week, 365 days a year. The bank site is available from everywhere, even mobile phones. If all transactions are electronic, that is, no checks or other paper in the system, the account balance will always be updated. All bills entered into the system will be paid on their due date, and the system can provide an overview of upcoming payments. An additional advantage of removing paper from the system is that the customer no longer has to archive manual transaction records. Instead, all historical data are available from the Web interface, in the customary chronological presentation or, for example, presented by addressee. With a button click, the customer can get a list of all transactions regarding the credit card company or any other institution or account. Earlier the customer had to do this himself, by going through a large number of printed bank statements.

The disadvantage of electronic banking is that the customer needs Internet access and the skills to perform the functions and do all the keying themselves. However, banking functions are formalized to a high degree, and with good user interfaces most people will be able to do this with ease. The data needed is minimal, such as amounts and account numbers, so keying is limited. As these services evolve, the need to key in data, such as bills, will be greatly reduced. Regular bills, for example, utility bills, can be entered for automatic payment, where the bill will be paid on the due date if the system is not told otherwise. Other requests for payment can be sent to the customer as an e-mail message and as an electronic record to the banking system. When the customer accesses the banking system to pay the bill, all data will be available so that the bill can be paid just by a confirmation, for example, by checking off the box next to the bill.

While a pure Internet bank is just a computer, in practice some personal services are needed to handle special cases. For example, when the customer has technical problems, when he does not understand the interface, or when the interface does not provide the functionality that the user requires. The pure Internet bank tries to handle these exceptions by providing customer service through telephone, chat, and e-mail. But this affects costs and the interest rates and fees that the bank can offer. The business model really requires that personal service be offered only for exceptions. Therefore, it is important that the bank monitor all personal requests to see which of these may be handled by an improved or extended user interface. In this way, similar requests may be avoided in the future.

This is not always possible. In principle, Internet banks use a cash-free model in which all transactions are completed electronically. But, even though plastic is replacing paper money for many transactions, cash is still more convenient in some situations. Cash withdrawals are handled by cash-back services when using the plastic card in a store, or by ATM machines. However, pure Internet banks, without physical offices, cannot easily offer the opposite service, inserting large amounts of cash into an account.[1] These banks may not be a good alternative for customers who are paid in cash, such as a newsstand agent.

An Internet bank may offer checks, but this violates the all-electronic business model and requires new channels between the bank and its customers, and between the receiver of the checks and the bank. Some countries, such as Norway, have a bank infrastructure that makes it easy to establish Internet banks. In Norway, checks are the exception: All bills are paid with bank-to-bank transfers using a nationwide system. Today, the Internet is the most common way of paying bills in Norway; handling 98 percent of the volume. Costs are an important

A pure Internet bank is just a computer.

Internet banks need a good **infrastructure** of internationally and nationally unique account numbers and simple cash-free payment systems. In addition, the proliferation of PCs with Internet connections needs to be high if large market shares are to be had.

issue here. The average transaction fee for paying a bill on the Internet is approximately three cents, compared with an average of sixty cents for paper-initiated transactions. With even higher transaction volumes, Internet-based solutions will be even more cost effective.

In many ways, this is an identical situation to the transportation example used in Chapter 4 on formalization. As discussed, the metro system must be formalized to a higher degree before a computer could replace the driver. Internet banks face the same situation since their business model needs a world where the formalizations are in place for all or most economic transactions to be performed electronically.

In this respect small countries may have an advantage since it is easier to agree on and establish national systems and standards, for example, for account numbers and bank-to-bank transactions. Such a formalized infrastructure, often established long before the Internet, can provide the foundation for an efficient all-electronic system, independent of cash and checks. With such a system, all deposits are made electronically as bank-to-bank transfers. Bills can be paid the same way, by an electronic transfer directly to the recipient's account—independent of his choice of bank. Start-up online banks also may find it easier to establish trust in small, homogeneous countries.

It is interesting to see that while some countries are well into the digital economy, others are lagging behind. Iceland and Norway are examples of the former. Here, nearly all transactions are electronic, Internet banking is the norm, all businesses accept card payments, and banks are closing their branch offices or turning them into cash-free offices. The US can be used as an example of the latter. Here, checks are still common and many banks have expanded the number of branch offices.[2] However, while a transaction costs just a few cents in Norway[3] on average, it is much higher in the US.[4] This gives the "Internet countries" a clear strategic advantage, similar to that gained by those countries that were among the first to develop good railway systems in the 19th century.

The "Internet countries" get a clear and strategic advantage, similar to the advantage gained by the countries that were among the first to develop good railway systems in the 19th century.

However, undoubtedly, the Internet soon will become the most-used medium for bank transactions in most countries. The advantages of online banking are so great that they will remove nearly any barrier.

The impact on society of a nationwide system for electronic payments is interesting to consider. Experience from Iceland

and Norway, shows that credit and debit cards are used also for quite small amounts. When point-of-sale terminals are in place and connected to the Internet, the cost of yet another transaction is minimal. Other systems are established that reduce the need for cash. For example, paper tickets for everything from a bus to a movie are being replaced by passes that can be paid by credit card. Several systems for "electronic cash" also have been proposed that can handle micropayments with a minimum of transaction overhead. Some of these systems require a new infrastructure of "smart cards," while others are based on the Internet or on mobile phones. (I return to the cash-free society in Part 9.)

The Internet-based pay services are ideal for transactions that originate on the Internet, where all the data needed are already in electronic form. Mobile phone based services can replace cash in many other situations, for example, to put a bottle of cola from a vending machine on your telephone bill by calling a number or sending a text message. The technology developed for electronic highway toll passes, based on radio transponders, also can be used as a basis for other payments, such as entrance to sport activities or bus tickets. A mobile phone can also be used as a very inexpensive point-of-sale terminal by attaching a small device that can read a credit card.

It may no longer be possible to create **revenue** just by providing basic retail banking services.

Some Internet banks try to create additional profit by selling other services, ranging from investment offers to travel packages, on their Web sites. This is viewed as an important business model for retail banks, as the possibilities of generating revenue on the traditional banking services decrease with increased automation. However, this business model may not be valid. Internet banks are used in a different manner than traditional banks. In an all-electronic world, it is so much simpler to set up an automatic bill payment system. For example, instead of having to pay a bill on the due date, the Internet bank can be told to perform this transaction automatically, if the customer does not interfere. Customers can still check their bills by going through the data provided in an e-mail, but in the normal situation, the customer will have no need to access the banking portal. Already, with the services that an Internet bank offers for automatic payments, most personal transactions can be handled automatically. The day of the complete automatic banking system may not be very far off, even if there will always be the odd bill that has to be entered manually.

In many ways, an Internet bank is **more secure** than a brick and mortar bank. While it is still possible to break in, electronic money can be traced more easily than physical money.

Trust is important in all banking. While traditional banks can rely on their long standing and can express solidity through their buildings, an Internet bank must find different ways of promoting trust, such as by providing reliable, good, and secure service. In many countries, the state guarantees deposits up to a given amount, which clearly has an impact in promoting new bank services.

Security is an important issue in these pioneering days of the Web. In the brick-and-mortar world, security is implemented with ID cards, guards, surveillance cameras, and locks. On the Web, users identify themselves with PIN codes, often also by additional codes from special paper cards or password calculators. The client computer can be identified by using certificates provided by the bank and downloaded to the client, and the communication itself can go over the more secure HTTPS channel, where data is coded using advanced cryptographic techniques. In many ways, these practices make Web banking more secure than traditional banking, where it is difficult, in practice, to check signatures. In traditional banks, an attack may be in the form of a forged check, unauthorized access to an account, or a physical attack in a branch office, but online, a hacker may attack the whole Internet bank, perhaps gaining access to a large number of accounts. In the worst case, this may cause the downfall of the bank. However, it seems that the banks have managed to implement the necessary security level. At least Internet banks have managed to avoid the serious consequences of the crimes that follow all other banking services—bank robbery, check forgery, credit card swindle,[5] and ATM break-in—at least for now.

Both in the physical and virtual world, a balance exists between security and convenience. Too many, too long, or too frequent changes of passwords are inconvenient, and may be counterproductive in the sense that we have to write them down to remember. Therefore, some banks rely on just a four-digit PIN code for access, which gives hackers a 1/10000 probability of gaining access to the account for each attempt. Is this secure enough? For example, let us assume that this book will get ten thousand readers, and that each one has two different PIN codes. If I guess that one of these codes is 6753, at least a couple readers should cry out: "How did you know that?" Or, in other words, the chances of "winning" are ever so much greater than in a state lottery.[6]

If a customer is concerned about **security**, why not offer a more secure system, personalized to the customer's needs?

Today, most Internet banks try to mimic the services offered by brick and mortar banks. However, as Amazon has shown for bookstores, there are many **new services** that can be provided on the Internet.

Perhaps each individual customer can better determine this balance between security and convenience than the banks (that is, banks should allow for customized security in the same way as a browser allows us to set the security level). For example, we can set up the browser to disallow scripts, cookies, or Java applets. Similarly, we should be allowed to specify that our bank account should be accessed only from the office or home computer; that a certificate downloaded to a new computer should not be active before we have given an e-mail confirmation; or that we want to provide an additional password for transfer of large amounts. Customized security recognizes that customers are different. While students may access the bank from many computers, some of us use only an office or home computer. Students often have small amounts in their accounts, but people in regular jobs may have larger amounts available. Of course, the bank has to require a minimum-security level, but if we can reduce the risk of an attack, and the hassle that follows, without any inconvenience at all, why shouldn't we have this option of customizing our own risk management?

Banks are conservative institutions. Even Internet banks that rely on new technology for their services have not implemented many of the new services that online information makes possible, that is, to work as "information banks," providing new information-based services for their customers as a replacement of the old cash-based services. These could be as simple as organizing and printing existing information, or more dramatically, using this information to act on the customer's behalf. For example, while businesses are required to have full accounting, few consumers are willing to spend the work needed, even if most of us would be interested to see an account of last year's income and expenditures. If we agree to use the bank account and accompanying credit or debit cards for a substantial part of our expenses, allowing the bank to retrieve information on what we bought from point-of-sale terminals and bills, such a full account could be made automatically. The same data also could be used as a basis for next year's budget, perhaps provided by the bank in the form of a spreadsheet so that we could adjust the numbers ourselves.

With additional data, a good banking service—or perhaps we should call it the automatic financial advisor—should be able to give us recommendations for how we could save money next year. For example:

- Save $234/year by changing utility companies.
- Change to a different account type and get higher interest rates.
- A customer card could have given us a $56 rebate on the five overnights we had at Hilton hotels last year.
- Credit card interest amounted to $1,260, with an average rate of 7 percent. Consider a second mortgage loan instead, with savings of up to $200.
- You had three visits to the Science Center, with a total of $290 in entrance fees. Consider a family membership that gives unlimited access for $110, of which $98 is tax deductible.

The bank could take an even more active role. For example, we could instruct our bank to find the best deal for utilities, let the bank automatically order preferred customer's rebates on travel, and bargain on our behalf for goods that we need. The banks will be in a good position to offer such services since they have the necessary data and the contact points both with customers and companies. But it is important that they are trusted.

To offer such services the bank needs information that will raise privacy issues. However, where we have earlier trusted banks with our money, we now have to trust that the bank will guard this information and not let it be used to our disadvantage. Today, we expect that the bank will compute interest rates correctly. Few take the time to check these calculations. In the same way, we may trust the bank to provide the services mentioned above in the future, for example, expecting that the bank will offer us the best utility contract.

As the standard retail banking functions are replaced by a computer, making it more difficult to get high revenues on these functions, banks will need these additional services to survive in the retail market. The futuristic Internet-based banks will still be in the trust business, but only parts of the bits on their disks may represent money.

45.2   Travel information and booking

Travel agency functions such as information and booking are in many ways another ideal e-business application. Static information, in the form of text, images, maps, and video can be presented over the open Web at low cost, using all the Web fea-

Booking is the ideal computer application: Data is formalized to a high level and there is a need for fast and continuous updates.

tures including hypertext links. As we have seen, this can be combined with dynamic information, giving the customer updated information on availability and prices, and finally, the customer can perform the actual booking herself using the Web as a database interface. I used booking as a case in Chapter 20 (on flexible user interfaces). Here we shall go deeper into the booking process itself.

Simplified and less expensive bookings are a necessity for hotels and airlines, which are in the strange situation that the cost of selling is often inversely correlated to the price of the product. For example, a full-price airline ticket can be processed in a very short time, as the customer usually will have exact data on her plans and there normally will not be a problem of availability. But for bargain tickets, several conditions have to be met, and bargain tickets are often used for leisure travel, where there may be many options for dates, times, and locations. Combined with limited availability, selling these tickets may involve a prolonged conversation with the customer, until the right flights are found. Therefore, the Web must seem to be a godsend to airlines, or perhaps it is the Web that has made cheap flights possible. At least Web sales has offered an opportunity for new airlines, since many of the incumbents tried to hold on to traditional models for selling tickets.

By replacing paper-based tickets, booking can be an **all electronic service**.

In principle, booking is an entirely symbolic service. Plastic cards or reference numbers can easily replace tickets and vouchers, and the whole booking transaction can then be performed via the Internet. Removing paper tickets has, of course, other advantages. Electronic media not only makes all the paper-oriented functions—such as printing, distributing, counting, and storing—disappear, but they also can provide automated check-in, both at airports and hotels. When a plastic card is used for boarding instead of a paper ticket, the system will know immediately that the passenger has boarded the aircraft. This makes it possible to have updated passenger lists available at all times, also for corporate headquarters. That is, data is available at any time about the actual number of passengers on the planes, where they are going, and what they paid for the ticket, important background information for planning new flights.

Electronic media have the disadvantage that they demand a working network connection, but downloading all bookings from the central hotel or flight reservation system to the actual

Travel data, available dates, flights, schedules are easier to present **visually**, for example, on a Web page, than orally, over a telephone.

hotel reception or boarding gate PC in advance can reduce the risk of failure.

To limit the input needed from the customer, the booking system should adjust to the customer's preferred language, capturing flight patterns of frequent flyers (if any), or allow the customer to enter this information and offering the option of choosing among these defaults, asking only for the date for a trip. Such systems not only offer the advantage of more efficient consumer-to-business communication, but also connect the customer more strongly to the company. The company that has updated and utilized customer data in the best way will have an advantage.

Therefore, travel is one of the major applications of e-business today. We expect all the major hotel chains and airlines to offer full electronic service today. In addition, we find the online travel agencies that give us access to many different service providers. These automatic intermediaries have the advantage that they can send our request to the online booking system of each airline, saving us the time of having to repeat our request to each individual booking system as we try to find the best offer. Some of these intermediaries also may be in the position to give us bargains that cannot be found within each service, for example, with their "block" bookings of hotel rooms and airline seats (similar to brick-and-mortar travel agencies).

The main advantage of online booking for consumers is that the cost of an intermediary is eliminated or reduced because customers perform the data entry themselves. Of course, this is only an advantage if the savings comes down to us in the form of cheaper tickets, not if they are retained as profits in other parts of the value chain. In addition, the Internet may give us faster access than waiting in line for a telephone operator. We also may find, especially in cases where our requests are difficult to fulfill, that the Internet may provide a better overview than we may get over a telephone from a travel agent. For example, an airline Web site can provide us with a calendar, marking the dates of available bargain flights, thus making it easier to find the best alternatives. Of course, if we visit a travel agency, we can get the same information, but we will—one way or another—have to pay for the agent's time. With the Internet we can review alternatives at leisure.

Will the Internet replace the brick-and-mortar travel agencies?

Will the Internet replace the brick-and-mortar travel agencies? To some extent, a large part of their business already has

Many of the services offered by a brick and mortar travel agency are formalized, and can easily be performed by a **customer** with access to the booking systems.

been lost to e-business. However, travel agencies have always competed with direct consumer booking. Calling a hotel or airline directly has always been an option. The question is to what extent does the Internet provide something different? To answer this question, let's consider the brick-and-mortar travel agency. Simplified, this intermediary provides the following services:

1. Advice
2. Information (brochures, schedules, etc.)
3. Booking services
4. Travel insurance
5. Billing

We will consider each of these functions, in reverse order. Previously, billing (5) was an important function for the travel agency. You confirmed your reservation by prepaying, receiving tickets, and hotel vouchers. With the ubiquitous use of credit cards, this service is no longer needed as hotels, rental agencies, and airlines can get a credit card number as a no-show guarantee. However, some customers may feel more protected by offering their credit card to a well-known travel agent than by providing this information via the Internet.

Many credit card companies include travel insurance (4) as a free service when using the card to pay for travel, and to a large extent, year-round insurance has replaced insurance for each trip. In addition, travel insurance can easily be offered over the Web, so this is no longer an important business area for the agencies.

Before the Internet, online access to booking systems (3) used private networks. In practice, access was restricted to heavy users, travel agencies, and perhaps some large enterprises. As consumers, we could access these systems only through intermediaries, such as airlines, hotels, car rentals, or travel agencies. The travel agencies' advantage was that they could access many different booking systems. Today, each and every one of us gets the same functionality, without the travel agency, if we have Internet access. But do-it-yourself is not cost free. Apart from paying for the computer and the Internet service, we "pay" with our time. On the Internet, we do the keying ourselves. Experienced travelers will soon learn the tricks, even if there are discrepancies between various sites. However, cus-

With the Internet and the Web, customers have access to the same data as a travel agency; the access **monopoly** to the booking systems has been broken.

tomers who travel seldom may get better results by letting an experienced travel agent do the job.

The travel agency can give us nice brochures (2) printed on glossy paper, but we can get the same information, with the latest updates, over the Web. With a connection to reservation systems, we can also restrict information to availability—not showing hotels, or flights that are sold out, and showing only discount fares, for example—clearly more convenient than what we can get from the static brochures.

Advice (1) can be given via the Internet, as I discussed in Chapter 20. For example, a good search system will help us find available flights and hotels within our price range, with the facilities we need. This will work as long as our needs can be formalized within the attributes that the search system provides, but will be more problematic if our needs are more open.

Web travel sites, especially with more flexible and customized user interfaces, should have the potential to take a large part of the travel market. For airlines, hotel and rental agencies, their own Web-based booking systems will act as an extension of previous telephone booking systems. However, the applicability of the Internet for these applications, notably the ease of searching and retrieving information, will attract new and larger groups of customers. For companies, such a development will have several advantages: Online booking is cost effective, as the customer herself does all the manual work. With direct booking, the company will avoid paying a percentage to an intermediary, and the increased availability of updated information may make it easier to fill up hotels and flights. Through e-mail, and perhaps through social networks, the companies have a fast channel for a last-minute sale, such as the bargain weekend offers from many airlines. Collecting data on customer profiles or preferences can enhance these sale efforts to the theoretical limit in which all customers who receive an offer also accept the offer. Although this is impossible in practice, the profiles may be used to identify the groups in which the probability of acceptance is highest.

Customers' **preferences** can be used to find the best offer, or to create the products that the customers call for.

However, as customers, we will often have to contact each airline to get information. This is very time consuming and cumbersome, and many may prefer leaving this work to a travel agency. But, today this agency may be an automatic Web-based system. In theory, such a system will be able to find the best deals if it has access to all available information, in the

Control over the **formalized part** the booking system may be more important than control over the physical part.

same way as a traditional brick-and-mortar agency. In practice, the situation may be very different.

Imagine yourself as a marketing director of an airline. Today, brick-and-mortar travel agencies have direct access to your booking system. Should you allow the Web-based agency the same service? Is this just a matter of another agency or could these electronic intermediaries have a greater impact on your business? The difference between a brick-and-mortar and online travel agency is not fundamental: Both offer the same type of services to customers. However, there is a difference in size. While a traditional agency may have a customer base of perhaps ten thousand people, limited by the population of their location, there will be no upper limit to the customer base of a Web-based agency. If a traditional agency favors another airline, this will not have any great influence on your sales, since there will probably be other agencies that favor your company. However, if the successful Web site agency is biased, that may have a major impact.

Therefore, a requirement will be that the Web system does not present your flights in any unfavorable way, for example, presenting competitors' flights before your own. But, even if fairness can be guaranteed, is that what you want? A Web-based agency with access to all booking systems will be able to present the customer with the best deal. For many of us, this implies the cheapest fare. In principle, customers will be able to obtain "best fare" price through traditional systems, either using the telephone or a traditional travel agency. If the telephone is used, all airlines must be called to fulfill the information need. In such a situation, many accept the first "reasonable" offer, knowing that further calling will take time and that the first offer may not be available later. Similarly, a human travel agent may not be willing to do much work to find a ticket that gives the customer an even lower price.

So here, as in other sectors of life, the first "reasonable" deal is accepted. But the computer can do an extensive search and find the lowest price, which creates a very different marketplace from what we have in the physical world. For example, if Web travel sites become successful and a large percentage of all flight bookings is channeled through these systems, the way will be opened for new low-cost airlines, as their bargain offers will come up first in any price-based rankings. Such a system will remove a major hindrance for these start-up com-

General, all inclusive, booking systems can be a threat to the core part of an airline, as it becomes easier to compare prices.

Price competition can be handled by making offers more **open**, less closed and formalized, for example, by frequent flier programs, different service levels, and so on.

panies—the struggle to be seen in the market and have customers evaluating their offers.

Established airlines can meet this potential competition by offering better service, frequent flyer programs, and other offers that complicate the search for the best deal—and, they can try to ensure that Web sites cannot find the best offer. This can be done by not offering access to their own booking systems to Web-based travel agencies, by offering limited access, by limiting the best deals to their own systems, and so forth. In this way, they may force the market and the customers to use their own systems, and create a situation in which we return to accepting the first "reasonable" deal.

While the functionality of individual airline booking systems may be as good as what we can get from online travel agencies (apart from price competition), when the trip can be confined to one airline only, these systems will be too limited if the trip involves many legs with flights offered by different airlines. Travelers usually want through-tickets that name all the different legs of a trip, for the convenience's sake. Therefore, a system that includes several airlines is needed. Is this a market opening for the online travel agencies? Possibly, but the airlines are meeting this challenge with mergers and alliances. By interconnecting the different booking systems, or offering a centralized system for the whole alliance, the group can offer the same, perhaps better functionality as a travel agency, while keeping competition under control. Consumers are offered frequent flyer mileage on all flights of participating airlines, to ensure customer loyalty to the alliance (or their booking system). That is, these companies will try to capture the customer at the earliest possible moment. Getting the customers to use their Web site and booking system will be as important as getting them on the plane.

Interestingly, most hotels are included in the general booking sites. It is probably too difficult to try to exist outside of these sites, perhaps only a real possibility for small hotels that have a loyal customer base. Of course, when sites include most hotels, more and more customers will start their booking there, making it even more important to be covered by the sites. Airlines and their alliances may be stronger than hotels or hotel chains, especially within their "home areas," but in the long run, we should expect a similar development here—existing outside of the general booking sites will be difficult.

This will have consequences for marketing. There will be little point in marketing hotel chains, airlines, or car rental agencies if all customers go to the Web, indicate their preferences, and then choose from the returned list based on the information offered and additional data, such as customer reviews. That is, there is a danger that many of these products will become commodities.

Notes

1   Some ATM machines also can accept cash, using the same technology as gas stations and other merchants have used to scan paper bills and detect coins.

2   See The Economist, Special report on international banking, May 19th 2012.

3   Norges Bank (2012) Årsrapport om betalingssystem 2011 (in Norwegian).

4   See Stiglitz, Joseph (2010) Freefall: America, Free Markets, and the Sinking of the World Economy, W.W. Norton & Company, New York.

5   Here criminals have been able to use new technology to copy cards and to get PIN codes, the latter often by the use of a hidden camera. This has forced credit card companies and banks to replace the simple magnet stripe cards of today with smarter cards that have a small computer on board.

6   Many banks use special password calculators that generate six- or eight-digit access codes. These reduce the risk of unauthorized access, but require that the user have access to the calculator when she wants to use the online system.

46 Long Tail

With very cheap storage space on computer disks there is **no practical limit** to what can be stocked of digital products.

If you own a physical store, you will have limited place for storing products. To do business, you will try to stock the stores with products that sell—in high numbers, you hope. Clearly you will stock all "hits" and popular items. To offer a reasonable range you will offer other products as well, but always products that you will expect to sell in some numbers. The cost of taking in more marginal products is high. They take up storage space, and there is the risk that these must be sold at a discount, or that they never will be sold. That is, in practice, the demand curve for physical products is cut off by what a physical store can stock.

But we face a very different situation for symbolic products that are digitalized. With very cheap storage space on computer disks, and with simple processes of storing and disseminating products, there is no practical limit to what can be stocked. Chris Anderson called this the "long tail" in an article in *Wired* and also in a popular book.[1]

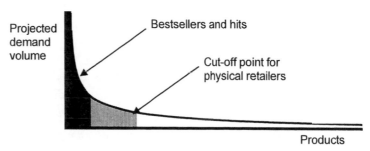

Figure 46.1 Long tail—there is no cut-off in the digital world.

As a retailer, you will have an idea of projected demand, or sales if you want, as shown in Figure 46.1 above. You will have a number of best sellers or hits that sell in high volumes (the black area), and then products that are expected to sell less but that you will store to offer a reasonable range (the grey area). The physical and economical constraints define a cut-off point. Therefore, an ordinary physical store cannot serve the latent demand, the white area shown to the right of the cut-off point.

For example, a music shop may carry around a thousand CDs; the largest stores, perhaps as many as five thousand. But online, Spotify, can offer nearly twenty million songs (2012),

The volume of the **latent demand** may run into high numbers, and when costs are low, this part of the demand curve can also generate a profit.

approximately two million CDs. The same is true for all other online music services: They have an inventory many times larger than any ordinary physical store.

Carrying inventory is one thing, but will these "long time items" sell? Using the online music service Rhapsody as a case, Anderson showed that even the track ranked number eight-hundred thousand, still has a number of downloads each year. That is, the volume of the latent demand (Figure 46.1) may run into high numbers, and when costs are low, this part of the demand curve can also generate a profit.

With books, large physical retailers such as Amazon can handle parts of the "tail" market by reducing costs of storage and by selling to the whole world. Amazon also has a print-on-demand solution, with which out-of-stock books can be printed and bound for each customer. But this is quite an expensive solution. Of course, the future for Amazon is selling books as digital files. That is, sometime in the future, Amazon will become a true long-tail retailer.

Chris Anderson offered movies as another example. Every night a theater will try to sell as many seats as possible, limited by the number of persons who:

1. Are interested in seeing the film
2. Live within reasonable driving distance
3. Are willing to pay for the show
4. Have time the night the film is showing
5. Make the decision to go

Reasonable enough; to get an audience, the theater owner will have to choose films that many of his customers want to see. That is, to have an audience left after point 5 above, point 1 must define a high number.

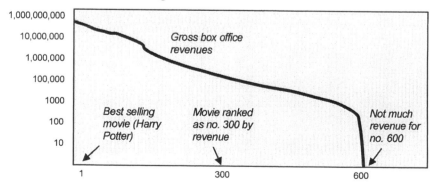

Figure 46.2 Hollywood box office gross (03.20.11–03.18.12).

Figure 46.2 presents a year of Hollywood box office revenues from theaters.[2] The gross is presented in a logarithmic scale, and movies are ranked according to gross income. The best-selling movie, number one on the graph above (*Harry Potter*) generated a gross of $381,011,219, while the last ranked movie (number 609) generated only $252. What we see is that there seems to be a cut-off point. The revenue curve drops dramatically after 600 movies.

However, there are many more interesting movies than these six hundred, and, based on interest, there is absolutely no reason for any drop in demand at this rank. The drop simply explains that theater owners have to make the hard economical decisions, but this drop will disappear as movies go electronic. Today streaming services for movies are limited, but with more bandwidth, we are likely to see a very different demand curve, a more natural curve that continues into the right side of Figure 46.2.

Nearly everything—every book, CD, or movie—may have a demand, but the problem is marketing. How can we find the customers? Marketing is not a problem for potential hits or best sellers. A new album from a famous performer, a new book from a well-known author, or a new movie with top actors will always get attention. In addition, sales or forecasted sales may be so high that the product can afford a large marketing budget (as with the Harry Potter movies). But what about products that cannot draw media attention and do not have huge marketing budgets?

The answer is the Internet where there are many opportunities:

- Using *search engines* to find the product. For example, a customer interested in folk music from Norway may search Spotify with these terms.
- Tell customers about the product on *blogs and social services*. If you tell your friends and they tell their friends, the news will spread.
- *Connections*. For example, nearly all Internet shops have features such as "frequently bought together" and "customers who bought this item also bought." In this way, hits can point customers to similar, but less well-known products.
- *Mailing lists*. By maintaining a customer profile based on previous contacts, a company can use

> Nearly everything—every book, CD, or movie—may have a demand, but the problem is marketing. How can we find the **customers**?

e-mail to promote products expected to be of interest. (However, this marketing should not be overdone. If these messages are seen as spam, customers may block all of these.)

Of these, connections are perhaps the most important. Anderson cited two books as examples: *Into Thin Air* and *Touching the Void.* Joe Simpson's 1988 book, *Touching the Void*, which described a dramatic climbing expedition in the Andes Mountains, received good reviews and sold reasonably well. However, *Into Thin Air* drew tremendous attention and became an international best seller. The author, Jon Krakauer, described a disaster on Mount Everest in 1996 in which eight climbers died. After Amazon connected the two books through its recommendation system, the ten-year-old *Touching the Void* also became a bestseller, even outselling *Into Thin Air*. That is, in a world of an abundance of products, recommendation systems become important. These systems may be in the form cited here, "frequently bought together," or in a more advanced form that considers individual preferences (an example was presented in Chapter 43.4).

Can we get long-tail effects also for physical products?

Can we get long-tail effects also for physical products? Of course, the problem is higher costs for large physical inventories. However, the Internet may open a very large market with a demand for nearly every product. Amazon has millions of books in storage and some companies that rent DVDs also have huge inventories, in large, central facilities with effective logistics. However, eBay offers millions of products without any storage facilities at all, because eBay is just an administrative solution—marketing and sales for millions of retailers.

Even with physical products, marketing is nearly always symbolic and digital. Newspaper and TV advertisements and printed brochures must be directed toward the main customer groups. But, as eBay and similar sites indicate, marketing on the Internet can be targeted toward quite small groups.

As an example, consider the Hurtigruten,[3] a costal steamer that traverses the Norwegian coast from Bergen to Kirkenes. Each day a ship will leave Bergen for the eleven-day round-trip. The steamer, which has a two-hundred-year history, has changed from an important transport solution for coastal communities to mainly a tourist attraction. Advertisements and brochures are, naturally enough, directed toward the mainstream market—selling the cruise, Norwegian fjords, and the midnight sun. However, with a good booking system, the Web can be used to market cruises toward small groups. For example, by connecting to hotels, guides, boat rentals, and local attractions, packages could be offered, such as cruise and deep-sea fishing, cruise and skiing, cruise and mountaineering, or cruise and museums. With good infrastructure, such packages could be put together in a couple of hours, including a Web presentation. An advantage of attracting many small groups is that the season will be extended. For example, winter is the best time for deep-sea fishing, when there is a lot of spare cruise capacity.

That is, even if the product is physical, as with a cruise, the administration and marketing are symbolic and can exploit the long-tail effects.

Notes

1   Anderson, Chris (2004) "The Long Tail" *Wired*, October and Anderson, Chris (2006) The Long Tail: Why the Future of Business is Selling Less of More. New York, NY: Hyperion. ISBN 1-4013-0237-8.

2   www.boxofficemojo.com

3   www.hurtigruten.no

47 Online Retail Shopping, Physical Items

Online shopping is one of the most profiled applications on the Web. The idea of shopping from home is not new, of course, as catalog sales have a long history.[1] Web advocates may not like a comparison with the very profane catalog market, but the basics are similar:

- shopping from a "catalog"
- submitting an order
- waiting for the goods to arrive

The difference is not in the principles, but in the implementation. Here the Web has several advantages. The Web allows for a more comprehensive product description than a paper catalog. A Web site is highly "updatable," in contrast to a catalog printed in huge numbers. The ability to update not only allows the store to introduce new items and remove sold-out items, but also provides the customer with detailed information on availability, if the Web system has a direct link to the underlying inventory systems. The dynamic nature of the media also allows the supplier to introduce dynamic pricing—giving a discount where sales are lower than expected or when there is additional packing capacity—all the way up the value chain.

The possibility of having an updated catalog at all times simplifies both marketing and logistics. While a catalog company must keep large stock and a steady supply of items, demand and supply can be better adjusted on the Web. Stock can be reduced to a minimum by providing customers with a date of availability. Sales may go down if the customer has to wait for a shipment, but as long as the products are delivered within the promised date, complaints may be avoided.

Some Web companies do not have their own warehouses. Customer orders can be directed electronically to suppliers that produce on demand or stock items. That is, the highly dynamic Web medium and electronic ordering allow for very flexible supply policies.

However, using the Web has a few disadvantages compared with catalog sales. The customers need Internet access, and they need a reasonable bandwidth to be able to browse the site and view product information presented as pictures, video clips, and so on. Customers also need the skill to find products

The Web makes it possible to create **virtual industries** that, at the extreme, may consist of only a computer program. This program can maintain a Web portal and communicate with other virtual and physical industries.

of interest and to place orders. Younger customers may have these skills, but many elderly people often find traditional catalog sites convenient and may have problems using the Web.

From a marketing viewpoint, the Web has the disadvantage that the *activation* is up to the user. A traditional catalog company can generate interest by mailing a catalog, but the Web site will have to wait until the customer accesses the site or will have to try to generate interest in other ways, such as by sending e-mail messages to the customer, posting banner ads on other sites, or sponsoring links on search engines. Some Web sites even present part of their product spectrum in paper catalogs, illustrating these disadvantages of the Web.

The most interesting question is not how Web sites will compete with traditional catalog sales (most catalog companies also offer Web access), but to what extent the Web will compete with brick-and-mortar stores. Although some of the initial enthusiasm for the Web has rubbed off and many have learned the hard way that changing customer habits is difficult, the Web has the possibility of being an alternative sales channel to physical stores. As we have experienced, there is no magic to the Web. Yes, the interface to the customers may be somewhat different from a brick-and-mortar store, but many of the other functions, such as making good deals with manufacturers and maintaining a good logistics system, are identical.

The online store will need even better logistics systems than brick-and-mortar stores. While both stores need to keep track of inventory, when the brick and mortar runs out of an item, it cannot sell that product. But an online store that lacks a close connection between stock and the catalogs may continue selling long after the last item disappears. Even if the catalogs show the number in stock for each item, a discrepancy may result in the customer buying what the store does not have.

While the brick-and-mortar store leaves the problem of transporting the products on the "last mile" to the customer, letting her negotiate rush-hour traffic on her way home, distribution will be the headache for the online store. Many have learned that a promise of delivery before Christmas is not easy to fulfill for an order taken on the 10th of December. These problems have to be solved to keep customers satisfied. In addition, the online store, like any other store, has to streamline its processes and reduce costs. The bottom line is to maximize profit (to generate revenues through efficient sales and minimize the cost of order fulfillment).

Where shopping can be **formalized** as:

- Select product
- Find best price
- Order
- Pay

the online stores will have a great future.

Personal cars have had a profound impact on the retail marketplace, even to the extent of changing cities, replacing active downtown areas with out-of-city malls. With the Internet the marketplace has expanded to a **global** level. Will this have a similar impact?

In theory, the Internet and Web provides a global **marketplace**. In practice it may be more local, especially when physical goods are involved.

In the physical world, there are some practical limits to how far the customer will travel to shop; the Web is a global marketplace in which the competitor is only "a click away." To some extent this is a new situation, but companies earlier have learned to live under very similar conditions. In the physical world, the competition may be next door or may be reached by a different telephone number. Before personal transportation, we had every variety of shop in the neighborhood. But cars made it practical to shop in a larger area. Did this increase competition? Initially, yes, but the car has transformed cities: There are no longer an abundance of similar shops within easy driving distance, and in many areas there may be only one store or mall. That is, we may still use the one grocer in the neighborhood, but that grocer is no longer a small shop on the corner, but a supermarket that serves a much larger area. As before, if this grocer does not serve us well, we may go to the competition, even if they may be farther away.

We may see a similar development on the Web, where businesses have to adjust to a virtual world in which communication goes at the speed of light. For entirely symbolic applications, with input and output in the form of bits, the marketplace can be the world, although regulations, currencies, taxation, and so on may impose restrictions for some applications, such as banking. For businesses that have a physical part, for example, product delivery, there may be practical limitations as to how far off we can go. Still, the Internet widens the size of the practical market. Where we previously had a choice of a few local bookstores, we now can choose between an abundance of stores offering Internet service. In the long run, we should expect a similar development as with local shops: Some will disappear and that others will expand. This may even go faster on the Internet where expansion is much easier and, in many ways, independent of physical factors.

While most businesses accept some form of competition, too much competition may affect profitability. To avoid such a situation, businesses have a variety of devices that diminish direct competition:

- *Differentiation.* Concentrating on a narrower market segment, for example, parts for veteran cars.

- Different *product specter*, but also variations on models and packaging. A product found in one store may not exactly match a product in another.

It is important that existing customers find it simpler to return than to go to a competitor. One way to achieve this is to retain all data on the **customer**.

- Different *service level*, from personal service to do-it-yourself.

- Different *store layout*, making shopping easier for the customer in a store that she knows. On the Internet the user will operate faster with a well-known interface.

- Proprietary *charge cards*, so that returning to this store may represent a savings.

- Retaining *customer data*, making it more convenient to shop from a store that has all details of names, addresses, and so on.

- The use of *sales, coupons, charge card rebates*, and time-dependent pricing to make direct price comparisons difficult.

- *Mailing of coupons* and special offers to customers.

Both brick-and-mortar stores and those on the Internet use these measures, but to differing degrees. On the Web, it may be more difficult to have a distinctive product specter than in a physical store, as the customer is less able to examine and try out the product. But methods such as dynamic pricing, customized offers, special (and customized) store layout, are often easier to implement on the Web than in the physical world.

According to Porter's generic competitive strategies,[2] a would-be competitor should go for cost leadership (lower costs, broad targets) or differentiation (narrower targets). The problem on the Web is that the incumbents try to use both of these strategies at the same time; they offer lower prices for hits, and at the same time, they are open for high diversity. While this would be a difficult strategy in the real world, it may be possible on the Web where automation makes it easier to handle diverse customer groups.

The retail landscape online may mirror that in the physical world. Larger stores will have their own locations, using a well-known name (URL). Smaller stores may be organized in "malls" (found within portals and marketplaces), both Amazon and eBay may be used as examples. Since trust is a strong issue on the Internet, these marketplaces should be somewhat more than just a collection of businesses. For example, the portal should be able to give some guarantee concerning the solidity of each store and payments should be processed through the portal.

47.1 Web advantages

An important task for an online store is to **formalize products** through exact descriptions. This may be easier for some products than for others.

The main advantage for the Web customer is that the Web offers shopping independent of time and, to some degree, independent of distance. A Web site can be accessed from any place in the world, twenty-four hours a day, every day of the year. For companies, the advantages are that they do not have to maintain expensive stores and that the degree of automation can be higher on the Web than in the physical world.

An online store provides product information that is *searchable*, which becomes useful when the collections are large or when product identifiers are formalized. Books are an ideal example. For other types of products, searching may be more difficult. Clothes may be described by general keywords, for example, by function (pants), material (cotton), users (men, women, and children), type (jeans), producer (Levi), and so on, but such searches cannot be used to pinpoint a certain product. Toys are in the same category, but here we may have an even greater discrepancy between the "need" and a formalized description of keywords. A fun birthday present for five-year-old John is not easy to form into search terms.

When searching breaks down, *browsing* is an option. The Web supports browsing by hyperlinks, menus, and navigation buttons. Since the whole idea of browsing is to retrieve, scan, and move on to other pages, a reasonably fast Internet connection is needed. If not, long download times will disrupt the whole process.

We have seen that several sites use customer input as a part of the information provided.

We have seen that several sites use *customer input* as a part of the information provided. Amazon and other sites provide customer ratings and reviews. You can e-mail a friend ("Thought you'd be interested in this item.") and see which groups bought a book, or browse the list of "customers who bought this book also bought." There is also the possibility of publishing a wish list, suggesting the kind of gifts that would be welcome for an upcoming event. Some stores even allow a customer to roam their physical store with a scanner, registering product codes. These are then stored on the Web as a gift list for an upcoming birthday, marriage, or other event.

Web ordering is more convenient both for the customer and the supplier than telephone, ordinary mail, or fax. On the customer side, errors are avoided by directly moving items into a "shopping cart." This provides the customer with a readable list of items, prices, and totals. On the supplier side, the main advantage is that the customer provides his order list in electronic format, with the correct item identifiers, and so forth. Thus the order can be passed along on the supply chain without human interference. The items ordered can immediately be withdrawn from numbers in stock, so that the next customer will get updated information on availability.

47.2   Web disadvantages

When **shopping** is something more than just buying a product, that is, if there are open parts ("shopping as an experience"), the online store may not be a good alternative.

On the Web, the customer has to rely on a description of a physical product, with no possibility of holding, feeling, trying, or testing. The physical store allows the customer to buy the item that she has picked up; the Web site will send her a copy of the product described. Web stores are restricted by the screen size; the physical store has a 3D world in which to display products—a simple storage space, a warehouse where goods are stacked on the floor, in an attempt to satisfy customer needs with as low overhead as possible. A quite different philosophy is to sell *shopping as an experience*. A mall may try to capture customers with luxurious surroundings, not only displaying products to their full advantage, but also adding atmosphere with gardens, fountains, and perhaps someone playing the piano.

The online store may compete with the "warehouse" model, as an online store does not have to take up space with huge piles of physical products. Shopping as an experience is much more difficult to implement on the Web than in the physical world, where so many more channels to the customer are available.

Of course, the customer may use the physical store to find a product and then buy it on the Web to save money. But this is perhaps more a theoretical than a practical possibility in the long run. The convenience of buying the product right there in the physical store will be overwhelming. The customer will have no guarantee that she will find the same product on the Web. In addition, if this situation becomes a problem, we can expect to see different product spectra in the physical and virtual world, since brick-and-mortar stores cannot survive as display spaces for Web stores.

Physical products must be **distributed** to customers, which can be a severe problem for online stores.

For many products, the Web may not offer a clear price advantage. Even with savings in employees and rental space, the distribution phase of online shopping is very expensive. Instead of mailing twenty-five TVs to a store, the distributor has to mail one TV to twenty-five customers. The Internet does not support the transportation phase to any great extent. A computer system can print labels, do some sorting, give information on the location of the package, and generate an e-mail when the package has arrived, but the most expensive parts are in physical transportation. Online stores are learning the hard way that not all sales generate profits. Unwieldy, bulky, or fragile items are expensive to stock, pack, and send—so expensive that the loss on each sale may be significant. Other products may be so difficult to assemble that they put a heavy demand on customer service. When the call of the day is profit instead of market share, online stores will remove these items from their catalogs.

A physical location in a mall or at a busy street corner may be expensive, but location also is a way to market the store. Online stores have to take some of these expenses with additional marketing—buying ads on TV, radio and in newspapers, by banners on portals, and so forth.

Clearly, these advantages and disadvantages of Web stores will vary depending on the product. In the following chapter, I will compare various product classes.

47.3   Brick and mortar or online, a comparison

Table 47.1 (next page) shows a comparison of brick-and-mortar (BM) and online stores (OS). As we have seen, online stores sell efficiency and convenience, while brick and mortar often work to give you a shopping experience. The two different models are very apparent in the business of selling books. Online stores offer large collections and discounts, and 24/7/365 availability from your office or home. Brick-and-mortar stores let you browse the actual books in a pleasant environment, let you take a cappuccino in their café, meet authors, listen to lectures, discuss books with their staff, meet friends.

If you know the book you want, you may locate it faster in an online store. If you are just browsing, you can get much information online, but the brick-and-mortar store may offer you the same information at an in-store terminal or from a customer service representative. The online stores can offer discounts due to larger sales, more automation, no need for expensive physical locations, and reduced inventory or no inventory at all.

Attributes	Brick-and-mortar store (BM)	Online store (OS)	Comments
Physical location	Very important, a way of marketing the store.	Anywhere	In principle, an online store does not need any physical space at all, but may have warehouses to have more control over delivery.
Finding the store	Location, marketing of store	Marketing of site (URL)	Heavy marketing will be needed to introduce and to maintain interest.
Availability	On location, within opening hours	From everywhere, 24/7/365	The main advantage of online shopping, customer transportation is not needed.
Inventory	Sell what you have	Sell what can be delivered	Products can be delivered directly from their suppliers, no inventory needed, in principle.
Stocking	Products must be transported to store	Not necessary (in principle).	Transportation cost per product for the BM store can be kept low by large volumes.
Product presentation	Through actual products	Description in text and images	The BM store allows the customer to see, hold, try on, test the product; the online store will have to present the product indirectly.
Search for product	Browsing through store, store organization	Organization, search tools, ads with links	Both stores try to organize products into well-known categories, allowing the customer to browse within each category.
Product information	Through product itself, staff	On page or by hypertext links	The BM store needs more staff to handle customer requests, many of which can be handled automatically in the OS.
Payment	Cash, check, credit card, store card. Manual.	Credit card. Automatic.	BM needs cashiers, but can handle cash and checks as well as credit cards. Most OS rely on credit cards.
Delivery	Usually performed by customer	Mail services, special delivery	The main disadvantage of online stores. Delivery is expensive and time-consuming.
Delay	None	Days, even weeks	Online shopping is not for the impatient.
Customer gets	The product she chose	A copy of the product described.	Copy variation may pose problems for the online store.
Customer profile	For customers with store cards, limited for others	For all customers	This represents an advantage for the OS, a disadvantage for customers that are concerned about privacy issues.
Customer relations	Store cards, coupons, marketing	Online contact	In this area both types of stores can use the same media, but a BM store will need to collect e-mail addresses manually from the customers.
Customer loyalty	Location, service, and pricing	Price, service, known URL	Location may be a means of retaining customers for the BM store; on the Web the competition is just a click away.

Table 47.1 A comparison between brick-and-mortar and online stores.

A large marketing effort will be needed to set up an online store—to give the URL to customers, while the location itself may attract customers to a brick-and-mortar store. However, when more books become digital, the online store is poised to capture the market. Many brick and mortar bookstores will not survive this transformation as they will loose a large part of their market.

The online store allows you to shop from home, but introduces an extra transportation phase to shopping. The customer will have to wait for the product, pay the cost of delivering individual orders, and may have to organize the acceptance of the goods, for example, by being at home to receive and sign for the package.

Product	Copy variation	Physical factor	Delivery factor
Music (CD)	0	Low	0 or low
Software	0	0	0 or low
Computers	0	Low	Low
Cameras	0	Low	Low
Daily disposable contact lenses	0	High/low	Low
Books	Low	Low/med.	Medium
Office supplies	Low	Zero or low	Medium
Wine	0	Low	Medium
Toys	0 or low	Medium	Medium
Car parts	0 or low	Low	Medium
Paint	0 or low	High	High
Clothes and shoes	Possible	High	Medium
Flowers	High	High	Medium
Furniture	Possible	High	High
Bikes	Low	High	High
Cars	Low	High	High
Paintings, art, antiques	High	High	Medium
Groceries, industrial products	0	0	High
Groceries, natural products	High	High	High

Table 47.2. Attributes of selected product classes (consumer sales).

On the Web, the customer has to rely on the product **description**, as the physical product is not available.

The brick-and mortar-stores allow the customer to view, hold, try on, and test the actual product. If you decide to buy, you can take this item with you immediately. Using an online store, the customer must rely on a product description, and usually will get only a copy of the product described. Table 47.2 presents these attributes for selected classes of products.

Note that the values given here have to do with consumer sales. (Procurement in a business-to-business environment is discussed later.) *Copy variation* indicates whether there are dif-

Copy variation tells whether there are differences between copies of a product.

The **physical factor** shows the advantage of holding, trying, and testing a product.

The **delivery factor** expresses the cost of delivery relative to the price of the product.

Products that are described mainly through **specifications**, such as a laptop, are often ideal for the online stores.

ferences between copies of a product, a factor that usually will be low or zero for high-quality industrial products. A high *physical factor* expresses the advantage of being able to hold, feel, try, and test a product. The *delivery factor* expresses delivery costs compared with total costs.

The advantage for the online stores will be in areas where all or most of these factors have a low or zero score; high scores will work favorably for brick-and-mortar stores. In addition, market opportunities exist in areas where the competition faces similar problems as on the Internet. For example, flowers have a high copy variation and physical factors that make it difficult for an Internet store to compete with a brick-and-mortar store, if the customer is able to visit the store. However, flowers are often used as gifts for relatives, friends, and business partners who live at a distance. In this case, the Internet has clear advantages over telephone ordering. The online flower shop can present pictures and can use text-based ordering to avoid errors. It may even be possible to show an image of the actual flowers, perhaps let the user pick these on the screen, using the factors above as an advantage instead of a disadvantage.

In general, we will have to rely on product descriptions online—text and images—instead of presenting the actual product. For many products this description may be as good as the real product, even better! When we buy an office PC, the specifications are more important than seeing the actual cabinet (buying a laptop may be different). Most books can be fairly well described by title, author, and additional textual information. Describing furniture and clothes may be more difficult. Customers would like to sit in a chair, try on shoes or pants, or feel the texture of a skirt. Color cannot be reproduced very well on a computer display, and size, weight, quality, and other attributes must be described indirectly. In these cases, we operate with a high physical factor. While these items can be sold online, customer dissatisfaction may be higher for these products than for those that can be described more accurately. In practice, this implies that the number of returns will be higher, too. Returns are very expensive in every way and may be the downfall of an online store. They represent lost sales, unnecessary expenses, and dissatisfied customers and need a reverse logistics system (a way to receive goods from customers) that may be difficult to implement efficiently.

Brand names and standardized products may be used as an alternative to evaluating the actual product. A customer could order a pair of blue Levi 501 jeans, size 32x34 knowing that they would fit.[3] Similarly, we would know what we would get when ordering a bottle of Heinz ketchup, a Playstation II, or a Jeep Grand Cherokee. This is not the case for many natural products. An apple is not an apple. Since the variability of natural products is so great, most customers would want to select the product themselves. Even if you trust the store not to give you outdated products, you may want your bananas softer and your tomatoes harder. In these cases, copy variation is high.

The disadvantage of transportation costs for online stores can be reduced where products are small and light (for example, CDs or contact lenses), where the cost of transportation is only a fraction of total costs (computers), or where the transportation phase is needed anyway (building materials, household appliances, and furniture). In the latter case, an online store will need local distribution centers, and this model may perhaps best be used for the online part of brick-and-mortar stores.

We could also have included a *wait* factor to Table 47.2, indicating the disadvantage of having to wait for delivery of the product. However, a wait factor will be very dependent on the customer. For a business, where procurement is planned, lead times of days or weeks between ordering and receiving are usually accepted. With a JIT (just-in-time philosophy) there may even be extra expenses incurred if the product is delivered ahead of time. In contrast, ordinary consumers usually will want the product as soon as possible. We may accept to wait for a product if the online store offers compensating advantages, such as discounts. For example, we do not buy a computer very often because it is expensive, and we may be willing to wait some days, perhaps even some weeks, to get the right model or a good bargain. Although we may want to read a novel tonight, we can wait some days for textbooks we need for the fall term. In other situations—for example, when buying a car or a house—the expense is so great that we usually have a prolonged buying process. Here the Web can be an important tool in the initial "information gathering" phase, even if the final deal will be performed in a brick-and-mortar office.

Based on these arguments, CDs and books seem to be better products for online stores than groceries. However, even within the more "ideal" areas, we see that some online stores have had problems getting a sales volume sufficient to keep prices low. What an online store saves on automation, small in-

Transportation costs are product dependent, and should be compared to the price of the product.

Online stores may be the only alternative in rural areas.

A **formalization** of the business environment (with standardization of products or clear specifications) may remove the disadvantage of the online store because there will be no need to examine the products.

ventories, and rent may easily be lost in the cost of delivery, returns, and marketing to get and keep customers.

There are exceptions to these factors. In rural areas with few brick-and-mortar stores, the Web may be the most convenient alternative. Online stores also can offer a larger product range than brick-and-mortar stores, and because of their worldwide customer base, may offer special products or collections. For example, to get clothes in certain sizes, a customer may find that the Web provides the only practical alternative. Some companies have even managed to establish successful online grocery stores, working hard to diminish the inherent disadvantages. For example, Terry Leahy, the long-time CEO of Tesco, describes[4] how his company carefully trained all employees involved in the online process, including the drivers and the staff who picked the groceries from shelves. An important market segment was people who stayed at home most of the day, and also small businesses. This simplifies delivery.

Procurement within a business-to-business environment follows different procedures than consumer sales. Here specifications may be more important than handling the actual product. When a company needs a 1/4-20 aluminum NC (a standard) hex nut it does not need to examine the actual item. Procurement will be based on specifications and standards, trusting that the supplier will deliver accordingly. If examining the products is important, this can be done through models, prototypes, or sample items. Clothes manufacturers will present their collection well in advance of the season. Actual procurement can then be performed based on product identifiers, sizes, colors, and other specifications. Even where copy variation is high, such as with natural products, formalizing product requirements can be accomplished through specifications for a minimum quality, or using arbiters in cases where quality is in dispute. For example, the grocer getting a shipment of produce from his distributor each day will have routines to handle cases where the tomatoes are too soft. This is usually not as simple for the customer who finds bad tomatoes in the package from the online store.

While online stores introduce an additional distribution phase—getting the goods from the store to the consumer—this phase is necessary for any procurement operation within a business environment. Further, the delay imposed by this phase has less impact in a business environment where procurement is planned ahead of time, not as an impulse action as in many consumer situations.

47.4   Auctions

Online **auctions** over the Web make it easier for consumers to take the opposite role, that of *seller*.

In established retail markets, a clear distinction exists between sellers and consumers. The sellers create the stores, choose the products, and set prices. However, in some situations we, as consumers, may take on the role of the seller, to get rid of an old car, the bike that our daughter has outgrown, or other goods we no longer need. In these situations, we can choose a direct marketplace such as a garage sale, a dealer, or a flea market. These have the advantage of allowing potential customers to examine the articles, especially important for used and old items. The disadvantage is that these methods are time-consuming and the market is limited to the customers who are physically present at the right point in time.

Indirect channels may be more efficient and may offer the potential of larger markets. Here we can post a notice on a convenient bulletin board or put a classified ad in a local newspaper, hoping that a potential buyer will call. For indirect sales, the Internet and the Web have several advantages:

- *Location independent*. A for-sale notice on the Web is not location-specific in the same way as on a bulletin board on some wall or an ad in a local newspaper.

- *Full product description*. A "classified" on the Web is not limited by a few lines of text.

- *Hypermedia description*. On the Web it is feasible to describe the item for sale using pictures, even sound and video.

- *Electronic submittal*. Sellers can submit all product information electronically.

- *Searchable ads*. On the Web, potential buyers can find the "ad" by keyword searching in addition to browsing.

- *Multiple organizational strategies*. While a newspaper uses only one organizational category, such as product class, a Web portal can use multiple strategies, for example, by price or location in addition to product class.

- *Updatable*. In contrast to a classified in a newspaper, the seller can remove the ad the second the item is sold.

- *Automatic auctions*. The Web site can automatically handle bids, using any type of auction policy. Auctions are an ideal form for selling used items, as the market will determine the price.

- *Simple communication.* Contact between buyers and sellers can be established using e-mail.

While the Web often removes **intermediates**, online auctions introduce an intermediate.

Auction sites, such as eBay, utilize all these Web advantages, even if they run counter to the idea of using the new technology to remove intermediaries, auction sites are really re-intermediation compared with direct sales between sellers and buyers.

With close to zero cost for entering, storing, and disseminating information, we can give grandmother's lamp a full description on the Web, including a picture and hypertext links to the manufacturer's site. Buyers can search and browse the site, and can sign up for automatic e-mail notifications whenever an interesting product comes up. The site can administer the bidding process automatically. But online bidding with a deadline is somewhat different from bidding over slower channels. Smart bidders use "sniper programs" that can help them give a bid in the last seconds before the deadline, ensuring a sale without having to raise the price significantly. False bidding also does seem to be a larger problem on the Web than elsewhere (that is, situations in which the seller or his associates can artificially increase the price).

The **Web auction site** can offer the possibility of submitting complete item descriptions.

The geographical independence of these sites is an advantage as ads are offered to everyone, all over the world. However, there are often practical limitations to the distance between seller and buyer. Some items may be difficult to send across national borders; others may be too expensive to transport, too bulky or too heavy compared to their overall value. The Web sites try to overcome this drawback by offering local trading, limiting presentations to a city or region. While this works technically, one may find very few items for sale after such a severe filtering, limiting the usefulness of local trading. Here, local newspapers still have an advantage. Many of these also present their classifieds online, offering the customer the advantage of both the paper and the electronic medium.

In contrast to online shops, the pioneer auction sites have an advantage over newcomers in their customer base. While an Amazon customer may find the same books at barnesandnoble.com, the eBay customer may find that only a few items may be listed on other sites. That is, eBay's advantage today is not its software or hardware, which is available for all, but its huge database of ads that attracts a large number of potential buyers, and in turn, more sellers, and more ads. Of course, this is nothing new. Start-up newspapers found it very difficult to compete with the incumbents that already had a large number of classified ads.

The heaviest competition for a site such as eBay comes from larger portals, such as Yahoo! and Amazon, which use large customer bases to offer auction services. In addition, we see the establishment of more niche auction markets, often created on the basis of established "meeting places" such as Web sites of professional and amateur organizations.

Notes

1   The first Sears mail order catalog was published in 1888. Seven years later the catalog had grown to five hundred pages.

2   Porter, Michael E. 1985. Competitive Advantage. The Free Press. New York.

3   Or, perhaps not? There is inflation in money, but also in sizes. Instead of telling a customer that she has to choose a larger size, manufacturers increase sizes but retain the size code. For many types of clothes, a size 10 today is identical to a size 14 in 1975 ("Dressing up," *Economist*, April 7, 2012).

4   Leahy, Terry. 2012. Mangement in 10 Words, Random House, London.

48 A Better Model?

The Internet and the Web have opened the way for a new method of doing business, even if calling it "a new economy" may be going too far. The successful business models in the consumer market have been in offering tools, from devices to search engines and social networks. In addition, automating existing services, such as retail banking, bookings, auctions, and to some extent shopping, has offered viable business models. Clearly, most of the success stories are in areas where the products are digital, such as for banking. However, while some services are performed fast and cheap on the Web, there are other, more open services that are difficult to handle through a Web interface. I use banking as an example to explore whether there are better models than just replacing the brick-and-mortar service with a computer.

Services have both open and closed parts. We need providers that can offer both.

As we have seen, banking is a prime target for Internet technology and online banks are getting solid market shares where they have the most advantage, for example, for bill payment. But will online banks with a full range of services be able to put an end to brick-and-mortar banking? The advantage of Internet banks is that all services are formalized to a degree so that they can be computerized, based on customer specifications. However, although banking is a formalized application area, some services and situations fall outside the programmed functions. We may need help when we are buying a house, exchanging foreign currency, performing cash transfers, and replacing a stolen credit card. In these situations, the Internet bank may not be able to provide the service we need. Their model is based on preprogrammed functions, and there may not be a function for the more specialized or ad hoc services. In addition, it may not be cost effective to offer functions online that are seldom used. Not only do an abundance of functions make the systems more expensive to develop and maintain, but they also may result in complex user interfaces that are difficult to understand for the ordinary user.

We need a model with automatic services at one end and **human support** at the other. In between, there is a place for computer-supported services (such as those in which the user performs the task with the help of the computer).

Internet banks will try to handle exceptions by offering a telephone, chat, and e-mail connection, in addition to the Web interface. But this will be an impersonal form of contact (we call the company number or use a generic e-mail address), and the range of services that can be provided probably will be limited, often set by the constraints of the call center's system, that is, constrained by another formalized system. In exceptional situations, we will probably be much better off with a local brick-and-mortar bank, where we may have a long customer relationship. Based on these relations, the bank can offer very flexible service.

How can a traditional bank compete with the **pure Internet banks**?

While most traditional banks offer online as well as traditional services, they have problems competing with the low fees and good interest rates of the pure Internet bank. But why should we have to choose? Why can we not get the best of both worlds—low fees for online services and flexible personal service when we choose to use traditional services, although probably at a higher fee? These combined services will be simplest to implement for a traditional bank that already has the local offices and personnel. These may serve customers that still do not have an Internet connection or that are willing to pay for personalized service. In the long run, however, we should expect a transition to more complex services in the brick-and-mortar part of the business. This part will handle the special services and exceptions that cannot be performed via the Internet. Over time the nature of the physical bank will change. Most of the services that are performed today at the counter will go online. Most customers may arrive with an appointment, and use the brick-and-mortar bank for the more complex cases where personal handling is needed. Fees will follow the service level, from low cost or free services online to the more expensive manual services.

Computer support can enhance and make more efficient the open and flexible services offered by human operators.

Customers will expect a personal level of service from such a bank. This is easy to provide to customers who use the brick-and-mortar bank frequently, as they will be known by face at the bank. Such a customer may get immediate attention the day he calls from Rome, Italy explaining that his wallet has been stolen and he needs an immediate cash transfer. Can the bank provide the same service to a customer that has only used their Internet service? With the right systems this should be no problem. Within seconds the operator should have all data on the customer available, for example:

- Predetermined questions and answers that can be used to verify identification.
- A list of the customer's accounts.
- A short automated history of relations between bank and customer.

As with the situation we discussed regarding an airline flight booking, a good computer system can help an arbitrary call center operator to provide personalized service (Chapter 45.2).

Humans will always be more flexible than computer programs. It is expensive, difficult, or sometimes impossible to develop systems that can handle all our wishes and peculiarities, while a professional human agent often can take these in stride.

An interesting model for a travel agency would be to offer both the formalized and unformalized service, combining the advantages of the computer and the human being as in our "idealized" bank above. On the Internet, the customer can provide the formalized data on airports and dates, do some preliminary study of destinations, and perhaps use the online booking system to choose a set of alternatives. To this formalized booking the customer can add a request for a hotel, for example, "suitable for kids and near the old part of the city." The agency could then use the formalized data directly in the processing, acknowledging flights, and so forth, and use the additional data to find the most suitable hotel. Profiles could be kept of each customer, from credit cards to travel patterns and requirements that could be used as background information. The agent could then use her experience and knowledge of the family's preferences (other profile data, non-formal data from the booking) to select a set of suitable offers that should be returned to the customer (e-mail or presented over the Web).

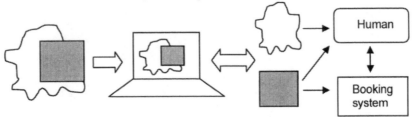

Figure 48.1 Formalized and unformalized parts.

This human/computer model with formal and informal parts is illustrated in Figure 48.1. The initial need, for example, for a booking, has closed and open parts, illustrated by a rectangle and the uneven shape, respectively. The user interface should capture both parts and transmit these to the booking system. The formal part can be implemented by check boxes, a list of alternatives, and data provided in separate fields, such as

Many services have both **open and closed parts**. While the closed parts can be handled by a computer, a human is often needed to take care of the open parts.

dates, name, address, and credit card number. Informal parts can be provided as annotations in text form. Both parts can be augmented with profile data that also have closed and open parts.

The booking service will get both types of data. Some services may fall entirely within the formalized range (booking of a simple ticket) others may be a combination of the two (as explained above), and there may be requests that fall in the informal range ("an inexpensive place in the Caribbean for a family with two kids ages eight and twelve, for a week during April"). The computer system can handle a booking that is completely described by formal data, without human intervention, while the travel agent will take care of requests that include open data. Of course, the computer will be an important tool for the agent when performing these parts even to the extent that the computer system may retrieve keywords automatically from the open part to get the data the agent needs. For example, based on the keywords "inexpensive," "week," "April," and "Caribbean," the travel agent may be provided with a list of alternatives the moment she gets the request.

The incentive for the customer to describe his wishes in a formalized manner is that the booking can be performed fully automated, fast, and at low cost. The manual service will be slower and more expensive, but here the customer can draw on the agent's experience to find the right place for a vacation or the best hotel. Brick-and-mortar offices provide these services today, but in this combined model, they may be provided more efficiently.

There will be no clear distinction between the formalized and unformalized tasks, between the closed and open applications. For example, with extensive hotel descriptions, the Internet application may directly suggest "suitable for kids and near the old part of the city" or suggest alternatives in the Caribbean. An important task for the developers of the online part of the system will be to monitor all services that the human agents provide. This information may be used to find functions that can be formalized, and then offered as a support tool for the agent or as an online function for the customer. In practice, this may imply adding additional data and more flexible search functions, as discussed in Chapter 45.2. In this way, an online agency can handle more orders without having to increase its staff.

Even if the Internet makes it possible, it is not always **cost effective** for the customer to perform all services herself.

In the age before computers, all these services were handled manually. Then, computer support made manual services more efficient. With the Internet, the customer can operate the system directly, but this does not imply that it is cost effective for the customer to do all the services herself. Professionals—in banks, travel agencies, and insurance offices—have always provided value outside of just operating the computer system. Therefore, the ideal model should be to retain the experience and know-how offered by these professionals, but use the Internet as another means of providing more efficient services.

This combined model may be efficient in other areas as well. As we have said, the expense of getting the product to the customer is a severe limitation for online shopping. But some of the advantages of shopping online can be retained when the online store works together with a brick-and-mortar store, for example, when the online store uses the logistics facilities that are already in place. In practice, this may imply that the more bulky goods are transported to the customer from the brick-and-mortar store, or that the customer picks up the items there, while smaller items can be sent through the mail. This model does not offer shopping independent of location, but many of the other online advantages are retained.

PART 7

Business-to-Business Applications

In **B2B** environments, we have a computer at either end of the communication line. This opens the way for automatic transaction handling, if the necessary standards are in place.

The advantage of having a person at one end of the communication line (as with B2C) is that we can utilize the flexibility and intelligence of human beings to adapt to nearly any type of user interface. While a common look and feel of the Web forms may simplify input, it is by no means required. Humans adapt intelligently to the purpose of a given interface, as long as it is flexible and well organized. Neither is it a problem that information is presented in different ways or that some use the shopping cart metaphor and others do not. This flexibility has allowed for fast growth in consumer services.

In principle, all types of business-to-business applications can be organized the same way, by asking customers to fill out online forms. While this has the advantage of being flexible, it often will be inefficient, as the data needed may already be stored in an electronic format. Also, where a private citizen or an employee ordering office supplies may send a few orders a year, we may have thousands of orders a day in a B2B (business-to-business) environment. Here a manufacturer, for example, will have full and detailed descriptions of all the components that go into a product. These may be stored within his ERP (Enterprise Resource Planning) system. A production order, or a plan to produce this product, will generate a set of procurement orders, many of which will go to external suppliers. Traditionally these may be printed on paper, sent by mail, or faxed to the suppliers. The manufacturer will certainly not see it as an improvement if he has to reenter all the data in the supplier's Web forms.

As an alternative, the manufacturer could send procurement orders as e-mail messages that his system could generate automatically. However, this would just move the problem to the receiving end, asking the supplier to transfer the order data from e-mail into its own order system. Without a well-defined format for these messages, this transfer would have to be performed manually, similarly to the retrieval of data from orders that have arrived by surface mail or fax.

The solution is obvious. We must let the two computer systems, the ERP systems for both the manufacturer and the supplier, communicate on a high formalization level. That is, on a level where both computers "understand" the format and the meaning of every data field.

General data exchange is discussed in Chapter 49, and formalized data exchange and standardization are discussed in Chapter 50. The traditional EDI-standard is presented in Chapter 51, and the newer markup language, XML, in Chapter 52. Interesting new applications of these B2B technologies, such as Web services, automated value chain, electronic marketplaces, and outsourcing, are presented in the last four chapters of this part.

49 Data Exchange

B2B solutions are not simple to realize. First, we cannot expect manufacturers and suppliers to use the same ERP[1] or database systems and even if they do, one system may not understand the data values of another. For example, the part identifiers and customer numbers may be proprietary to each company. A diameter may be in millimeters in one system and in inches in another; an amount may be in dollars or any other currency; and so on. In some cases, conversion may be possible, for example, by multiplying inches by 2.54 to get centimeters or a dollar by 5.7 to get Norwegian kroner. However, the one-inch bolt may not have a 2.54 equivalent in centimeters, and today's exchange rate may change tomorrow. That is, even if each system is formalized, the formalization is only valid in a given context. When data is transferred from one company to another, they are taken out of context. Therefore, we must establish a common area for both the manufacturer and the supplier, ideally a context that will work for all manufacturers and all suppliers.

Technically, we will have the simplest case if we define a standard high-level formalization that all companies could use. Then B2B communication would be just a matter of sending bits. However, this is a utopian situation. Not only must we expect that companies use different systems, but also that they store different data and use different formats. The idea is then to define standards for *transmitting* data. That is, each company has the freedom to do whatever they want internally, but when they want to communicate with others in a high-level form, data must be converted to the overall standard. Still, this is just the technical part. Businesses must take care that they transmit only data that can be understood at the other end.

We implement this concept by establishing a "transfer format" where each field of the data set is clearly identified. In addition, we need to describe which fields need to be included in a valid data set, and perhaps also allow optional fields. This has to be done for every document that we want to pass electronically between manufacturers and suppliers—purchase orders, transport documents, invoices, and so on. For each field, we have to determine the range of allowed values, and the measuring units that are to be used. For example, we can determine that all lengths will be given as millimeters; that both the manufacturers' and suppliers' part numbers will be included; that references to another entity (for example, a customer number), will be replaced by detailed data on this entity; that amounts will be given in dollars or, where other currencies are involved, given by the currency code and the exchange rate.

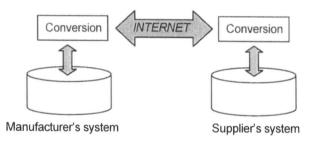

Manufacturer's system   Supplier's system

Figure 49.1 Formalized data exchange based on a common format.

This idea is illustrated in Figure 49.1. Data is retrieved from the manufacturer's database and converted to a common electronic format that both systems can understand before transmission. The data package is then transferred electronically to the supplier using the Internet, where a similar conversion process will retrieve the various data items and store these in the supplier's database, such as an order file. Such a system will be fast, reliable, and very efficient, but it requires the parties to agree on and develop the necessary formalizations.

Of course, when firms start to use B2B applications, we also will see a tendency to follow more global standardization within each company. Until now, the task of database administrators has been to define standard formats for each company, to avoid unnecessary formats and duplication of data. With more communication to outside partners, the conversion process will be simpler if data already follow more global standards. This is quite similar to the development of railways and other communication systems. As long as these are developed on a local scale, each developer can use the gauge that is most suited for his application. But as these expand, the value of the local network increases if it can be connected to other networks, and the need for standards emerges.

B2B communication formalized to high levels can do away with most of the paper that is used to communicate between businesses. Instead of printing an order, sending it by mail or fax, and requiring the receiving party to key in the necessary

In the first phase, B2B allows us to go from paper to all **electronic communication**, where orders and invoices can be handled automatically or semi-automatically.

In the next phase, we can organize **partnerships** in ways that we can do without these messages (that is the information can be retrieved directly from the underlying information).

data in their own system, the order can now be stored accurately in the supplier's ERP system a split second after it has been sent from the manufacturer.

While the first phase of B2B will be to make existing processes more efficient, the main advantages may lie in the second phase in which we utilize the technology to build new and closer relations between businesses. We will then see that many of the messages that are sent today, such as purchase orders and invoices, may be quite unnecessary. For example, a car manufacturer may generate purchase orders to a tire supplier based on an overall production plan. However, if the supplier has direct access to the plan (to the manufacturer's ERP system), no purchase order will be needed. The plan will provide the supplier with all the data necessary for accurate deliveries. With these data, the supplier can be connected virtually to the assembly line, with no need for the car manufacturer to stock tires, except for the supplies needed until the next delivery. Since the supplier has all the data, and will know immediately if there is a change in the plan, batches can be reduced to a minimum, for example, to a situation in which tires are supplied every day. Furthermore, we see that there will be no need for the supplier to send an invoice to the manufacturer. Since we can assume that all cars have tires, the supplier can be paid based on the number and type of cars that leave the assembly line.

The process that we see here is typical of the way we use computers. At first, technology is used to speed up manual processes, for example, by replacing surface mail with electronic communication. In the next phase, many of the processes from the old, paper-based world are no longer needed and the world can be remodeled based on the new technology.

The foundation of this evolution is a formalized system. This enables the computer to perform high-level operations automatically. However, as we have seen, many of the operations within the business world are already formalized, especially within larger businesses. Here high transaction volumes, the need for efficient and secure handling combined with regulations (tax, industrial, others) have made strict formalizations necessary. Therefore, parts of the infrastructure needed for B2B applications are already in place.

From the 1960s, banks, insurance companies, airlines, and other large businesses established proprietary networks for internal electronic communication. Today, these organizations

B2B requires a high **formalization level**, but in many businesses, especially the larger companies, part of this formalization is already in place.

have a long history of transferring money, database records, documents, orders, and invoices using proprietary formats or formats that have been established through national and international standards, such as EDI (Electronic Data Interchange). We should bear this in mind when we discuss new possibilities. In contrast to B2C applications that were enabled by the Internet, computer-supported B2B applications have been here for nearly sixty years. We must assume that many companies, especially the larger, have already realized a large part of the B2B advantages. Therefore, it is incorrect to see B2B as something new. This is an ongoing process that started many years ago, long before the advent of the Internet.

What Internet technology provides is a general network that is so inexpensive that all firms can be connected. With XML (eXtensible Markup Language) we have a common format for the messages and with the accompanying SOAP (Simple Object Access Protocol) protocol we have a standard for transmissions. These developments offer the opportunity for medium and smaller companies to participate with B2B.

B2B requires a high level of **IT maturity** within each business. The job for B2B is to connect these IT systems.

B2B applications assume a high level of computerization within each company. If the supplier's order processing were manual, there would be no advantage to receiving an electronic order since a fax or e-mail would have been just as good, perhaps even more convenient. However, when the receiver has the logistics systems in place, an electronic order can be inserted directly into his ERP system. The data can then be used to refine production plans, purchases, and so on. That is, in a world of many automated and formalized islands, B2B offers the possibility of automating the communication between these.

Note

1   ERP systems handle product descriptions in the form of bill of materials. Based on these data structures and a production plan, the ERP system can automatically generate procurement orders to suppliers and job orders to the production and assembly facilities. The ERP system keeps track of inventory, generates invoices and payment orders, and so on. In short, an ERP system is one huge software package that can handle all administrative information services in a company. Some well-known vendors of ERP systems are SAP, Baan, Oracle, and PeopleSoft.

50   Formalized Data Exchange

Business-to-business communication is traditionally performed using telephone, fax, letter, or e-mail. The data itself may be entered in free form—for example, given orally over the telephone or in an open e-mail message—or it may be more structured as an order form. Flexibility is maintained by having human beings at both ends of the communication line. This allows us to handle nearly any type of exception. We can send an order for a hundred units, and ask for delivery by truck, but can add a comment that five units should be sent immediately by air. The supplier may call us and say that he can deliver seventy within the deadline, but needs two more weeks to produce the last thirty, alternatively we can get these in a compatible model. We can argue and bargain and persuade him to work overtime in order to give us at least eighty within the deadline. In everyday communication, these "exceptions" are frequent, but cause few problems because both the form of the data and the processes are flexible.

The drawback is that manual handling is time-consuming and inefficient. Routine orders can be handled much more efficiently with business-to-business communication, keeping the human beings out of the loop. That is, if we view the human being as an intelligent and flexible but slow "machine," it is inefficient to use this expensive "machine" for routine cases that can be handled by the less flexible but very efficient computer. However, the computer requires formalized data and processes. Not only do we need to agree on low-level exchange formats, such as using the SOAP protocol and XML format, but we also need formalization of semantics. For a purchase order, for example, we must agree on which data should be included, in what format, and how the data is to be interpreted.

This task is very similar to what a database administrator performs. Before a company can set up its internal systems for storing data, someone must determine the format of the different record types. This is not an easy task, especially in firms that have exploited the freedom of using manual routines. For example, what kind of data should describe a customer, a supplier, or a product? One will usually find that different departments have very different opinions of what is needed. The job of the database administrator is to find the structures that fulfill the requirements from all parts of the organization, and that can be used to describe all the customers, suppliers, or products. Clearly, this formalization process is complicated and will require several meetings with the involved parties and good diplomatic skills to find the right balance between conflicting interests.

While difficult, this formalization has the advantage that data may be stored once within the legacy system of the company and then can be used for all applications. The idea is "store once, use many times." The value of the data increases as it can be made available for the whole organization and used for many different purposes. Not only do we get more in return for making the effort to store the data in the first place, but data quality also will improve as it is used in more applications. With the Internet and the Web, these data also can be made available outside of the business premises, for example, by Intranet and Extranet implementations.

Note that this standardization is not without costs. Many enterprises that have installed ERP systems have found that the company as a whole may benefit, but each department or production line may be dissatisfied with what the general system can provide. Often the ERP system replaced proprietary systems developed to meet one department's needs. Replacing a good solution with a mediocre one is not easy. These problems will be most severe in diverse enterprises, which may incorporate very different business units, each with their own culture and business models. In these cases, one overall system (one overall formalization) may not work, and a better alternative may be to use Web services (see Chapter 53).

Standardization is also necessary in data communication between organizations. But here we have the additional complication that we have stakeholders from several institutions who may have different ways of doing business. In trying to connect these different worlds, we may encounter different vocabularies, processes, formats, ways of encoding data, and so on. We see the same type of problem when we go from one country to another. We may find a different currency, keyboards, and standards for mobile phones, voltages, videotape, and TV format —even different ways of presenting date, time, numbers, and postal codes.

Formalization is context dependent: What is clear and unambiguous within a department, company, or country—within a given context—may not be as clear in another. For example, the supplier identifier in an order record will reference a local

We need **translations** when moving from one formalized system (context) to the other.

On isolated "islands," people enjoy the freedom to design their **own systems**. This can become troublesome when the islands are connected to other parts of the world.

supplier file. If this record is to be transferred to another company or context, the supplier file has to be sent along with the order or the identifier has to be replaced by the contents of the supplier record. If we look at the record itself we may find that one company registers different data than the next, that addresses and telephone numbers are given locally, that one firm offers two address fields, another only one, and so forth.

While the post office may force some standards for addresses, at least within a country, businesses often have complete freedom in how they represent internal data. For example, when doing some consulting work for a foundry that produces ship propellers (as presented in Chapter 26), I found that the foundry's customers used a number of different coordinate systems. While all had an axis parallel to the propeller shaft, it might be called x, y, or z; the positive direction could be forward or backward; and the origin could be on the axis or having an offset from this. Some customers even used several coordinate systems within their organization, an inheritance from engineering firms that had been acquired or merged with the company.

The foundry's customers enjoyed and utilized the freedom to make a choice, one that was unproblematic as long as the drawings were used only internally, but that created problems when the specifications were used outside, especially within a B2B setting. The foundry addressed the lack of standards with a system that identified the coordinate system used and mapped these into a common in-house system—yet another coordinate system. An alternative would have been to try to work out standards, perhaps involving manufacturer organizations or international standards committees. But standardization work is a long and tedious process. Even if such standards were accepted, it would have taken years to implement them in every engineering drawing and in every specification. For example, while the foundry gets most specifications in electronic form, there are situations in which it receives old paper drawings, such as when an old ship, perhaps launched as much as thirty years ago, needs a new propeller blade.

Computer technology has offered efficient and error-free communication between businesses, but has offered little help in the standardization process itself.

Computer technology has offered efficient and error-free communication between businesses, but has offered little help in the standardization process itself. Standardization is a social process in which participants define a common ground. The process is somewhat simplified in the cases where a large manufacturer or service provider can set the requirements,

Computer technology, especially the Internet, offers great rewards when the formalization process has been performed, but may not offer **significant help** in this process.

Control over "de facto" standards is a very important competitive advantage.

forcing its major suppliers to follow its standards. While this is an efficient way of establishing the data formats, it has the drawback that suppliers may have to conform to different formats for different customers. The manufacturer also may find that the "take it or leave it" policy does not work for all suppliers. If the manufacturer is not a major customer, the supplier may just "leave it," not finding it worth the effort to conform to the new formats.

In some cases, de facto standards emerge. For example, many businesses exchange data electronically using Adobe's PDF format, Microsoft Word documents, Excel spreadsheets, or Access databases as "attachments" to e-mail. Of these, only PDF is an official standard.[1] The data can be read manually, or imported into other programs. In the latter case, Excel and Access define what is called a medium-level formalization, providing a name, a format, and a value for each data element. On a higher level, the trading partners must agree on which data elements should be included and the overall record structure. Still, spreadsheet and database formats provide a useful way of formatting data, and may offer a convenient method for simple B2B transactions until higher-level standards are accepted.

The value of a company such as Microsoft is not in its products alone. We can get word processing, spreadsheet, and database systems that are as good from other vendors.[2] Microsoft's advantage is the fact that many of their file formats have become de facto standards. Therefore, we may send these files to the world and assume that everyone can use them. If we use another system, often a conversion to the "standard" Microsoft format may be required (the conversion job usually falls on the organization using the less common formats). While this may be implemented as a "save as Word format" instruction, automatic conversion never manages to be 100 percent. There will always be effects that are not reproduced identically in the two systems.[3]

But we cannot expect to get these de facto standards in every area. Then standards have to be developed, approved, and—the most difficult part—used. As we will see in the next chapter, the work to establish B2B standards started more than thirty years ago, and has been an ongoing process since then.

Notes

1   PDF (Portable Document Format) was created by Adobe Systems as early as 1993. It became an ISO standard in 2008.

2   An example is OpenOffice.org. This office package is provided for free, and we can even download the source code.

3   Earlier, simple ASCII text files were used as a basic medium for transmitting documents between all types of programs. Today, HTML and other standards that retain layout information are offering better alternatives, allowing for a somewhat higher formalization level than ASCII. In the coming years XML may provide a higher-level document form, but even with XML we cannot expect that 100 percent of a document will be preserved from one system to the next. Therefore, Microsoft will most probably retain their "standard advantages" for a system such as Word and Excel.

51   Electronic Data Interchange (EDI)

The work to formalize and standardize **EDI** started in the early 1970s.

From the moment computers were used to store data within businesses, the inefficiency of making a printout, sending the printout by mail, and letting the receiver key the data into his computer system was recognized. Therefore, the first networks for electronic transmissions were established very early in the history of computing. These used proprietary formats, for communication within one enterprise or between business partners. The actual communication took place using private networks, for example, by dial-up communication over ordinary telephone lines.

Formats were established within an enterprise, or between an enterprise and its major suppliers. The disadvantage was that many different formats were in use. A supplier could find that each of its major customers had its own data interchange format. Efforts to work out standards started as early as in the 1970s when the Transportation Data Coordinating Committee developed the initial EDI (Electronic Data Interchange) formats for data transportation. Today, there are two widely accepted EDI standards: X.12 developed by the American National Institute of Standards and Technology (ANSI) and EDIFACT,[1] developed by the United Nations. EDIFACT has been used mainly in Europe and the Pacific Rim.[2]

The standards are based on a transaction set that equates to a paper form, for example, an invoice or a purchase order. Each transaction set specifies the actual data items that are included, the fields in the paper form, and a computer-readable format to allow the business-to-business interchange of the transaction.

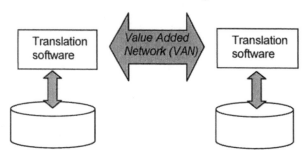

Figure 51.1 Translation software.

The EDI standard requires complicated **coding**, is only readable for machines, and is most often implemented using proprietary networks.

Although these standards set strict requirements for the interchange, each business may still use its own database systems and in-house formats. The mapping to and from the EDI standard is performed by translation software, as illustrated in Figure 51.1. The communication software itself will be quite similar to that of an e-mail system and can be implemented as an extension to such a system.

EDI transactions can be transmitted over any type of network. Until the Internet emerged, expensive Value Added Networks (VANs) have been used. While VANs provide a high level of security, the expense of establishing and maintaining these networks has limited the use of EDI, especially for small and medium-sized businesses. Further, EDI requires a unique solution for each pair of trading partners, where the implementation of the standard may be complicated by the use of different versions, even by different interpretations of rather complex guidelines.

EDI with its fixed commands and rigid structure is not an open tool. To make implementation and operation of an EDI system cost effective, large transaction volumes are needed. These volumes are found in larger businesses that may also have the advantage that they can force their trading partners to use EDI. Still, on a world basis, EDI is used only by a fraction of the businesses that are potential users of business-to-business systems.

The EDI records is made as compact as possible to save bandwidth.

Since the EDI standards were developed at a time when bandwidth was an expensive commodity, care was taken to make the EDI records as compact as possible. This compressed form makes it is quite complicated to develop the translation software and to perform the complex coding into the EDI standards. An even larger problem is that this coding makes EDI records unreadable for human beings. That is, EDI records are designed for business-to-business communication, and can be used only in this context. In practice, this is clearly a limitation to the wide acceptance of EDI usage. A firm may have to create two different types of record formats, EDI records for the suppliers or customers that support B2B and other solutions for the rest.

Today, we have a different communication infrastructure than the one for which EDI was developed. Instead of expensive private networks, we have the Internet. This does not imply that EDI must be abolished, but that we need EDI on the new Internet platform. This can be done by using EDI on top of the new Internet standards, getting the advantage of the Internet at the same time retaining the results from the development of the EDI standards.

Notes

1 United Nations/Electronic Data Interchange For Administration, Commerce and Transport (UN/EDIFACT)

2 Efforts are under way to harmonize the two standards, not an easy task because of fundamental differences in both syntax and semantics.

52   XML

The Internet, with its global addressing scheme and the relatively inexpensive connection and usage fees, is an important part of the infrastructure for business-to-business applications. However, new standards for a formalized description of data on a *semantic* level are required. HTML, as a layout-oriented language, cannot provide the functionality needed.

52.1   A common format

XML is a tool for describing structured documents and data records, a tool that can be used to define new languages for storing and transmitting data on a high formalization level.

XML,[1] which has become the common format for exchanging data over the Internet, is a vehicle for describing markup languages. That is, while HTML is a specific markup language, XML is used to construct such languages. In XML, users introduce tags (such as <order_no>); these are not specified in XML itself. Further, XML has tools that make it possible to define the structure of a document.

XML is a subset of SGML (Standard Generalized Markup Language), an ISO[2] standard. In principle, SGML will provide the functionality needed to describe semantic documents, but SGML is a fairly complex language with a large number of constructs both for creating and presenting documents. Because of its complexity, SGML has never been a success, and the scaled-down XML version was developed to retain much of the functionality with limited complexity.

```
<?xml version="1.0"?>
<!DOCTYPE address SYSTEM "address.dtd">
<address>
        <street>2000 Fifth Avenue</street>
        <city>Pittsburgh</city>
        <zipcode>PA 15260</zipcode>
</address>
```

Figure 52.1 XML document (example).

With XML, the individual data elements are marked (tagged) according to a schema, typically DTD (Document Type Definition) or XML Schema. A simple example is shown in Figure 52.1, an XML document with address information. Here we use DTD as an example for a schema language.

Since XML will be used across boundaries, whether of enterprises or countries, it is important to ensure the uniqueness of **namespaces**—the vocabularies.

```
<!ELEMENT address (street, city, zipcode)>
    <!ELEMENT street (#PCDATA)>
    <!ELEMENT city (#PCDATA)>
    <!ELEMENT zipcode (#PCDATA)>
```

Figure 52.2. XML Document Type Definition.

This document refers to the DTD shown in Figure 52.2, the type definition, or form, that tells which fields are included in the address. From the DTD, we see that the address type, as we have defined it, consists of three elements, each of the basic type, PCDATA (basically text, with markup references sometimes included). If we compare this example to traditional paper forms, Figure 52.2 will be the blank form and Figure 52.1 the completed form. In XML, the field descriptions are given as named fields, not as boxes and lines. XML also allows us to describe more complex "forms" than are possible on paper.

Note the generic nature of the language. Tag names are not static as in HTML. Instead, these are introduced in the DTD, which also determines the structure of the form or document, for example, that an address consists of the three elements: *street*, *city*, and *zipcode*. XML is a language for defining markup languages, such as the simple "address language" described here.

52.2   Schema

XML started out as a system for describing **documents**, but has moved toward also encompassing data records in newer versions.

A schema offers a set of basic data types (string, decimal, date) that lets the user restrict the values of elements and also build new types based on the basic types. We can specify the cardinality—the number of occurrences of elements—and can include choice statements, for example, stating that a name can be given in one field or as separate entities for first name, last name, and initials.

The idea behind the schema concept is to extend XML so that it can be as useful for handling data records as for structured documents. With schemas, XML has taken a great step in the direction of programming languages and database systems.

52.3   Namespaces

In this example, names, such as address, city, and street, are introduced directly in the DTD or schema. This works fine for simple cases, but what happens when enterprises start to create their own vocabularies? For example, we may get many different definitions of "street," similar to what may happen when different companies create their own paper forms. For example, some companies may have name and street number in the same field, others may have separate fields for each entity, and so forth. Therefore, we need a system for creating unique vocabularies. In XML this is done through the concept of a namespace, an identifier that is unique on a global basis. A name in XML will then consist of a local name, for example, *street*, from a given namespace, for example *invoice:street* in the example below.

```
<item
    xmlns:invoice=http://www.acmeinc.com/inv
    xmlns:delivery=http://www.acmeinc.com/deliv>
    <invoice:street>
        P.O.Box 5440
    </invoice:street>
    <delivery:street>
        45 Main St
    </delivery:street>
</item>
```

Figure 52.3 A XML document using namespaces

In the example shown in Figure 52.3, we have identified two namespaces, *invoice* and *delivery*, using an URL-like syntax to define unique identifiers. Note that there may not be any files at the given URL locations, as we apply this syntax only to ensure that invoice and delivery have globally unique identifiers.[3]

In XML, it is assumed that a parser, for example a browser, will know the location of a schema (this will be the case for standard vocabularies); if not, the location can be offered in a special schemaLocation element. Within the document we then prefix each name with the name of the namespace, here *invoice* or *delivery*. Thus *invoice:street* will be a reference to the name "street" within the namespace *invoice*.[4]

Note that namespaces also clear up the problem discussed in Chapter 36.4 regarding to an overload of acronyms and names in the real world. While the acronym SAS is overloaded in a global context, SAS as a value to the element *airline:name* (*name* within the namespace *airline*) should be unique. That is, namespaces help us define a formalized context, an area delimited from other parts of the world.

52.4   Validity of documents

XML documents will be read by a computer, and therefore, must abide to strict **syntactical requirements**.

With a schema, it is possible to check the *validity* of the document. That is, we can require that every element used within an XML document be declared in a DTD. Alternatively, the document description can be defined through the document itself, without any explicit DTD. Thus, a DTD is not a required part of an XML document. However, without the type definition, it is only possible to check if the XML description is well-formed, that tags have an end tag, and so forth.

The requirement for a well-formed, possibly also validated document, distinguishes XML from HTML. While HTML browsers ignore unknown tags and accept documents that do not follow the syntax, for example, where end tags are missing, XML will give an error message in these cases. Flexibility is an advantage for a presentation language, where the output is for human beings, but when "dumb" computers must read documents, a higher level of formalization is needed. If not, we cannot ensure a correct interpretation.

52.5   Application Program Interface

A supporting specification called the Document Object Model (DOM) offers XML documents an interface that is independent of platform and language. The DOM provides an API (Application Program Interface) to the XML documents that can be used by, for example, a Java program or a Visual Basic script to update a document's structure and content or to retrieve the various data elements. In many ways, the DOM works both as a query and a programming language, enabling programs to work on the underlying data using high-level concepts. This is especially important for XML, since most XML documents will be created and read by programs in business-to-business communication environments.

52.6   Tools

The tools provided for implementing the DOM model are Xpath, XSLT (for document-oriented XML) and XQuery (for data-oriented XML). Xpath is a tool that allows us to navigate the document structure, for example, to select all headers from a document, or all courses that student "John Doe" is enrolled in. That is, if we are writing programs that work on XML documents, this tool will aid us in retrieving all elements of the document or just the parts we need.

The standardization work needed on top of XML will be as tedious and complex as all standardization always is.

XML does not contain layout information. However, in those cases where XML documents are to be presented to human beings, an accompanying description— provided by the XSL (eXtensible Stylesheet Language)—will explain how the document is to be formatted. XSL consists of two parts in addition to Xpath, a transformer (XSLT) and a formatting language that describes how the document is to be rendered in a browser on a PC, a tablet, a smartphone or on a high-quality printout. In this process, some information may need to be removed (for a smartphone), or added (a table of contents or an index for a printed form).

These transformations are possible because data is stored in a high-level, structured form: The XML version contains more information than the lower-level forms of HTML or PDF. With XSLT, documents can be differentiated for internal use in an organization, in much the same way as a database system lets different applications access or view different parts of a record. Therefore, documents and other types of data formalized as XML may be used for many different purposes.

52.7   A tool to define standards

XML is a tool for **defining standards**; the Internet is the vehicle for implementing XML applications.

XML provides a formalized syntax and a framework for defining semantics, but not the higher-level standards needed to make the applications. As discussed in the introduction to this chapter, formalization within one area—a country or a company—may not be valid in another. An important task for standardization committees in the future will be to define both the syntax and the semantics of standard vocabularies. That is, each type of document will require a schema, defined namespaces, and a description of the type of data that goes into each element. Ideally, these descriptions—at least the syntactic parts— can be stored in repositories, global databases in which both senders and receivers can find schema descriptions. Repositories also will guarantee that the parties use the same version of a DTD.

The standardization work needed on top of XML will be as tedious and complex as all standardization always is, but the work does not have to start from scratch. There are efforts underway to create an XML/EDIFACT, utilizing the forty-year effort to develop EDI. In this format the EDIFACT vocabulary and grammar are presented with XML syntax. A clear advantage to this work is that both XML and EDI have recognized the need for sublanguages (vocabularies defined for groups of organizations). Just as EDI has standards for the transportation business, for airplane maintenance, and for customs handling, work is under way to establish standard XML vocabularies for a large number of areas—chemical data, mathematics, data on mining, geographical data, and so on. Therefore, the EDI sublanguages, or transaction sets as they are called within EDI, can be accommodated within the XML philosophy.

In order to move EDI to XML, schemas and namespaces for all the EDI transaction types must be defined. While the schema development will be a technical translation from EDI to XML structure, the namespace definitions will be more of a social process in which political issues such as language independence will be a major factor. If successful, this effort will make EDI more readily available for small and medium-sized businesses. Translation software, from internal formats to XML/EDI, will be much simpler than the old encoding programs because the DOM will offer a convenient interface. Transactions can be sent via the Internet, reducing the need for special Value Added Networks or, where the greater VAN security is needed, the competition from the Internet will reduce the cost of using these networks.

With an integration of EDI and XML, we can bring along thirty years of standardization efforts.

The XSL formatting also will be an important part of an XML/EDIFACT standard. A large manufacturer would be able to format all its business transactions using XML/EDI. The larger suppliers would then process these transactions automatically on a business-to-business basis, while smaller suppliers could choose to have the data presented as a form in their browser or printed on paper for manual in-house processing. This can be done by using different transformation and formatting descriptions.

52.8   Standardization

The long and complex process of developing official standards is not the only way toward standardization. As we have seen, a winning product may define a de facto standard. Monopolies may have disadvantages, but they are perhaps the only way that we could have established "standards" in many areas. The process of determining a format within the scope of one system is always simpler than defining a standard for all systems. A monopoly may curb fair competition for licensing fees and functionality, but the advantage of knowing that MS Word (an unofficial standard) or PDF (a standard) documents can be at-

The long and complex process of developing official standards is not the only way toward standardization. As we have seen, a winning product may define **a de facto standard**.

The real problem is not to define XML nor to define suggestions for standards, but to have these standards **accepted** by the user communities.

tached to e-mail messages and received without conversion errors is tremendous.

Many word processors allow documents to be saved as XML, which enables XML to piggyback on the de facto document standards. The advantage of publishing documents as XML instead of HTML on the Web is that this will allow for somewhat higher-level searches, for example, for attributes such as date, author, headings, language, and number of pages. However, other parts of a document—the text—will be represented in proprietary format; XML will just define the "envelope" of these parts.

What we need is an advanced "save as XML" function with which the user can choose a document template, for example, a template for a scientific paper. The word processor could then extract titles, authors, affiliations, keywords, references, and so on, from the document under the user's supervision. These data could then be formatted using a "scientific paper" vocabulary, which would allow for higher-level searches, at least within the vocabulary covered by this type of document. Similarly, XML documents can be created based on the standards used for database systems. New versions of these systems offer converters from their own internal formats to XML. An enterprise can then export data as XML. The receiver will need to have the same database system to do the opposite conversion, or will have to build a program that processes the XML record directly.

Clearly, XML is a flexible tool that can be used to capture existing standards, both official and de facto. It will encourage and simplify the work of defining new high-level standards in many areas. But the real problem is not to define XML nor to define suggestions for standards, but to have these standards accepted by the user communities. Acceptance of standards implies a change of routines and software; legacy data may become outdated or must be converted to new standards, which may be an expensive process.

Not everybody benefits from the acceptance of standards. Standards imply leveling the playing field, which may provide leverage for some companies and disadvantages for others. I discussed this problem in Chapter 45.2 regarding airline reservations. Identifying the cheapest fares would be easy with a standard for describing available airplane seats (destinations, dates, prices, and restrictions), a clear advantage for a new bargain airline and a clear disadvantage for the established compa-

Not everybody benefits from the acceptance of standards. Standards imply **leveling the playing field**, which may provide leverage for some companies and disadvantages for others.

The **acceptance** of standards may be a threat to established companies, even to the society as a whole in the cases where standards are a barrier against innovation.

nies. Therefore, the latter may find it more convenient to keep their own reservation systems, using proprietary formats, restricting access from other computer systems, and also perhaps using pricing policies, restrictions, and frequent flyer programs that complicate direct comparisons. Standardization may be a means to run society more efficiently, but also a threat to many businesses. Since the standardization work itself is complicated, there may be many ways for major companies to impair standardization efforts wherever these threaten the existing power structure. In today's tough market, it is vitally important to control the channels to the customer. If these are lost, the company may end up as a subcontractor, in fierce price competition with others that can perform the same service.

Even for society as a whole, standards may pose a threat because they may have a tendency to freeze progress and technology and to be a barrier against competition. Each of us may benefit from the de facto standards of Adobe and Microsoft products, but these established formats make it nearly impossible for others to enter the market. A competing product will have to be dramatically better, perhaps based on a new disruptive technology,[5] to persuade customers to leave the convenient position that the standards provide. The power of ownership of a standard occurs in countries as well as businesses: Today the American GPS (Global Positioning System) defines a standard for navigation, but the European Union is creating its own system[6] to avoid the American dominance.

Large enterprises may use a monopoly position to force everybody to accept a standard, which was the case when AT&T, the parent company of the Bell System, reshaped the American telephone network around 1920. But this monopoly also served as a lid on new business models and creativity within the communication area for voice and data. Today, we have many businesses in this area, but have lost many of the standards; for example, mobile phone systems are not universal. However, with active involvement both from governmental and international standards organizations, it should be possible to merge the advantages of standards with the advantages of free competition. Without this involvement, we will get incompatible systems and a situation in which effectiveness can be achieved only by having a dominant player in the market. I discussed these issues in Chapter 12.

Notes

1   The development of XML can be followed on www.xml.org and on the www.w3.org websites. There are also several good textbooks out on XML, but be certain to get a new edition.

2   International Standardization Organization.

3   This is a really smart idea, with the drawback of confusing users as we normally view a URL as a pointer to a file.

4   To avoid too many prefixes (really not a problem in most cases since a computer program normally will produce XML), XML allows us to have a default namespace.

5   A technology that creates new markets and as such is better suited for start-ups than for the incumbents.

6   Galileo, a European navigation satellite system costing more than three billion euros.

53   Web Services

XML is a tool for creating standardized data exchange and storing formats. When a vocabulary and a document format have been established for an application, we can create a document on one computer and send it to another. We are then ready for the next step, to define services on a computer system that can be accessed from the outside. For example:

- We can offer an automated weather forecast system. Based on a location (name or coordinates) from the calling computer, we return a forecast for this area.

- A point-of-sale system can call a Web service of a credit card company, providing the card number, the date, and the amount, and receive a verification code.

- With an article number as input, a Web service can return the number of items in stock.

- With a request for an offer, including article number, quantity and delivery terms, a Web service can return an offer.

But aren't all of these simply the things this book already has discussed: services that have been established using Web browsers and HTML? No, this time we are within B2B applications, with a computer at both ends of the communication line. That is, instead of just presenting the returned data on a Web page, the calling computer can use these data for further processing. For example, when the weather forecast is received in XML format, the calling computer can reformat this and present it to the user in any conceivable way—translating it to another language (perhaps using yet another Web service), sending out a warning to drivers if certain parameters in the forecast are present, storing it for statistical reference, and so forth.

53.1   Protocols

A set of protocols and standards are established to handle these Web services. The SOAP[1] protocol, for example, defines an envelope that contains the data transferred between the two computer systems. WSDL[2] defines the details of the services, and the idea behind UDDI[3] is to provide a "yellow pages" system to describe services. We also have a new version of devel-

Web services can be used to model the information interface between various parts of an enterprise. Thus, it offers an alternative to the "total" system approach.

opment tools that helps developers to implement these services. A well known example is Microsoft's dot-net architecture.

In principle Web services are nothing new. From the very start we had the ability to call procedures or subroutines (services) within a computer program. In this case, the administration of the call—sending the data to the routine, transferring control, returning the results—was handled within one programming system. Later, we were able to call "services" within other programs on the same computer system, for example, using Microsoft's OLE[4] feature or standards such as CORBA.[5] However, with Web services, we can call services on other computer systems, independent of the program language used, independent of the operating systems, and independent of location. In practice, this makes it much simpler to use computer resources and data at different locations. We can concentrate on the services, independently of how these are implemented.

There are those that believe that Web services will revolutionize the way we do business.[6] But, as with XML, the tools only offer a way of creating these services; the job of establishing the standards are as difficult as ever. In addition, companies may fear they will lose control over their information resources by opening their computer services to anyone.

53.2 Within a company

Independent of this discussion, Web services may have a great impact on how we organize the computer systems within a company. From an early beginning and with a large number of independent programs, many companies have tried to control their data and computer services by installing one total system (an ERP system that takes care of everything). That way, they could store data in only one place and make these data available to the whole organization through this one system. This goal is not easy to achieve. There have been many failures on the ERP path, and those that have succeeded have used very large resources to accommodate the system to the enterprise. The ERP system is a general system, and sometimes each division within the company was happier with their old proprietary systems that were tuned to their needs. (I discussed ERP systems in Chapter 24.4.)

An alternative to implementing one system for the whole company is to use Web services. Now divisions can keep their own systems, but each system must implement a Web service

Web services may offer the better of two words.

that can offer data to the head office and other divisions. Instead of standardizing on an ERP system, "interfaces" between the various parts are defined. For example, the CEO will need financial data from each division, and a Web service that retrieves these data from the divisional systems must then be implemented. A transport division will need information on which goods that arrive—container types and weight—and all other divisions must provide these data through a Web service.

Of course, defining what services are needed, the data they are to provide, and the data formats will be a major task. But companies usually have the mechanisms needed, from a management, social, and technical view. These services can be called through a Web interface, in which in and out data are most often described as XML documents. It offers a flexible way of invoking services.

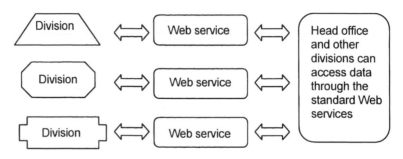

Figure 53.1. Web services

Each division can use their own systems, and at the same time, important data is made **available** to other units.

Illustrated in Figure 53.1, this alternative yields the better of two words: Each division can use their own systems, and at the same time, important data is made available to other units. The disadvantage is that each division will have to maintain its own system. But, this is not a necessity. If this system implements the division's idiosyncratic business processes, it is a good idea; however, if this allows the division to perform standard routines in a peculiar way, the best practices enforced by the ERP system may be a better solution. Or, one may do as in some companies, allow the divisions to use a standard system or, where necessary, implement an idiosyncratic system.

Web services may also have a great future for government agencies. Today, for example, my college must use a government designated student administrative system so that the Ministry of Education can get the data it needs. A more flexible option would be for the ministry to define a set of Web services that each institution had to offer (number of students, credits, grades) instead of imposing one system. Behind such a standard interface, each institution could have its own system, opting for a standard system or developing something on its own. The only requirement would be that the Web services should be able to retrieve the data they need from the internal systems. But there would be nothing to hinder an institution from typing in these data whenever the Web service was called, as long as they conformed to the required data format.

While Web services clearly are a part of our discussion on formalization (that is, "closing" the world), we see that they also open the possibilities for greater "computing freedom." Within an organization, we can maintain basic ideas of storing data only once, for making data available to all, for defining standard processes, and so on, and at the same time, allow each division to choose the computer system that best fulfills its needs.

Web services open the possibilities for greater "computing freedom."

Notes

1 SOAP (Simple Object Access Protocol) is a protocol intended for exchanging formalized and structured information in a decentralized environment, such as between independent computer systems. The message within a SOAP envelope is described using XML. The protocol contains all information needed to transmit, receive, and process messages.

2 WSDL (Web Services Description Language) describes how to access a Web service and what operations it will perform.

3 UDDI (Universal Description, Discovery, and Integration protocol), acts as a directory model for Web services.

4 OLE (Object Linking and Embedding) is Microsoft's proprietary mechanism for allowing documents and applications to access data and subroutines in applications.

5 CORBA (Common Object Request Broker Architecture) is an ISO standard for managing distributed program objects in a network. It allows communication between programs at different locations and developed by different vendors.

6 Hagel III, J. (2002). Out of the Box: Strategies for Achieving Profits Today and Growth Tomorrow Through Web Services, Harvard Business School Press.

54 Automated Value Chain

The real advantage of B2B is that the whole **value chain** can be automated, based on the availability of data records with a high formalization level.

With high-level, B2B communication, the front-end company can be **all symbolic**, for example, handling customer contact only and relying on subcontractors for all other operations.

Seconds after the customer has hit the submit button, an online store receives the order and it is entered in its database system. The Web interface has ensured that this is a complete order, formalized by including unique product identifiers and specifications, such as size and color. Probably the Web site also has checked to see if the products are available. The online store's computer system verifies credit card information by sending transaction records with credit card number, expiration date, and the amount electronically in XML format to the credit card company's Web service. The result, an approved/not approved status, is returned to the online store also, in XML, with an electronic signature, a code that the store uses to verify its claim in case of a dispute.

The online store may have its own warehouses or may just pass the order on to a manufacturer or distribution center. The order will be directed to the most convenient warehouse, depending on product availability, distance to the customer, and load factor. The products will be collected, packed, and sent to the customer using the postal system or any other delivery service. The date and time of the sending will be noted in the online store's system, which will initiate another electronic transaction to the credit card company, this time to get credit for the full amount. The customer can check the status of the order over the Web interface, until the delivery truck arrives. All order data will be retained in the database system of the online store. These data are needed if there is a dispute or if the customer decides to return the products; they also will provide important background information for overall statistics and can be used to create a customer profile.

At all times, the store's ERP system will keep track of what is in stock. The system will be preset with different replenishment procedures for different products. For some items, the system may generate a replenishment order when stock levels go beyond a preset safety point; for others, it may need confirmation before a reorder is sent or it may be instructed to remove the product from the Web site when there are no more items. The decision as to which procedure to use will depend on type of product, its popularity, availability, demand variation, time to replenish inventory, and so forth. The ERP system may use historical data to aid the procurer (purchaser) in determining a replenishment scheme and to set reorder points, and so forth, but this is not a closed process. Historical data may be an indicator for future demand, but new models, new technology, or a shift in trends may cause abrupt changes. There are no formalized methods to determine these events, and a human procurer has to use all his skill to predict future demand.

For example, a replenishment order may be coded as an EDI transaction and transmitted to the supplier on a special network, as an XML-coded transaction on the Internet, or perhaps printed out and faxed to the manufacturer. While many online stores have impressive Web sites, the technology behind the scene is not always as modern. Some suppliers still rely on manual systems; only a few may have implemented EDI, and the promise of new standards is still just that. That is, the infrastructure of a fully automated value chain is still not in place for most firms.

The idea is to capture the data in a formalized form as soon as possible (such as, directly from the customer), then utilizing these data through the whole value chain.

However, let us assume that suppliers have XML/EDI, and that the replenishment order is sent automatically the moment the stock number falls below the replenishment point (reorder level). We now have a similar situation to the one above, but the customer is the online store. The routines of payment, pricing, and so on will be different in this case, probably regulated by agreements set up in advance. These agreements will be part of the ERP systems of both the store and the supplier, and will be used to determine discounts, forms of shipment, and so forth. Based on these agreements, both systems can handle all transactions automatically, without any intervention of human beings. However, for control purposes, many companies put a person in the loop, to verify the transactions.

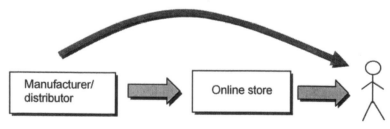

Figure 54.1. Product delivery to customer, through store or directly from supplier.

The supplier can fulfill the replenishment order by taking products out of stock and sending these to the online store or by creating orders for having the products produced, similar to the situation with the online store. Now the value chain can be simplified, as shown in Figure 54.1, allowing the manufacturer or distributor to send the product directly to the customer instead of through the online store—thus, we avoid a shipment (from the supplier to the store) and having to handle products at the store.

In this case, the online store will be nearly virtual, without any products or warehouses. Therefore, its business model must be to make money on its Web site and its customer base alone, a valid model if the store can maintain its customer base and does not give too much control to suppliers. But, the model also has some logistical problems, especially for exceptions. The customer order may include products from different suppliers. Without a central warehouse or packaging center, the order will have to be sent as several packages to the customer, who may find this inconvenient, especially when items must be collected at a post office or a distribution center.

Inverse logistics can be a problem for online stores.

Returns will pose another problem in these cases, handling what we can call "inverse logistics." How should the items be returned? The customer may be given preprinted return labels, but she must be sure to keep the labels and connect the right label to the right product.

Information technology may be used to streamline processes, keeping stock levels to a minimum.

The need to keep products in stock may be reduced by JIT (Just-in-Time) techniques, which use the flexibility of modern manufacturing plants to avoid large production batches, reduce work-in-process inventories, and maintain direct ties to vendors that offer a "streaming" supply line. With smaller set-up costs, lot sizes can be reduced to a minimum, perhaps making it possible to produce on demand. A book that we order from the online store could be printed and bound based on our order, making it unnecessary to print large editions, keep volumes in stock, and hold bargain sales to get rid of large inventories. However, for many products the economics of scale are valid and produce-to-order may not be acceptable. In most cases, ordinary consumers at the end of the value chain expect to get what they buy immediately and at the lowest possible price.

Henry Ford's "any color as long as it is black" philosophy worked at a time when consumers bought their very first cars. Today, we emphasize diversity, and are open to new features, designs, and products. Most of us have satisfied the need for

With modularization of products or efficient manufacturing processes, it is possible to produce or assemble based on **specifications** from the customer. With IT technology, these individualized products can be produced as effective as serial products.

transportation and look for more when we buy a new car. Since people come in all types and shapes, one product—or even a range of products—will not fulfill all customers' needs. The answer is customization, which allows the individual customer to specify what he wants. While some engineer-to-order manufacturers may allow the customer a high degree of control (for example, to determine the capacity and design of a pump, a crane, or a ship), others offer the customer the choice between predetermined variants. This is the production model for many car manufacturers: Customers specify color, engine type, size, air conditioning, audio system, configuration of seats, and so on.

This assemble-to-order production philosophy is ideal for PC manufacturers. Here the actual assembly process may be performed in a short time, since a PC has high-level components that may be inserted in a rack, and the time of delivery can be kept within an acceptable range. Instead of just placing an order for a premade PC configuration, the Web site gives the user the option of customizing, for example, specifying processor, the size and type of memory, accessories such as sound and video boards, operating system, and application programs. The store will have a manufacturing plant that assembles these PCs based on customer's specifications. The great advantage is that these components may be used to produce a large variety of products, in some cases the variety may be so large that the average number produced may be less than one for each possible product variant. For example, if there is a choice of five cabinets, five processors, ten memory configurations, five operating systems, ten displays, five keyboards, and twenty different software configurations we have a set of 1,250,000 possible configurations. Such a product range is often needed to accommodate the needs of demanding customers, and can only be implemented on the basis of an assemble-to-order philosophy.[1]

Customization has two parts. First we create a **virtual product** in collaboration with the customer, and then this product description is "copied" into a physical product.

The Web offers excellent support for customer specifications, whether the product is a PC, a car, or an insurance policy. We can view the specification process as a virtual assembly line,[2] where the idea is to create a virtual product (description). For a PC specification, the virtual process will precede the physical; for others, the virtual and physical assembly processes may be simultaneous, to some extent, which is the case for constructing a ship or a building. Here the detailed design and specification process can be performed at the same time as the

The **virtual parts** of production, such as design and marketing, are becoming more important than the physical manufacturing.

physical processes, of course, with the specification process ahead of the physical.

In many cases the virtual parts of production are becoming more important than the physical. The creativity, complexity, and greatest rewards are in the virtual process. In many cases, we may view the physical process as copying from the virtual original to the physical reality.

While the Web can support the specification phase of customization, this production philosophy may require very flexible production and logistics systems, and also will be product dependent. Although a computer manufacturer can insert almost any board in a rack, a printer company may delay putting a power supply in a printer until the destination is known, and a manufacturer of paint may postpone putting in the dye to the last possible moment (often in the shop), these methods cannot as easily be used when variations are more deeply integrated in a product. An air-conditioning unit in a car, for example, cannot easily be offered as an add-on item, but has to be integrated into the car through the production phase. Car manufacturers handle these cases by using advanced logistics systems that control production according to customer specifications. That is, cars often are not produced before the order is in. The production facilities and suppliers are then controlled directly by the order sequence. While this may be known days in advance, exceptions may occur. In some cases, both inside and outside suppliers have to be able to deliver components with a lead time of a few hours.

An alternative is to accommodate customers' need for personification of products by offering superficial variation, that is, hiding a standard product in "packaging" with high variation. Snap-on, "individualized" covers for mobile phones are a typical example. However, while it is easy to get a mobile phone in the color we want, we may have more problems finding a telephone that allows customized functionality, for example, one with large keys, higher speaker volume, and simple functions for the elderly. We are offered the McDonald's variant of customization (meal number, type of drink, sizes) instead of the more expensive restaurant model that allows for more custom control.

The customer's click on the submit button may create an automated chain reaction through a large value chain.

When the computer systems are in place, handling customized orders as efficiently as mass production becomes a reality for many industries. The customer's click on the submit button may create an automated chain reaction through a large value chain, with each system using the data for its own purpose, accepting messages at one end and creating new messages at the other.

If all processes and all data are formalized, then the complete value chain can be controlled automatically without human intervention. With flexible, computer-controlled machinery, we may even set up the machines and control the production based on data that the customer originally sent.

Notes

1   Interestingly, many PC manufacturers do not utilize fully the advantages of customer specifications. Both my office and home computers run the next-to-last version of the operating system, and I naturally want this on my new laptop. However, only one manufacturer out of the five I considered offered me this choice. Yes, I may be in a minority group, but the sum of all minorities over all options may be quite a large group.

2   These ideas are discussed in more detail in Olsen, K. A. & Sætre, P. 1998. Describing products as programs, International Journal of Production Economics, vol. 56, no 1.

55　Electronic Marketplaces

Instead of taking the products to the marketplace, we offer the symbolic **descriptions** of the products. In this virtual setting, it is possible to inverse the process, letting the customers specify their needs as well as letting the producers specify what they have for sale.

In their simplest form, electronic marketplaces may be based on the same technology as retail shopping, database access through an HTML-based interface, using forms to provide input data. These marketplaces may be "sellside," organized by groups of vendors, or "buyside," in which a number of purchasers go together to define joint requests for quotes. Marketplaces also may be organized as automated brokerage services that match buyers and sellers on common ground. As with other forms of electronic shopping, electronic marketplaces have the advantages of global access, larger markets, and simplified transactions.

In the early stages of Internet and Web technology, many firms successfully used electronic marketplaces for the procurement of nonproduction goods (that is, materials needed for administration such as office equipment, supplies, and computers). While having an unimportant percentage of accounts payable, these items may take up a large part of the total transaction volume. Often the cost of handling an order will be higher than the cost of the products. Therefore, the savings of automatic procurement in this area may be high and involves simple products that are easy to specify. Through the Intranet, an employee can request articles by browsing catalogs from the firm's approved list of vendors, adding items to her shopping cart. This request is forwarded to her boss for approval, and then handled automatically by the procurement system. When the employee receives the goods, she will be asked to verify quantity and quality—online, of course. With verification, the system can automatically transfer the right amount to the vendor, based on predetermined contracts. No invoices or manual handling are necessary. Since all transactions are electronic, this automatic system may give a more comprehensive view of all costs than a manual system in many ways. As most transactions are automatic, the procurement department can use their resources on a higher level, to search for vendors, negotiate contracts, and handle exceptions.

The Internet and Web are ideal for implementing virtual, all-symbolic **marketplaces**, organized as sellside, buyside, close partnerships, or as auctions.

Of course, this model also can be used for production-related goods. Establishing companywide portals achieves a centralization of buying power that can be used to leverage the purchase process, lower prices, automate transactions, and get faster cycle times. Companies within the same field may establish common portals to create greater buying force, but at the same time, having to acknowledge that procurement will no longer be an area of competition, at least for the goods covered by the portal. Similarly, sellers may present themselves through a common portal, to offer a larger variety of materials and, perhaps, reduce internal competition.

Online auctions have the advantage that sellers and buyers do not have to be physically present at the same time or in the same location. These are an ideal application for the Web, utilizing inexpensive ways to describe items and global access in a system that can organize the bidding process automatically. With a sellside auction, the vendor gives a description of what he has and buyers bid for the products in a forward auction, with prices moving upward. In a reverse auction, a buyer specifies his needs, and sellers bid to fulfill these needs, with prices moving downward. Each auction goes until a preset deadline.

In practice, the sellside and buyside partnerships could not have been established on a broad basis without modern communication technology. While input via forms works for retail shopping or auctions, it is not practical for general B2B transactions. Therefore, the next step for these marketplaces is to accommodate business-to-business transactions, making automatic procurement processes possible.

As an example, let's say a manufacturer sells bikes via the Internet. His business idea is to allow customers to "design" their own bike, based on the principles explored in the previous chapter, using an advanced generic (general) product structure that describes all the possible variants of a bike. On the Web interface, the customer is led through the design process, getting a choice of components and add-ons for each part of the bike. When the process is complete, the manufacturer has a description of the virtual bike with all its components. A due date for delivery is promised based on the availability of these components. However, let us assume for simplicity that the manufacturer guarantees a one-month deadline for all bikes.

The job of the MPC (Manufacturing Planning and Control), often a module in an ERP system, is to get these items within the deadline, taking into account the time needed for assembly and transport to the customer. Some components may be in stock; if not they must be produced in-house or ordered from a supplier. In-house production requires complete production plans, and triggers a need for lower-level components, perhaps in several layers. With the necessary data, the MPC system per-

---

Online auctions have the advantage that sellers and buyers do not have to be physically present at the same time or in the same location.

*To be efficient, electronic marketplaces will demand a high degree of **formalization**, both in the communication between organizations and within organizations.*

forms these tasks automatically. The materials are ordered from individual suppliers based on predefined procurement contracts that specify delivery times and prices, while others are obtained on the open market. In the latter case, the manufacturer's computer sends out a request for quotes, or bids in an auction marketplace. Bids, purchase orders, and other data are transmitted as XML documents, using a standard vocabulary so that the computers at the other end can understand the data on a semantic level. The supplier's computer performs an identical process, setting up in-house production orders and generating orders to its suppliers.

Ideally, we can envision a streamlined value chain from the customer down to the producers of raw materials, in which all communication is electronic. In practice, it will take time to get the necessary infrastructure, the computer systems, and the standards needed in place. But firms that succeed will have a clear advantage: They can allow customers to specify individual variants, experience great savings through automatic electronic transactions, and be able to utilize data updated to the last moment. When the customer hits the submit button, her order is communicated through the whole system. The whole value chain can base forecasts on data updated to the last second. The standards and connectivity offered by the Internet and Web technologies may have a tremendous impact in this area, but a high degree of formalization is required. The standards must be in place before the different computer systems can understand each other, not only the underlying communication protocols, but also the syntax (for example, XML) and the semantics (vocabularies and more).

Formalization offers a more streamlined world, but something may be lost when we try to mold an open world into a closed system. This problem can be reduced by having two systems, a formalized and automatic system for routine transactions and a manual system for exceptions. The efficiency of such a system will be determined by the transactions that can be set up automatically and how easy it is to perform the manual tasks. In a B2B environment, one would expect a larger part of all transactions to be formalized than in consumer applications. In B2B, it may be possible to formalize even the exceptions, for example, setting up formal procedures for quality control and for product returns that do not conform to these requirements. In a B2C setting, the only practical solution may be to let the

---

Ideally, we can envision a **streamlined value chain** from the customer down to the producers of raw materials, in which all communication is electronic.

We formalize to **automate**, but at the same time we reduce flexibility in the handling of exceptions. These often have to be handled manual channels, but for efficiency, we would like to use these infrequently.

Are we willing to formalize and automate all parts of a business process, or do we also require **informal** knowledge, experience and intuition (that is, manual handling as a part of the processes)?

consumer determine quality, for example, with a liberal return policy.

There also may be limitations to formalization. Auctions or price negations are like a game of poker. Information may be incomplete and subjective, and psychology is an important part of the decision process. While formalized methods have a part, the indeterminism of human nature plays an important role. In fact, one may argue that negotiations and bidding can be performed only in an open world. Even if it is possible to implement some unpredictability in an automatic bidding system, it seems that the more natural direction for an automatic system will be to use all the available information to calculate rather than negotiate a price, or to use this information to support a human negotiator.

The formalization itself will have a deep impact on how we do business. In a more open world, competition may be based on special products and features, add-on services, high quality, low prices, reliable deliveries, good service and customer support, personal relations, and so on. A formalized world will allow for fewer competitive parameters. For example, if the bike manufacturer's computer requests a quote for one hundred battery-powered headlights, a formalized way to handling quotes may be simply to accept the lowest bid. But in the real world functionality, technical solutions, and quality play an important part, as well as personal connections and trust. Of course, some of these attributes may be incorporated in the procurement process, but they complicate an automatic system. For example, how is quality expressed in formalized terms and how do we define a formalized function to balance functionality and price? How do we determine trust, and can we ascertain a cost for the possibility of a delayed order? For B2C applications, we may not get the best price from the nearby garage, but we know that vendor will be willing to help us out the day the car breaks down. Similar considerations apply to B2B worlds.

We conquer the world by using **both** manual and automatic processes, using the human being in the more open parts (negotiation), the automatic processing on the closed parts (transaction processing).

When we use the computer as an assistant to human activities, we can get the benefits of both open and closed systems. In this scenario, the human procurer negotiates the contracts with the suppliers, does the bidding, and selects the best offers, while the computer automatically takes care of the "paperwork"—the secretarial work—such as creating and transmitting purchase orders based on contracts, or requesting quotes based on the procurer's specifications. In the latter case, the computer will receive and present the quotes, allowing the human operator to

For many applications, the computer should be viewed as an **assistant**—the human makes the decisions and the computer takes care of the "paperwork."

make the decisions. This balance between flexibility and automation takes advantage of both the open and closed world.

Within some domains, full automation may be possible to achieve in a painless manner. These are domains with rigid standards or products that can be described completely by specifications. Some raw materials and simpler products fall in this category. However, even then, there may be distinctions between products (eighty gram, white, A4, laser printer paper does not tell the whole story), but we may choose to ignore the differences to get the efficiency of an automated procurement process.

56   Outsourcing

B2B applications make it easier to **specialize**, to fulfill the demands of a more complicated business environment in which each part covers a very narrow area. The whole, a large organization or a project, can then be created out of these specialized parts, such as groups, departments, or individual companies, using B2B techniques.

Emerging companies in the early part of the twentieth century had to do everything themselves. Car manufacturers had rubber plantations, produced tires, and owned ships to transport goods and materials. This approach was necessary to reduce uncertainty and because companies lacked a working business infrastructure, but it was also a way of making another buck: Companies could implement their business models in the whole value chain. Today, the need for more specialization makes it difficult to master all activities. Businesses try to concentrate on core functions, outsourcing everything else to suppliers and service providers. The doorman may no longer be a company employee, but someone hired from a security company that can offer the necessary training and compliance with laws and regulations. The call center functions can be outsourced, perhaps to quite another part of the world where the company can draw benefits from low wages.

A business no longer needs to run its own computers or software, but can let an ASP (Application Service Provider[1]) handle these functions or use applications in the cloud—applications that are available over the Internet. Shipyards in industrial countries may concentrate on design, planning, and perhaps refitting of ships, leaving simpler jobs, such as welding, to underdeveloped countries where wages are lower. Similarly, software companies in Europe and the US may have programming groups in India. Manufacturers of everything from computers to bikes may leave the actual production of parts to others, concentrating on core functions such as design, marketing, sales, and assembly.

Fundamental to outsourcing are processes that can be formalized. This may be easy when setting up a contract with the security company. We want a guard at the door at all times during office hours. The call center functions may be as simple as taking telephone orders and entering them in a computer system. Manufacturing of parts that are clearly specified may be moved from an in-house facility to an outside supplier. However, even with such simple functions, there may be informal parts that may be lost when a process is outsourced. The firm's own doormen were able to provide directions, knew employees and major customers personally and could let them in without a pass, could say if someone was in or not, and were an extra re-

Outsourcing requires services to be formalized, such as in a **contract**. The advantage is that specialists can perform the services; the disadvantage is that open functions may be unfulfilled.

source for special events. Although only personnel who know the company well—not an outside agency—may perform many of these functions, we could try to incorporate some of them in the outsourcing contract. However, we may run into the same problems we have discussed earlier—the complexity of foreseeing every possible situation.

The situation is similar for a call center. When giving the next order, customers may comment on the service given on previous orders, thereby providing valuable information that may be lost if the collection of this additional information is not a part of the contract. Outsourcing manufacturing may cause problems, too. When this was performed in-house, we had opportunities to modify plans and handle emergencies that may not be allowed with an outside supplier. With close contact between designers and production, the latter may also have important feedback, for example, in order to modify a design to make it easier to produce.

Trust is also an important factor in outsourcing. A firm may find it cost effective to outsource the operation of servers and databases to an ASP or to a cloud service. But this is like choosing a bank. The firm must rely on the provider to offer the necessary service level and keep all the company data secure, just as they must trust the bank to guard their money. But while banks may be working under strong government regulations and guaranties, there is no such thing for the ASP. The ASP may not be able to maintain the service level, may fail to protect the data, or may go belly up. Either way, our firm may be in a critical situation.

Electronic communication makes some of these outsourcing activities possible and simply facilitates others. For example, outsourcing call-center functions or computer operations cannot be done without computer networks. Manufacturers rely on these networks to have efficient communication with suppliers, for sending purchase orders, specifications, drawings, and so on. The faster and cheaper that we can perform these transactions, the easier it will be to outsource activities. Some predict that Internet and Web technologies may lay the foundation for completely new business models.

Not all functions are good candidates for outsourcing. Core competencies should be kept in-house. If we lose track of these parts, we also lose track of the business. Core competencies should be the value that we add to the chain, those being man-

> With **global access** to information, more and more processes and services can be performed in any location, by any type of organization.

A danger of **outsourcing** is that it is very difficult to outsource manufacturing without also outsourcing competence and knowledge.

agement, marketing, a patented design, or production techniques.

Some years ago a Norwegian company received the prestigious Norway Design price for a new porcelain coffee set.[2] This caused some embarrassment when one found that the products were not only manufactured in Bangladesh, but were also designed there. A danger of outsourcing is that it is very difficult to outsource manufacturing without also outsourcing competence and knowledge. Smart people in other countries soon will learn how to copy products, and also how to make better products. Japan is a good example. After the Second World War, Japan rebuilt its industry based on copying products, such as cameras, electronic equipment, and cars. They soon learned how to improve these, and then to design their own.

Notes

1   Not to be confused with Active Server Pages, Microsoft's technology for implementing dynamic Web pages, discussed in Chapter 39.

2   See www.skup.no/Metoderapporter/ SKUP-metoderapporter_for_2004/1017Metoderapport.doc (in Norwegian)

PART 8

Cloud Computing and Large Data Repositories

Modern computer technology is able to handle and store huge amounts of data. An ordinary consumer can get a two-terabyte disk (a terabyte is one trillion bytes) for just a hundred dollars. This technological advance makes it possible for companies, such as Google, Apple, Amazon, Yahoo, and Facebook to build large data centers. Instead of using sophisticated computers, they employ millions of very simple units, each with its own processor, memory, and disk. These units are mounted on large racks within an open container; a data center consists of a large number of these containers. Data centers are situated all over the world, and their main operation costs seem to be energy, to power the machines and for cooling. The same data is stored on several disks, which creates robust systems independent of failures in a few computers.

These huge data centers have been used to offer a variety of services. For example:

- *Indexing the Web.* This makes search facilities such as Google possible.
- *Social networks.* With 800 million users demanding fast access, Facebook needs large data centers.
- *Map services.* Google, as an example, provides extensive 2D and 3D map services, with maps, terrain profiles, and satellite images for most of the world.
- *Google Street View* offers panoramic views along many streets all over the world. Initially made for roads, the service is now extended to bike trails, ski slopes, and even the Amazon River.
- *Streaming and download services for* music, books, movies, and so on. Examples are Spotify, Wimp and iTunes.
- *Large repositories*, of books, pictures, scientific articles, etc.

As many companies discovered that they had more computer resources than they needed, they took the next step—offering computing services to external customers. Amazon, a pioneer here, launched Amazon Web Service in 2006. Today, many companies are offering such cloud services. According to Wikipedia, the name comes from the use of clouds as an abstraction for the complex infrastructure described in system diagrams. Another interpretation could be to view the computing resources being somewhere "in the cloud," that is, we do not really know where they are situated.

Chapter 57 takes a look at cloud computing. Then, in Chapter 58, we discuss all the origins of data that we have today and how these can be collected. Next we examine applications that can utilize the enormous data repositories that are collected. An example is natural language translation (Chapter 59). As discussed earlier, natural languages are not formal, and efforts to implement translation based on dictionaries and grammar rules have failed. However, Google can offer a better translator based on the idea of comparing similar texts in many languages. That is, Google implements a cut-and-paste strategy, using the work of human translators, which is possible because of the huge repositories of text that Google indexes and stores. A detailed case, showing how such text repositories can be used, in this case for proofreading, is presented in Chapter 60.

As all types of background data become accessible, designing "smarter" systems is possible. Smarter systems are not a way of programming intelligence, but rather a way to organize, compute, and present data in the right form. I present a case of an adaptive system in Chapter 61, that is, a system that can learn.

With data and applications in the cloud or in a location that everyone can access over the Internet, collaborative systems are possible, in which many can participate in a task. Wikipedia is a good example of this "crowdsourcing." These issues are discussed in more detail in Chapter 62.

This part ends with a look at how cloud data, GPS, and smartphones may be used to implement a personal assistant (Chapter 63).

57　Cloud Computing

Computing services, both the hardware and the software, traditionally have been offered as products—something we buy and install in our own locations. "Cloud computing" presents computer services as any other utility, comparable to electricity, based on a grid of resources that customers do not see. When we need a service, in this case a computer application, we plug in and get what we want. Since data and applications are accessible over the Web, it is not important where the facilities really are. Cloud computing can offer cheaper, more efficient, and reliable services.

57.1　Service models

Cloud computing offers a set of services, storage resources, computation, and data management over the Internet.

Cloud computing offers a set of services, storage resources, computation, and data management over the Internet. The cloud service is accessed using a terminal, which can be a PC, a tablet, or a mobile phone. The interface tool is often a standard browser or an App. Advanced cloud services use virtualization, implementing "virtual" computers on top of a software and hardware facility. That is, customers can then run their own operating systems, and applications easily can be moved from one physical location to the other. There are three fundamental service models:

- *Infrastructure as a service (IaaS)*. Cloud providers offer implementation of a virtual machine. Customers have the same experience as running their own computer systems, but the basic hardware and software are provided in the cloud. In this case, the customer is responsible for maintaining the virtual machine, that is, installing operating systems, databases, and so on. The advantage is that the basic resources may be better utilized than if each virtual machine were running on its own hardware. For example, a local system must be able to handle peak loads. On a large cloud facility, the peak loads for different customers may vary, especially if customers are in different time zones.

- *Platform as a service (PaaS)*. Cloud providers offer a complete computer platform, with an operating system, databases, Web server, and perhaps a software development platform. The advantage for consumers is that they can run their own software, without the cost of buying and maintaining their own computer system.

- *Software as a service (SaaS).* This is often what we are offered as end users, complete services from the cloud. An example is Google Docs, a full office suite. Customers avoid having to install or maintain software themselves and can have access to data and services everywhere. Collaboration with other users also is possible, as documents, spreadsheets, and presentations can be available to all.

Most end users are familiar with the SaaS model through Facebook, Google, or many other Internet applications. The other two models are more interesting for businesses.

57.2   Advantages

The **advantages** of cloud computing are better utilization of resources, more reliable systems, and services that can be accessed everywhere.

Applications are more robust when they can be run independent of servers, memory units, and networks. For example, in the cloud, more than one instance of each application, provisioned over different infrastructures, can be operated. If one of these infrastructures has technical problems with power, servers, memory units, or basic software, the load can be shifted to another instance. Similarly, if the load increases for one application, additional resources can be assigned, such as processing power or memory, or more instances can be created. Similarly, when the load decreases, the number of instances can be reduced and resources offered to other applications. To save energy, infrastructure, such as servers, can be shut down when the load is low, and remaining applications can be moved to other servers.

Cloud computing gives us an additional layer between the infrastructure and the applications. With this layer, we can run virtual machines on top of the infrastructure. These machines will, of course, need basic resources to run, but they will be independent of any specific device. This is similar to the power grid. If a power station closes down, another part of the grid takes over, and we will still have electricity (we hope).

The advantages are better utilization of resources, more reliable systems, and services that can be accessed from everywhere. Companies that need additional computer resources for a limited time can rent both processing power and computer space in the cloud, or can choose to have all their facilities there.

The latter may cause problems with regulations. Many countries demand that important data, such as accounting data or other sensitive data, must be stored within the country. Then a hybrid model can be the solution, such as operating some services on the company's computer systems and others in the cloud. In the long run, cloud providers may be able to guarantee that data will be stored under a given jurisdiction, for example the United States or European Union, and that they comply with all requirements of this legal region.

Some companies also chose to use cloud techniques to run their own systems, to achieve more robust systems and better utilization of resources. By joining together with other cloud providers, they can have low-cost backup resources. For example, if there is trouble in one infrastructure, critical services can be migrated to the other. If one company needs additional resources at a given time, these can be offered by the other cloud. The idea is to have applications that are completely location free and that can be deployed on every cloud.[1]

57.3   Disadvantages

A problem with cloud computing today is the lack of standards. If a cloud provider goes belly up, it may not be easy to move to another provider. Another problem may be privacy. As long as data is stored locally, we are in full control, but how can we be sure that cloud providers will protect our privacy? Data protection from a technical perspective also is an issue. The cloud providers run complex systems. Can we, at any time, be sure that data will not be lost and that the integrity of databases will be maintained?

Many of these questions may be answered satisfactorily in the long run. Already, the pioneers of cloud computing are less concerned about these issues than about those who have not tried the technology.[2] Standards are emerging, and most cloud providers offer well-documented systems.

57.4   Discussion

The alternative to using resources in the cloud is for customers to maintain their own computer resources. For a private individual, this can be as simple as running a PC, implementing the basic software that is needed, and storing data locally. For a company, it implies running a full server with an operating system, databases, and application programs. At one time, this implied severe hardware and software maintenance costs in addition to software licensing fees. Today, plug and play, automatic updates, and more reliable hardware have reduced these costs. When software providers get competition from free or cheap cloud services, we also can assume lower licensing costs. Therefore, the balance between local and cloud services will be maintained. The local solution offers the highest control over data, and will probably be the main option for many years to come, especially when privacy is important.

However, cloud applications have many advantages, and hybrid models may offer the best of both worlds for businesses: running sensitive applications in-house and all other services through the cloud. As we have seen, an option for larger companies is to organize their own infrastructure as a cloud, which will offer reliability, good resource allocation, and a flexibility that the standard client-server models cannot provide.

The cloud may be a good alternative when extra resources are needed, when it is important to have access from everywhere, and when reliability is important. Even private persons and small companies can get an advantage by avoiding the task of maintaining their own systems. The low cost of cloud solutions may also be an important argument for many.

Notes

1 Rochwerger et al (2011) Reservoir—When one cloud is not enough, IEEE COMPUTER, March and Armbrust et al. (2010) A View of Cloud Computing, Comm. of the ACM, vol. 53, no. 4, April.

2 For example, see Narasimhan, B. and Nichols, R. (2011) State of Cloud Applications and platforms: The Cloud Adopters' view, IEEE Computer, March.

58 Collecting Data

On the Web and in the cloud, we find huge amounts of data. Where does all this come from? At one time, in the early days of computing, punch operators were required to type in the input to various programs. The world was still one of paper, and the transformation from paper to electronic form was expensive.

But, this changed with online systems. Now data originates in digital form, and all types of symbolic data can be digitalized. Since storage is cheap and the capacity of modern devices is nearly unlimited, there is no reason to delete. Therefore, many of use keep photos, documents, and e-mails "forever." Privacy regulation may mandate deleting data, such as administrative data on phone calls or credit card transactions, after a time. However, the unidentifiable parts of such data may be retained for statistics. For example, an online store or an airline may keep impersonalized data on all transactions for planning purposes. This is one of the advantages of introducing customer cards. The customer is offered some discounts or payback, while the company receives valuable data about buying patterns and preferences.

Many new devices, sensors, and monitors provide large amounts of data for scientists—everything from simple sensors that collect data on temperature to satellite systems that offer high-resolution images. Again, since storing these data is relatively cheap, large repositories can be built. While an X-ray apparatus may take a few images of the patient, MRI (magnetic resonance imaging) machines may collect many hundred images or slices, which can be used to provide 3D images.

When it is possible and cheap to collect more data, it will be done.

When it is possible and cheap to collect more data, it will be done, not only in science and in medicine, but also by individuals. For example, we take many more photos with digital than with analog cameras.

Google has been a pioneer in recognizing the value of data, which began with indexing the Web. Since then we have seen a lot of new services, such as photo indexing and world maps. One of the most impressive is the street-view system, with which Google has captured 360-degree consecutive photos on all major, and many minor roads, all over the world. The service also has been extended to bike roads and ski tracks. Other providers present a similar service for walking trails, and

Google soon will present photos on the Amazon River and the Great Barrier Reef (underwater).

Special cars with nine directional cameras mounted on top collect the street views, providing the 360-degree panorama. Position is determined by GPS. In addition a laser will measure distances, so that the data can be presented as a 3D model. The amazing thing with this service is not the technology, but the fact that so many roads are included.

Another way of building large repositories is to engage the public. Wikipedia, YouTube, and photo sites such as Flickr and iStockphoto are good examples. (I cover these issues in Chapter 62 on crowdsourcing.)

Figure 58.1 The first edition of Aftenposten (May 14, 1860), on the Internet in image form.

Data generated prior to the digital age and the Internet is not lost. Many efforts are underway to convert these data into digital forms. A simple method is to store paper as images. An example is the Norwegian national newspaper *Aftenposten* that offers digital versions of nearly every issue from 1860 until today (Figure 58.1).

Project Guten-berg is a volunteer effort to digitize books, mostly public domain books, those for which the intellec-tual property rights have expired or been forfeited.

Project Gutenberg is a volunteer effort to digitize books, mostly public domain books, those for which the intellectual property rights have expired or been forfeited. Many of the books are classics. Books are stored as plain text, but often with formats suitable for different types of e-book readers. Today Project Gutenberg offers around forty thousand e-books.

Google Scholar also offers e-books, along with scientific papers. Most of this material is copyrighted, but Google solved this problem by offering only abstracts of papers that are not openly available in full text form and directing the user to sites where the full text can be obtained.

59   Automatic Translation

Automatic translation of natural languages is something people dreamed of since the early days of computing. Large resources, from the US military, and later from the EU, have been used to master this task, with unimpressive results. Perhaps one needs to be a human to translate a text correctly from one language to the other. However, Google has managed to make a translator that can provide a rough translation, at least for simple text. Google's translator uses a cut-and-paste method, accessing large text repositories in many languages.

59.1   Natural languages

In some respects the **ambiguousness of natural language** may be a disadvantage, but in most cases it helps us to deal efficiently with a dynamic and complicated world.

Natural languages are not formalized, which is perhaps their great strength. In contrast to a formalized programming language, a natural language allows us to introduce and talk about concepts and processes that we cannot define, perhaps that we do not fully understand. Further, natural languages are very effective. By relying heavily on context, we do not have to say everything. "I'll see you at noon" is enough. It is not necessary to give the place and the date; "Have you called Bob?" may be perfectly clear, even if there are many Bobs.

Natural language formalization has been an area for intensive research, as the reward of success will be enormous. In our economy, language is a huge barrier to effective international cooperation. The European Union may have programs to support language skills and for internationalization, but even at academic conferences, the deficiency of foreign language skills impedes effective communication.[1]

In the 1960s, the US Navy presented the first primitive versions of an English-Russian translation system, which are easy to create. As an example, the code for a simple Norwegian-English translating system based on an electronic two-way dictionary, stored in a database table, can be as simple as:

```
function translate(inputword as string) as string
   dim stdset As Recordset, query As String

   query="SELECT English FROM dictionary
      WHERE Norwegian ='" & inputWord & "'"
   Set stdset=CurrentDatab.OpenRecordset(query)
   translate=stdset!English
end function
```

This simple function (written in Visual Basic) receives a word ("inputWord") in Norwegian, makes a query to the dictionary database table, selects the English translation for this word, and returns the result, translating one word at a time. With a few more program sentences, a continuous two-way translation can be achieved. In testing the program, we find that the Norwegian sentence "Her er jeg" is translated to "Here is I," which is understandable but not quite correct.

Natural language is in the open realm, and is impossible to formalize in the general case.

Are such minor details just a matter of more effort and more capital? We will soon find that synonymy (different words, one meaning), polysemy (one word, different meanings), and the dynamic effects of language complicate our efforts. Some words cannot be translated easily; expressions and metaphors have different interpretations in different languages; and the structure of languages may be quite different. The correct translation of a word will not always lie in the word itself. We may have to look at the sentence, the paragraph, or, in the worst case, the document type. As an example, the word "web" has many meanings. We must work on a semantic level to be able to perform the correct translation. We also have to consider style: A personal letter requires a different selection of words than a formal document, and a one from a teenager, an elderly person, and a professional person may include different terminology.

The problem remains to develop systems that can give a fully correct translation. Some approaches try to use a combination of automatic and manual translation, in which a human translator modifies the computer output. In many cases, this results in a strange sentence structure. My students often complain that the "help text" provided with US software is unreadable in the Norwegian version, and that the only way to understand the text is to translate back into English. That is, the words are Norwegian, but the sentence structure is English.

59.2   Translations with cut and paste

Today, we find translators on the Web that try to handle English, Spanish, French, German, and many other languages. An example is shown in Figure 59.1 where we have used Google's translator tool on this paragraph, translating into Spanish and then back to English. As seen, the results are reasonably good.

Hoy en día, nos encontramos con traducto-
res en la Web que tratan de manejar el
inglés, español, francés, alemán, y muchos
otros idiomas. Un ejemplo se muestra en la
Figure 59.1, donde hemos utilizado la herra-
mienta de Google Traductor en este párrafo,
su traducción al español y luego de vuelta a
Inglés. Como se ve, los resultados son
razonablemente buena.

Today, we find on the Web that translators try to handle
English, Spanish, French, German, and many other languages. An example is shown in Figure 59.1, where we
have used Google Translation tool in this paragraph, its
translation into Spanish and then back to English. As
seen, the results are reasonably good.

Figure 59.1 Example of natural language translation using Google's translator.

Google enhances the automatic translation by comparing
the text to manual translations. Google has huge archives of
text in many languages, for example from EU documents that
have been manually translated into other European languages.
Thus most of the translation may be performed with cut-and-
past techniques using this text repository. In addition, Google
asks the user to provide alternative translations; thus, it has the
ability to learn. In many situations, Google provides good translations, and even if there are errors, it is most often possible to
get an idea of what being said. However, the translation is far
from foolproof.

There are exceptions. Machine translation has been very
useful within closed worlds, such as translation of weather
forecasts. With some discipline when creating the original text,
a limited vocabulary may allow for a high-level formalization
that can facilitate automatic translation.

Machine transla-
tion has been very
useful within
closed worlds.

Note

1   At a conference I attended, the Finnish speaker could not understand the question posed by an Italian. An American saved the day by translating the question from Italian-English to English and the answer from Finnish-English to a version that the Italian could understand. While citizens of smaller countries are forced to have foreign language skills, citizens of the larger European countries can manage only with their own languages, until the day they participate in international work. One can understand why language skills and student exchange are prioritized areas for the European Union.

60 Case: Proofreading

Proofreading is simpler than translation. Spelling and grammar checkers help us to some extent, but these cannot remove semantic errors from a document, such as when the words and the grammar are correct but have no meaning.

Here I will present a case to show how this task can be performed, using a similar strategy to Google's, that is, to compare text to a large repository.[1]

60.1 Automatic proofreading

An automatic system for proofreading can be devised that works by comparing the user's text offered to that of a large text repository. While a full system can be offered in the cloud, I will present a prototype that uses a local text repository. This has the advantage that we also can study the inner parts of such a system.

Proofreading is both tedious and difficult. It is expensive to hire a professional to do the job, and finding a competent person also may be difficult. Newspapers skip proofreaders to save money and most writers try to do the job themselves. The consequences are clearly seen—from errors in text written by professionals to incomprehensive e-mails and blogs—which create misunderstandings, offer false data, and, in the worst cases, may give a very bad impression. As an example, a university will not be eager to admit a master student after receiving this e-mail:

> I am a student of MSc Logistics and Supply Chain Management from ... University, London. Last weel I had the presentation regarding Molde University and I heart that you are the module leader of Management of value. I am wondering if you may write me back more about that module, because it not really clear for me? In particular, when I am considering to go foe the second semestr to Molde. I will be really approciate for it.

While we can offer very good arguments for spending more time on proofreading it seems that this is all in vain. Few are willing to spend much effort here. Online media with continuous deadlines often do not have the time needed for careful proofreading.

A solution could be to automate the process. As a first step, we can use the spelling and grammar checkers that are a part of modern word processing systems. But these are limited. The spelling checker marks a word that is not found in a dictionary, while the grammar checker is based on a set of very simple rules. For example, the grammar checker in Microsoft Office will detect the error in "Jim have a red car," but not in "Jim, my oldest son, have a red car." And, of course, a typo such as "Jim has a red far" will not be found. Had our student used the proofreading tools in Microsoft Office, the spelling checker would have indicated "weel," "semestr," and "appreciate"; while the grammar checker would suggest "going" instead of "to go." However, several of the more serious errors would not be found (for example, "I heart" and "foe").

Another option for this student would have been to ask someone else to check her work. But there may not have been any candidate who had mastered English to ask. Instead she could have asked the whole world using a search engine. For example, when writing in a foreign language we may wonder if it is "in," "on," or "at" "the west coast." By offering the alternatives to Google, using exclamation marks to get a frequency count for the complete phrase, we will find that "we live at the west coast" has one occurrence, while "on" has three million and "in" six million occurrences.[2] We can then conclude that both "in" and "on" can be used, but we may end up with the more frequent choice, "in."

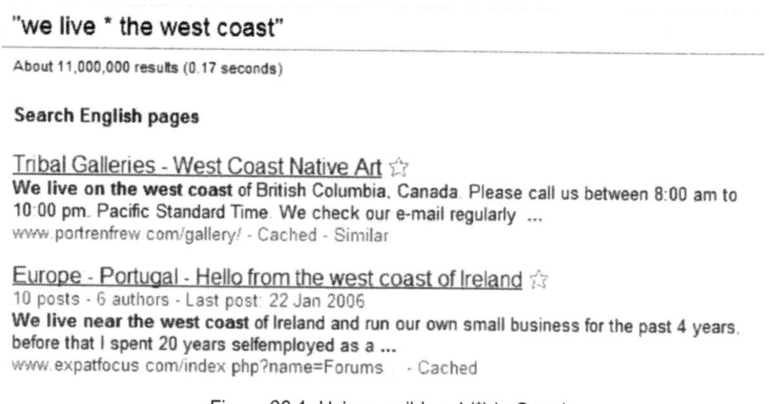

"we live * the west coast"

About 11,000,000 results (0.17 seconds)

Search English pages

Tribal Galleries - West Coast Native Art ☆
We live on the west coast of British Columbia, Canada. Please call us between 8:00 am to 10:00 pm. Pacific Standard Time. We check our e-mail regularly ...
www.portrenfrew.com/gallery/ - Cached - Similar

Europe - Portugal - Hello from the west coast of Ireland ☆
10 posts - 6 authors - Last post: 22 Jan 2006
We live near the west coast of Ireland and run our own small business for the past 4 years. before that I spent 20 years selfemployed as a ...
www.expatfocus.com/index.php?name=Forums - Cached

Figure 60.1. Using a wildcard (*) in Google.

If the alternatives are unknown, a wildcard (*) may be used in the query. An example is shown in Figure 60.1. The possible alternatives can be extracted from the result pages, and we can use the method described above to get the number of occurrences with each alternative word in the sentence—a tedious process. In addition, we have to find the phrases where we are uncertain. Many write "we had ice cream for desert" and are quite happy with their spelling.

60.2   An automated proofreader

An automated proofreader system will find and offer suggestions for corrections for many types of errors, from spelling mistakes to semantic errors, based on a large text repository. The idea is to compare the user's sentence to what everybody else has written. Instead of using Google or another search engine, we will build our own text repository for this case. We will have the advantage of full control over the underlying data, for example, to correct punctuation and numerical errors. Also, Google and other search engines often block programmable access, a practice that follows from its business model—real users click on ads, programs do not.

Using full sentences requires very large text repositories to find constructs similar to the one the user may offer. We can reduce this problem by looking only at parts of a sentence, but the more context considered, the better the system's suggestions will be.

The case prototype is based on large text repositories caught from the Web. The prototype includes examples of text in both English and Norwegian, but the system will work in any language. The system consists of three parts:

1. A *spider* that traverses the Web to build a text repository.

2. An *index builder* that creates indexes for fast access. For each word an index will show the file numbers where the word occurs. For each file and word, another index will show in which lines (in the file) the word occurs.

3. An *analyzer*, that analyzes the user's sentences.

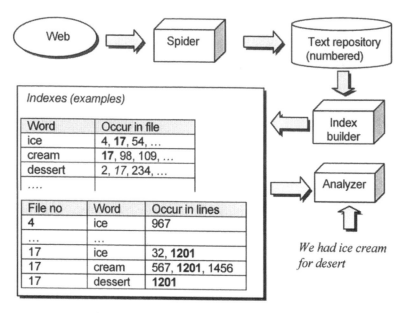

Figure 60.2 Spider, index builder, and the analyzer.

Figure 60.2 shows the data flow from the Web to the text repository, and the indexes that are built based on the text files that are stored there. The analyzer will use these indexes (a few examples are presented) to evaluate alternative wording in the user's sentence. Each of these parts is described in detail below.

60.3   The spider

The spider traverses the Web, downloads text, cleans the text of formatting data, and stores the result in consecutively numbered files. An identifier (a hash-code) for each Web page (URL) is calculated and stored in a database to avoid downloading a page more than once. Links found in the text are remembered for later downloads. The spider handles text in HTML, PDF and doc formats.

Initially, the spider is given a seed, a collection of Web-addresses. I have chosen to use links to newspapers, universities, government agencies, and large companies. By parsing these pages, the spider will find new links that can be tried. To simplify, I let the spider consider Web sites with text only in one language. For example, in English we look for extensions such as .com, .edu, or .org. In Norwegian, the spider will only consider .no sites. This works reasonably well. A better alternative would be to use automatic language detection, as the extension only distinguishes the origin of a site, not the language. In this prototype case, the spider has created approximately 2,500 text files of 1 MB each, both for English and Norwegian. That is, the text repository is 2.5 gigabytes in each language.

60.4   The index builder

An index structure is created to avoid traversing all files for a given sentence. The index shows in which files each word is found. Then, for each file and each word, a new index will give the lines in the file where the word occurs. To avoid too many spelling mistakes, we may set a frequency limit on the words we index. For this case, I set this value as ten, ignoring all words with a lower frequency. Since a word is defined as a string of letters enclosed by spaces or punctuation, I ended up with approximate two hundred thousand "words" in each language. Interestingly enough, even with the limit of ten, a lot of spelling mistakes pass the filter, indicating that Web writers make a lot of common mistakes. To achieve fast access these indexes are stored in simple text files, approximately forty million for each language, a number that poses no problem for a modern PC running on Windows.

When the user provides a sentence with N words, the first index is used to find the files where at least N-1 of the words occurs. That is, since we are looking for alternatives for each word in the sentence, we have to perform N queries, in which one and one word is replaced by a wildcard. For each alternative query this will give a list of files. For each file, we will check to see if the N-1 words of the query occur in the same line in the file. If this is the case, the file will be parsed, the sentence analyzed, and alternatives for wildcards will be retrieved.

60.5   The analyzer

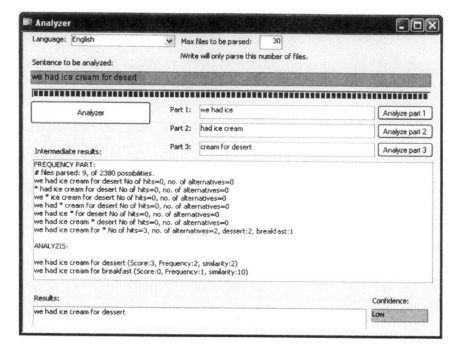

Figure 60.3 Screen shot of the analyzer.

A screen shot of the analyzer is shown in Figure 60.3. Here the user has provided the sentence "We had ice cream for desert." The system suggests correcting this to "We had ice cream for dessert." From the intermediate results, we see that the first alternative received zero hits, and the latter, two. One occurrence of "We had ice cream for breakfast" was found.

The analyzer offers a "confidence value" based on the difference of frequency between the original sentence and the suggestion, the similarity of the words, and the frequency for other alternatives. In this example, the confidence level is considered low.

60.6   Parallel data processing

The prototype works on a single PC, and requires building an index structure. Even then, the prototype will use everything from a few seconds to over a minute to process a sentence. It works especially slowly on long sentences with most common words, as this requires parsing a large number of files. This

The system **transforms** knowledge of writing into knowledge of reading.

slow speed is unsatisfactory for a product version. Further, while a 2.5-gigabyte repository is suitable for testing, a much larger one is needed to offer enough samples for comparison. We could improve the prototype by keeping more of the index structure in memory, but it still will not scale to a full product version in which large repositories will be needed to serve many users simultaneously. The solution is to use parallelism, a set up of many (thousands) computers each working on a part of the text base.

The *MapReduce* method[3] seems a promising candidate. Here the *map* operation is applied to each record and produces a set of intermediate key/value pairs. For example, in an application to count the number of words in a document collection, the operation can map from documents to a list of value pairs, each a word, and the number of occurrences of this word in the document. The *reduce* operation is then applied to the results, all pairs that share the same key, which gives the total frequency for each word in the collection. The advantages of this set up are that the operations can be performed on large sets of simple computers, and the "parallelism" is hidden from the application developer.

In our case we could choose to apply the user's queries directly to the text repository, that is, to the one megabyte text files, mapping the occurrence of each alternative sentence to an intermediate sentence/frequency pair and then running a reduce to get the total frequencies with alternatives. Each single computer then would handle a map or a reduce operation, which should enable a large number of user queries to be served in real time, given that there are a large cluster of servers.

60.7   Discussion

Should we follow the **norm**, or go our own way when writing?

The system presented here is based on the idea of following the majority. If others write "in London" instead of ours "at London," we have the option to change. This will not work in all cases. The system may suggest that the sentence "we eat avocado" be changed to "we eat apples," because the latter may has a higher frequency than the first. Such false alternatives can be a drawback; however, with large repositories, the correct alternative may have enough occurrences to be accepted.

Even with a large repository, the system never will be able to correct language automatically. As with spelling and grammar checkers, it can offer only suggestions for improvements. These systems, along with thesauruses, transform knowledge of writing into knowledge of reading. Since most of us are more proficient in reading than writing, we can use such tools to our advantage.

A more philosophical argument can be made against tools that let us follow the norm. Is this really what we want, to be only as good as the majority? For many the answer is yes. When we write in a foreign language, or if we are not too proficient in our own, getting closer to the norm is just what we want to achieve. However, in the end, these tools offer suggestions only; the user must decide to follow the suggestion or not.

Note that the tool also will correct facts. If we write that Mount Everest is 9,000 meters high, our facts will be corrected to 8,848 meters. But we may get into problems with time-dependent data, for example, with sentences such as "The prime minister of Great Britain is ..." In practice these cases will seldom be problematic as they often will address an area where the user is competent. However, false suggestions will always be a nuisance.

The prototype implementation is based on text from the Web, which is not the ideal source, as many texts on the Web are of low quality with an abundance of spelling and other mistakes. Another problem is that the same text may be found in many different sites, for example, articles that may be presented by a chain of newspapers. The ideal solution would be to get access to large, high-quality text repositories, such as bibliographical databases for books, journal papers, or official reports. With these, one could build a high quality repository with little effort.

Open sources also could be explored, from Project Gutenberg[4] and similar sites. The problem is that really large repositories are needed, probably terabytes of data. We find these amounts of text on the Web, but we would need to perform a quality check on each paragraph before adding it to the repository. For example, one could ignore the paragraph if too many common spelling mistakes were found, or if it had been stored previously.

Even with large high-quality repositories, there will be cases in which there is no match for the user's sentence. A remedy is to split the sentence into parts, checking each part independently. The prototype can do this, but the disadvantage of this approach is that the system ignores context information that may be valuable for a good suggestion.

While the prototype presented here has limitations, especially as it runs on only one PC, a full product version could use a cluster of many machines. This is the "Google way" of data processing. We can expect, perhaps not too far in the future, that these proofreading tools will be offered as cloud computing, similar to the other language tools offered today. Ideally, we would want proofreading functions to be part of the word processor, offering advice as we write—just as with today's spelling and grammar checkers. The text repository and the necessary indexes for the language that we use could then be stored locally or in the cloud.

A learning system is also a possibility. If few users correct "We eat avocado" to "we eat apples," the system may stop offering this suggestion. If many change "desert" to "dessert" in combination with ice cream, we could offer this suggestion with a higher confidence. Letting the system learn also will help to avoid other false suggestions, for example, with time-dependent data. Such adaptive systems are used in many applications; an example is presented in the next chapter.

A full system needs to be backed up by a large cloud computing facility.

Notes

1   This chapter is based on Olsen, K. A., Indredavik, B. (2011) A Proofreading Tool Using Brute Force Techniques, IEEE Potentials, Vol. 30, issue 4, 2011.

2   See for example Olsen, K. A., Williams, J. G. (2004). Spelling and Grammar Checking Using the Web as a Text Repository, Journal of the American Society for Information Science and Technology (JASIST), Vol. 55, no 11.

3   Dean, J. and Ghemawat, S. (2010) MapReduce: A Flexible Data Processing Tool, Communications of the ACM, Vol. 53, No 1.

4   www.gutenberg.org

61   Case: An Adaptive System

The technical
ability to store
large amounts of
reliable data, such
as data collected
from automatic
systems, offers the
possibility of
developing sys-
tems that **adapt** to
current situations.

The technical ability to store large amounts of reliable data, such as data collected from automatic systems, offers the possibility of developing systems that adapt to current situations. This case presents such a system, one that can learn from experience. It is used to estimate time of arrival (ETA) for a regular boat service on the northwestern coast of Norway.

Since the route also includes exposed areas where the relative small craft may meet heavy seas, bad weather may delay vessels. This makes it difficult to perform ETA calculations. To handle all cases a database is built based on sampling position and speed at regular intervals for each trip. This will give useful information for subsequent trips.

Using this database, the system gives very reliable ETA values, even in extraordinary situations. The system is based on a very simple and easy to understand model. ETAs are displayed on harbor terminals, and also on the Web. The system is a fast learner, and with experience, can handle many types of exceptions.[1]

61.1   ETA calculations

German trains are renowned for their punctuality. Although it may be an exaggeration to say one can set the time by the trains, 97 percent of Germany's trains run on schedule. A railway has the advantage of full control over the tracks. When buses are stuck in traffic or boats delayed by bad weather, timetables are no longer reliable, and we need a sophisticated means of calculating ETAs. In this case of the Norwegian boat service, boats run on time in good weather. But in bad weather, with strong winds and heavy seas, they have to slow down, and in some cases, may even change route, taking a longer inshore course to avoid a stretch of open sea.

Our job is to give reliable estimates for time of arrival, which are displayed at each stop along the route and also are available on the Internet and on mobile phones. With this information, passengers can use the waiting time more efficiently than by standing on a weather-beaten dock looking for the boat. The Internet service will be helpful for those who may be meeting a vessel to collect passengers or freight. While

The **timetable** is the first generation method for estimating ETAs.

With a **GPS,** we get a second-generation system in which we can take the actual position into account.

this case concerns a boat route, the methods can be applied to any type of scheduled transportation.

A timetable can be considered a first-generation method for finding ETA. The schedule is set up for a year, month, or for a certain day. It will tell when we leave and when we arrive, but is based on an optimistic view of the future. It may include data from experience, for example, that buses run somewhat slower during rush hours, but only if these delays can be anticipated. Naturally enough, we have no means of including more irregular events, such as the weather or road closures. Therefore, a schedule will work best when we have a formalized and predictable environment, which implies that we know and control the variables that influence the schedule. German Rail is a good example of such a system.

In systems in which we lack full control, or when events such as bad weather and very heavy traffic cannot be reliably forecasted, something more sophisticated is needed. A GPS system (Global Positioning System) is the key component in a second-generation system. GPS will not help us run on schedule, but we can get a better idea of ETAs based on an accurate positioning of the vehicles. Most of the GPS systems that are in use, for example in private cars, estimate time by the simple formula that we learned in school, $v=d/t$, where v is velocity, d distance and t time. Time is then given by $t=d/v$. Of course, velocity is an unknown.

Car navigators use a standard average velocity for each type of road, for example, 50 mph on a busy freeway. Often the calculations are based on speed limits, which may work well for good roads but breaks down when roads are narrow or winding. Then the speed limit is only a theoretical value. A similar case exists when other traffic, weather conditions, or roadwork necessitates a reduction in speed. A car navigator will recalculate the ETA every minute based on position, using the fixed velocity, but this could be overly optimistic if the bad conditions persist. An alternative would be to use the average speed for the first part of the journey, which may work— sometimes. But what if most of the time has been spent in a queue entering the freeway? In a few seconds, it will be our turn to join the fast-moving traffic, and the rest of our trip will go at full speed.

We need something smarter, a third-generation system, that will be able to use data from previous journeys to say

A third-generation system can use **previous experience** to estimate an ETA.

something about the future. Such a system will work best for transportation that follows the same route every time.

Another possibility would be to gather data on the conditions ahead and use this to give a good estimation. That is, instead of looking back into previous data, we can try to gather as much data as possible on the current situation. Such a solution may be viable in the future. When all cars have GPS and all positions are available in the cloud, the expected wait time on the ramp as well as the average velocity on the freeway can be calculated based on data from other vehicles. However, instead of waiting for a better infrastructure, let us study what we can do today. But, first, let us return to the Norwegian boat service.

61.2   Boat routes on the Norwegian coast

The western coast of Norway is mountainous and riddled with fjords—narrow stretches of sea that may extend hundreds of miles inland—following the "valleys" carved out by the glaciers during the ice ages. This geography makes road construction difficult. Roads often follow the coastline on the narrow strip of land between fjord and mountain. In this part of the country, there are no freeways, and roads are narrow. Driving takes time. For example, it is 85 miles between the cities of Kristiansund and Trondheim, as the bird flies. The road is 125 miles long, and the bus will take five to six hours. A boat route is a faster alternative, making the journey in three and a half hours. A catamaran boat takes close to three hundred passengers and run at a speed of 33 knots (approximately 40 mph). They make several stops along the route, servicing island communities.

These vessels, like most other ships, will send an AIS (Automatic Identification System) message every thirty seconds. This electronic signal gives vessel ID, position, course, speed, destination, and several other parameters. Sent over VHF radio, it is captured by antennas on shore or on other boats. In this way ships can exchange data with nearby ships and costal stations. Vessel movements can be monitored and collisions avoided. In our application, we are interested only in position, speed, and course from the AIS data. Since these are received from each vessel every thirty seconds, we have a formalized environment with very accurate data. We may then consider an adaptive system, one that can learn from experience.

61.3   Adaptive systems

An adaptive system can learn and then respond to the situation at hand.

An adaptive system can learn and then respond to the situation at hand. The term comes from biology, describing how an organism adapts to its environment under natural evolution. The phenomenon was first applied in computing science in control theory and cybernetics. The application of adaption may be considered a form of computer intelligence. In the 1960s, there were great expectations for this field, but these beliefs were based on a very simplified view of how tasks are performed in the real world. The problem with artificial intelligence, in the form of adaptive systems or other methods, is that the computer seldom gets the whole story; it does not get the context. This is also the fundamental problem when developing learning systems. Do they "understand" what is happening; do they have an adequate system model? (I discussed these issues in Chapters 3 and 4.)

The idea of adaption will work best in situations in which the system model gives a good approximation of the application area.

The idea of adaption will work best in situations in which the system model gives a good approximation of the application area. Many applications for adaptive methods are found within technical environments, such as for steering robots, tuning wireless systems, network control, recognizing visual images, or traffic surveillance. In these examples, we find the level of formalization needed for an adaptive application to work well.

Our application is similar. First, the vessels have a timetable to follow and an incentive to keep to this. If there are too many delays, the boat company will be punished by a reduction in the financial support they get from the state. Second, we have formalized data from the AIS system, position, speed and course every thirty seconds. Therefore, this application looks like a promising one for an adaptive system.

61.4   The solution

When developing IT systems, it can sometimes be helpful to study how the problem would be solved in the real world. Let us assume that we are onboard a vessel. After leaving the harbor, the boat accelerates to a speed of 33 knots. We look forward to arriving at our destination in three hours time. Suddenly we are out in heavy seas, and the boat slows down to half speed. Will we arrive on time? Let us ask the captain, who has years' of experience on this route. He tells us, "No problem. With winds from the southward we have to slow down just on this short stretch. In five minutes time, we will be at full speed again." In practice, the captain may not always be available, or he may not remember all details from previous trips. However, we can develop a system that monitors everything and registers all the details. Based on this information, the system should be able to give even more accurate information than the captain.

In its simplest form, the world of this model consists of positions, speeds, and delays. That is, we expect to be able to forecast a delay based on the boat's position and the speed it has at that position. These values will be stored in a database every thirty seconds, with small discrepancies in both of these values from one trip to the next. Therefore, the values are rounded before they are stored. Speed, for example, is considered within tolerances of ± 3 knots (± 4 mph).

This simple model is sufficient for our case. In the following examples, we will make things easier by only considering ETA for the final destination. But the model can, of course, also be used to calculate arrival times at stops along the route. We also ignore data on compass courses, assuming that the route is only serviced in one direction (in practice we have to consider that a boat can be at one position at a certain speed, but following different courses).

On the very first trip, we have no data in the system. The ETA is then based on the timetable. Still, every thirty seconds we store position and speed for use later on. Let us assume that we are four minutes late on arrival. Then, we go into the database and register these four minutes for every entity of position and speed. Now we start a second trip. If this follows the same pattern as the first, we will operate with an ETA that assumes a four-minute delay, that is, when we perform a lookup based on the actual position and speed we will find the four-minute value in the database.

The current trip ends up being six minutes late, and the database is updated with this new value. On the third trip, we experience strong winds and heavy seas. The vessel has to slow down and when we look into the database, we will not find any entities of position and speed for the current situation. We could then base the ETA on the timetable, but it seems more prudent to use the maximum delay experienced until now (six minutes). In fact, we end up with a twenty minute delay on this trip. This journey will give new entities of position and speed to the database, all of which get a delay value of twenty minutes.

On the next trip, you are invited to calculate an ETA. Let us assume that the weather is nice and that the boat follows the track of the very first trip. You will probably suggest a four minute delay; perhaps less if you find that the captain is keeping a somewhat higher speed than on previous trips. But if weather is bad, a twenty minute delay may be a better estimate. As you see, even based on only three examples, you have learned something about running a boat schedule on the Norwegian coast. Although this example is limited to a few cases, the system acquires large amounts of data every single day.

61.5   **Exceptions**

The system handles all normal cases, but from the discussion above, we should be aware of extraordinary situations. A hurricane could be an example. On this day, the captain prudently decides to take a longer inshore route instead of the shorter, more exposed course. We are now in unknown territory. The system will have to resort to the timetable to present an ETA, but also may set a question mark behind this value to indicate uncertainty. Later on, when we are back on track, we may again find positions where we have been previously. An improved ETA can then be offered.

Fortunately, hurricanes do not appear often. Some months later, however, the vessel is again forced to take the inshore route. This time the system is in familiar territory: It can calculate an accurate ETA based on previous data on speed and positions for the inshore route.

The system described here has been in use for two years. It was a fast learner. After just a few trips, it gave very accurate ETA values, and today it can handle most exceptions.

A limitation of the current system is that the only data available before the journey starts is the timetable. As we have seen, the system needs data from the current trip, such as position and speed, to make ETA estimates. On days with strong winds and heavy seas, we may expect delays, but since weather is not included in the model, we have no way of forecasting these delays. However, with wind sensors or weather data captured from the Web, we can get additional information, which can be used in the model to predict delays before departure, similar to the way we use position and speed in the current system.

61.6   Discussion

In applications in which the adaption model is a good approximation of the real world, there are clear advantages to using learning systems.

In applications in which the adaption model is a good approximation of the real world, there are clear advantages to using learning systems. One of the main benefits is that the same general system with its very simple model can be applied to new applications without manual customization or an extensive setup. By learning, the empty system will soon build up a sufficient data repository to adapt to the current application and act as an experienced player.

The system described here can be applied to other transportation systems, for example to buses. Where boats are dependent on the weather, buses are influenced by traffic, rush hours, roadwork, and road closures. Whenever the bus is running late we will get new data on positions and speed. These will be used to give an updated ETA for the next trip. When the roadwork is completed and traffic runs faster, we will again return to previous values in the database for our calculations.

Note

1   This chapter is based on Olsen, K. A., Fagerlie, E. (2011). Adaptive Systems – A Case for Calculating Estimated Time of Arrival, IEEE Potentials, Vol. 30, No. 2.

62 Crowdsourcing

Crowdsourcing is inviting users to participate in offering information or solving a problem.

With data in the cloud accessible to everyone, a new type of service becomes feasible—engaging users all over the world to build an application. Perhaps the best example is Wikipedia, the huge collaborative and multilingual encyclopedia for which everyone can be an author and everyone an editor. The idea was radical. Until the Internet age, encyclopedias were written by professors, edited by a team of professionals, and printed in large volumes by a respectable publisher. In 2001, Jimmy Wales and Larry Sanger offered an alternative. They invited volunteers to write articles for an online encyclopedia (see Chapter 43.5 on wikis).

However, a closer examination shows that Wikipedia is not the work of a crowd, at least not in the literal sense of the word. For Wikipedia, and many other applications, the work is divided into parts (articles in Wikipedia's case), and knowledgeable individuals volunteer to take on a number of these jobs. Most Wikipedia articles are written by one person only, and there are reasons to believe that a rather small group of people writes most of the articles.

The following section presents a number of applications for crowdsourcing, divided into what I choose to call direct (explicit) and indirect (implicit) participation. Direct participation is when the user actively engages in a crowdsourcing activity, as with Wikipedia, YouTube, or the many photo sites. Indirect participation is when we can use data from the crowds to build interesting applications. For example, Google translation and the proofreading system presented in Chapters 59 and 60 are as examples of implicit crowdsourcing. In these cases, text from many human writers was used to improve the applications. I shall offer several more examples in this chapter.

62.1 Direct participation

The idea of crowdsourcing is to engage users, often from all over the world, to participate in solving a problem or a set of problems. The reward may be personal pride ("this job was done by me"), a community feeling ("we managed to solve this problem"), monetary, or any other form of credit. In the open-source movement—clearly a crowdsourcing activity—all of

Open source is crowdsourcing.

rewards may be present. There is a personal reward in solving part of the problem, a clear community feeling when one has managed to develop a complex product as a group, and also the more implicit reward of experience gained. The people who participated in developing the Apache Web server should have no problem getting jobs in companies that employ this server.

Often crowdsourcing is an activity that is controlled by special purpose software. Wikipedia, for example, relies on its MediaWiki software for writing, editing, and automatically checking articles. This software application is also available to other wikis.

A crowdsourcing activity is set up and controlled by individuals or an organization that define the main structure of the problem. For example, the open-source movement that developed the operating system Linux was heavily influenced by an individual (Linus Torvalds).

There are other examples: eBird allows participants, professional or recreational bird watchers, to register their observations, submit photos of rare birds and explore maps and graphs. The data is shared with scientist, educators and ornithologist all over the world. NASA has its Clickworkers project in which they recruit volunteers to perform tasks that are difficult to do automatically. The original task was to identify craters on Mars based on images returned from the Viking orbiter.

Amazon's Mechanical Turk is a site for simple tasks.

If such applications are to work in practice, the problems left to the "crowd" must be clearly stated and the solution must be well defined. While Wikipedia fulfills these requirements, Amazon's Mechanical Turk (MTurk) may not. The name of this beta application is inspired by an eighteenth-century hoax, a chess playing automation that toured Europe and, according to Wikipedia, beating the likes of Napoleon Bonaparte and Benjamin Franklin. Later on, it was revealed that a human chess master had been hiding inside the seemingly mechanical machine.

With this experiment, Amazon aimed to use their site to offer simple jobs to humans, unformalized tasks that cannot be performed by a computer. For example, a museum may have thousands of photographs of people at work that it wants to publish on the Web with tags. The tags may be something like farming, fishing, transportation, building, and so on. This is a job best done by experts, but experts are expensive. Instead, the museum can present the job on MTurk, offering a small reward for each picture. The museum can set requirements for worker competence, or have an open participation. Of course, the problem is the same as we always encounter when we outsource a task—how do we ensure than we get the quality we need? How do we prevent a worker from tagging the pictures at random by using software? The museum can check the final results, but this may take as much time as tagging the pictures in the first place. An indirect way of ensuring quality may be to engage only history students, or only persons who are affiliated with a historical society.

Similar sites offer problems to professionals. The requesters may be companies that have problems that they do not manage to solve themselves, either because they lack the skills or do not have the capacity for the task. The problems are posted on a Web site, and "workers," often professionals, can make a try. The limitations are that the problems must be stand-alone—independent from other processes in the company and well documented. To simplify verification, the problems must have a clear solution, as ideas for solutions are not enough. Often rigid testing and experimentation is needed to check if the idea will work in practice. The advantage for a company is that crowdsourcing opens the way for new views on the problem from people outside the company with varying forms of expertise.

The simplest forms of crowdsourcing—the application with a well-defined purpose and a well-defined division into simple parts—seem to flourish. The Instagram photo sharing program is a good example. It allows user to take a photo on the mobile phone, apply a filter and present in a grid or a list on a social networking site. Photos may be tagged and commented. Other examples are photo sites such as iStockphoto and Flickr, video sites such as YouTube, and social sites such as Facebook.

The photo sites present an interesting example. Previously, publishers had to go to professional agencies to get illustration photos; now these can be downloaded from photo sites at just a fraction of the former price. In addition, Web sites have a much wider range of photos than any professional agency. Of course, pictures taken by professional photographers may have a higher quality. But the amateurs that stock the various photo sites are experienced and use excellent cameras, thus the quality may be good enough for most purposes.

We see a similar development on YouTube and other video sites. With modern, high-quality equipment and excellent

*The advantage is that crowd-sourcing can open the way for **new views** on a problem.*

editing software, gifted individuals may produce viral videos—clips that become popular through sharing on the Internet. Today, some TV shows even use these viral clips as their main source of material.

Both the photo and the video applications are interesting examples of how modern technology—from cameras, editing software, to dissemination sites—let amateurs compete with professionals. Yes, there is a difference between posting a one-minute video clip on YouTube and making a full-length movie, but customers who watch YouTube are not in a movie theater, neither are they looking at TV.

Social networks also can be seen as a form of crowdsourcing because the system is based on participation from many, even if most often the audience is limited.

In the end, this is a question of motivation. When an idea is new, many may be willing to participate just to see what the idea is. In the end, people will ask "what is in it for me?" Many of the applications described above offer some reward. Professional and amateur ornithologists will find that sites such as eBird can enhance their work or hobby. Amateur photographers may earn revenue from the photos that they submit to Flickr or iStockphoto, and you may gain fame with a viral video clip on YouTube.

62.2   Indirect participation

When activities such as shopping and bookings are performed on the Internet, important background data are generated. These patterns made by other users, have been exploited for many years. An example is the message to customers of Internet bookstores: "Customers who bought this book also bought…" In fact, this simple technique has established new market patterns for books, as discussed in Chapter 46.

In 2006, Netflix initiated a $1-million competition, the Netflix Prize, to improve its algorithm for making recommendations. The size of the prize shows how important these systems are. A small improvement in a recommendation scheme will have a huge impact on sales or rentals.[1]

GPS devices, combined with Internet communication, offer the possibility of launching a set of new applications based on crowdsourcing. Displaying trails on maps are a good example. While photos from airplanes and satellites have offered improved topological maps, the imprints of trails on the photos are often too weak to be retrieved automatically. In practice, it

While standard GPS receivers may help us pinpoint our location on the map, a two-way system also could be used to gather trail information.

With a two-way connection, an **adaptive** navigation system could be implemented.

has to be entered manually. Thus we often find that this information may be lacking or erroneous on many new maps for hikers.

While standard GPS receivers may help us pinpoint our location on the map, a two-way system also could be used to gather trail information. If we could retrieve locations of hikers, a simple system could be used to set up trails. That is, we could create virtual trails (to be drawn on the map) in just the same way as physical trails are made, by collecting the cumulative data from many individuals. As in the physical world, only trails that many hikers have followed would be presented in the virtual world.

Similar systems could be set up for driving. In typical navigator systems, we start by typing in our destination, and the navigator will then suggest a route, offering detailed directions. This works fine, until the navigator directs us the wrong direction down a one-way street or tells us to make illegal turns. I once had a navigator directing me to drive down a ski slope, a challenge even for an SUV. Another time I was stuck in the center of Malaga, Spain, and no matter which direction I tried to go, the navigator always steered me to a street clearly reserved for pedestrians.

The problem is, of course, that the electronic maps are full of errors. There also may be temporary closings that can affect our choice of route. While some of the initial errors may be removed, it is very optimistic to expect that we will get error free maps, and that the navigator will know all closings and changes in the road system. However, with a two-way connection, an adaptive system could be implemented, similar to the one presented in Chapter 61. When we go straight ahead instead of taking the left turn as directed, the system could register this as a possible closure, a one-way street, or perhaps a place where a left turn is not legal. Of course, we may have simply changed our minds and are going to another destination or choosing another route. The navigator can soon eliminate the "closure" or "one-way" alternatives if data from other cars shows that this road is open, but it cannot determine between "illegal left turn" and "a change of mind." That is, one person does not make a trail. However, the next time a driver circumvents the navigator's instructions at this location, we have a stronger case for the "no left turn." In the end, we may have enough data to determine that we have a trail. Then the navigator can avoid directing a left turn at this point. It may, however, revoke its decision at a later time, if it sees that some drivers really do take a left turn here. When we get trail data from other cars, we can be presented with the "trails" that are best at this time of day—roads where traffic is moving faster.

Below, I use these "trails" as a metaphor to show how we can improve Internet searches, that is, by following in the path of others.

62.3   Case: Internet trails

The **trail** is the incarnation of the cumulative decisions made by people who have walked there before.

Let us say we are on our way to a mountaintop, negotiating the terrain, finding our way up steep cliffs and through the vegetation, following the bank of a river to locate a place to ford. Then, suddenly, we find a trail going in the right direction. Now everything becomes easier. The trail offers the best route, avoiding all the difficult spots. Coming to the next river, the trail leads us directly to the best place to cross.[2]

The trail is the incarnation of the cumulative decisions made by people who have walked there before—crowdsourcing from the pre-Internet world. By simply following the trail, we can exploit others' knowledge and effort. There may be side trails, for example, where someone has tried an alternative route, but these are most often weaker trails. By always choosing the trail with the strongest impression on the ground, we can follow the majority. Utilizing additional information, we may decide to branch to a side trail, when we recognize that this may offer a shorter alternative or we assume that the side trail may take us to a nice viewpoint. Even without this information, we may want to explore alternatives, perhaps when we take this trail a second time. Note that even if the majority has taken another route, many persons must have used side trails: One person wandering off will not make a trail. That is, trails represent common decisions, not individual choices.

In the virtual world, implemented by the Internet, Web, satellite navigation, and other technologies, people also are roaming around, many of whom share similar objectives. These groups may leave virtual trails that we may follow. As in the physical world, we can exploit the knowledge of others by following their trails.

The term trail offers a nice metaphor, and was used by Vannevar Bush in his seminal paper, "As We May Think," published in *The Atlantic Monthly* in 1945.[3] Bush described a "physician, puzzled by her patient's reactions, [that] strikes the trail established in studying an earlier similar case." In this section, I will exploit the idea of trail, presenting a set of examples to discuss the concept's application in the virtual world.

The advantage of utilizing trails is that they are adaptive, systems can catch all types of trails, and the program only has to distinguish trails—it does not have to comprehend the common goal all these users may have.

62.4   Utilizing virtual trails

Virtual trails on the Internet can be as useful as trails in the physical world.

Although fast indexing and powerful servers make it possible to search large volumes of data, the main issue—considering the vastness of the Web—is to find relevant pages. Traditionally, keyword frequency was an important parameter in the task of determining relevance. However, frequency is a very indirect means of finding what pages best conform to a query, and also are easily subject to biased by Web page designers. Google has a better idea—using Web structure, the linkage between pages, to determine relevance. A page to which many other pages link gets a high score, especially if these other pages also have high scores. To stretch the point, we could say that Google uses trail information in the static sense; that is, it uses the cumulative decisions of Web designers when setting up links.

However, why not add dynamic trail information? This could be done by offering users the experience of others—taking advantage of the crowd. An example may clarify. There has been an election in Italy, and we want to know the results. Our query could consist of the three keywords: Italy, election, results. The search engine would then give us a long list of Web pages, sorted according to its relevance criteria. After looking at several pages, perhaps trying to refine the query, we may find a story in a newspaper that presents up-to-date results in easy to understand tables, perhaps with an interesting analysis. Later, when a friend later asks us if we have seen the election results, we can direct him to this page.

This same search also can be done by an automatic system. That is, all users who give a similar query could be directed to an "other-users-found-these-pages" list. The search engine could prioritize the pages with which other users ended their sessions or spent most of their time. These trails would be created dynamically, by data from all previous users with a similar request. The results could be offered in addition to the standard results sorted by relevance.

Trail information
could be offered
directly on Web
pages.

"Trails" could be presented for any type of Web page, linking requests to products or information. Today data on these operations may exist at the server level only, but it is quite easy to implement Web pages that can collect the necessary statistics. With such features, we could strengthen the trail if the user performed some action at the end. For example, a trail to a certain page for the query "lightweight, digital camera" would be stronger if some of the users ahead of us actually bought the camera offered on this page. Similarly a trail would be reinforced if the user copied or printed page information.

Trail information could be offered directly on Web pages. Today, links that we have used previously are shown in a different color to tell us where we have been, but what if the browser could indicate how large a percentage of Web surfers had used this link? This information would show where the main trail goes. Of course, Web designers can use this information to put the most frequently used links first, but this may not always be so easy. For example, menus may be in alphabetical order. Further, changing the order may confuse frequent users of a Web page. Weighting links according to usage will offer a very dynamic solution. Weights could be presented by using bold types: the fatter the type, the larger percentage of users on the site has previously taken this trail, like tag clouds presented in collaborative tagging systems (see Chapter 43.4).

62.5 Discussion

In some cases we clearly do not want to follow the trails of others, such as when we search for one-of-a-kind products or a secluded beach where we can be alone. However, even in these cases, trails may be useful, as we will know what to avoid. That is, if you are looking for a secluded beach, you do not want to follow the most traveled trails.

One may argue that trails advocate a flock mentality; we follow in the paths of others instead of taking a more individual direction, a similar discussion to the one on proofreading (Chapter 60.7). However, this argument may easily be turned upside down. Today most Web users go to well-known sites, such as Facebook, CNN, BBC, Amazon, and eBay. Trails may help us to find the less known, but perhaps also interesting sites.

As discussed earlier, we are most inclined to follow trails when we are in new and unknown territory. This may be the case when we want information on which prepositions to use when writing in a second language, or when we want a quick solution to a problem. With more experience, we may follow our own routes that may take us to the goal faster, and more according to our own special interests.

Trails may also be misleading. When finding a trail in the mountains, we have to decide if this will take us in the right direction or not. We may follow it for a while even though it does not go exactly in the right direction, but may abandon the trail if the discrepancy increases. If we are lucky, there may be a side trail at this point, made by others who have made the same decision. Similar problems may be encountered on the Web. The sentence that we are writing in English may be "at a boat gangway," thus the "on a boat" search takes us down the main trail, missing the correct side path. The users ahead of us with the digital camera query may want specifications only, while we want to buy one. However, a difference of goals may soon be apparent; the "information scent" given along the way to the goal or at the goal will tell us that it could be more profitable to follow other routes.

As with other search strategies, commercial interests may try to (mis)lead us into trails that lead to certain hotels, airlines, or other products. But this problem can be solved if sponsored trails are separated from organic trails found by usage data only.

Trails may disappear. The Web page of the newspaper giving the results of the Italian election may no longer be there, but a trail may still lead to this page. This should be no problem; the trail can be removed in the same way as it was established. If users going to this page, after giving the query for "Italy election," immediate return to other alternatives, then that is an indication that the trail is misleading. However, the trail itself will help to stabilize the system. Web developers want traffic to their sites, and trails will be viewed as an advantage. Therefore, it is more likely that the newspaper, if it recognizes that trails are leading to this page, will improve the page rather than remove it.

Just as with our metaphor, we have to follow trails conscientiously, not as the last sheep of the flock running over the cliff along with the others. However, as in the physical world, we will have additional data also in the virtual, data that may help us to decide if this is a profitable trail to follow. The advantage that we have in the virtual world is that goals are stated more explicitly. We do not know that the people who have made a physical trail have the same goal as we have. But on the Web, each of us may have declared our final destination.

Notes

1 Netflix had to cancel this contest in 2010 because of privacy concerns. The data the contestants were offered, basic data on rentals, had been anonymized; still it was found that it was possible to identify individual users. The lesson is that one should take care when using indirect crowdsourcing data.

2 Parts of this chapter are based on Olsen, K. A., Malizia, A. (2010). Following Virtual Trails, *IEEE Potentials*. Volume 29, Issue 1.

3 Bush, V. (1945). As We May Think, *The Atlantic Monthly*, Vol. 176, No. 1, 1945, pp. 101–108.

63   Cloud Data for the Individual—a Personal Assistant

Smartphones have the possibility of knowing the position of the user. By combining time, position and data in the cloud it is possible to make smart deductions as to what information the user needs. These deductions can be performed by an automated assistant that have access to the user's e-mail and SMS messages, calendar, phone book, notes, etc., as well as to the position of the user. The assistant can present the information in an "I feel lucky" display on the user's smartphone. This is somewhat similar to the push services that I presented in Chapter 38, but here we shall explore a set of new possibilities. [1]

63.1   A personal assistant

A **smartphone** may do the job, but often requires too much input.

We are in the middle of an unknown city. The hotel should be nearby, but we can't find it. We have two options: One, take out the smartphone, open an Internet connection, find the map service, input the name of the city, download a city map, change to a convenient map scale, type the address of the hotel, and let the GPS system lead us to our destination. Two, ask a passerby.

We go for option two. Our smart devices can do the job, but in most cases, they require too much effort. Keying comes at a cost. This is especially the case when we have to use on-screen keyboards. Even where input is as simple as a button click, small displays make everything time consuming and irksome.

By using **context information** much input can be avoided.

Often systems ask for input that could be found from available data, or inferred from context information. As an example, consider a common situation: You are in a meeting that drags on and on. At some point it is clear that there is no chance of catching the five o'clock plane back home. So you will have to leave the meeting, get an Internet connection, log in to the Web site of your airline, give IDs such as name and booking reference and change the booking to a later flight. Some airlines even require you to make a phone call in these circumstances.

However, if the booking system could use context information, you would be able to perform the whole operation without interrupting the meeting. A text message to the airline with "later flight" should suffice. Their system should be able

An **agent** running
on a smartphone
can work as a
personal assistant,
aiding us in provid-
ing the information
we need.

to identify you by phone number, retrieve the booking for this evening's flight, and return a set of options for later flights, asking you to choose one. It could even book the next flight automatically, letting you change to another if this is not suitable.

However, the airline may not offer such an option. Instead of waiting for this to happen, we could use an agent running on our smartphone to help us in these situations. Based on data from the initial booking this personal assistant should be able to change the flight. This would be easy if it made the booking in the first place, but should be possible if data on our bookings were available, such as in the cloud. Perhaps it also could initiate the rebooking, for example, when it understands that you will not be able to catch the flight. The agent could be implemented as an App, but since it would require access to nearly everything, it would be simpler if it were embedded in the operating system.

The idea of having a computer system that could act as a personal assistant has been around for many years. As early as 1987, Apple CEO John Scully described in his book *Odyssey* a device called the "Knowledge Navigator" that used software agents to assist the user.[2]

The concept was depicted in several videos from Apple. The assistant was shown to have human properties, envisioned as a bow-tied butler. It had natural sounding speech generation, speech recognition, and the ability to understand what the user was saying, that is, to grasp the underlying semantics.

However, these were only mock-ups; the real world assistants were more primitive. A well-known example is the assistant that came with Microsoft Office between 1998 and 2003, depicted as everything from a paper clip to an Einstein caricature. This feature got a negative response from users; some went as far as to develop applications that allowed the user to shoot (sic) down their assistant. It had the bad habit of popping up in unexpected situations, even when the user had turned the function off. The *Smithsonian* magazine called it "one of the worst software design blunders in the annals of computing."[3]

The problem was that the assistant took its cues from a skerrick of context; for example, just a keyword. If you started by writing "Dear" the assistant could tell you "It looks like you're writing a letter. Would you like help?" The advice that it could offer was often irrelevant, downright silly, or too trivial to be of any use.

Even if speech generation and recognition may be useful in some cases, communication with the assistant can be dealt with via a smartphone keyboard and display. Thus, there is no need to give the assistant humanlike capabilities or to let it "understand" the user. Today we can implement a "knowledge navigator" without the magic parts, leaving the role of the human to the user.

63.2   Contextual data

What if we offer the assistant the word "hotel"? Is this a meaningful command? Of course, there are many different interpretations, such as:

1. We want to book a hotel.
2. We need to view a booking, change or delete it.
3. We need directions to a hotel.

However, with contextual data things are clearer. Let us assume that the system has an overview of all your bookings, your current location, and home address. If you have booked a hotel in Rome starting today and your current location is an airport or any place in Rome, the system could retrieve the booking, offer the name, address, and phone number for the hotel, and give directions from the current location. If you have a rental car booking, the directions should be for travel by car. If you are close to the hotel, it could be for walking or, if you are further away, the assistant could offer suggestions for transport.

Context, time, keyword or location can be used to determine what information the user needs.

If you are away from your home town, and do not have a booking, the system should choose the first alternative above, offering you a selection of nearby hotels that have a room available and that are within the price range that you normally select. If you are at home, the system should let you choose between alternatives 1 and 2. That is, in most cases a simple word such as "hotel" can be given a meaningful interpretation when context information is available. If there are other interpretations—for example, you may want to translate the word "hotel" into Arabic—these could be offered as secondary options, or you may have to add more keywords.

In the early days of computing, an interface was an empty line on a teletype or a blinking ">" on a display. Nowadays this has been replaced by apps and their form-based input. The drawback is that the user has to choose the right App for the function, and then fill out forms, provide codes, and so on. Perhaps we should reintroduce the command line interface, but this time letting an assistant parse the data?

63.3   Automatic assistance

As discussed in Chapter 19.3 the best interface may be the one that does not require any input—an interface that takes its cues from the data that are available. This becomes possible for many applications on smartphones that use time and location as clues.

Let us assume that we are on our way to the bus stop. With time of day, our location, the location of the bus stop, and bus route data, the assistant could present the bus schedule on the phone display automatically, or better yet, count down the minutes until our bus arrives. Route data could be entered explicitly or the assistant may be able to deduce this from our history of commuting. The data can be presented on an "I feel lucky" display on the phone. That is, we can just take a look at this display to get all the information we need. But if we go past the bus stop on our way to the grocer, the data will be cleared. When entering the grocer the system will, of course, present our shopping list.

The ideal interface can be the **input-free** interface.

As another example, imagine yourself driving to the airport. The weather is bad; traffic is dense and moving slowly ahead. You wonder if you will miss your flight, or maybe the bad weather also has delayed departures. All you need to do with a context sensitive interface is to look at the "I feel lucky" screen on the mobile phone. The system already should have deduced what information you need, such as an updated departure time for your flight or directions that may avoid traffic congestions.

Or, on the way to a meeting, the assistant has computed that you will be fifteen minutes late. It could then offer to send a text message notifying the other participants of your delay.

63.4   Formalized data

Storing data in the cloud allows access to all relevant information, a necessity if a personal assistant is to understand the context of what the user is doing. A "later flight" or "hotel" command will be interpreted incorrectly if the assistant does not have access to all bookings. Today, when we use computers for nearly everything, these data are available, but access to data is not enough. They must also be presented in a useful form.

This is the great challenge. It is possible to extract the necessary information from an e-mail confirmation of a booking, such as the hotel name, arrival date, departure date, and reference number. However, it would be more convenient if a version of the booking were stored in the cloud in a standardized format. Thus, to get full benefit of an assistant, we need a more formalized infrastructure than we have today. This will require agreements on standards.[4]

Standardization is not easy to achieve. Technical, economic, and political issues can hamper the work. However, the promise of new services may be an incentive for defining new standards.

Further, the assistant's interpretation of the context may not always be correct. There may be cases in which the assistant does not have the most recent data or makes the wrong deductions. However, since the system is working as a personal assistant to the user, these cases will most often be recognized as erroneous, even if they can be annoying. The fact that most advice is on current events, often on what is happening right now, also will be useful in detecting erroneous help.

63.5   Conclusion

The assistant's **interpretation** of the context may not always be correct.

In the history of computing, we have seen computers leaving the centralized data center, moving into local centers, then to the desktop, to the laptop, and today—into our pocket as smartphones.

As with other technology, the smartphone's evolution initially focused on new functions. Now there is a need to consider the user interface. But this time it is not a case for organizing the input, or for developing convenient forms or menu systems, but to find the cases where we can *avoid* input. A personal assistant can do this for us. As we have seen a humanlike assistant is not necessary; in many cases, background data from the cloud, time of day, and the user's location should be sufficient.

The requirements are that the assistant have access to all data, and that it can use selectors such as time and location to deduct what the user needs. Patterns and user's routines may also be important input in deciding what information to present at any time. It is also central that what we present is information for the individual. This makes it easier to recognize the cases where the assistant has misinterpreted the situation. Then the "I feel lucky display" will be recognized as an assistant, not as unimportant spam.

Maybe the job for computer professionals in the next decade is not just to add functions and new gadgets to current devices, but to ensure that users get the full benefits of the new technology. One way of achieving this is to go for the "free" solutions in which the user gets valuable information without having to pay with button clicks.

Notes

1   Parts of this subchapter are based on Olsen, K. A, Malizia, A. (2011) Automated Personal Assistants, IEEE Computer, November.

2   Sculley, J. (1987) Odyssey: Pepsi to Apple: A Journey of Adventure Ideas and the Future. HarperCollins.

3   Conniff, R. (2007) "What's Behind a Smile?," Smithsonian, pp. 46–53.

4   See: The Problem with Cloud-Computing Standardization, Computer, July 2011 pp. 13–16.

PART 9

A Digital World

In the introduction of this book, you were welcomed to the virtual world, a world of symbols. By digitalizing these symbols and by representing processes as computer programs, many functions can be automated. For the less formal services, the technology provides power tools to the human user.

These changes are dramatic. Many jobs have disappeared as they are taken over by computer technology. Intermediates have been removed when customers perform services themselves. Productivity in the jobs that humans have retained has increased many times with the new tools. However, efficiency is just a part of the impact that computer technology has left on society. IT offers new forms of interactions between humans. In the small, this affects our social life. We have Facebook friends that we communicate with every day, but who we may seldom see in real life. In the large, new services also may influence how we govern cities and countries, and important issues such as democracy. Some also have questioned how this new way of working—being continuously online and multitasking—is affecting our brains.

This last part of the book explores these issues. To some extent this is speculative, as we try to foresee the effects of a new technology on society, a technology that has shown many surprising sides in its short lifespan. However, we are well armed. We have a throughout knowledge of concepts such as formalization and digitalization. We have studied the technology itself, its advantages and disadvantages. We know the constraints and are armed with experience from a large set of cases.

I will discuss the effects of being continuously online in Chapter 64. The Internet and democracy is covered in Chapter 65. In Chapter 0, I will discuss how IT is changing the world, and present a case on the cash-free society, before summing up all effects of IT technology in Chapter 67.

64 Continuously Online

New devices have made it possible to be continuously online. We can be on Facebook, receive e-mail, send Twitter messages, surf the Web and receive phone calls—all at the same time. At a meeting, we put or smartphones, tablets, or laptops on the table. Students have their laptops open when they attend lectures. In seminars, many seat themselves in the back of the room, open their laptops, and seem to concentrate more on their e-mails than on the lecture.

Multitasking may give us a shallow way of working. This may also affect our brains.

Multitasking is nothing new. Before being continuous online, we could be interrupted in our work by phone calls, or by people knocking on the office door. While the digital services have reduced these disturbances, there are so many other interruptions today. In his book, *The Shallows* (2010), Nicholas Carr warned that multitasking may give us a shallow way of working, and that it may also affect our brains. Modern research has shown that the idea that the adult brain is a fixed thing is wrong. Instead, there is strong evidence that the brain has the ability to be tuned to the tasks that we perform. Despite interruptions, we move from task to task. We become more proficient in handling many tasks at one time, but the drawback may be that we miss the ability to concentrate on one task. For example, we may get better at scanning documents, but less proficient in studying them in depth—we may develop a shallow brain.

However, if concentration and in-depth studying are important aspects of survival—for example, to get a job, to perform the job, and to get better jobs—we should assume that the situation would change. This balancing is something that we often see. For example, when I got my first graphical workstation back in 1990, it had a hundred fonts. I tried to use them all. The word processing system that I use today also has as many fonts, but I use only a few. That is, I am over the initial joy of using a new technology, and I now concentrate on using fonts to fulfill a purpose. When novel users make Powerpoint presentations, the slides come in from left or right, exploding and imploding, and all the various backgrounds are used. After a while, users concentrate on using the effects to improve communication, and simpler presentations appear.

When I participate in a meeting, I may be the only one that does not put a smart device on the table. That is, I am there to concentrate on the meeting, and I have the privilege of not having to be online at all times. Similarly, I have removed the beep that announces incoming e-mail, knowing that I do not have to either read or answer mail immediately.

An English theater has a bucket of water at the entrance with a sign: "Put your mobile phone here." We have to relearn to concentrate on the one task we are doing. The idea that someone can do many things at the same time is fiction. Either we go to the theater or we stay at home. In the theater, we concentrate on the play. Of course, we always have the option to leave and to find another task that we can concentrate on.

> The idea that someone can do many things at the same time is **fiction**.

We may expect (or hope) to see a reaction to the continuous online idea. Just as some people are deleting their Facebook accounts because they have too many "friends," get too many uninteresting notices, and find that they have spent too much time on this application, others may slow down, read their e-mail just a few times every day, put phones in silent mode, and concentrate on the tasks they are doing. I have stopped taking my laptop to seminars. Either I stay there and follow the lectures, or I return to my office to work.

Socrates was afraid that writing would affect our brains, that it would reduce our ability to remember and to explore ideas without the limitation of putting these in writing. Well, writing—and later, the printing press—has changed our society and perhaps also our brains. Socrates was right, every tool or technology will change the way we work. However, while writing may have reduced our ability to remember, it also had many important advantages.

> **Socrates** was afraid that writing would affect our brains, that it would reduce our ability to remember and to explore ideas without the limitation of putting these in writing.

When motor ships replaced sailing ships, much of the knowledge about winds, currents and sailing big ships disappeared. Now that we all have GPS devices, the ability to locate our position by other means may also disappear.

Information technology will affect the way we work and the way we think. Some knowledge will become superfluous; we can rely on the calendar application to remind us of meetings and birthdays, and if we don't remember we can always find what we need to know on the Internet.

As with other technologies—guns, drugs, cars—there are both advantages and disadvantage for individuals and for society. After the initial euphoria of using a new technology, we can perform some cost-benefit analysis: What do I get out of this? Is it worth the time? Are there alternatives? Societies can also try to regulate the use of new tools and technologies, as they try to do with everything from guns to atomic weapons. But restraining new technologies that many consider advantageous is difficult. In the small, however, we can have areas were mobile phones are forbidden; we can take away the WLAN from lecture rooms; prohibit students to open their laptops in class, and so on. At one time, everyone smoked in meetings. This is now forbidden and respected by all. Perhaps we will get to the situation in which it is impolite to be on the Internet in presence of others.

65   Internet and Democracy

When the Web first emerged, the initial hope was for a democratic system in which everybody was both an information-provider and a consumer. These opportunities in the technology have been taken to the point where everybody can have a home page —but to what effect? As we have seen, large institutions are as powerful on the Internet as elsewhere.[1]

65.1   Technology for democracy and suppression

Social networks and blogs seem to be an answer for the individual. Here we have a more level playing field. On Facebook, we are all peers, all are providers, and all are consumers, even if most of us have a limited audience.

Many bloggers have managed to establish large audiences. Some fifteen-year-olds have as much traffic to their blogs as well established newspapers have to their Web sites. Politicians, political activists, and many others have found that blogs are an efficient way of communicating ideas: There are no restrictions, dissemination is fast, and readers often have the ability to comment.

Totalitarian dicta-
torships will use all
means to maintain
control.

Facebook, Twitter, and text messages have been important tools for people in undemocratic societies. The threat to regimes from the Internet and these services are so great that many regimes attempt to limit access or have surveillance systems that monitor traffic. This is nothing new. Totalitarian dictatorships will use all means to maintain control. For the Nazis, this implied having vast archives with data collected before and during the war. They introduced passports, permissions, war currency, and rigorous control of all travel. Newspapers and radio were under severe censorship. They also used all available technology in their suppression, everything from typewriters to telex and punched cards.[2]

A suppressive regime today will, of course, also use all available technology, perhaps including DNA, video surveillance, and control of movements. They may use computers to monitor communication and, for that matter, to follow monetary transactions. No country has a full DNA archive of their citizens, but at some point could pass laws stating that everybody has to offer a sample—in order "to protect society." If anonymous cash is important for a resistance movement, a regime can try to supervise transactions, perhaps also making the transition to a fully digital economy. However, we should remember that the Nazi regime of Germany did not need either computers or DNA to persecute ethnic groups or political opponents; neither did Joseph Stalin to murder Polish officers or his fellow citizens; nor Pol Pot to kill his countrymen in Cambodia.

Laws for protecting privacy will work only as long as we have democratic governments that recognize the importance of free speech.

Of course, laws for protecting privacy will work only as long as we have democratic governments that recognize the importance of free speech. We also need a proficient free press and an independent judicial system as additional safeguards to protect democracy.

65.2   Open channels

Today, Internet and mobile phones are important channels, both to get information out of a country and into a country. Videos, captured by smartphones, can show regime brutality, and are important for democracy movements. Most of Nazi Germany's atrocities were performed under secrecy, and there is strong evidence that concealment was a necessity. Today, this would not be possible. Thus, even the most brutal regimes have to consider the risk of losing support by angering their citizens. Excessive brutality also may turn the outside word against the regime, inviting sanctions, or in some cases, an invasion.

Technology can be the means either to suppress or to liberate.

Technology can be the means either to suppress or to liberate. Personally, I am an optimist; I see computer technology—whether the Internet, Facebook, Twitter, or smartphones—as an important tool for advocating democracy. Regimes trying to restrict access to the Internet or turn off cellular networks may face problems since these restrictions also may hamper efficient business operations. There also are technical problems. One can get software that bypasses the Internet filters or antenna systems for mobile phones that can connect to cellular networks in a neighboring country. As satellite phones become easily available, communication with the outside world may be possible without the risk of surveillance.

65.3   A threat to privacy

Technology also can be a threat to privacy, even within the realm of a democracy. Video surveillance can be used as an example. Cameras are mounted to secure banks, shops, or to make it safer for us to walk the streets or ride safely on a bus. At the same time, these cameras may threaten privacy. A camera in the parking lot of an apartment building may reduce car theft or make it easier to find who bumped your car. At the same time, we do not want these videos to be used to see who came home drunk or with the wrong woman. But we can have the one without the other. By requiring that all data from cameras be stored on locked servers that only the police or an accredited security company can open, we can avoid many privacy problems.

The need for storing data has to be **balanced** with the risk of violating privacy rights.

Law authorities often want access to communication records to follow the track of criminals and terrorists, and governments are passing laws to ensure that these data are stored by communication companies. These requirements have to be balanced by the right to privacy—what is to be stored and for how long. The EU, for example, requires communication companies to store administrative records of phone use and Internet access (dates, phone numbers, duration of call, location data for mobile phones, and URLs), but not content. These records are retained for six months to a year, before they are deleted.[3]

While the EU's data storage requirements have been an important political issue, the collection of data by private companies often goes unnoticed. When Austrian student Max Schrems eventually managed to obtain a transcript of what Facebook had stored during the three years he had used the site, the transcript ran to 1222 pages. It seems that Facebook has a policy of storing everything—times, dates, IP addresses, invitations to be a friend, rejections, locations, etc.—in the hope that it can be used for something at some time. Personally, I am not afraid that Facebook will misuse this information. Users tend to react negatively when they feel that a company or other entity has violated their privacy. But there are other dangers. In special cases, Facebook may be required to offer the information it has to the authorities, and there is always the chance that someone will manage to break into its systems. Hopefully, these companies will see the risk and reduce what is stored. If not, we have to ask for stricter laws.

Transparency is important. The requirement that a user can obtain a transcript of all personal data that is stored should be implemented as an automatic option on every site.

Transparency is important. The requirement that a user can obtain a transcript of all personal data that is stored should be implemented as an automatic option on every site, so that the data can be seen by just the click of a button. Perhaps we also should ask to be able to delete data?

Not all privacy problems can be solved by technology, and as we see it is often necessary to balance between different needs. However, there may be technical solutions that can offer a win-win solution in which both privacy and public safety are considered. Of course, it all ends up with a question of trust. Do we trust the authorities, as well as the private companies that store our data to ensure our right to privacy?

Notes

1 Parts of this chapter are based on Morris, C., Olsen, K. A. (2011) Democracy and Technology, IEEE Computer, April.

2 The Nazi regime of Germany had Hollerith machines from IBM that could search through punched cards electronically. See Black, E. (2001) IBM and the Holocaust, Crown Books.

3 The Data Retention Directive, adopted by the European Union in 2006, mandates that telecommunication providers store all administrative data on a transmission (phone or Internet) for at least six months. Efforts in the US to pass similar legislation have not succeeded.

66   Changing the World

Most earlier successful IT projects have had a limited scope, a limited time span, and a limited budget. These projects could be to develop a system for sending text messages between universities and research centers (1969); manufacturing a chip for a calculator (1971); setting standards for electronic communication (1974); designing a computer system that offers an improved user experience (1981); simplifying access to scientific papers (1990); developing new technology for ranking Web pages (1996); or creating an online student directory with photos (2003).

I suspect that few people involved in these projects had any idea that they were changing the world. But in retrospect, that is what they did. The Arpanet project gave us the first e-mail system (1969); Intel developed the microprocessor (1971); an international effort gave us the TCP/IP standard for data communication (1974); researchers at Xerox Parc designed the first complete graphical workstation (1981); Tim Berners-Lee defined the basis for the WWW at CERN (1990); Larry Page and Sergey Brin laid the foundations for Google (1996); and Mark Zuckerberg created Facebook (2003).

66.1   Changing the lives of millions

Computing projects have **changed** the lives of millions all over the world. In the industrial countries, we work in front of a computer, shop from a computer, play and socialize using a computer.

These computing projects combined have changed the lives of millions all over the world. In the industrial countries, we work in front of a computer, shop from a computer, play and socialize using a computer. Whole business areas are going through a revolution. Music, movies, and books are now separated from their physical representation, with huge impact on the industry. Photography has gone digital. The analog products, such as film and cameras, and the connected services, such as development and printing, are disappearing. Newspapers that have existed for more than two hundred years are closing down, or in danger of closing down, as competition from the Internet becomes too tough.

Physical libraries, with collections in the form of clay tablets, papyrus, or books, have been an integral part of educational institutions for thousands of years. Today digital collections are taking over, and the physical library has an uncertain future in many domains. Companies that hardly existed five to ten years ago, such as Google, Facebook, and Twitter, are household words. New services and applications are offered every day to make our lives more effective, perhaps also more interesting. A comparison with politics is tempting: While many state leaders struggle to implement significant changes, a bunch of computing professionals achieves profound changes as a side effect.

66.2   A catalyst for change

Clearly the computing industry is the main catalyst for **change** today.

Clearly the computing industry is the main catalyst for change today. No other industry has a similar impact; no other industry is as dynamic. When *IEEE Spectrum* magazine presented the top eleven technologies of the decade in 2011, six of these were IT technologies (smartphones, social networks, IP telephony, multicore CPUs, cloud computing and digital photography), while two were strongly IT-related (drones and the rovers that explore other planets).[1]

IT is clearly shaping the world—the hope is into something better. The question remains: Are these changes something of the past, or can we expect further impact? Some argue that computing has become a commodity, like electricity. Something you need, but which has lost its competitive advantage. However, the Googles, YouTubes, Wikipedias, and Twitters show that the pace, if anything, has accelerated. So what can we expect in the next decennium? I will try to answer this question by offering a case.

66.3   Innovation

Computer technology supports innovation. With this technology many traditional tasks can be performed in new ways, and the technology can open for a long range of new applications. With a PC in every home, a smartphone in every pocket, and broadband networks available everywhere the necessary infrastructure is in place for an abundance of new applications.

However, innovation is a risky sport. Your new App may not be recognized by anyone, and for the more complex products, in depth and expensive research may be needed. Products must be tested, and tried in real markets. While existing standards simplify product development, they also offer a means for the competition to catch up. For example, many of the components that go into a modern smartphone, such as display, processor, and memory can be bought off-the-shelf. In addition, we see that even the software can be standardized, for example with standard applications on top of the Android operating system.

In this environment many companies have seen the advantages of copying, or in other words, "stealing" the ideas of others. Apple did not develop the first user friendly interface, neither was Facebook the first social network. The advantage of being an imitator is that one can learn from the mistakes of the pioneers, reduce costs for basic research and use more resources in improving the product.

While novel ideas are important, the real test is in implementation. Facebook succeeded by managing to maintain service levels at all times, in the start by implementing the service at one university at a time, only opening for the general public when the capital and the servers were in place. Apple succeeded by combining standard technology with impressive design, both in the units themselves and in the user interface.

Imitation plus innovation equals **imovation**.

Oded Shenkar, the author of the book Copycats,[2] calls this process imovation, a word made out of imitation and innovation, and shows that many businesses thrive by being imitators, not by copying outright but by improving the products and services that have already been tested in the marketplace. However, few companies will admit that this is can be an important way to success, and many companies do not have a plan for exploiting the ideas of others. The copycat is not the hero in Western culture, unlike the East where improving an existing idea is the basis of many products. Shenkar use the minivan as an example, innovated by US car makers. But the idea was imitated by the Japanese, that have been able to capture most of the market.

That is, while new technology offers many possibilities for innovation, it may be smarter to be an imitator or perhaps an imovator. We shall present a case below, showing how a country can get substantial benefits by taking standard technology one step further.

66.4　Case: A cash free society

Payment is a formalized service. With POS terminals everywhere we may **remove cash**.

The technology that forms the basis of this case is the simple POS (point-of-sale) terminal. This technology was not developed to change the world, just to make monetary transactions simpler. By using a credit or debit card, the terminal lets us perform a digital transaction, with no cash

Small countries
are at an advan-
tage and can often
offer high dissemi-
nation numbers for
new technologies.

involved. The advantages are so substantial that in many
countries a large percentage of all monetary transactions are
digital, based on POS terminals or credit card usage on the
Internet. Data is captured automatically and can be transferred
almost with no cost. At the same time, the information can be
used directly for inventory control, accounting, and statistics.

In my home country, Norway, you can avoid cash
altogether because all shops, hotels, restaurants, gas stations,
cabs, and many buses allow digital payment. Even the pizza
boy brings along a wireless POS terminal. Most banks offer
free service, and cards also are used for very small amounts.
Based on value, 98 percent of all monetary transactions in
Norway are digital.[3] Based on number of transactions, we can
assume that more than 90 percent are digital today.

As we discussed in Chapter 45.1 small countries are at an
advantage and often can offer high dissemination numbers for
new technologies. National standards are easier to implement in
a small rather than a large country; fewer installations make it
easier to update equipment and a homogeneous population
make it simpler win acceptance of new services. However,
larger countries are following suit in the digital economy. A
few years ago, you needed cash in cities such as Rome and
Madrid; today nearly all businesses there accept cards.

When only a small
fraction of all
transactions are in
cash an interesting
question turns up:
**Can we remove
cash altogether?**

When only a small fraction of all transactions are in cash,
an interesting question arises: Can we remove cash altogether?
Money, in the form of coins has been here for nearly three
thousand years. Paper bills have been used in Europe for nearly
four hundred years, and much longer in China. It seems
dramatic to convert to a true digital economy. However, there
are many advantages. Business can achieve great savings if we
avoid storing, counting, handling, and transporting cash.

The advantages for society as a whole may be even greater,
especially if cash is removed altogether. As we know from the
daily news, cash encourages crime. A wallet may be stolen
from a pocket, or more severe, someone may be the victim of
armed robbery. Institutions such as banks and security
transports must spend a lot of resources for protection,
sometimes not successfully. Both physical and psychological
injuries may be the consequences of having all this "bait" in the
form of cash.

But it would be naive to expect crime to disappear in a
digital economy. Credit card fraud is a daily occurrence.
However, the criminals who steal credit cards are spurred by

the possibility of using the cards to retrieving stolen money in cash from ATMs. Without cash, it will be much easier to follow the transactions.

We could hope to make it more inconvenient to be a criminal. A monetary economy is much more effective than bartering—that was understood thousands of years ago. It was easier to sell the horse for money that could be used freely, than to trade it for a cow and some chickens on the side. The seller may not need chickens or the potential horse buyer may not have a cow for sale. By going digital we could expect to remove the advantages of the monetary system from criminals. The pusher down the street would have problems if customers no longer had anonymous cash for the transaction. He could accept gold, PCs, TVs, or appliances instead, and get all the hassles of a barter economy.

Of course, criminals also can go digital, which would require computing competence, and today, with improved information security systems, the criminal would need competence at a fairly high level. As we all know, this competence can alternatively be sold in the open economy at quite acceptable prices. And digital criminals can be met with digital police. Some tasks, such as detecting whitewashing, may even be performed by automatic systems. At any rate, we should consider it an improvement if bandits replace guns with keyboards—there will at least be fewer injuries.

Do we see Big Brother here? Cash is anonymous; digital money can be followed. For ordinary law abiding citizens this should not be considered a threat, that is, as long as good laws to protect public privacy are in place. However, tax authorities now will have a weapon against the black market economy. It will not be so easy to pay the carpenter off the record without cash. Some may view this as a disadvantage, but we will get a fairer tax system and increased income from tax.

The process towards a cash-free society will be accelerated when the real costs of using cash are placed on the individual cash-paying customer.

Willing or not, we are moving slowly but smoothly into a cash free society. Today the $100 bill is the highest bill in circulation, the $500, $1,000, $5,000 and $10,000 bills are no longer in use. And as inflation takes a percentage of the real value of the $100 bill every year, we soon will have cash only as small change. On the other end, it is interesting to note that the US still has a one-cent coin. In Norway, the lowest valued coin is now one krone (approximately fifteen cents), up from the one øre (1/100 of a krone), which was removed from circulation in 1972. The highest denomination is still the thousand kroner bill, which was introduced as early as 1877. That's inflation!

The process towards a cash-free society will be accelerated when the real costs of using cash are placed on the individual cash-paying customer, not split on all customers. The growth of pure Internet banks, where all transactions are digital, is a severe threat to banks that still have high cash-handling costs. It may also become more awkward to use cash. Many countries are now requiring a national bank notification whenever large sums are withdrawn or deposited as cash. One could go further, perhaps placing a risk tax on the use of cash, to compensate for public injury and other expenses that follow from robberies.

We may be concerned about the risk of getting to a situation in which there is no longer any cash as backup. The answer is: We are already there! Look into your wallet and count the bills. Is it sufficient for food, rent, gas and all the other expenses? For how long? While there have been incidents of hacking credit card and banking systems, computer security is improving. As with cars, safety only became an issue late in the development history of the technology. First we had to solve the "important" problems: getting the vehicle to run, making it affordable, offering a fancy design, and adding functionality.

Government and regulators have a job here. They should ensure that businesses and organizations that handle critical tasks, power systems, communication networks, Internet banking, and so forth, should have the necessary independent backup systems in place.

One of the smaller countries is likely to take the first leap towards an all-digital economy. Large countries such as the United States have huge incomes from seigniorage, printing and "selling" dollar bills to other countries. Also, it is easier to get the necessary infrastructure in place in a small country—to issue debit cards to persons who do not qualify in a commercial bank, to implement improved ID systems, and so forth. It is also easier to remove cash from a currency that is in use on a national level only, i.e., not as with dollar and euro that have widespread acceptance.

Since there are clear advantages in being the first country to go completely digital, we can expect this to happen in not so many years (10 years is my guess). Criminals will be foiled and national industry and service providers will get a home market for technologies that may be in widespread use in the near future. This transition to a digital economy can be performed step by step, starting by removing the high denomination bills and imposing the cash-handling costs on the cash-paying customers. The process may go on until the economy is all digital, or one may see a benefit in keeping small denomination bills and coins.

Notes

1   IEEE Spectrum no 1, 2011. The other technologies were high quality sound, LED's and flexible power grids.

2   Shenkar, O. (2010) Copycats: How Smart Companies Use Imitation to Gain a Strategic Edge, Harvard Business Press.

3   Statistics from Norges Bank, Norway's central bank, "Årsrapport om Betalingssystem 2010" (in Norwegian).

67 Effects of IT Technology

When new technologies emerge, the focus is naturally on the possibilities. Prophets see helicopters as common as cars, drugs that can let us live much longer, interplanetary travel, home robots, cars that steer themselves, lightweight roll-up displays, thinking computers. However, when these technologies face the real world, the limitations and drawbacks become apparent. The new technology is often adapted, but technical, practical, and social factors limit the application. Technology can be successful in some areas, but not in all. Sometimes improvements in the incumbent technology offer a better solution. Technological revolutions are not common.

With all the technological advances of the last century, we tend to believe that everything is possible, that it is just a matter of having enough resources. To some extent this is true. We can move technology ahead by concentrating resources and a focused research, but there are limits to what we can achieve. Decades have passed since the first men walked on the moon, but it is still a sensation when an ordinary (but very wealthy) citizen gets a week in outer space. Interplanetary travel is still science fiction. We have some of the technology in place, but the challenges ahead are enormous. We use helicopters today for many functions. They are expensive, however; the technology is complex and needs expert maintenance and expert pilots. The idea of a people's helicopter is perhaps further away today than when the technology was invented. We still use motor cars for personal transportation, vehicles quite similar to the first models that hit the road more than a hundred years ago.

A powerful and lightweight battery could define the market base for a range of new products, from functional long-range electric cars to clothes with built-in heaters. But advances in battery technology seem to go slowly, although the economic incentives are enormous. Similarly, a display screen with the same quality and flexibility as paper could revolutionize the presentation of printed material. The LCD (liquid crystal diode) displays that have replaced the CRT (cathode ray tube) are thinner, lighter, and use less power than their predecessor, but still cannot compete with paper in quality. The first versions of "electronic paper," e-ink with paper-like letter quality, offer a promise of radically new displays in the future. These displays, such as Amazon's Kindle, use ambient light and are nearly as comfortable to read as paper. They can be made very thin, flexible, and requiring little power. The drawback is that they are currently only offered in black and white,[1] it takes time to change the contents of the display, and they have limited display size.

If we assume that advances in e-ink technology will provide high resolution color displays (which seems to be just around the corner), as well as faster screen refresh rate and larger formats this will have a high impact in many areas. Then even today's *paper* newspapers will be disseminated electronically. Without paper, printing, and manual distribution, subscription fees may be significantly reduced. With excellent displays, printers will disappear, being as unnecessary as telex machines, typewriters, or faxes. The postal services are already seeing a decline in letters. With a move from paper to electronic media, only package services will remain.

Other applications that may utilize an improved display technology are maps. Today, paper maps offer both an overview and detailed information at the same time, and the format is handy and can be taken along everywhere. New e-ink displays may change this. These may be flexible screens that can be rolled up, can have high resolution, and—the big advantage—can include a GPS unit to pinpoint the user's current location on the map. To speculate further, such a display could be offered with touch features, opening the way for various dynamic functions: show route to, calculate distance to, zoom in, zoom out, and so on.

With improved displays we will take a long step towards the paper less society. With everything digital—tickets, money, maps, newspapers, journals, reports and so on—paper will no longer be used to carry information.

That is, with improved displays we will take a long step towards the paper less society. With everything digital—tickets, money, maps, newspapers, journals, reports and so on—paper will no longer be used to carry information.

Other changes are possible if these displays can be produced in large sizes. For example, virtual walls can be installed, such as those found today in some laboratories. Current technology uses many displays, is expensive, and consumes a lot of power; but e-ink may offer more flexible and lighter screens that are power sparing. These walls can be used for presenting information or just to improve the view. Perhaps one day you can sit down with a cup of coffee in your living room, surrounded by walls that display a street scene from Rome or Paris. When enjoying a glass of beer, perhaps you would prefer a south island scene or a view of the Sahara Desert.

New display technology can be used to build virtual environments.

A more fundamental problem is the **open nature** of our world—it has so many different facets.

A more fundamental problem is the open nature of our world—it has so many different facets. Scientists and engineers have developed ground vehicles that run on Mars, but imagine the difficulties of developing such vehicles for Earth, which could negotiate any type of terrain: high mountains, rivers, jungles, the open sea, glaciers, and deserts. The diversity is even greater when we look at social functions and the way we perform work. Developing technology that can be used by all types of people of all cultures is a great challenge.

We see this in our homes. While gadgets simplify housework, helping us cook and do the cleaning, we have yet to see a home robot that automates these functions. We can cook a meal in three minutes with a microwave, but this does not imply that the process of making a meal is automated. The microwave helps with only parts of some functions, and may be a disappointment compared to the early predictions of the automatic kitchen. A vacuum cleaner may be more efficient than a broom, but we still have to operate it ourselves. Most of us would give a fortune for a machine that could clean the whole house while the family was off at school or work.

Why can we not get this product with all the advances in sensor and computer technology? In fact, the technology is here, as well as the very first products—the robot vacuum cleaner discussed in Chapter 1. The problem, if we can see it this way, is in our homes. They come in too many forms and shapes and are furnished in so many ways that it is still impossible to make a gadget that serves them all. A modern warehouse with automatic robot trucks is impressive, but that environment is customized for the robots: plane surfaces, infrared or wire controls for direction, standardized shelves, standardized loads, and everything in its right place.

The greatest technological breakthroughs have often come in areas where there is a formalized environment already in place. A new technology for computer memory does not have to conform to all facets of an open world, but has to adjust only to the electronic standards that are already in place. Mobile phones can rely on the technical and social standards of telephony established over more than a hundred years.

– These atoms are supposed to make everything superfluous...
– Sure enough, but give me a glass of beer anyhow!

(Storm P.)

The Internet and the Web were introduced to a world where most of the physical environment needed was already in place, a proliferation of computers, a very large group of "computer literates," and the means of electronic communication (data and telephone networks). The important standards, TCP and IP,

The **openness** of the Internet is an important idea, exemplified with everything from the View Source button via programmable devices to the open-source movement.

were already in place. Then HTML and HTTP defined the base for establishing new applications.

The openness of the Internet is an important idea, exemplified with everything from the View Source button via programmable devices to the open-source movement. Most of the tools we use are open in the respect that they can be programmed. As discussed in Chapter 19.2, the tendency today is to hide the underlying data structures—the files and folders—from the user. If this becomes the norm, the creativity in establishing new functions, often initiated by individuals more than companies, will dwindle.[2]

The most important contribution from Internet and Web technology is its two-way communication within a global system. This advantage is utilized fully for e-mail, chat, text messages, and social networks. The asynchronous and text-based message systems are taking over both personal and business communication, as they are flexible, fast, simple, and cheap.

Web technology opens the way for many different applications. Some of these can be implemented using HTML only, like home pages of institutions. Others can rely on existing formalization, such as online banking, travel services, and some B2B applications. For others, society will have to adapt, for example, by establishing new standards, before the new applications can be put to use. As we have seen, this can be a difficult process.

As an information provider the Web has to compete with existing media channels, such as TV and newspapers. But the Web provides the possibility of interaction. While this ability allows the user choice (for example, by clicking on links or providing search terms), it demands more active involvement from the user, and the information requested must be available. Broadcast channels such as TV and newspapers can put more effort into creating the information because they have only one or a few streams, and users limit their involvement to selecting channels. We solve this as Winnie the Pooh does, by saying yes to all offers. The Web will be used when two-way communication is important and when we wish to specify our needs. In other cases, traditional channels will prevail.

It is difficult to predict what new technologies the future may offer. The encompassing nature of the Internet and the Web is something that few could have foreseen, even if most of the underlying technology has been in place for a long time.

It is difficult to predict what new technologies the future may offer. The encompassing nature of the Internet and the Web is something that few could have foreseen, even if most of the underlying technology has been in place for a long time. In other areas technological breakthroughs have given us broad-

Formalization is a requirement for automated processes. The lowest levels offer great flexibility and are easily accepted. Higher levels offer greater advantages in efficiency and automation, but often will require changes in the application environment.

band services and extremely powerful and affordable computers. But independent of the technology, we know the applications must "interface" with users and their societies.

In this book I have focused on the part of the interface that has to do with formalization. Formalization is a requirement for automated processes, but it can be performed on different levels. The lowest levels offer great flexibility and user freedom, and therefore, are easily accepted. Higher levels offer greater advantages in efficiency and automation, but often will require changes in the application environment. The need for these changes in the technological interface may slow the acceptance rate, and in some cases, be a barrier against technology adoption.

The advances in IT technology have given us everything we need for most applications: fast processors, large storage capacity, high broadband networks, and an abundance of applications. The "with faster computers we will achieve..." statements have lost their value for most applications, as we already have the fast machines. Of course, if everybody begins streaming high quality video to PCs or mobile phones, higher bandwidth may be needed as well as more capacity in the backbone networks. However, these are services that we already have, and we can expect capacity to be extended as needed.

67.1   Digital representations

Digital versions are becoming the **representation of choice** for everything symbolic.

Digital versions are becoming the representation of choice for everything symbolic: music, movies, maps, tickets, documents, and books. As we have seen, a digital format has many advantages: It is compact, can be stored nearly without cost, and can be transmitted over a network. Also, the format is flexible, can be handled by standard equipment, edited, or sent to a player or a viewer. Producing an initial digital format can be important for some content because transferring from other representations often reduces quality, limits further editing, and incurs costs.

It is a reasonable expectation that everything symbolic will be digitalized. There may be a few exceptions, but the advantages of digitalization are so great that it will eliminate other formats. Music is becoming digital, and music lovers will no longer need a CD player. Movies are going in the same direction, even if this development will demand more bandwidth. As we have seen, even the paper version of a

As we have seen, even the paper version of a newspaper will be distributed in digital form and the electronic format will soon be the default for books.

newspaper will be distributed in digital form and the electronic format will soon be the default for books. However, there is a difference between traditional music and movies on one side and books, newspapers, and maps on the other. The first need a device to be heard or viewed, and the latter come with their own "viewer," for example, the paper book and the paper map. While electronic newspapers and maps may be augmented by other services, it is difficult to envisage what additional functions we would need when reading a novel. Even with the general advantages offered by digitalization, there will be cases in which the paper representation is useful. For example, it is more convenient to take a book to the beach in paperback form, than having to carry along an iPad or a Kindle. On the other hand, it is easier to buy the electronic version of a book, and it comes at a lower price.

A consequence of new representations is that we get new business models and new distribution channels. Stores that sell CDs and DVDs are closing down and will be closed down. Bookstores will have a tougher time as the market is moving to e-books. Even libraries, one of the fundamental parts of an educational institution, may have an uncertain future. Not many years ago, we went to the library to do literature searches. Today all needed background information is on the Internet, in various bibliographical databases. And e-books do not need shelves. Even the shelves in our homes, stocked with CDs, DVDs and books may diminish and disappear, when everything can be streamed from the net.

67.2   When everything is available

When everything is available, we can search *all* scientific papers to see what has been published on a topic, perform a search over *all* hotels or *all* flights, and find interest rates for *all* banks.

When everything is available, we can search *all* scientific papers to see what has been published on a topic, perform a search over *all* hotels or *all* flights, find interest rates for *all* banks, and so on. However, there are constraints both from a business and a technological side.

As we have seen, not all businesses may be willing to share their data with others. Airlines, hotels, or car rental agencies may chose to sell their products through their own systems. Yes, the large sites may have many customers, but within these, each producer ends up by being a generic producer, as the general sites dilute the brand names. For example, if we use a general site for hotel bookings, our specification may be for a three-star hotel in the center of Barcelona for a specified weekend. Each hotel that fulfills our requirements will be presented along with many others. Now, it matters less if this is an independent hotel or part of a chain. Similarly, when the general site can give a good offer for a rental car, it matters less whether Avis, Hertz, or any other company delivers the service. These generic services are attractive for customers because they simplify searching. Instead of checking the Web sites of each airline, hotel chain, or rental agency, we can search all together. The producers may have few alternatives. Either they have to surrender to these sites, or they have to rely on heavy marketing to attract customers to their individual sites.

Formalization and lack of standards are another problem. We need formalized data, as well as standard representations, to be able to collect and compare data from many sources. Some of the applications we have presented in this book, such as the personal assistant in Chapter 63, do require standard representations of data to be useful. What we can hope is that the advantages of standardization may force companies to agree on common representations and common formats.

67.3   Automation

Everything is constrained by the need for formalization.

Faster, cheaper, smaller, and mobile are important factors in the advancement of computer applications, but as we have seen, everything is constrained by the need for formalization. A formalized description of procedures is necessary before we can use the computer to perform a task—quite naturally really, since we know that this machine in the end executes fairly simple numeric statements, such as load, store, add, subtract, multiply, and compare.

In our world, many tasks fall into the formalized category. Some are simple, such as an alarm clock. Here the program (the formalization) may be expressed as one that checks every minute to see if it has reached the time setting for the alarm and performs the necessary steps to sound the alarm when this is the case. A few lines of code can express such a program, as described in Chapter 4.2. Other programs may be complex financial transaction systems that consist of many millions of code lines.

Formalization was an issue long before the advent of computers. Formalized procedures enabled processes to be streamlined, large volumes of data to be handled, and control procedures to be enforced. These things were necessary for the first large warehouses and banks. But the need for formalization is not limited to data and administrative

Computers allow us to **automate processes** based on data as long as the processes are formalized.

processes. In 1764, James Hargreaves built a spinning machine that spun a thread from eight spindles. That is, he formalized the process of spinning. Later, these hand-operated machines were powered first by steam and then by gasoline and electrical engines, opening the way for automation. A tremendous advantage was gained whenever a mechanical process was formalized and implemented in the form of a machine.

Similarly, computers allow us to automate processes based on data as long as the processes are formalized. Banking has been used as a primary example in this book, both for automation and for replacing intermediates. In less than fifty years, most banking operations have been automated, taken over by the computer. In theory, it is possible to handle all common banking operations today by a computer (that is, a bank is a computer). In theory, no manual operations are needed, but in practice we may need some manual support for special functions and exceptions.

The computer has increased the **reward** of formalization.

While it is as difficult as ever to formalize processes, the computer has increased the incentives (the rewards are higher). The advent of the Internet and the Web has increased the possibility of practical computer-based solutions, for example, by allowing the customer herself to do the job. In addition, the data that is needed are now often in a digital form.

The computer's way of performing a task may be quite different from that of a human.

Note that the computer's way of performing a task may be quite different from that of a human. Instead of navigating by the stars, we send up artificial "stars" that transmit electronic information which quite simple devices can use to calculate a position anywhere on the surface of the earth. An advantage with digitalization is that data in an electronic form can be processed automatically.

While we have used machines for many hundreds of years, computer controlled machines offer more flexibility and can perform larger parts of the job. Manufacturers run machines twenty-four hours a day, often without anyone present. An operator has prepared the jobs with parts and tools on a pallet. The machine processes each pallet, mounts the part, selects the tools, and performs the operations defined by a program for the part. If anything happens, the machine sends a text message to the operator.

With computer controlled machines and robots, manufacturers can increase output while decreasing the number of employees. Therefore, we have seen a decline in the number of people employed in industry over the last decenniums.

Can the development go too far? Is it smart for a modern society to replace professional journalists with amateur bloggers?

Computer automation is taking over jobs in many other areas. Every task that has a detailed and formalized job description with input and output in digital form is in the danger zone. Tollbooth operators are now replaced by a computer system that reads the license plate of the car or uses a radio transponder.

Many tasks fall into this category—simple, often low-paid tasks that can be automated. However, even well paid, skilled individuals such as stockbrokers are facing competition from the computer—the algorithmic trading systems which come in several forms. One system uses robots to perform high frequency trades, exploiting minor changes in the stock prices. Of these, there are low-latency trading systems where the idea is to react before anybody else. Here it is important that the computers are installed physically close to the stock exchange systems to be able to react faster than anybody else. There are also systems that perform the detailed bidding and asking needed to perform a larger operation, such as buying a thousand shares at a given average price. The end result of these systems is that banks and other financial institutions are expelling human traders whose jobs are too formalized to last into the computer age.

Financial institutions are expelling human traders whose jobs are too formalized to last into the computer age.

67.4   Removing intermediates

Computers and automation decouple intermediates from many tasks. At one time only the employee behind the counter in the bank or travel agency had access to the computer systems; today we can access these at home, performing the tasks ourselves without needing any intermediate. This is also the case for many other applications. Instead of calling the insurance company to ask for a change in a policy, we can perform the task directly in their system. In many countries we are now able to apply for schools, enroll in kindergarten, apply for a marriage license, register a car and to perform many other administrative tasks—online.

The effect of putting many journalists out of work is that fewer people are engaged in information gathering and information presentation.

In some cases, this development may go too far. Newspapers are closing down as people get their information from blogs, Web pages and other news services. The effect of putting many journalists out of work is that fewer people are engaged in information gathering and information presentation. The more superficial services that have taken over may not have the resources, the ability, or the interest to use time to investigate complex cases. The hope is that new technology, such as displays that support readability, may make it cheaper to disseminate high-quality newspapers, leaving more resources to be used in the newsroom. There also may be a reaction to a more superficial news coverage when people understand the value of in-depth information.

A simpler example of how new automated services are not covering all aspects of the old, is automatic phone answering systems that replace human operators. When a customer calls a company, he must hit 1 for this, 2 for that… System designers must be careful that the selection menus cover all aspects of business. One good way of doing this is have an option to wait for an operator because the formalization (here the menu) will seldom cover all types of calls.

Some forms of automation fail. For many years, there were high hopes for computer-assisted learning, replacing teachers by offering lectures, text material, and so on the Web. These services have been implemented to a certain extent, especially for distant learning. However, the majority of teaching is still performed in the traditional way, with a teacher and students together in a physical classroom. While the automated services can perform a similar task, the environment is different. Being together physically is often more important than we think for discipline, socialization, motivation, and creativity.

67.5   Power tools

Earlier, before the advent of the computer, human beings performed an abundance of simple jobs. For example, a new architect right out of school might be assigned simple tasks at his firm, such as to draw windows and doors in building plans. With experience, the architect could move to the more creative and complex tasks. Today, however, a computer can perform all the simple processes, automatically inserting details in drawings for a building. Similarly, engineering programs can perform the detailed calculations, and, of course, we no longer need human "computers," the persons who did the arithmetic before the arrival of computers.

A computer can handle bookkeeping, a task that needed many employees at one time, much more efficiently. Some high level tasks are still performed by experienced bookkeepers, but all the simpler tasks are handled automatically. We also see a chain reaction here. When payments are made electronically, the data needed for the bookkeeping will nearly always be in digital form, thus making

Printers, who have been needed since the Gutenberg press around 1450, are no longer necessary to the printing process.

it simpler to automate the job. An increase in formalization also will simplify bookkeeping.

Thirty years ago, many people held jobs as typists, but word processing systems have eliminated these intermediates. Computer systems also can handle other parts of administrative work, reducing the need for clerks, a job title that many held only a few years ago. Similarly, printers, who have been needed since the Gutenberg press around 1450, are no longer necessary to the printing process. Computer systems can set a book or newspaper in type under the direction of a journalist, the author, or an editor. These have been given power tools that handle all the details that were in the realm of the printer just a few years ago. We no longer see the large rooms with many architects, engineers, or administrative personnel performing similar tasks, as most of these have been replaced by a computer.

67.6   Business models and competition

The advent of the virtual and digital world is manifested by the fact that Facebook's initial stock market valuation surpassed that of General Motors in 2012 (before it plunged). While GM has more than 200,000 employees, Facebook has only a few thousand. The virtual becomes more important than the physical. Even with automation, GM needs many employees to design, manufacture, and market its products, but because Facebook handles only digital data, a few employees can run its systems, which are used by more than 800 million people all over the world. We see that the virtual nature of companies such as Facebook and Google makes it possible to attract new customers fast and to increase turnover fast. Even Apple, the biggest ever U.S. Company,[3] is more virtual than physical. The value is in design more than production, illustrated by the fact that Apple outsources production, even the development of its underlying technology.

Digital products may pass borders without being stopped by custom officers

For a company to go global is a complex task. If its products are in physical form, the company will encounter barriers such as customs, regulations that vary from country to country, and cultural and language differences. But for companies with digital products, such as Facebook, Google, Spotify, Flickr, and Twitter everything is much simpler. They will have to handle many different languages, but apart from that, most digital products may pass borders without being stopped by custom officers.

Computer systems and the Internet also support companies that have physical products. For example, improved communication makes it possible to outsource separate processes. Many shipyards in high cost countries have found it convenient to manufacture the hull (the cutting and welding functions) in low cost countries. The Internet is then an important channel for synchronizing manufacturing of the different parts.

With the Internet, local companies face competition both from national and international firms. When buying a book, I can use the local bookstore, a national Web site, or an international one. Although the percentage of physical products purchased on the Internet is still low, this proportion may increase as the Internet services become more efficient and can offer lower prices. For example, the EU is working to simplify cross-border transactions so that online stores can compute and handle payment of national taxes. I was impressed when I ordered a Kindle from Amazon just a few days before Christmas. It came from Phoenix, Arizona, to me in Molde, Norway, just three days after I submitted the order, and Amazon also had taken care of VAT and custom duties.

In a controversial paper, "IT Doesn't Matter," Nicholas G. Carr[4] advocated that as information technology has become a commodity, its strategic importance has been lost (I discussed this in Chapter 25). While this may be true in the general sense, businesses will have to adjust their business models to the new technologies. As with any other technology or market trend, it is important to get things right from the very start. There may be many implementations of Web presence or of B2C systems, but offering flexible and simple-to-use systems is important. Looking to the competition in the air, we see that new emerging airlines are employing the Internet better than the incumbents. Early birds in other areas, such as Amazon, eBay, and Yahoo! that offer well-designed applications, have a strong foothold. In some cases new methodologies may give a latecomer a chance. Google came later than most of the other search engines, but has become the most used through its smart implementation of relevance rankings.

An Intranet solution may offer huge benefits. It may be used to streamline business processes, to reduce administrative costs, and to build a community feeling. Contact with customers can be improved through Extranet and B2C solutions, and B2B offers a promise of effective interchange of data. This is

---

An **Intranet** solution may offer huge benefits. It may be used to streamline business processes, to reduce administrative costs, and to build a community feeling.

With the Internet, local companies face **competition** both from national and international firms.

especially the case were one company or group is in control of the complete value chain; then the difficult questions of standardization are somewhat easier to solve.

In the airline business, a first effect of Internet booking is that customers do the job themselves. This requires a reengineering of the business. First, a major group of employees are no longer needed; at least, there will be much fewer jobs than before. Second, to facilitate Internet booking, the airline needs a simple price and discount policy. Complicated discounts (for example, when couples get a discount if one of them pays full price) are not easy to implement over the Web because the two tickets must be linked. Third, with Internet booking, customers get very price conscious. We normally ask to get the cheapest offers up front. Then other factors, such as service, meals, or seat space, may be ignored. That is, today the Internet and bargain airlines are determining the rules of the game, and the incumbents have to adjust their business models to this situation. (But this may change.) Finally, we have seen that the Internet and Web offer new possibilities for marketing. We can notify customers whenever we have something to offer that may be of interest (based on profile data) or may design new offers in accordance with customers' wishes.

The incumbents will be forced to play along, like it or not. They may see existing business models threatened by new technology, and they may try to hold back the advent of new business models. However, in the end, they will be forced to follow suit. If they are reluctant to offer new services, a startup will always emerge to take that market niche.

Will computer technology result in more unemployment?

The Internet and the Web have, and will have, disruptive effects in many markets. I have used airlines, banks, travel agencies, record companies, publishing houses, and software firms as examples, but good examples can be found in many other areas.

67.7   Employment

The Internet will have disruptive effects in many markets.

Until now, industrialization has put many people out of jobs, but also has been able to create a similar number of new jobs. Are we in a different situation today? Is IT so effective, so flexible and encompassing that it will remove jobs faster than new ones can be created? Unemployment figures from many countries are rising. Is this temporary or a new trend?

Computers, the Internet, and the Web have had an effect on nearly all jobs—some eliminated, others radically changed.

If you can give an exact, **detailed description** of your job, you are in the danger zone because your job can be formalized, and then automated with the help of a computer.

To survive in the workplace we need to be good in areas where the computer does not perform well.

Automation may move against outsourcing. Many companies choose to implement a high level of automation in their processes. With fewer employees, the wage differences are less important.

Still others are indirectly affected, for example, with the possibilities the new technologies have for outsourcing tasks.

If you can give an exact, detailed description of your job, you are in the danger zone because your job can be formalized, and then automated with the help of a computer. This may happen for jobs as different as metro train drivers, cash register operators, and stockbrokers. That is, the automation we have seen in industry is now continuing outside of the plants.

In this book, I have given many examples of jobs that are affected by the fact that the customer herself gets access to the "internal" systems using Internet and Web services. While the threat of automation has been here for many years, this is a new way of removing "unnecessary" jobs. With direct access to company systems, many intermediates are no longer needed. With improved user interfaces, we can expect customers to perform more tasks themselves as the complexity of the tasks is reduced. Better back-office systems—the internal systems of businesses—also may open the way for new applications with which customers may do the jobs themselves.

With improved communication—virtual on the Internet, and physical on air, road, and sea networks—outsourcing parts of the administrative and production jobs to low-wage countries becomes easier. In principle, many types of jobs can be affected, but in practice, outsourcing is easiest for the simplest and most formalized tasks. For example, a programming task that is clearly specified may be performed anywhere in the world. For other more open tasks, continuous discussions with users may be necessary. This requires command of the language spoken, and it will be useful if the programmer participates in the same culture as the users. These factors also will influence other types of tasks. Even simple call center tasks can involve situations in which a thorough understanding of the customer's problem is needed. In practice, this understanding may be difficult to obtain for a person living in a different country and culture.

Call center operators, are also affected by other mechanisms. With the Internet and the Web, the customer may retrieve some information directly (Web-based directory services, user manuals, FAQ), avoiding a telephone call. The relatively formalized call center functions that serve customers who do not have Internet access or the ability to find the information for themselves, often can be outsourced to another country. However, with improved user interfaces and a more Internet-experienced population, these jobs will be of a temporary nature.

Automation may move against outsourcing. We see that many companies choose to implement a high level of automation in their processes. With fewer employees, the wage differences are less important. Also, there are advantages to producing in-house. Important knowledge is kept in the company. The distance between designers and production will be short, so that production can influence design, for example, to present solutions that are easier to manufacture. For products that change rapidly, such as fashion, production close to main markets has the advantage of offering short lead times, making it possible to tune manufacturing to demand. For example, Zara, a Spanish clothing retailer, has success with this model.

To survive in the workplace, we need to be good in areas in which the computer does not perform well. In other words, we need to concentrate on the open, unformalized tasks, which can be anything from driving a bus, teaching, working in health care, law enforcement, or to offering help with complex banking services. While both physical and administrative routine tasks in business may be in danger of being computerized, executive positions are not. Here the strong ability of humans to make decisions based on overall strategy and with incomplete data is important.

The advantage for workers and jobseekers is that many parts of society are not yet formalized. Often, changes in infrastructure are necessary before they can be automated. While some stores are experimenting with do-it-yourself cash registers, more standardized packaging of all goods is probably needed to automate all cash registers. We can check in ourselves at airports, but counter staff are still needed to handle exceptions or serve customers who do not manage to use the check in terminals. Some of switchboard tasks may be better handled by Web pages or telephone menu systems, but most companies would still need a human operator to handle special requests. However, employment in these areas will be reduced as automatic systems take over most of the traffic.

In the long run, formalization and the following automation will always be a threat. Internet banks, Internet shops, Internet auctions, digital solutions on the Internet will all have a competitive advantage of greater efficiency compared with traditional services. Some customers may enjoy the personal service they get in the bank, but this bank faces competition from the

---

*The advantage for workers and jobseekers is that many parts of society are **not yet formalized**. Often, changes in infrastructure are necessary before they can be automated.*

real Internet banks that do not have to handle cash, and where every operation is automatic. In the long run, all banks will be forced to either adopt the automation idea, or to ask customers to pay for the manual service.

67.8   Effect on society

The Internet and the Web is accelerating the process of establishing a **global economy**.

We have seen that computer technology along with the Internet and Web standards have affected both jobs and businesses, sometimes causing minor changes, and sometimes disruptive ones. Some of the same categorizations can be used to discuss effects on society (formalization, removing intermediates, and changes in the job market).

The change from a cash-based to an electronic economy offers new possibilities, as presented in the case study in Chapter 66.4. Today the US government is leading an effort to move paper to electronic passports, with some of the same arguments arising as with the discussion on cash. An electronic passport is difficult to forge and offers the possibility of automatically retrieving background information and travel patterns. As with electronic money, electronic passports raise privacy issues, which may be used both to support individual rights and to threaten them.

Just as businesses develop systems in which the customer does part of the job herself, state agencies also are offering B2C systems. In many cases, government organizations have been ahead of the private sector here. They have opened internal databases and offered all types of information to citizens over the Web. In many countries, we can e-mail politicians and administrators, and we can fill out many types of applications over a Web interface.

Electronic voting systems are under discussion. Such systems may make voting more reliable and efficient, but they also raise important questions on security, privacy, and accessibility that need to be discussed before this becomes an option. This is absolutely one area in which we should be extremely cautious. Also note that telephone-based voting has never been an issue, even if such systems could have offered a more effective process. (I discussed these issues in Chapter 16.)

Today the Internet and the Web are accelerating the process of establishing a global economy, the process that was started by dramatic changes in the world in the last decades: establishing of the European Union, opening of China, breakdown of the Soviet Union, and new trade agreements. This rapid transition has created the huge wage differences among countries very apparent, and manufacturing of simpler products has gone to areas where the wages are lowest. No problem, many economists say. This will give cheaper products that will open new markets and create incentives for making new businesses. There may be short-term disruptive effects, but in the long run the boost in productivity growth will counter the negative effects.

We should not be so sure. Within every country are areas with high unemployment rates, areas that have been left behind because of changes in the economy, transport networks, or technology. In a more global economy, industries and businesses can move freely across national borders. Today they may move where labor is inexpensive; tomorrow they may move to areas that have the highest growth, thus accelerating the processes.

In the end, more global communication and cooperation should result in lower entropy (we should expect that the differences among countries will be reduced). In the meantime, we will have to live with these differences, accepting that some jobs can no longer be performed in areas with high wages and a high standard of living. We need systems in place that can handle these effects of a dynamic and global economy. Remedies may be educational systems, for basic education and for retraining for new jobs. A good education normally leads to an unformalized job, one in which the danger of being removed or outsourced is less than for simpler tasks. Retraining may be necessary when jobs have a short life span, often so short than one job will not last a lifetime.

More global communication and cooperation should result in **lower entropy** (we should expect that the differences among countries will be reduced).

Notes

1   The Kindle Fire version has color, but has a backlit display, i.e., it does not use eInk technology.

2   See Santini, S. (2010), Is Your Phone Killing the Internet?, *IEEE Computer*, December.

3   On Monday 21. August 2012 Apple surpassed Microsoft as the most valuable U.S. company ever, measured by stock value. However, this is in nominal terms. Taking inflation into consideration, Microsoft's closing high of $616 billion in 1999 was higher.

4   Carr, N. G. 2003. IT Doesn't Matter, *Harvard Business Review*, May, pp. 41–49. See also his book, "Does IT Matter? Information Technology and the Corrosion of Competitive Advantage," Harvard Business School Press (April 2004).

68 Afterword

In 1976, my first job was to lead a project for using IT in primary health care. As a project leader, I was responsible for writing plans and other reports. I started out using an electric typewriter, but soon found that this was tedious, especially as the reports needed continual update. As a first project, we wrote a simple word processing system for a PC, one of the very first in its kind. It had all editing functions, but only a single font and no graphical capabilities. The development time was soon covered by the word processor's greater efficiency, even if this one was a very simple version. I learned my first lesson: Interactive computer systems are effective and flexible.

Soon, many other university departments bought PCs and started to use this word processor as an alternative to word processing on the central, timeshared mainframe computer. The PC had one important advantage, it could offer fast and reliable response times. My second lesson is one clearly understood by Facebook: Offering excellent response times at all times is an important ingredient in success.

In addition, my project team developed a simple statistical system. At that time, data entry in most systems was in a line format, with tabs or another delimiter between each item. Our system allowed the user to design a data entry form, similar to what we use today. While we had developed this system for general practitioners who wanted to do research, we were astonished to see that the system was used all over the university as well. Even if university researchers had access to a very advanced statistical package on the university mainframe, they chose to use this simple system. This was the third important lesson: Offer systems that users are able to master!

The project's main task was to develop a medical journal system for general practitioners. Since we had success with our PC solutions, we skipped the plan to use a minicomputer to run the system. Instead, we used a set of simple PCs, one in each of the four doctors' offices and one to handle the database. The system was installed in a health center in northern Norway in 1979. It had a 20 MB disk (20 million bytes), probably one of the first disks ever to be connected to a PC. This worked very well. We learned a fourth lesson: Many small computers that work together can do the job. Today, of course, we are not connecting five PCs, but millions through the Internet.

Lesson 5: Intuitive user interfaces are advantageous, often a necessity.

In the system's first year, more than thirty doctors used it. Recruiting doctors for this rural area far beyond the Arctic Circle was a challenge; some physicians stayed only a couple of weeks. Of course, offering extensive computer training was not possible. On the first day at work, a new replacement doctor was told: This is your office, this is your computer, and here comes the first patient. That led to our fifth lesson: Intuitive user interfaces are advantageous, often a necessity. Many of these doctors had never used a computer system, but still managed to use ours. Similarly, when it comes to offering booking, banking, and other systems to the general public on the Web, training is not possible. Instead, the intuitive interface is the norm.

Lesson 6: Keep it simple.

In 1991, Tim Berners-Lee got the very first Web page up on his display, using a very simple system for describing Web pages. Thus, lesson six is important: Keep it simple. Today, there are countless numbers of Web pages, and more than five hundred million people all over the world are connected to the Internet. Many Web pages are written and updated by the general public, which means we are learning another lesson, number seven: Engage the public wherever possible.

Lesson 7: Engage the public wherever possible.

Lesson 8: Automatic systems can do the job when tasks are formalized.

The most effective of all systems are automatic systems. These are important in industry, but also help to simplify our everyday lives. We have seen that many formalized applications can be automated, saving money and reducing errors. This is lesson eight: Automatic systems can do the job when tasks are formalized.

Lesson 9: In the virtual world computers may do most of the work.

The advance of Google, Facebook, and other virtual companies has demonstrated that dramatic successes can be achieved very quickly in the virtual and digital world. Computers can do most of the work, at least the work that runs up the huge numbers, which is lesson nine.

Lesson 10: Systems that enhance communication between people are important.

The Web allows for direct communication among people, an advantage displayed through the different social networks. In a modern world in which socializing in the physical world often can be difficult, these systems offer new important opportunities. We have learned lesson number ten.

Lesson 11: The input-free interface is the simplest.

Even simpler than the intuitive interfaces are the input-free user interfaces that may get their clues from context. This is our last lesson.

Index

Numbers in bold refer to the central discussion of the topic.

About the Author

Kai A. Olsen is a professor of Informatics (Computing Science) both at Molde College and University of Bergen, Norway. He is an adjunct professor at the School of Information Sciences, University of Pittsburgh. Olsen's main research interests are user interfaces, IT strategy, and logistic systems. He has been a pioneer in developing software systems for PCs, information systems for primary health care, and systems for visualization. He acts as a consultant for Norwegian and US organizations.